Jews, Turks, Ottomans

Modern Jewish History

Henry L. Feingold, *Series Editor*

JEWS, TURKS, OTTOMANS

A SHARED HISTORY, FIFTEENTH THROUGH THE TWENTIETH CENTURY

Edited by Avigdor Levy

SYRACUSE UNIVERSITY PRESS

First Edition 2002
02 03 04 05 06 07   6 5 4 3 2 1

The paper used in this publication meets the minimum requirements of
American National Standard for Information Sciences—Permanence
of Paper for Printed Library Materials, ANSI Z39.48–1984. ∞™

Library of Congress Cataloging-in-Publication Data
Jew, Turks, Ottomans : a shared history, fifteenth through
    the twentieth century / edited by Avigdor Levy.—1st ed.
p. ; cm.—(Modern Jewish history)
Includes bibliographical references and index.
ISBN 0-8156-2941-9 (pbk. : alk. paper)
    1. Jews—Turkey—History. 2. Jews—Turkey—Politics and government.
    3. Turkey—Ethnic relations/ 4. Jews—Middle East—History. 5. Middle
    East—Ethnic relations. 6. Turkey—History—Ottoman Empire, 1288–1918.
    I. Levy, Avigdor. II. Series.
DS135.T8 J53 2002
956'.004924—dc21
2002011481

Contents

Appendixes

Illustrations

Figure

Table

Map

Acknowledgments

Generous support for the publication of this book has been provided by the Provost's Office and the Department of Near Eastern and Judaic Studies at Brandeis University, by the Institute of Turkish Studies, Washington, D.C., and by the Quincentennial Foundation, Istanbul.

Special thanks are due to Barbara Petzen for her editorial assistance and for patiently typing the entire manuscript. Elisheva Darcy prepared the bibliography; Tobe R. Tsarfaty and Stephanie Gerber verified the accuracy of many of the references.

A Note on Transliteration and Pronunciation

Due to the diversity of the articles in this volume, strict consistency has not always been possible. Hebrew terms and proper names have been transliterated according to a simplified method intended to approximate their pronunciation in modern Hebrew.

The spelling of Turkish terms and proper names follows modern Turkish orthography. Please note that the Turkish *c* is pronounced as the English *j*, *ç* as *ch*, *ş* as *sh*. Thus, *cizye, çelebi, şura* are pronounced *jizye, chelebi, shura*. In general, wherever feasible, familiar anglicized forms have been used.

Contributors

Feroz Ahmad is Professor of History at the University of Massachusetts at Boston. He is the author of *The Young Turks: The Committee of Union and Progress in Turkish Politics, 1908–14* (1969); *The Turkish Experiment in Democracy, 1950–75* (1977); and *The Making of Modern Turkey* (1993). He has published numerous articles on late Ottoman history and modern Turkey.

Jacob Barnai is Professor of Jewish History at the University of Haifa. His publications include *Hasidic Letters from Eretz-Israel* (in Hebrew; 1980); *The Jews in Palestine in the Eighteenth Century* (1992); *Historiography and Nationalism* (in Hebrew; 1995); and *Sabbateanism—Social Perspectives* (in Hebrew; 2000). He also coauthored *History of the Jews in the Islamic Countries* (in Hebrew; 3 vols., 1981–1986) and *The Jews in Izmir in the Nineteenth Century* (in Turkish and Hebrew; 1984). He is the author of numerous articles on Jewish history in the Middle East and North Africa.

Amnon Cohen is Eliahu Elath Professor of the History of the Muslim Peoples at the Hebrew University of Jerusalem and Director of the Harry S. Truman Research Institute for the Advancement of Peace. He has written extensively on the history of Ottoman Palestine. Among his works are *Jewish Life under Islam* (1984); *Economic Life in Ottoman Jerusalem* (1989); *A World Within—Jewish Life as Reflected in Muslim Court Records from the Sijill of Jerusalem* (1994); and *The Guilds of Ottoman Jerusalem* (2001).

Daniel Goffman is Professor of History at Ball State University. He is the author of *Izmir and the Levantine World, 1550–1650* (1990); *Britons in the Ottoman Empire, 1642–1660* (1998); *The Ottoman City between East and West: Istanbul,*

Izmir and Aleppo, with Edhem Eldem and Bruce Masters (1999); and *The Ottoman Empire and Early Modern Europe* (2002), as well as many articles and book reviews. He has served as editor of the *Turkish Studies Association Bulletin* and as president of the Turkish Studies Association. He currently is editor of the *Middle East Studies Association Bulletin.*

Nedim Gürsel is a Turkish writer who is the author of more than twenty books, including novels, collections of short stories and essays, and travelogues. His works have won several prizes and awards, and they have been translated into French, German, Italian, Spanish, and other languages. He divides his time between Turkey and France. In Paris, he is a senior researcher at the Centre National de la Recherche Scientifique and Professor at the Ecole des Langues Orientales. His most recent works include *Paysage littéraire de la Turquie contemporaine* (1993); *Le roman de conquérant* (1996); *Retour dans les Balkans* (1997); *Un turc en Amérique* (1997); *Mirages du sud* (2001); and *Le roman d'une transition* (2001).

Halil İnalcık is Professor of History at Bilkent University, Ankara. He also taught for many years at Ankara University (1943–1972) and the University of Chicago (1972–86) and served as a visiting professor at Columbia University and Princeton University. He is founding editor of the journal *Archivum Ottomanicum* and has published extensively on all periods of Ottoman history. Among his publications are *The Ottoman Empire: The Classical Age, 1300–1600* (1973); *Studies in Ottoman Social and Economic History* (1985); and *The Middle East and the Balkans under the Ottoman Empire* (1993). He is the principal author and coeditor, with Donald Quataert, of *An Economic and Social History of the Ottoman Empire, 1300–1914* (1994). His most recent book is *Essays in Ottoman History* (1998).

Jacob M. Landau is Professor Emeritus of Political Science at the Hebrew University of Jerusalem. Specializing in the history and politics of the modern Middle East, he has written twenty books and numerous articles. His most recent books are *Jews, Arabs, Turks* (1993); *The Arab Minority in Israel 1967–1991* (1993); *The Politics of Pan-Islam: Ideology and Organization* (1994); *Pan-Turkism: From Irredentism to Cooperation* (1995); and *Politics of Language in the Ex-Soviet Muslim States* (2001, with Barbara Kellner-Heinkele).

Avigdor Levy is Professor of Near Eastern and Judaic Studies at Brandeis University. He has also taught at Tel Aviv University and served as visiting professor at the University of Chicago and the University of Haifa. He has published several books and numerous articles on Ottoman and modern Middle Eastern history and on the history of the Jewish people in the Middle East. He is the author of *The Sephardim in the Ottoman Empire* (1992). He has also coauthored and edited several books, including *The Arab-Israeli Conflict: Risks and Opportunities* (1975) and *The Jews of the Ottoman Empire* (1994).

Moshe Ma'oz is Professor of Islamic and Middle Eastern Studies at the Hebrew University of Jerusalem. He has published several books and numerous articles on various aspects of Middle Eastern history and politics, among them *Ottoman Reform in Syria and Palestine* (1968); *Syria and Israel: From War to Peacemaking* (1995); and *Middle Eastern Minorities: Between Integration and Conflict* (1999).

Rhoads Murphey is Reader in Ottoman Studies at the Centre for Byzantine, Ottoman and Modern Greek Studies at the University of Birmingham, England, and associate editor of the journal *Archivum Ottomanicum*. He has published extensively on Ottoman historiography and on pre-nineteenth-century Ottoman social, economic, and cultural history. His principal publications are *Aziz Efendi's Book of Sultanic Laws and Regulations* (Harvard University, Sources of Oriental Languages and Literatures no. 9, 1985); *Regional Structure in the Ottoman Economy* (1987); and *Ottoman Warfare, 1500–1700* (1999).

Donald Quataert is Professor of History, the State University of New York at Binghamton. He has written numerous books and articles on Ottoman social and economic history. His principal publications are *Social Disintegration and Popular Resistance in the Ottoman Empire, 1881–1914* (1983); *Workers, Peasants and Economic Change in the Ottoman Empire, 1730–1914* (1993); *Ottoman Manufacturing in the Age of the Industrial Revolution* (1993); and *The Ottoman Empire, 1700–1923* (2000). He is also coauthor and coeditor, with Halil İnalcık, of *An Economic and Social History of the Ottoman Empire, 1300–1914* (1994). He is the editor of *Consumption Studies and the History of the Ottoman Empire: 1550–1922* (2000) and other books.

Daniel J. Schroeter is Professor of History at the University of California, Irvine, where he holds the Teller Family Chair in Jewish History. A specialist in Moroccan history, he has published numerous articles on the Jews of Morocco and the Middle East, and he is the author of *Merchants of Essaouira* (1988), which was translated into Arabic and won a national book award in Morocco for best translated work (1997). He also is the author of *Israel: An Illustrated History* (1998) and *The Sultan's Jew: Morocco and the Sephardi World* (2002). He is presently conducting research on Jews among Berbers in Morocco, and he recently published "Jewish Communities of Morocco: History and Identity," in *Morocco: Jews and Art in a Muslim Land,* The Jewish Museum, New York.

Stanford J. Shaw is Professor Emeritus of Turkish and Judeo-Turkish History at the University of California, Los Angeles, and Professor of Turkish History at Bilkent University, Ankara. Recipient of numerous awards and fellowships, he was also awarded honorary Ph.D. degrees from Harvard University and the University of the Bosphorus, Istanbul. He was the founding editor of the *International Journal of Middle East Studies,* published by Cambridge University Press for the Middle East Studies Association of North America. He is the author of numerous books and articles on Ottoman and Turkish history, including *History of the Ottoman Empire and Modern Turkey* (2 vols., 1976–77; second volume with his wife, Ezel Kural Shaw); *The Jews of the Ottoman Empire and the Turkish Republic* (1992); *Studies in Ottoman and Turkish History: Life with the Ottomans* (2000); and *The Turkish War of National Liberation, 1918–1923* (5 vols., 2000).

Rachel Simon is Associate Fellow of the Foundation for Turkish Studies at Princeton University. A specialist in Libyan history, she has published numerous articles on the Jews of Libya and the Middle East. Her principal publications are *Libya between Ottomanism and Nationalism: The Ottoman Involvement in Libya during the War with Italy (1911–1919)* (1987) and *Change within Tradition among Jewish Women in Libya* (1992).

Frank Tachau is Professor Emeritus of Political Science at the University of Illinois at Chicago, where he served as chairman of the Department of Political Science and coordinator of Jewish Studies. Recipient of numerous awards and fellowships, he was a visiting professor at the University of Chicago as well as at several universities in Israel, Turkey, and Canada. He has published several books and numerous articles on the politics of Turkey, Israel, and the Middle East. He is the author of *Turkey: The Politics of Authority, Democracy, and Development* (1984). He has also coauthored, with others, and edited a number of books, including *Political Elites and Political Development in the Middle East* (1975); *Electoral Politics in the Middle East* (1980); and *Political Parties in the Middle East and North Africa* (1994).

Israel Ta-Shma is Professor Emeritus of Talmud at the Hebrew University of Jerusalem and former Director of the Institute of Microfilmed Hebrew Manuscripts at the National and University Library in Jerusalem. He has published numerous articles on rabbinic history and literature and is the author of *Early Franco-German Ritual and Custom* (in Hebrew; 1992); *Rabbi Zerachya Halevy and His Circle—Rabbinic Literature in Twelfth-Century Provence* (in Hebrew; 1993); *Ha-Nigle She-Banistar—The Halachic Residue in the Zohar* (in Hebrew; 1999); *Ritual, Custom and Reality in Franco-Germany, 1000–1350* (in Hebrew; 1996); and *Talmudic Commentary in Europe and North Africa* (in Hebrew; 2 vols., 1999–2000).

Marie Christine Varol teaches Judeo-Spanish at the National Institute for Oriental Languages and Civilizations (INALCO) in Paris. She is a member of the research laboratory "Languages—Musics—Societies" of the National Center for Scientific Research (CNRS) in France. She has published numerous articles on Judeo-Spanish (Ladino) language, culture, and literature. She is the author of *Balat—Fauburg Juif d'Istanbul* (1989) and *Manuel de judéo-espagnol, langue et culture* (1998). She has edited several volumes, including a special issue of the journal *Plurilinguismes* (no.7, Paris, 1994) on diaspora languages and, together with Winfried Busse, *Hommage à Haïm Vidal Sephiha* (1996).

Introduction

Avigdor Levy

The purpose of this volume is to make a contribution to the emerging field of study on the Jews of the Ottoman Empire and modern Turkey. Only a few years ago, while editing a similar volume of articles, I felt compelled to write a lengthy introduction, amounting to an extended historical essay on Ottoman Jewish history, that first appeared as a separate volume.[1] At the time of writing there was no modern, updated general history of the Jews in the Ottoman Empire and modern Turkey that could be used as a frame of reference for the specialized articles published in that volume. My introduction was intended, therefore, to provide historical context, to point out the results of recent research, and to identify current controversies. During the last decade, however, the field has changed considerably, due in no small measure to the interest engendered by the commemoration in 1992 of the quincentennial of the expulsion of the Jews from Spain and the settlement of many of them in the Ottoman Empire. Within months of the publication of my introductory essay appeared the books by Stanford J. Shaw[2] and Walter F. Weiker,[3] and shortly thereafter the volume coauthored by Esther Benbassa and Aron Rodrigue.[4] This and the ongoing research on different levels make it possible to say that, by the beginning of the twenty-first century, the field of Ottoman and Turkish Jewish studies has received a measure of recognition.

Nonetheless, we still are in the early stages of a full appreciation of the history of Ottoman and Turkish Jewry. As the present volume demonstrates, this history is an integral part of Ottoman and Turkish social, economic, political, religious, and cultural history. Accordingly, what is needed is the in-

tegration of all kinds of primary research based on a wide range of sources—
Jewish, Ottoman, Turkish, Arab, and European. Indeed, a glance at the
sources used in this volume would reveal that the contributing authors have
utilized materials written in Hebrew (rabbinic and modern), Judeo-Spanish,
Turkish (Ottoman and modern), Arabic, and European languages. These
sources fall into several categories: published works, unpublished manuscripts, and documents from the national and private archives of Turkey, Israel, Britain, France, Italy, Austria, Germany, and the United States. Few
scholars, if any, can be expected to have command of all the languages and
kinds of sources required to produce those basic studies necessary for establishing an authoritative account of the history of Ottoman and Turkish Jews.
It is obvious, therefore, that what is needed is an ongoing collaborative effort
among specialists in many fields, and especially in Jewish, Ottoman, Turkish,
Arab, and Balkan studies. Such cooperation would benefit not only Jewish
studies, but also all those other areas. Regrettably, so far we have seen only a
few attempts to engage in collaborative work that would cut across the
boundaries of fields of study.

◆　　◆　　◆

The story of the Jews of the Ottoman Empire and modern Turkey deserves
to be better known. For hundreds of years the Ottoman Empire was home
to one of the world's largest and most vibrant Jewish communities. It is commonly believed that throughout most of the sixteenth and seventeenth centuries, more Jews lived in the Ottoman Empire than in any other state in the
world. Even as late as 1900—following two centuries of Ottoman retreat
from territories that included important Jewish centers, on the one hand,
and migrations and other demographic changes that completely transformed the Jewish diaspora, on the other hand—the Ottoman Jews,
400,000 strong, constituted the fifth-largest Jewish community in the world,
after those of Russia, Austria-Hungary, the United States, and Germany. At
the time, more Jews lived in the Ottoman Empire than in Great Britain and
France combined. Besides their numerical importance, for a long time Ottoman Jewry constituted a major center—materially, spiritually, and culturally—of the world Jewish diaspora. In the fifteenth and sixteenth centuries,
Jews fleeing from Spain and other European countries found in the Ot-

toman Empire a secure and friendly haven, which became home to the largest numbers of Jewish refugees from those countries. The European Jews brought with them their community life, institutions, culture, and scholarship. The resulting contacts and cross-fertilization between Jewish groups coming from different cultures and traditions, together with the unprecedented individual and religious freedom and long periods of material comfort, security, and prominence that they enjoyed in the Ottoman Empire, led to the emergence of a uniquely vibrant society, rich in culture and scholarship. The great Jewish historian Salo Baron described this period as another Jewish Golden Age. Indeed, in the sixteenth century the Ottoman Jewish communities effectively succeeded Spanish Jewry as the most important centers of Jewish scholarship and learning in the world, a position that they maintained for a long time.

Within the Ottoman sociopolitical order for much of this period, the Jews occupied an important, perhaps unique, position. In the fifteenth and sixteenth centuries they were instrumental in developing and expanding the Ottoman administration and economy, and they continued to maintain a prominent role in those areas for a long time thereafter. Jews performed important services as government advisors, ambassadors, tax farmers, financial agents, scribes, international and interregional traders, and in a wide range of urban industries and trades. They also made significant contributions to Ottoman society in science, medicine, technology, culture, and entertainment.

The Ottoman Jews also knew periods of material and spiritual impoverishment, reflecting the general decline of the Ottoman state and society. What makes their experience unique, however—especially when compared with that of European Jewry—is that over a period lasting six centuries, in good times or bad, Jews were never singled out for persecution or oppression because of their religion. In fact, for much of this period they enjoyed the status of a favored minority. Most Jews appreciated the security that they enjoyed in the Ottoman Empire and the plural character of its society, and these evoked among them sentiments of loyalty and patriotism. These sentiments could be quite eloquently expressed, as, for example, in the following refrain from a Judeo-Spanish folk song that became popular at the time of the Young Turk Revolution of 1908:

> *Turkos, djudios, i kristianos,*
> *Todos ottomanos,*
> *Mos tomimos de las manos,*
> *Djurimos de ser ermanos.*

> (Turks, Jews, and Christians,
> All Ottomans,
> Hand in hand
> We swear to be brothers.) [5]

The "special relations" between Jews and Turks have continued to the present. Today the Jewish community of Turkey is small, numbering about 20,000 and concentrated mainly in Istanbul. It is, however, one of the largest—and certainly the most vibrant—of the Jewish communities remaining in the Muslim world. The Jews of Turkey are well integrated in Turkish society, and at the same time they maintain close ties with the world Jewish community.

Halil İnalcık explores the underlying causes for the close cooperation between the Jews and the Ottoman Turks. These relations were shaped in the fifteenth and sixteenth centuries by a conjunction of historical circumstances. The Ottoman conflict with Christian Europe over political and economic hegemony in the Mediterranean and southeastern Europe often assumed the characteristics of a holy war. This same period also witnessed widespread persecution of Jews in European countries. Thus Ottomans and Jews regarded each other as allies, and the former entrusted to the latter key positions in developing the administration and economy of newly conquered territories. As a result, Jews acquired a disproportionate place in the Ottoman economy and financial administration, and on occasion, individual Jews rose to positions where they were able to influence government policies. Although pragmatic considerations were at the heart of this relationship, İnalcık cautions that one need not discount such intangibles as mutual trust and loyalty.

Daniel Goffman continues to discuss the role of Jews in the Ottoman economy from the point İnalcık left off. As long as the central Ottoman government maintained tight control over the empire's main commercial centers, the predominance of Jews in the Ottoman economy and financial administration was assured by government support and the wide-flung networks that the Jews themselves developed. During the late sixteenth and seventeenth centuries, however, a conjunction of changes and transformations undermined the position of the Jewish networks. On the one hand, the Ottoman central government gradually lost its grip over wide provinces to local notables and brigands, and as a result its control of the economy also weakened. On the other hand, changes in international commerce enabled European traders—Dutch, English, French, Venetians, and others—to bypass central government controls and deal directly with the increasingly independent local notables. Because the Jewish networks were so closely identified with the central government, both European merchants and the local authorities preferred to bypass the Jews and deal with members of the Ottoman Christian minorities, mainly Greeks and Armenians. By about 1650 the Jews were in full retreat, although they did not entirely disappear from important positions in banking and international trade. Goffman argues that in some measure the Ottoman Jews, by failing to adapt to the new circumstances, were responsible for their own decline. These transformations, leading to the erosion of Jewish influence, first became evident in Izmir, a trading center that developed in spite of the Ottoman government's opposition and where the central authorities could exercise little influence. But these changes quickly spread to other trading centers, such as Aleppo, Alexandria, and even Istanbul.

Jacob Barnai also takes a close look at the Jews of Izmir, but from a different perspective, that of community life and leadership structures. The economic ascendancy of Izmir attracted Jewish settlers as of the end of the sixteenth century, and the community quickly developed to become one of the leading Jewish centers in the Ottoman Empire and modern Turkey until the twentieth century. Because Izmir was a major regional and international trading center, its population was generally quite diverse, comprising not only different Ottoman religious and ethnic groups, but also Europeans of various nationalities. The same was true of Izmir's Jewish population, which hailed from different parts of the Ottoman Empire as well as from Europe. This diversity led to various cleavages within the community, particularly between the Ottoman Jews and the so-called Portuguese Marranos, who returned to normative Judaism following their settlement in the Ottoman Empire. The tensions among the Jews in Izmir led to the formation of a joint chief rabbinate so as to satisfy competing interests within the community. This arrangement remained in force in Izmir, as well as in other Jewish communities, until the *Tanzimat* reforms. Barnai also discusses some aspects of the Sabbatean movement, which had originated in Izmir and made a long-lasting impact on its Jewish community. He suggests that Portuguese Marranos, who were themselves influenced by Christian millennarianism, played an important role in fostering the intellectual and spiritual climate in which the movement thrived.

Israel Ta-Shma traces the early history of rabbinic literature in the Ottoman Empire and its intellectual and literary origins. He argues that in the fourteenth and fifteenth centuries the Jewish communities in the Balkans were increasingly coming under the influence of Franco-German Jewish legal traditions and thought. This found its expression in the writings and legal decisions of leading rabbis, such as Moses Capsali, the chief rabbi of Istanbul (d. ca. 1496). These processes had a lasting influence on the development of Jewish law in the Ottoman Empire by contributing to the emergence of a careful equilibrium between Ashkenazi and Sephardic legal practices. This is exemplified in the classic *Beit Yosef* by Rabbi Yosef [Joseph] Caro (d. 1575), a work that became a widely accepted legal guide throughout the Jewish world.

Rhoads Murphey deals with another aspect of Jewish scholarly and professional activity in the Ottoman Empire: medicine. He argues that the unique aspect of the Jewish contribution to the medical profession in the Ottoman Empire was not only its ability to produce a few outstanding figures who served sultans and high state officials, but rather the domination of the medical profession as a whole, especially after the mid-sixteenth century. Jewish prominence in the field of medicine was due, in the first place, to the migration of talent from Europe, but also to the proliferation of the profession within the Ottoman Jewish community. He challenges the accepted wisdom that after the sixteenth century Jews no longer played an important role in Ottoman medicine. He demonstrates that, to the contrary, Jewish physicians—and sometimes Jewish converts to Islam—continued to play a major role in the profession down to the nineteenth century. Murphey further argues that medical standards in the Ottoman Empire were equal, or close, to those prevalent in the West at the time and that Ottoman physicians, including Jews, were not isolated from their Western colleagues and they could, therefore, keep abreast of new advances in the profession.

The second part of this volume deals with the nineteenth and early twentieth centuries, a period that witnessed much social and political change and a considerable overall improvement in the condition of the Ottoman Jewish communities. A key issue in Ottoman Jewish historiography of the period is the impact of the Ottoman reforms on Jewish life. Using Ottoman Egypt as a case study, Jacob Landau discusses the changes affecting the structures of the Ottoman Jewish communities and their autonomy. During this period the institutions of the Jewish community—as well as those of other minorities—became better defined through state legislation and the adoption of internal community regulations. At the same time, however, the community's autonomy and the authority of its traditional leadership declined as a result of pressures coming from two different directions. On the one hand, the state began to interfere increasingly in the appointment of chief rabbis so as to secure that influential position for those most likely to follow and advocate its policies. In addition, through the legislative process, the state strictly limited the community's legal autonomy. On the other hand, as a result of rising educational standards and increased secularization, the community's membership began challenging the religious authorities and demanding broader representation in the management of community affairs. Landau argues that the pressures from above and those from below often militated against each other, and as a result the traditional leadership continued to exercise somewhat diminished, but still considerable, authority.

Daniel J. Schroeter also discusses the impact of the Ottoman reforms on Jewish life, examining the cases of the Jewish communities of Syria, Palestine, Iraq, and Libya. But he is concerned primarily with the question of Jewish self-identity. He argues that the Ottoman reforms, by articulating the concept of a Jewish *millet* equal to other *millets*, served to reinforce the notion of communal self-government and strengthened the formal corporate status of the Jews in the Ottoman Empire. In addition, the absence of a broad secularization of society prevented the emergence of an autonomous, non-state civil culture with which the Jews could identify (this last aspect was, of course, somewhat different in the major Ottoman urban centers in the Balkans, Anatolia, and Egypt, where in the empire's last decades a civil culture was noticeable, as reflected in the articles by Feroz Ahmad, Donald Quataert, Avigdor Levy, and Jacob Landau). Therefore, continues Schroeter (and this was probably true throughout the empire), adherence to the community in its universal and local sense defined the identity of most Jews. Consequently, although the Jews were greatly affected by the processes of modernization, this did not lead to wholesale assimilation, as in the West. For the most part the Jews of the Ottoman Empire could accommodate themselves to modernity without severing their ties with their community and religious culture.

Concerned with intercommunity relations in Syria and Palestine, Moshe Ma'oz writes that throughout most of the nineteenth century Jews benefited from a closer and better relationship with the Ottoman authorities and with the Muslim majority than did their Christian neighbors. This resulted in economic advantages for Jews. The close Jewish-Muslim relationship was based largely on age-old Muslim perceptions that Jews were apolitical, weak, unattached to European interests, and therefore loyal. On the other hand, Jewish relations with their Christian neighbors were generally unfriendly due to deep religious animosities and bitter economic rivalry, as Jews and Christians often competed for the same government contracts and in the same trades. This pattern of relations changed only toward the end of the nineteenth century. At that time there emerged a growing community of interests between Muslims and Christians. Both Muslim and Christian Syrian intellectuals took part in the Arab cultural renaissance and the awakening of an Arab national consciousness, while the apolitical Jews did not. At the same time, while Ottoman Jews continued to profess their loyalty to the state, the rise of political Zionism accompanied by the first Zionist agricultural settlements in Palestine tainted all Jews with disloyalty and further strengthened Muslim-Christian bonds.

Related to some of the issues discussed by Ma'oz, Amnon Cohen's contribution is concerned primarily with the relationship between the Jewish community of Jerusalem and the Muslim religious court, which also operated as a state court. Jerusalem attracted Jewish pilgrims and settlers from all corners of the Jewish diaspora, and consequently the city's Jewish population was very diverse. Perhaps this condition accounted in some measure for the fact that the Jews of Jerusalem were prone to litigate one another. Rather than settle their disputes among themselves, they apparently preferred to bring them before the Muslim religious court, and this relationship continued into the second half of the nineteenth century. Cohen demonstrates that while much is known about Jewish life in Jerusalem during this period from many Jewish and Western sources, the records of the Muslim court still contain an abundance of information on the Jewish community that cannot be found elsewhere. The lengthy and complicated lawsuit discussed by Cohen sheds light on living conditions in Jerusalem, the rising cost of housing, details of real estate transactions, relations between Sephardic and Ashkenazi Jews, and other facets of daily life.

Rachel Simon deals with a key issue in the modernization of Jewish society: the education of women. Using examples from different parts of the Ottoman Empire, she argues that modern Jewish female education began in the mid-nineteenth century, primarily as a result of the activities of Western organizations. First on the scene were Christian missionaries, who directed considerable efforts at attracting Jewish girls and young women to their institutions. Fear of conversion facilitated the intervention of Western Jewish philanthropic organizations, which aimed not only to avert the missionary threat, but also to improve the general condition of the Ottoman Jewish communities. Modern female Jewish education developed quickly, although it always lagged behind that of males. Simon argues that because traditional Jewish society had not provided for the systematic education of females, the new girls' schools encountered less opposition on the part of traditionalists than did boys' schools. Furthermore, girls' schools did not have to incorporate in their curricula elements of traditional education in the same way that boys' schools were required to do. Consequently, maintains Simon, those women that attended the new schools became the only segment of Jewish society that received a thoroughly modern education. Modern education transformed the position of women in many communities: it improved their economic condition and allowed them to become educators and civic leaders, roles that traditionally had been the domain of men only. In breaking new ground, however, women encountered a great deal of opposition, and although they made progress, the process was difficult and slow.

In some ways Avigdor Levy's article could be regarded as a case study illustrating some of Simon's arguments. Using the unpublished journal of the directress of the Alliance Israélite Universelle school for girls in Edirne as his main source, Levy discusses the frequent clashes between the directress, on the one hand, and the all-male Jewish community leadership in Edirne, on the other. Levy's main objective, however, is to describe the daily life of the civilian population in the besieged city of Edirne during the first Balkan War (October 1912-March 1913) and discuss the consequences of that war with particular attention to the Jewish community. In a wider sense, this article portrays the final days of the plural character of Ottoman society, underscoring Jewish preferences for continued Ottoman administration in the Balkans. Edirne could be said to have been a microcosm of Ottoman society as a whole: at the outbreak of the war, about half its population was Turkish and the other half consisted of minorities—Greeks, Jews, Bulgarians, Armenians, and Europeans. Although the city's population suffered greatly from bombardment, hunger, and disease, throughout this ordeal public order and personal security were maintained, and there were no incidents of intercommunal strife until after the city's fall to the Bulgarian and Serb armies. In fact, during the siege there was considerable intercommunal cooperation, and acts of basic human decency that cut across religious and ethnic lines abounded. The Balkan Wars, however, by exacerbating nationalist animosities, delivered a severe blow to the possibility of plural coexistence and foreshadowed the Ottoman Empire's total disintegration. The wars also led to the dramatic decline of the city of Edirne, to the disappearance of its Christian minorities, and to the gradual decline and final demise of its Jewish community.

The plural character of Ottoman society is also a central theme in Donald Quataert's article. In its last decades as an Ottoman city, Salonica experienced exceptional economic growth and social transformation. It became a major center of regional and international trade, with a corresponding growth in its industrial infrastructure, which at the time was perhaps the largest in the Ottoman Empire. Jews, who were the largest ethnic group of the city's population, played a major role in Salonica's economic development and modernization. They constituted the majority of the city's entrepreneurs and factory founders. The industrialization of the city also created a large working class, and here again Jews played a major role in forming and leading the labor movement, which was multiethnic and multireligious. Because Salonica's Jews strongly opposed separation from the empire, the labor movement as a whole adopted an Ottomanist position. The movement tried to remain above nationalist politics, and it appealed to the working-class identity of its members. Quataert argues that the most successful efforts to overcome national differences in the Ottoman Empire took place in Salonica.

Feroz Ahmad discusses the relationship between the Committee of Union and Progress (CUP), the principal Young Turk group that dominated the political scene from 1908 to 1918, and the Ottoman Jewish political leadership. In the process he also makes a contribution to the current debate over the significance of Zionism among Ottoman Jews. Following the Young Turk Revolution of 1908, the new regime sought to overhaul the government and regulate the relations between the state and the non-Muslim communities. It was at this point that the political differences between the CUP and the political leaders of the Greek and Armenian communities came into sharp focus. In contrast, the Jewish political leadership cooperated with the CUP, because Jews and Turks largely shared the same aspirations: both wanted to build a strong, centralized Ottoman state and break the hold of the Great Powers since neither benefited from the foreign protection provided by the Capitulations. The Jewish political leadership, argues Ahmad, was the only non-Muslim, non-Turkish group to fully cooperate with the CUP. Although the Zionist movement succeeded in introducing its ideology to the Ottoman Jewish communities in such centers as Istanbul and Salonica, the Zionists were not as well organized as the Greek and Armenian nationalists. Furthermore, for most Ottoman Jews, Zionism was more an amorphous quest for cultural and national identity than a well-articulated political program. In any event, the Jewish communities did not elect any Zionists to the Ottoman assemblies; in fact, all the deputies they elected were members or sympathizers of the CUP. The cooperation between the CUP and the Jewish political leadership continued through the Balkan Wars as well as World War I, when Jewish officials represented the Ottoman government in a variety of diplomatic missions abroad.

The common denominator of the articles in the third part of this volume is that they are all concerned with modern Turkey's relations with Jews. The first two contributions deal with Turkey's attitude toward European Jewry during the 1930s and World War II, while the last two are concerned with issues related to Jewish identity and acculturation in modern Turkey.

Frank Tachau traces the emergence of a German Jewish community in Turkey to a remarkable historical coincidence. Adolf Hitler's rise to power in Germany in January 1933 placed in immediate danger Jewish scholars and all opponents of the regime. At precisely the same time, the Turkish republic, under the leadership of President Kemal Atatürk, undertook a major reform of its system of higher education as part of a massive effort to modernize the country. This undertaking created an urgent need for scientists and scholars to take on the task of building the new universities and scientific institutions. The result of this historic coincidence was that several hundred highly talented individuals fleeing Nazi persecution were able to find shelter in Turkey, in spite of German opposition. These refugees helped to develop Turkey's universities and established and directed new research institutions. The absorption in Turkey of hundreds of scholars, most of whom were unfamiliar with the Turkish language or with living conditions in the country, was not an easy task, as Tachau demonstrates. On the whole, however, the experiment proved highly successful and benefited both parties: Turkey was able to modernize its academic institutions and enrich its cultural life, while for most of the refugee scholars the Turkish haven provided an escape from almost certain death and an opportunity to continue with their professional careers.

Stanford Shaw discusses Turkey's role in assisting European Jews to escape the Holocaust. Although Turkey remained neutral during most of World War II, it was forced to formulate policies and pursue an active role on matters related to the Holocaust when these began to affect its own Jewish citizens living in Europe. Shaw focuses mainly on the activities of Turkish diplomats in France, where some 10,000 Jews who were Turkish citizens, or former citizens, lived. Although the German and French authorities insisted on applying racial laws against all Jews residing in France, irrespective of their nationality, the Turkish government refused to accept this position. Turkey argued that these policies violated the treaties it had signed with

France, which provided that Turkish nationals were to enjoy the same civil rights in France that French citizens enjoyed in Turkey. In addition, the Turks argued that the racial policies discriminated among Turkish citizens of different religions, which violated Turkish constitutional law. The steadfast vigilance of Turkish diplomats resulted in the rescue of thousands of Jews, in France as well as in Greece, from deportation to extermination camps. Shaw also discusses Turkey's policies in permitting its territory to be used for rescue operations of Jews from Nazi-occupied Europe.

Marie-Christine Varol discusses linguistic aspects of Sephardic popular cultural traditions as they persisted among the Jews of Istanbul in the late twentieth century. She focuses on the linguistic manner through which traditional magic-religious medical practices were transmitted. The modern practitioners of this kind of medicine were always women, and most were well educated and familiar with modern medicine. These women would use magic-religious practices only as a last resort, after modern medical procedures had failed. Varol demonstrates how the practitioners of this knowledge would express their belief in the efficacy of these practices and at the same time maintain their distance from them through an intricate use of language, alternating between Judeo-Spanish, a language of tradition, on the one hand, and French and Turkish, languages of modernity, on the other hand. Varol is concerned with the question whether the practice of this knowledge will survive the disappearance of Judeo-Spanish and the multilingualism of the Jewish community.

Through an analysis of the literary work of Mario Levi, whom Nedim Gürsel describes as "the first modern Turkish-language writer who has openly flaunted his Jewish identity," Gürsel demonstrates that it is possible for Turkish Jews to become fully acculturated and integrated into Turkish society and at the same time maintain their ethnic-religious distinctiveness. While the balancing of the two may result in a certain tension, Mario Levi, for one, considers it an advantage in his mission as a Turkish writer. While Levi considers the Turkish language to be his "true homeland," he writes mainly about minorities and the "psychology of exile." His narrative abounds with uprooted characters who live between different countries, different cultures, and different languages. Gürsel argues that Levi's most important contribution to Turkish literature lies in exposing the world of the minorities, their sensitivities and anxieties, to the Turkish public, contributing thereby to the diversity and enrichment of Turkish literature. Gürsel's article, which deals with what is perhaps the last chapter in the relations between Jews and Turks in contemporary Turkey, is a fitting conclusion to this volume.

PART ONE

Jewish Society and the Ottoman Polity,
Fifteenth through Eighteenth Centuries

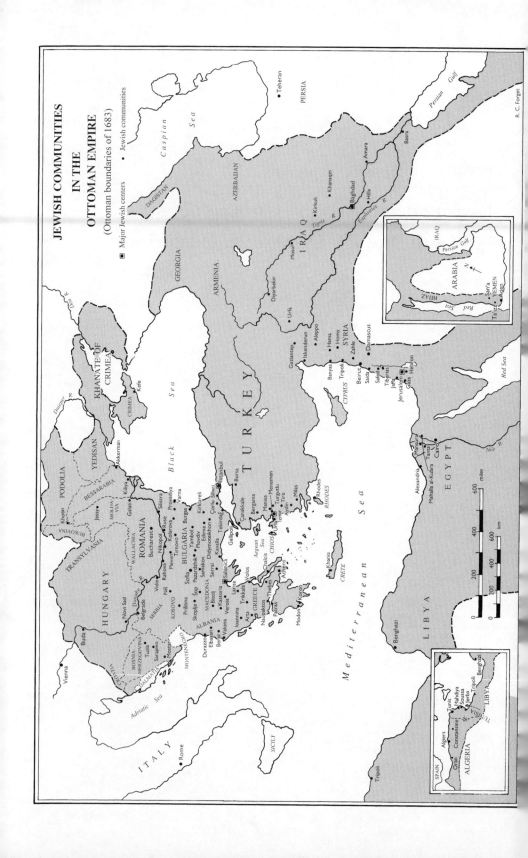

JEWISH COMMUNITIES
IN THE
OTTOMAN EMPIRE
(Ottoman boundaries of 1683)

■ Major Jewish centers   • Jewish communities

CHAPTER I

Foundations of Ottoman-Jewish Cooperation

Halil İnalcık

The records of the Ottoman archives clearly indicate that in public life Jews performed important functions as advisors to the government, tax farmers, financial agents, and scribes. In economic life, in international and interregional trade, as well as in urban trades and industries, Jews also played a role of importance far beyond the size of their community. One can see the Jewish presence in all kinds of Ottoman archival documentation: in the *Mühimme,* or proceedings of the imperial council, in the registers and papers of the finance department, and in the court records of the *kadi,* or judge, which deal with legal and commercial transactions and administrative matters. On the activities of Jews only a fraction of these vast collections has so far been the subject of investigation.[1] The question before the historian is to explain why at a particular period of time the Ottomans demonstrated an exceptional interest in European Jewry, an interest that was indeed without precedent or equal in Islamic history.

The community of interests between Turks and Jews had a long history, going back to the early days of the Ottoman state. It was, however, the confluence of certain circumstances in the second half of the fifteenth century that led the Ottomans to show a particular interest in the Jews expelled from Spain. First, it must be recalled that following the Ottoman conquest of Constantinople, the crusading fervor in Europe had reached its peak. On the other hand, the Spanish *reconquista,* resumed against the Muslims of al-Andalus, stirred an intense spirit of *jihad* in the Islamic world. In 1492 the fall of Granada was celebrated with religious processions throughout Europe. Ear-

3

lier, in 1490, the pope had invited all the Christian states to send delegates to Rome to discuss a full-fledged crusade against the Ottoman Empire. Prince Cem (Jem), the son of Mehmed II, the conqueror of Constantinople, was at the time held as a captive at the Vatican, and the Christian powers had intended to use him as a tool in their crusade. At the same time, Andalusian and North African Muslims attempted to attract the attention of the Ottoman sultan to their impending conquest by a crusading Spain. In 1477 they had sent a delegation to Mehmed the Conqueror to solicit his aid and protection. After the fall of Granada in 1492, the North African Muslims, fearing that the same fate would soon befall them, redoubled their efforts to secure Ottoman protection. Thus, in the Ottoman mind, Spain was a major antagonist, and the Ottomans made little distinction between the plight of the Andalusian Muslims and that of the Jews when both communities were threatened by Spain and both appealed for Ottoman aid and protection.[2]

By 1492 the patterns of Jewish immigration to Ottoman lands had been established for more than a century. Ever since the year 1360, when King Louis the Great of Hungary issued a decree expelling the Jews from his dominions, European Jewry had begun to look to the Ottoman territories as a sanctuary.[3] The Jews of Central Europe may have become aware at that time of the favorable conditions that existed for Jews in the Ottoman Balkans before 1453. Although this awareness did not result at the time in a mass Jewish migration to the Ottoman dominions, the Ottoman sources testify that there were prosperous, and growing, Jewish communities in Ottoman Balkan cities such as Edirne and Salonica in the period prior to 1453. It was, however, after the conquest of Constantinople that the Ottomans demonstrated their particular interest in the Jews by encouraging their immigration. This was the outcome of a rational and deliberate policy on the part of the Ottomans in response to a crusading Europe, where religious intolerance and persecution of Jews were on the rise. Mehmed the Conqueror must have been aware of the plight of the Jews in Europe when he encouraged them to take sanctuary in his territories. This attitude corresponded to the general policies of Mehmed II, who was then deeply preoccupied with the resettlement of his depopulated and ruined new capital, Istanbul, with a population possessing skills and financial resources.[4] The well-known circular letter of Isaac Sarfati (Yitzhak Tzarfati) gains credit when placed in this context. Incidentally, this letter belongs, I believe, to Mehmed II's reign (1451–81), although Salo Baron is inclined to trace it back to the reign of Murad II (1421–51). Himself a refugee from Germany, Sarfati, in his letter, vigorously encouraged the Jews of Europe to immigrate to the Ottoman Empire, where "every man may dwell at peace under his own vine and fig-tree."[5] In view of the circumstances following the conquest of Constantinople, it is quite plausible that the sultan himself had Sarfati send out this circular to European Jewry.

At the time, Mehmed II's first and principal concern was to repopulate and restore the economic vitality of Istanbul. He wanted to bring and settle in his new capital as many Jews as possible. The Venetian district and the trade depots of the Latin nations, in the port area in particular, were completely destroyed during the capture of the city. These trading nations had formerly been in control of, and responsible for, much of the economic prosperity of the Byzantine capital. The well-to-do of Bursa and other Anatolian cities did not respond to Mehmed's order to come and settle in the ruined city. Also, as the Ottoman census of 1455 reveals,[6] many Turkish settlers soon returned to their original homes in Anatolia and Rumeli. For the reconstruction of the city, the sultan realized that he needed people with mercantile skills and capital. The same census shows that many abandoned houses and entire districts were then taken over by Jewish settlers from Balkan and Anatolian towns. Driven from their homes under the Ottoman resettlement (sürgün) system, many of these Jews were settled in the port area from Çıfut-Kapı or "the Gate of the Jews" to Zindan-Kapı. This was the business center of the city, and it had been formerly occupied principally by Venetians.[7] The sultan prohibited the return of the Venetians to the area and, no doubt, intended the Jewish businessmen and traders to replace them. It is interesting to note that Mehmed II demanded from the doge of Venice to allow Venetian Jews, who before and during the siege had fled from Constantinople's port district to Venice, to return to Istanbul. The Ottoman survey of 1477 lists 1,647 Jewish households in Istanbul but no Jews in Galata. The earlier census of 1455, however, records a group of 44 Jewish families in Galata, many of them quite wealthy. Apparently the Jews of Galata, too, were selected for resettlement on the Istanbul side of the Golden Horn. Similarly, all the Jews of Salonica were resettled in Istanbul. Furthermore, the census of 1492 reveals that 380 new families had joined Istanbul's Jewry since the census of 1477. This clearly indicates that Mehmed II considered the Jews, even those Venetian Jews who had fled the city during the hostilities, as trustworthy subjects, and he believed that they were indispensable for the economic development of his new imperial capital.[8]

The policies that Mehmed II's successors adopted toward the Jews, the Sephardic Jews in particular, were based on the same principles. This explains why the Ottoman bureaucracy demonstrated particular sympathy toward the Jews, just at the time when the Sephardic mass immigration into the Ottoman dominions was at its peak.

Along with these particular circumstances, we also have to take into account the established norms of Islamic law, the *Shari'a,* in regard to religious minorities, the so-called *dhimma* law. In return for the payment of a poll tax by the minorities, the *jizya,* the Islamic state assumed the responsibility of providing the same protection for its non-Muslim subjects as for Muslims. It was a strict religious duty for Muslim rulers to abide by this law. True, under the Islamic tradition non-Muslims were subject to various restrictions. They were, for example, prohibited from dressing as Muslims, riding horses, owning slaves, and practicing religious ceremonies in a way that might be offensive to Muslims. These restrictions were all designed to underscore the social inferiority of non-Muslims in relation to Muslims. Ordinarily, however, such restrictions were overlooked by the Ottoman authorities, and, I believe, it is an exaggeration to interpret these social limitations as reducing non-Muslims under Islam to the status of second-class subjects. Thus we learn from imperial Ottoman orders, issued at times when popular feelings against non-Muslims ran high as a result of military defeat at the hands of Christian powers, that wealthy Jews are described as indistinguishable from the Muslim elite with their costly caftans, richly harnessed horses, and their slave attendants. In brief, Islamic law and the state generally accepted non-Muslim communities, including the Jews, as part of the larger Islamic society.

Furthermore, the Turkish state tradition practiced Islamic law with regard to non-Muslims in its broadest and most liberal interpretation. Since the eleventh century, when the Seljuk Turks seized control of the Islamic lands in the east, Turkish states introduced new concepts of government and law into the Islamic world. The Turkish states down to the Ottoman Empire jealously guarded the independence of their political action and secular state laws in the face of Islamic law and its interpreters, the *ulema*. In fact, the Ottoman sultans went so far as to issue their own imperial codes of law. The dominance of sultanic authority and law in Muslim Turkish states most likely originated from the Central Asian *törü* or *yasa* tradition. As a kind of constitutional law, *törü* or *yasa* regulated the imperial organization under a charismatic leader. In the Euroasian steppe empires, all those elements that provided information, skills, and wealth for the empire, particularly traveling merchants, were given special attention and protection. Those who produced wealth for the ruler's treasury or provided him with luxury goods or with information were believed to be indispensable for his power. Ottoman sultans, like the Turco-Mongol rulers of Central Asia, were most concerned with these aspects of government, considered as directly involving their own interests and power.[9]

In sum, special historical circumstances led to a kind of solidarity and cooperation between European Jewry and the Ottomans in the face of a crusading Christian Europe. The Turkish state tradition of Central Asia favored those subjects who could provide skill and capital to the empire. Finally, Islam's constitutional *dhimma* law provided the religious minorities with strict guarantees for their lives, property, and freedom of religion. All this made it possible for the Jews of Europe to immigrate, settle, and develop prosperous Jewish communities in the Ottoman Empire.

As I noted earlier, after 1453 Mehmed the Conqueror resorted to forced resettlement of Jews from Balkan and Anatolian towns to Istanbul. It soon became evident, however, that this measure disrupted the economic well-being of those towns. In 1492 the opportunity arose to resettle these same towns with new Jewish immigrants from Spain. Although it is impossible to determine with any certainty how many Jews emigrated from the Iberian peninsula in 1492 and after, all the evidence suggests that a majority of these refugees settled in the Ottoman dominions and that their numbers were in the tens of thousands. These immigrants settled for the most part outside Istanbul, in Salonica, Valona (Avlonya), Patras, Edirne, Bursa, and many other towns throughout the empire.[10]

Once established in the urban centers of the Ottoman Empire, the

Sephardic Jews first formed congregations (*cema'ats*) on the basis of their towns of origin. Over time, however, these congregations were integrated into already existing Jewish quarters, or they formed separate quarters around a synagogue of their own.[11] The Ottoman government allowed the immigrants to maintain their traditional community organization and autonomy in their internal affairs. Moreover, they protected the Jews, as they did other minorities, against acts of fraud and oppression. In the case of the Jews, the Ottoman government demonstrated particular concern to protect them against ritual murder accusations (the false allegation that Jews kill non-Jews, especially Christians, to use their blood for the Passover or other rituals), then common in Europe and also among Ottoman Christians.[12] Thus, under the guarantees provided by Islamic law and Ottoman state law (*kanun*), as well as the supervision of a vigilant central bureaucracy, the Jewish communities prospered. These conditions are well recorded by the vast Jewish responsa literature and travelers' accounts.[13]

As the Ottomans had expected, the Jewish contribution to the Ottoman economy, finances, and urban development proved to be most substantial and diverse. Sephardic Jews made spectacular contributions to the development of the empire's industries, especially to the manufacture of woolens in places such as Salonica, Safed, and Istanbul.[14] In this article, however, I will focus on Jewish activity in the areas of tax farming and trade.

As the Ottomans sought to undermine Venetian and Genoese economic domination and exploitation of the Levant, they pursued a deliberate policy of favoring and protecting their native minorities, including Greeks, Armenians, and Jews. Having become an important segment of Ottoman society, the Jewish community occupied since the fifteenth century a particularly influential position in tax farming and in interregional and international trade.[15]

In the fifteenth and sixteenth centuries, Ottoman Jews, Turks, and Greeks were competing for tax farm contracts, and Jews were particularly active in this area. Extensively applied in the Ottoman Empire even at this early period, tax farming was one of the most profitable economic activities for those who had accumulated cash capital. Short of steady and regular cash resources to meet current needs, and lacking the complex tax collection system of a modern state, the Ottoman government generally depended on cash advances from individuals who had accumulated capital through commercial activities. The registers of tax farming, the so-called *mukata'a defterleri*, from the second half of the fifteenth century contain many names of Jewish "capitalists" serving as tax farmers.

We find Jews undertaking all kinds of tax farms everywhere in the empire, particularly in the big cities and at important sea ports, but also in many smaller towns in the Balkans and Anatolia. At the auctions of the tax farms, keen competition between Jewish, Turkish, and Greek bidders took place.[16]

In October 1477, outbidding their rivals by 400,000 *akçe,* the partnership of the Jew Altina, the Turk Seyyidi Küçük of Edirne, and an Italian by the name of Nikiroz won the right to collect the customs dues from the ports in the Istanbul customs zone for the enormous sum of 20,400,000 *akçe* (45 *akçe* equalled one gold ducat at this time). They thus outbid the previous offer made by the partnership of the Greek Palaeologus of Istanbul, Palaeologus Kassandros, and Lefteri Galyanos of Trebizond. Anyone engaged in tax farming had to provide at least two sureties with assets large enough to meet the debt in case of default. In our records, the sureties designated by the Jewish bidders are all from the Jewish community. But, as seen in the above example, Jews also joined in partnership with Muslim Turks. In this connection we should not forget that the latter group included many Jewish, Greek, and Italian converts.[17]

Because of its crucial importance for state finances, the tax farm of the Istanbul customs house conferred on its holders a great deal of influence in affairs of state. During the fifteenth and sixteenth centuries, this position was quite often held by Jews. Jews also held tax farms outside Istanbul. For example, in 1483 a Jew, Sabbetay son of Avraham, offered 1,200,000 *akçe,* outbidding all competitors, for the tax farm of the saltworks of Thrace. In addition to the rich merchants and money changers, there were also enterprising Jews who brought together investors with small savings or inherited money, and they became quite prominent in tax farming. Jewish tax farmers were assisted mostly by other Jews who acted as scribes and assessors.

By the second half of the sixteenth century, Jewish bankers and tax farmers had gained a predominant place in Ottoman finances and long distance trade. Perhaps the best-known case is that of the famous Marrano-Jewish family of Mendes in the mid-sixteenth century.[18] Many Marrano

Jews, victims of the Inquisition in western Europe, immigrated to the Ottoman Empire in the sixteenth and early seventeenth centuries. Among them was the house of Mendes, which controlled a large share of the international spice trade and had accumulated enormous capital in Europe. Under the protection of Sultan Süleyman the Magnificent, the head of the family, Doña Gracia Mendes, settled in Istanbul in 1552. Her nephew and partner, Don Joseph Nasi, became the most prominent member of the family. Initially, his spectacular rise was due to his financial services to Prince Selim, who had made him one of his intimates, a *müteferrika* (distinguished attendant), in his provincial palace. When, in 1566, Selim acceded to the Ottoman throne, he appointed Don Joseph as the duke of Naxos (Nakşa Dukası), which comprised a group of islands in the Aegean, producing rare wines for export. This appointment must have been related to Joseph's control of the tax farm on wine exports to the northern Black Sea countries, Poland in particular. The tax farm on the dukedom was fixed at 6,000 gold pieces. Joseph's control of this trade was of course a loss for Venice. The former duke of Naxos, a Venetian, did not give up his claim and continued to harass Don Joseph. The tax farm on customs dues on the wine exported from the Aegean and Venetian Crete to Poland also came under Joseph's control. This secured for him a virtual monopoly of the wine trade, since under the Ottoman tax farm system the government put strict controls on the traffic in goods to prevent smuggling and to realize the highest revenue possible. Joseph Nasi's annual income from the monopoly on the export of Cretan wine was estimated at 15,000 ducats a year. Around 1575 it is reported that one thousand casks of wine were exported annually from Crete alone.

Don Joseph is reputed to have influenced Ottoman policy toward Venice regarding Cyprus, which was another center of wine production. Considered an expert on European political affairs, Don Joseph became at this time one of the sultan's most trusted counselors. Apparently Nasi was among the supporters of Vezir Lala Mustafa's plan to conquer Cyprus, in opposition to Grand Vezir Sokollu Mehmed, who objected to the plan and wanted to continue the war against Muscovy in the north. The plan to colonize the island with Jewish settlers is also worth noting in this context. The Ottoman conquest of Cyprus led to the formation of the Christian Holy

League in the Mediterranean, resulting in the Ottoman disaster at the Battle of Lepanto in 1571. In spite of that, however, it appears that Don Joseph continued to enjoy the sultan's favor.

It has been suggested that the Marrano Jews introduced into the Ottoman Empire the techniques of European capitalism, banking, and even the mercantilist concept of a state economy.[19] International trade, tax farming, and banking operations were all interconnected at this time. The financial operations of the Mendes family were carried out through a wide network of agents in the principal centers of Europe. Thus, the Mendes family controlled a large portion of the commerce between the Ottoman Empire and Europe, which mainly consisted of the exchange of European-manufactured woolens for Ottoman wheat, pepper, and raw wool. Also, investments by Jewish merchants in the treasury's tax farms seem to have been quite high during this period. In 1555, when Pope Paul IV confiscated the possessions of Jews in the papal territory, the sultan protested, claiming that many Jews of Salonica and Istanbul had gone bankrupt and were unable to meet their financial obligations to the treasury, amounting to 400,000 gold ducats.[20]

Under the management of Doña Gracia (d. 1568 or 1569), a Jewish bank, or *dolab*, appears to have involved Ottoman finances and capital investments in European markets. Don Joseph became a big creditor to the kings of Europe. His large loans to the king of Poland procured for him various commercial concessions. Under the sultan's protection, he obtained, for example, a monopoly on beeswax exports from Poland. In 1555, when King Henri II of France was pressed for money, Don Joseph floated a loan in France in which the interest ranged from 12 to 16 percent. Little wonder that many Turks invested money in the loan through Don Joseph.

Later on, in 1588, Alvaro Mendes, who like Joseph Nasi was an archenemy of King Philip II of Spain, came to settle in Istanbul, reportedly bringing with him capital of 850,000 gold ducats. He received the same favors once enjoyed by Don Joseph. Esther Kyra, a Jewish favorite of the women in the imperial palace and a liaison between them and Jewish interests outside, also became involved in tax farming and trade and amassed a large fortune during her long relation with the seraglio. However, she met with a tragic end at the hands of the Sipahis. Her fortune at the time of her death was reported to have amounted to fifty million *akçe* or 300,000 gold ducats.

In sum, Jews played a crucial role in the relations of the Ottoman Empire with Western Europe, politically as well as economically. Joseph Nasi, for example, played a decisive role in developing Ottoman–Dutch relations. Since he had once been active in the Antwerp banking house of Mendes, the Prince of Orange, William I, sent a secret envoy to Nasi, seeking Ottoman support for the Dutch revolt against Philip II. There was even some talk of a Dutch alliance with the Ottomans. In a letter to the "Lutherans" in Flanders and other Spanish provinces, the sultan promised to send troops to their aid at a time to be determined by them.[21] Indeed, to counter the Catholic front in the Mediterranean, the Ottomans took the initiative in reaching an accord with the Dutch, whose powerful navy had greatly impressed the Ottomans.

A little-known case illustrating how the Jewish enterprising spirit led to the economic development of an entire region is that of the Jews of the Adriatic. Benjamin Ravid's inquiries demonstrate that with the help, and under the protection, of the Ottoman government, Jews were able to promote their trade and legal status in Venice in the course of the sixteenth century.[22] Moreover, during the period 1492–1520, the Ottoman government actively encouraged Sephardic Jews to settle in Adriatic ports and develop their trade there. Consequently, Jews emerged as the most active partners, and rivals, of Dubrovnik (Ragusa) in regional trade. Valona, one of the most important Ottoman sea ports on the Adriatic, was a case in point. In Valona, the Ottoman government settled Jews expelled from Spain in 1492, from Portugal in 1497, and from Italy in 1510–11. By 1520 they numbered 527 households, constituting one third of the city's population. The court records of Valona demonstrate that the Jews dominated the city's economic life and enjoyed great freedom of action.[23] The Jews of Valona were principally engaged in long-distance trade. That they dominated the city's trade with Venice is attested by Venetian insurance documents. The insurance register for the years 1592–1609 lists sixteen Valona Jews as residing in Venice.

In the late sixteenth century, Valona's role in the Adriatic declined in favor of new ports closer to Venice. Many Jews moved to Dubrovnik during the Ottoman–Venetian war of 1570–73, when woolen cloth imports from Venice shifted to this neutral port.[24] Meanwhile, the Ottomans resettled a great number of Sephardic Jews in Nova (Herzegnovi), further north on the Adriatic, when they reconquered the town in 1570. In the last decades of the sixteenth century, many Ottoman Jews, chiefly those engaged in the cloth trade, preferred to settle in Venice or moved to Split (Spalato). Clearly, there had been large Jewish emigrations from Valona to the northern Adriatic ports. In Valona, the Ottoman tax registers of 1583 still list 212 Jews, but only 50 in 1597.[25]

In the wake of the Ottoman-Venetian peace of 1573, an enterprising Jewish merchant, Daniel Rodriguez (Rodriga), proposed to the Venetian senate to develop Split into a free port by improving its facilities and abolishing or reducing customs dues. Venice was hesitant; then Ottoman Jews approached the council of Dubrovnik and, for a while, obtained a privileged tariff. In the end, with the support of Ottoman Jews residing in Venice and the active involvement of the Ottoman governor of Bosnia, the Venetians finally decided to proceed with Rodriguez's plan. On 20 June 1590, the senate decided that Split would become a free port, that customs dues on imports from the Ottoman dominions to Venice through Split would be reduced by half, and that dues on the export of soap, rice, and some other goods would be totally abolished. Furthermore, Ottoman Jews arriving in Venice would not be subject to any residential tax and could settle in the old Jewish quarter. Rodriguez's plan could be regarded as part of a Jewish attempt to organize an international trading network under Ottoman protection. At Split, Venetian-Ottoman trade based mainly on Ottoman exports of wax, moroccos, timber, silk, mohair, and hides rapidly flourished. From 1590 onward, Split surpassed Dubrovnik and Valona in the Ottoman trade with Venice and assumed a very important role in the overall Venetian commerce.[26]

◆   ◆   ◆

It is only fitting to conclude this article with the eloquent words of the great Jewish historian Salo Baron, who described sixteenth-century Jewish life in the Ottoman Empire as follows:

> The Sephardic and Romaniot [Jewish] communities now lived almost exclusively under Ottoman rule and its system of legislation characterized by

great stability and basic protection of human rights. The Jews reciprocated with a growing sense of Turkish patriotism. . . . With the great freedom of movement guaranteed by legal and administrative enactments, communication between the various Jewish communities became very intensive. . . . Making use of the vast opportunities offered by Turkey's Golden Age, the regrouped Mediterranean Jewry, too, now enjoyed a new efflorescence. It, too, may have legitimately classified the sixteenth century as another Golden Age of its own.[27]

As a historian, I tried to focus on the historical, rational motives and causes for Turkish-Jewish cooperation, setting aside the role of intangible sentiments such as compassion, sympathy, and loyalty. But I think I was mistaken. Sometimes human relations are shaped and moved by forces that are deeper and more significant than mere rationality. Shared experiences and positive memories, interwoven through centuries of coexistence, have made Turks and Jews one family united in friendship.

CHAPTER 2

Jews in Early Modern Ottoman Commerce

Daniel Goffman

The integration of Jews from Iberia and elsewhere into Ottoman society accompanied the Ottoman expansion into southeastern Europe,
the Fertile Crescent, and Egypt. In the fifteenth and sixteenth centuries,
Jews created new niches in the Ottoman economy. They also joined other
Ottoman subjects in many urban pursuits and became influential in industry,
banking, administration, and, most notably, international trade. The Ottomans' early triumphs, both military and commercial, also benefited that
empire's Jews.

In the late sixteenth and seventeenth centuries, however, rival Ottoman
subjects dislodged the Jews from many of those very occupations in Ottoman industry and international commerce that they had helped create.
Other Jewish employments simply became less pivotal in the eastern
Mediterranean marketplace. This decrease in Jewish activities at the heart of
transcontinental exchange had several roots. As patterns in Mediterranean
commerce changed, Jewish merchants were displaced. Transformations in
the Ottoman state and society forced Jews out of administrative positions.
The emergence of new economic, cultural, and demographic centers served
to redefine the Ottoman Jewish community's bonds to the world in which it
lived. Perhaps the most profound (and certainly the most visible) change was
the atrophy in Sephardic communities such as Salonica, Istanbul, and Safed,
and the attendant founding of a new and metamorphic nucleus in Izmir.

The nexus of these alterations rested in international commerce. Earlier,
the abilities and power of Ottoman-Jewish industrialists, tax collectors, and

15

merchants had compelled traders—both subject and foreign—to negotiate with and even hire Ottoman Jews as brokers and translators.[1] Thus, even the French and English, neither of whom tolerated Jews in their own lands, utilized that community, often without the approval of their company directors or home governments, to lodge themselves within the Ottoman economy. Because of innovations and transformations in global commerce, however, it became increasingly possible, and even advantageous, to circumvent the Judeo-Ottoman network. There are several key factors in understanding the position of Ottoman Jews in early modern international commerce. One should examine the routines and methods of the Ottoman government, the long-term implications of Jewish dominance in decreasingly effective governmental services, the tactics of Atlantic seaboard governments and trading companies, the transforming place of the Ottomans in the international economic order, and the minutiae of relations between Jews and others in Aleppo, Istanbul, and elsewhere in the empire.[2]

◆　　◆　　◆

The settlement of Jews in the Ottoman Empire occurred in surges. First came the small Romaniot and Karaite communities that existed in pre-Ottoman Anatolia and the Balkans.[3] Most of these Jews had faced severe persecution under Byzantine rule, and the Ottoman takeover significantly ameliorated their condition. Even before the Ottomans and these Jews had attained a full *modus operandi,* however, other settlers followed. Ashkenazis from the north migrated into the fledgling empire, melding with Romaniot Jewry even as they helped alter the structure of that community. More immigrations followed. Soon after the Ottoman conquest of Constantinople—which became the hub of the expanding state—Sephardic Jews from Spain and their Marrano compeers flooded the small Jewish communities of Istanbul, Salonica, and Palestine.[4]

These settlements attended the foundation and establishment of the Ottoman Empire, a coincidence that engendered a unique relationship.[5] No other ethnoreligious group (other than the Turks themselves) had had to adapt to a new land and a new socioeconomic order even as it blended itself into the imperial system that the Ottomans were creating. True, the Ottoman onslaught engulfed Greeks, Arabs, Armenians, and others. But

whereas the Ottomans embraced various aspects of these peoples' social systems, political structures, and economies, even as they integrated them into
their empire,[6] the new realm accommodated the Jews hardly at all, simply
because there was no need.[7] It was the Jews who did the accommodating.

It may seem that this peculiarly one-sided relationship would have put
the Jewish community at a disadvantage. It did not. Despite the fact that the
Ottoman state did not adapt itself to Jewish needs, the Jews became more a
part of, contributed more to, and flourished more within the Ottoman
economy and society than any other group.[8] This resiliency and achievement derived from three main causes. In part, it came from the fierce ongoing persecution of Jews in both Europe and the Middle East. It also occurred
because of the Jews' lack of alternatives. Thirdly, it derived from the absence
of an established Jewish social and political system for the conquering Turks
to undermine or transform.

This last point perhaps is the most important. After the Ottoman conquests of the fourteenth through the sixteenth centuries, most Christians
and Arab Muslims continued to live much as they had. In the case of the
Balkans, the Ottomans were faced with the peculiar prospect of encompass-
ing a population that in many regions was overwhelmingly Christian. The
state had to accommodate this mass of infidel subjects or face chronic re-
sentment or even rebellion. In the case of the Arabs, by the time the Ottomans had penetrated the Arab/Islamic heartland in 1516–17, they felt
secure in their legitimacy as the preeminent protector of Islam and confident
in their system of government. They felt little urge to oppress or harass their
new subjects. Although the Ottomans would profoundly influence the Arab
world for over four centuries, the Turkish dynasty did relatively little to fashion the Islamic heartland in the Ottoman image.

Jewish society, however, had to modify itself enormously, often traumat-
ically. In order to survive, Jews from the Balkans, the German and Italian
states, Iberia, and even those who had undergone harsh treatment at the
hands of the Ottomans' Byzantine predecessors had to find the economic
and social cracks and crevasses in an emerging kingdom and exploit them.[9]
Although Jewish innovations in textile manufacturing, medicine, banking,
and international commerce profited both the Jews and their Ottoman
rulers, the underlying bases for those commercial achievements were myriad

and complicated. In fact, the relative generosity the Ottomans displayed toward Jews from Spain and elsewhere was not solely or even principally responsible for that community's success.

Instead, fundamental to Jewish achievements was the linkage between Jewish contributions to international trade in the empire and their innovations in other fields. Jews displaced Italians in the textile trade in the eastern Mediterranean and the Black Sea in part because of Ottoman distrust of their Christian rivals and because of the trading diaspora that in the sixteenth century linked the Dutch, Italian, and Ottoman Jewish communities.[10] A homegrown Jewish textile industry that was based upon technologies imported from Spain and Italy and that emerged particularly in Salonica and Safed also severed the dependence of Ottoman Jewry upon Christian Spaniards and Italians.[11]

Jews had many reasons to flock to Istanbul after 1453. Not only did the sultan ruthlessly resettle there Jewish populations from the Balkans and Anatolia, but the conquest reunited two halves of a water-linked empire and Istanbul reemerged as the center of the eastern Mediterranean world.[12] Salonica's metamorphosis into a Jewish city during the sixteenth century, however, depended upon Jewish ingenuity and innovation in both the production and marketing of textiles. By the mid-sixteenth century, broadcloth from Salonica dominated the Ottoman government's purchases and fiercely competed with European manufactured textiles in the empire and the West.[13] This success stimulated other segments of the city's economy, briefly transforming it into an economic, cultural, and political mecca.

Important innovation is also apparent in Jewish control over the international wine market. The mastery over this trade arose from, first, the realization that there was a market for Ottoman wines in northern Europe; second, the presence of a familial network that could exploit it; and finally, Ottoman willingness to support it. The best known but not the only such merchant was Joseph Nasi, who spun his wine interests into vast commercial and political power, centered upon Sultan Selim II and the islands of Naxos.[14]

Such transformations allowed Jews to construct a network of international commerce centered in Istanbul. Its threads reached out far—via Crimean ports to Russia; via Zagreb and other Balkan cities to the Habsburg

Empire and Poland, via Salonica, Dubrovnik, and the Aegean islands (as they fell one by one under Ottoman control) to Italy and the western Mediterranean; via Bursa and Trabzon to Persia; and via Aleppo and Alexandria (after 1516–17) to the Indian Ocean and the East.[15] These routes brought bullion, woolens, leathers, silks, and spices into the Ottoman Empire in exchange for other goods.

Jews shared with others profits from these trades (silks with Armenians and Muslims, spices with Italians and Muslims, woolens with Italians, wines with Greeks). Nevertheless, Jewish merchants had several advantages. They benefited from the diversity defined by the inchoate merger of Romaniot, Ashkenazi, Sephardic, and Marrano cultures; they were helped by the presence of friends and relatives throughout the European, Middle Eastern, and even South Asian worlds; and they were strengthened by the evolving symbiosis between the Jewish community and the Ottoman state (especially in the realm of tax farming). The Jews singularly were able to leap across cultural and religious boundaries and compete in all spheres and with virtually all groups.

The dynamic economic growth of Jewish communities in Istanbul, Salonica, and Palestine continued during the reigns of Mehmed II, Bayezid II, Selim I, and Süleyman I. Other spheres reflected this strength. Rabbinic and kabbalistic thinkers met, argued, and invented new theosophies in this stimulating and multicultural milieu. During the sixteenth century, they helped transform Jewish concepts of man's relationship with God, and they provided the basis for the explosive eschatology of the mid-seventeenth century.[16] Leadership within the Ottoman Jewish community also changed due to both international and domestic migrations and a maturing Ottoman authority. The traumatic squabbles within the Jewish community over ritual, language, and ultimately power and legitimacy at first stimulated economic and intellectual growth. It is no mere coincidence, however, that resolution of many of these conflicts in Istanbul, Salonica, and Safed coincided with economic and intellectual stagnation. Nor is it happenstance that in the seventeenth century such disputes subsided in Istanbul, Salonica, and Safed, none of which had sustained the growth of the previous century, even as they arose in the new city of Izmir.

Salonica's atrophy was the most precipitate. Between 1550 and 1600,

Salonican textiles lost many of their markets.[17] The city's merchants also had to contend with an increasingly severe monetary crisis in Istanbul and throughout the empire.[18] Most notoriously, the government, striving to control its deficit, imposed debilitating price controls over purchases of textiles for the janissary corps.[19] In an earlier epoch, the close association between Jewish merchants and the Ottoman military, which was voracious and flush from a series of triumphs on the battlefield, had stimulated and strengthened the Jews' position in international trade. In the markets of Istanbul, Jews had competed with Venetians, Armenians, and others to provide the textiles of the imperial retinue.[20]

That association now proved a liability. The charge to sell broadcloth to the government at fixed prices undermined Salonica's ability to compete not only with Italians but, more alarmingly, with the innovative and assertive northern European companies that simultaneously entered into competition with Salonica, Safed, Manisa, and other Ottoman centers of textile manufacture.[21] The representatives of these European states gobbled up those markets in Europe, and even in southwestern Asia, that Jewish industrialists and merchants had earlier wrested from others. Their exertions helped precipitate a crisis at the economic core of the Ottoman Jewish world.

Salonica was a center of production; Aleppo was one of the ancient centers of redistribution in the Islamic world.[22] Just as Jews had found a niche in industry in sixteenth-century Salonica, so in Aleppo had they discovered a function as commercial agents and tax farmers.[23] In the late sixteenth century, however, the same paralysis that affected other Jewish centers also struck in Aleppo. Changes in the relationship between Istanbul and outlying regions in the Ottoman Empire, as well as the insertion of new communities of traders, broke the delicate bond between state, production, and distribution that Ottoman Jewry had constructed.[24] Aleppo rebounded more successfully than Salonica from the resultant slump. The city's Jews, however, recovered less fully than others. One short-term consequence was to drive some Jews to emigrate from this trading capital. Many of those who remained were thrust inexorably to the fringes of the Aleppan economy—not without a fight, however.

Well into the seventeenth century, the Jews of Aleppo labored to maintain their positions. At times they were able to exploit rivalries between foreign nations, as in 1639, when shots were fired during a dispute between English and French ships riding off the coast of Alexandretta, after which harsh words flew between the allegedly inebriated French and English assistant consuls residing in the port town.[25] According to the English consul of Aleppo, the assistant French consul—"little more than a boy"—complained against the English sailors before the *kadi* stationed in Alexandretta. The French obtained from him a "sigill" [*sic*] (ruling from a *kadi*) condemning the warlike action of the English vessel anchored in front of the sultan's port. This document

> was sent up hither to the Aga of the Scale, who is a Jew that has a Bro. in great credit with the vizier. This aga comes to me with pretence of a great deal of Jewish friendship, shows me the sigill, and urges the heinousness of the fact, to use hostility on the G[rand]. S[ignior].'s ports, and against his friends. . . . But with all as a great friend to us, offered to compose it privately, that it might not come to the Bassa's [vizier's] ears, who was expected daily from the wars, needy and destitute of money, and would make a heinous matter of this.[26]

Wherever the truth may lie (and it is certain that the Frenchman's and Jew's viewpoints differed profoundly), the English believed that they had been wronged and that their situation was precarious.

The Jewish customs official demanded 10,000 lion dollars[27] in order to "compose" the incident; the English feared he would be able to draw upon his network of compatriots, one of whom apparently held the ear of the powerful and feared pasha, who was about to descend upon the city after a military campaign to Baghdad. Ottoman commanders returning from wars or naval patrols were notoriously rapacious, and the customs official's insinuation that he could unleash the pasha against the English community of Aleppo was probably not idle. However, the eighteen English merchants who gathered in a "Court" to discuss the matter exhibited an extraordinary lack of will. They first (9 Dec. 1640) resolved that they would not fight the extortionary demand, which they referred to as *avania,* by asking the English ambassador, Sir Sackvile Crow, to take the matter to the imperial divan.[28]

Rather, they would offer the Ottoman official 4,500 lion dollars. Then in another court (28 May 1641), they equivocated about offering this bribe and, after presenting gifts of 500 lion dollars to the *kadi* of Aleppo and 1,000 to the vizier, they called the "Jew Customer" before the vizier to complain "of the wrongs and oppressions we suffered by him, to the great decay and almost ruin of our trade, detaining by force our estates from us, and committing many other insolences against us."[29] This stratagem also proved unavailing, for the Jewish official was able to rebut, and the dispute escalated until the highest Ottoman and English officials in both Aleppo and Istanbul became involved.[30] The muddle was resolved (at least temporarily) only when the English community in Aleppo procured a *hatt-i şerif* (a decree carrying the sultan's signature), at considerable expense.[31] Thus, the Jewish customs official never received his money. This incident fully reveals the *political* nature of commercial dealings in Aleppo and elsewhere in the empire. Jewish dominance clearly depended upon Ottoman support. As that support slackened in the face of potent Atlantic seaboard companies, the Jewish network became increasingly marginalized.

The political undercurrents of commercial power are further manifested in an incident that occurred two years later. In 1641, Hayim, the Jewish collector of customs in Aleppo and its port of Alexandretta, explained to the imperial divan in Istanbul that French, Dutch, Venetian, and English vessels long had anchored at Syrian Tripoli (which had flourished since the late sixteenth century as the center of a customs zone),[32] and there paid duties of 2.5 percent for lengths of cloth, 3 percent for goods sold by weight, and 7.5 percent for goods sold by item.[33] Now the English wanted to reroute their commerce through Alexandretta in order to avoid such customs. Although the Sublime Porte ordered English ships to continue paying these charges, they resisted doing so. In fact, in 1647 the English Levant Company instructed its new ambassador in Istanbul, Sir Thomas Bendysh, to proscribe all English factors in the Ottoman Empire from trusting "out cloth to Jews."[34]

Five years later Bendysh had to confront in Istanbul the dangers of involvement with Jewish merchants. On 11 October 1652, he received a petition from three merchants, Roger How, Nathaniel Man, and John Hurt, protesting the intention of a compatriot, William Pearle, to take recourse to an Ottoman court of law in order to achieve redress against a Jewish firm owned by Benjamin Perists.[35] Pearle, it appears, believed that his friends among Ottoman officialdom would ensure the success of his suit. The three petitioners, however, feared the resultant semblance of disarray within the English community ("the nation") in the city.[36] They also suspected that Pearle would be out of his depth before "Turkish Justice" because the Jews' experience and influence in that arena were far greater than his, and worried that the judge's acceptance of verbal testimony would further advantage the Englishman's adversaries (they presumably could rely upon their coreligionists, who enjoyed the powerful advantage of knowing Turkish, to support them). How, Man, and Hurt insisted that "whereas Mr. Pearle's chiefest hopes are to prevail by making friends, it may justly be feared that the Jews will be too hard for him therein, having already gained the Vizier's [ear], & his Jew being also most likely to favor those of his own tribe."[37] Finally, they deemed it likely that both sides would resort to bribery; the Jews' pockets were considered deep.[38]

The Englishmen's fears were not mere speculation. In 1649, John Ridley accused William Osborne, factor in Istanbul for the London merchant Francis Read, of cheating him and his master. In his defense, Osborne claimed to have been compelled to forge a commercial agreement with two Jews, Samuel Saguien and another individual known only as Sermony, because the witnesses to their first agreement had been "only Jews, and such as by the experience I had found, would not give in testimony against their own nation."[39] Two years later, Osborne protested the stratagems of the Jewish partnership of Isaak Cargashan, Abraham Hekem, and Isaak Useph.[40] When that company of Jews became insolvent, Osborne maintained, Useph dragged him before the *kadi* of Istanbul, where he unjustly demanded from him 3,587 lion dollars as payment for 644 buffalo hides. When Osborne balked, Useph procured an order to seal the Englishman's house with all his goods inside. Osborne rejoined on the next Saturday, when he went to the public divan. Here, Useph again outmaneuvered him "with a bribe of $300.00." Osborne was dragged to the house of the chief religious magistrate (*kadiasker*), clapped in irons for five days, and forced to acknowledge not only that he had received from Useph the 644 buffalo hides, but still owed four and one half dollars for each. Osborne escaped from his predicament only after a payment of 1,200 lion dollars. He called this disbursement an *avania* and requested repayment from the English Levant Company. It is doubtful that the company did so, for it always was reluctant to pay such bills, which occurred often and which it termed "private" avanias. Ambassador Bendysh likely responded by imposing a battulation (commercial boycott) against the Jews, a recourse to which the English often, if apparently futilely, resorted.[41] This incident suggests that foreigners often found themselves at a disadvantage in the Ottoman legal morass and thus hired natives, whether as dragomans or in other capacities, to represent them.

A dispute between two local officials with whom the English of Aleppo had to contend in the early 1650s, the Jewish customs collectors Daniel Chelebi and Davud Chelebi, shows that the procurement of an imperial decree a decade earlier had only temporarily quelled Jewish resistance to English incursions. This dispute also provides a hint of the universality and ferocity of the war then being fought over commercial terrain.[42] Both the English consul, John Riley, and Bendysh derogatorily labeled Daniel and Davud the "Jew Customers," railed against their abuses (such as their impositions of avanias), and threatened them with a public hanging, the ignominious fate of one of their infamous predecessors two decades earlier.[43] Riley first ordered a series of battulations against Daniel and Davud, their supporters, and their servants. Then, in April 1652, an English court in Aleppo decided to "henceforth Battelate all Jew Brokers and all Jews whatsoever from all Employment by the English Nation, upon the penalty of $500.00."[44] This sweeping action proved no more effective against Jewish administrators than earlier ones, however, because of the customs collectors' impenetrable network of patronage, particularly among those Jews who acted as brokers and middlemen for the English. Riley and his nation also appealed to Bendysh, their ambassador in Istanbul, who secured a series of decrees in their favor from the imperial divan.[45] The Jewish customers, however, utilizing their own connections in Aleppo and its surroundings, simply ignored the orders. The English finally settled their debilitating dispute by appealing to "some great men of the place to interpose in their differences," which they did for the rather heavy fee of $2,700.00.[46]

The struggle extended beyond the walls of Aleppo. Both the English nation in Aleppo and the Jewish customs officials installed representatives in the port town of Alexandretta. These agents supervised the transfer of goods and monies to and from ships and Aleppo. During an earlier dispute, mariners and assistant consuls in Alexandretta had instigated the difficulties. In 1652, however, the crisis began in Aleppo, but soon also encompassed Alexandretta. The customer not only blocked the departure of the English caravan from Aleppo for Alexandretta, but also prevented goods already in the port from being laden upon ships. The frustrated English nation reacted by battulating trade with any "Turk, Armenian, Jew or any Stranger or Native of this Country."[47] Such an action not only implies an inability to distinguish between various "others," but also must have paralyzed English trade, encouraged Dutch, French, and Venetian rivals, and even tempted headstrong and despairing English factors to break the boycott. The English "factor marine" (or assistant consul) in Alexandretta, whose function was to negotiate with the customer's representatives, expedite trade, and protect against smugglers, meanwhile worked, without much success, to undercut the customer's influence there.

An Ottoman decree issued fourteen years later indicates the chronic nature of this struggle. The French consul made a complaint against the embezzlements and inflated duties imposed by Mustafa (the collector of customs in Aleppo), Hüseyin, and Halil Kethüda (the *nazir*, or supervising watchman, in Alexandretta).[48] He insisted that because of these exactions, caravans did not pass from Aleppo to Alexandretta and trade was frozen. It is perhaps significant that although the grounds for dispute had changed little, by 1666 (the very year that Sabbatai Sevi [Shabbetai Tzevi] proclaimed himself messiah), Muslims rather than Jews seem to have occupied the critical ground as intermediaries between the Ottoman government and European merchants.

Both Ottoman and English archival sources stress these tensions between various authorities.[49] It is apparent, however, that generally both English traders and Ottoman notables worked together and resisted Istanbul's interference in their affairs. They also learned to circumvent the vigorous Jewish network rather than attempt to rout it. At first they had to negotiate. In the long run, however, it proved possible, and more profitable, to force Jews from their positions as brokers and translators than to pay them to negotiate with their coreligionists on the waterfronts and in the bureaucracies. In other words, the Aleppo-Alexandretta trading corridor, as well as other emerging networks within the empire, rewarded local notables, and those foreigners who were willing to negotiate with them, even as these groups eroded the position of Jews and impeded centralized management. Jewish collectors of customs and Jewish brokers, who depended more upon Istanbul than their rivals did, suffered as the bond between Istanbul and Aleppo, Izmir, and Alexandria weakened. As early as 1606, in fact, Istanbul had attempted to reestablish its authority along that commercial artery by reducing Alexandretta and relocating Aleppo's port to Syrian Tripoli,[50] which sporadically served a similar function. The relative inconvenience of the latter port and fear of officialdom along the Lebanese coast, however, led to massive resistance, and within a year Alexandretta regained its status.

One associates the Jews of Salonica, Istanbul, Aleppo, and Safed with the establishment and development of Ottoman rule. These religious communities are said to have ridden the wave of Ottoman expansion, flourished during the celebrated Ottoman heyday, and more devotedly than other socioreligious groups accompanied the Ottoman Empire into old age and ill health. Izmir, another great center of Ottoman Jewry, does not share these associations. At the time when other Ottoman commercial and industrial centers flourished, Izmir hardly even existed; it was only as other centers faltered that Izmir was born.[51] This inverted image of other Ottoman cities was no coincidence. Sixteenth-century Aleppo, Istanbul, Salonica, and Safed owed everything to Ottoman strength; their fates, no less than the Jewish communities they nurtured, mirrored the empire's. The same governmental policy that helped advance these cities, however, had stifled Izmir. The Sublime Porte sought to retain western Anatolia as a provisioning zone; Izmir grew in reaction against the capital city, and as a response to peoples and forces that lay beyond Istanbul's control.

The Sephardic settlement in the Ottoman Empire had been the result of the classic "push-pull" of migration.[52] The "push" was not subtle at all; it was dispossession and expulsion from Spain and elsewhere. The "pull" was in part Ottoman clemency—the famous invitation to settle—and in part the lack of alternatives. Izmir was a little different. The "push" there was not persecution, and the "pull" was not clemency. The economic factors that propelled the Jewish reshuffle—which earlier had been generated by Ottoman expansion—were in Izmir's case largely external to the Ottoman Empire, while the migration of Jews—which earlier had come from outside the empire—was now almost exclusively intra-imperial.

The principal economic factor in the growth of Izmir was the global realignment in commerce that occurred in the late sixteenth and early seventeenth centuries.[53] Before about 1620, Bursa, Aleppo, and Alexandria had retained their positions as middle cities in the ancient spice trade that dominated global commerce. After 1620, however, pepper, cinnamon, and even silks and porcelains became less of a factor in Middle Eastern trade. Commerce began focusing more and more on bulkier goods that were dependent upon quick access to the sea, such as woolens, cottons, and fruits. Izmir's location along the western Anatolian coast attracted merchants seeking these products.[54] Consequently, the city grew economically and demographically even as other Ottoman ports contracted.

Furthermore, in the sixteenth century western Anatolia had served as Istanbul's "fruit basket." Sultanas from the districts (*kazas*) of Manisa and Marmara, figs from the *kaza* of Izmir, and raisins from the *kaza*s of Izmir, Menemen, and Nif dominated the markets of the capital city. Izmir, as an urban concentration in western Anatolia that increasingly competed with Istanbul for the same foodstuffs, posed a particular threat to the capital's provisioning network. The Ottomans strenuously resisted Izmir's growth. Whereas sixteenth-century Jewish centers had emerged in part *because* of Ottoman policies—at Istanbul because of forced resettlement (*sürgün*),[55] at Salonica because of janissary clothing, at Safed because of taxation policies[56]—Izmir emerged *despite* Ottoman opposition and because of an erosion in the government's control over its provinces.

It is important to realize that lack of governmental control does not equal decline in economic activities.[57] There *was* economic, intellectual, and political development in the empire during this period. This growth, however, was not necessarily instigated in or even approved by Istanbul. It was more likely that transformations outside the control of the central government stimulated change, particularly economic change. The Sublime Porte's control over western Anatolia loosened, the lines of authority became fragmented and localized, and the Ottoman provisioning network weakened. At the same time, new trading states in search of new commercial opportunities—principally England and the Netherlands—used innovative techniques to exploit change within the empire.

In the case of Izmir, the states of northwestern Europe ushered in the growth. From 1610 to 1630, Dutch and English merchants, and then French and Venetian ones, repudiated Istanbul's commands, dealt independently with local brigands and notables, probed the Anatolian hinterlands, and carved out trading networks.[58] They strove, quite successfully, to redefine commerce in western Anatolia. Now the world of Anatolian commerce no longer revolved almost exclusively around Istanbul. Izmir's fate depended as much upon policies, even attitudes, formulated locally, or in London, Paris, and Amsterdam.

The Jewish settlement in Izmir, no less than the concurrent Armenian, Greek, and Turkish settlements, reflects these global transformations. The proprietors of the consulates and homes that sprang up along Franks Street demanded servants, brokers, money-changers, customs collectors, and tavern keepers. Representatives of every ethnic group filled these positions. Jews, who were prominent as governmental representatives in Istanbul, Aleppo, and Alexandria, naturally worked to acquire similar posts in the new city. Indeed, between 1610 and 1650, most collectors of customs in Izmir were Jewish;[59] and Dutch, English, and French merchants felt compelled to surround themselves with the coreligionists of these officials.

Ottoman letters of appointment (berats) from that period reflect this Jewish dominance. For instance, in 1638 "some people" demanded the removal of a Jew named Isaac from his position as dragoman of the merchants of Antalya. The French community resisted this pressure and secured a command confirming him in his post.[60] Two years later, the French ambassador vigorously campaigned at the Sublime Porte for the appointment of the Jew Avraham veled-i Yusef as dragoman to the French consul in Izmir.[61]

It obviously was not compassion for the Jewish people that prompted such appointments. In fact, the French at that time were notoriously hostile toward Jews, and had expelled them from French lands some three centuries earlier. Perhaps the merchants' enthusiasm for Jewish employees derived from personal friendship or from the exemplary linguistic and commercial abilities of these Jews. More likely, though, the appointments represented a form of protection from official coreligionists and from potential lawsuits. At exactly the time the French ambassador was supporting Jewish drago- mans (that is, in 1638–40) a Manisan Jew named Rab initiated a lawsuit in the Ottoman courts against the French consul in Izmir and his merchants.[62] Although the Ottoman capitulations then in place proscribed foreign mer- chants from turning to Ottoman courts in lawsuits against each other, the agreements did not yet provide much protection against Ottoman sub- jects—particularly Muslim, but also Christian or Jewish—who chose Is- lamic justice.[63] The foreign consul caught in a legal quarrel with an Ottoman subject could not easily flee to the protection of the capitulatory umbrella.

The intimacy of these cross-cultural relationships not only drove for- eigners into Ottoman law courts, but even more often compelled ambassa- dors and consuls to call Ottoman witnesses in internal feudings. In 1645 the English ambassador in Istanbul, Sir Sackvile Crow, heard testimony regard- ing a contest between Gyles Ball and Henry Hyde over control of the cur- rant trade and the consulship of the Morea.[64] In the preceding few years, their complex maneuvering had drawn in not only many English merchants and sailors, but also a Jew named Salla (who served as Hyde's factor); three Jews named David Cohen, Abraham Sachée, and Aaron Tereachi (who served Ball); two Turks named Abisutt Effendi and Mehemet Agra (who were powerful dealers in currants); and the *kadi, kaymakam,* and pasha in the town of Patras. Salla seems to have been the key figure in Hyde's negotia- tions for currants and in his representations before various Ottoman officials.

As Crow worked to unravel the labyrinth of intrigue, witnesses included not only compatriots, but also Saphiere Philorito (the Greek commissioner of Patras), Nicolo Villeroy (the French consul for the Morea), and Moise Levi (Ball's Jewish dragoman). Levi contended that Ball not only had bribed the kadi at Patras in order to acquire a decree against Hyde, but also unnec- essarily caused a rise in the price of currants and consequently sabotaged the earnings of the English Levant Company (a grievous sin in the eyes of com- pany directors). Levi's testimony proved Ball's undoing and set the stage for a lengthy alliance between Crow and Hyde, which ended only with Crow's incarceration in the Tower of London and Hyde's beheading.[65] Significant here is that Jews were involved in these intrigues from the very beginning.

Local Jews and foreign merchants settling in Izmir and elsewhere in the

Ottoman Empire bargained with, swindled, and conspired against each other. Their acumen and the networks upon which they depended decided their lots. Sometimes their schemes produced fortunes; at other times their plottings exploded in their faces. Such an end assaulted all the concerned parties in 1639.[66]

In that year, one of the first tasks for the new English ambassador in Istanbul, Sir Sackvile Crow, and the new English consul in Izmir, Edward Stringer, was to rule on a lawsuit between two merchants, Richard Lawrence and Frances Reade, and to unravel the roles of both Jews and Armenians in their bitter clash. Two or three years earlier, three of Reade's principals in England—Sir Morris Abbott, Mr. Edward Abbott, and Mr. Lewise Roberts—had become suspicious of his ventures on their behalf. Roberts asked Lawrence (who then was consul in Izmir) to investigate. The consul wrote back that Reade had lost 20 percent on poor investments in pepper and freighting costs, and that faced with the choice of ruin or wronging his principals, he decided on the latter course and sold Mr. Roberts's cloths at 73 lion dollars per cloth while reporting that he had received only 66 dollars. Lawrence also detailed an illicit deal for indigo Lahor, in which, the consul charged, Reade had taken a bribe of 2,000 lion dollars from an Armenian, Hoggia Toma, and connived with the man who brokered the deal, a Jew named Simsson Cress. Cress ostensibly confirmed Reade's treachery before some rabbis and two Jewish witnesses, Mosse Morell and Joseph Morian. Lawrence also secretly forwarded these Jews' depositions to London. Significantly, Cress was said to have been in partnership not only with another Jew, Mayer Bevenias, but also with two Armenians, Hoggia Toma and Hoggia Murat, and a Turk, Hoggia Achmett. Toma, Lawrence contended, demanded his 2,000 lion dollars back from Reade.

On 10 September 1639, Reade complained to Crow that these documents, which Lawrence had sent to his principals without consulting the English nation in Izmir, were slanders that severely damaged Reade's reputation, made it difficult for him to find patrons, and lost him at least 12,000 lion dollars. On 4 November, the merchants of Izmir confirmed Reade's contentions. Lawrence responded by attacking the entire English nation of Izmir for raising false witnesses against him and illegally entering his home and seizing papers. The English ambassador ordered the English consul in

Izmir to convene twelve of the "chief of the nation" in Izmir to investigate the case and appoint four "indifferent" (presumably meaning "impartial") men to decide it.

The nation found Lawrence, who had initially informed against Reade, to be the villain. The four indifferent men concluded that Reade had in fact earned the difference between the 66 and 73 dollars lost to his patrons by dealing in finished garments. They interviewed Simsson Cress about the indigo. The Jew not only denied having condemned Reade, but insisted that Morell and Morian were his enemies. The latter two, Stringer informed Crow, "are in repute in their own Nation, as honest men as [Cress] who indeed is not a man of the best fame."[67] The consul and his merchants surmised that Cress had merely tried to ingratiate himself with Lawrence in order to drum up business.

Their investigation of the Armenian Toma proved equally barren. He now denied the claim that Reade had received a bribe in a deal for indigo. Even the breaking into Lawrence's home had been undertaken legally, so the nation claimed, by the consul's dragoman and under the supervision of six merchants. They removed from the premises only an incriminating letter-book, which the dragoman had properly sealed. This volume was fully intact and was waiting for Lawrence to reclaim.

This event tells us much of the intricate economic relations binding together the various socioreligious communities in an Ottoman commercial center, as well as the realities that blurred the religio-communal lines said to define Ottoman society. Armenians, Jews, Turks, and Greeks formed combinations against Dutch, English, French, and Venetian merchants. The foreign nations sought to counter such alliances by living and working together, and keeping each other abreast of their commercial activities. A gamut of religious and linguistic loyalties, and penalties such as the battula-tion, endeavored to seal these combinations of religious groups and foreign nations. But petty jealousies and greed often defeated the endeavors of these groupings.

In this case, if we tentatively accept the findings of the English nation in Izmir, we can conclude that Cress chose to break with his coreligionists, and perhaps even perjure himself before his own rabbis, in order to gain admittance into the English network of trade; Toma resorted to bribery or perjury, and perhaps even blackmail, to complete some deal involving indigo; and Lawrence broke every rule governing proper behavior in the English nation, exhibiting even a willingness to shatter the integrity of English trade in Izmir, in order to undercut Reade, his fellow countryman and rival. In each case, communal solidarity proved elusive. It is not hard to imagine the lengths to which each of these men would go to "buy" Ottoman officials.

◆　　◆　　◆

A Jew, an Armenian, a Greek, or a Muslim who was related to or had influence over a customs collector enjoyed an enormous advantage over his compatriots and rivals. In Izmir this advantage existed in two spheres. First, he could use the position to penetrate the Ottoman network of commerce that had expanded and evolved with the empire's fifteenth- and sixteenth-century conquests and that still existed in the seventeenth century. This Ottoman sphere had been the principal concern of both the Armenian and Jewish networks in sixteenth-century Aleppo, Istanbul, and Salonica, and both groups owed much to their ability to work within this Ottoman edifice. In Izmir, however, the position of Jews also eased their entrance into the international sphere that the English and other European states were then creating. This new network did not destroy Ottoman commerce, but rather integrated it into a new, larger system. Men such as Reade and Lawrence needed local merchants to help them against their competitors in this new world, and chose those who seemed to have the best connections within the Ottoman economy.

In an earlier era, dominance in customs collecting had denoted Jewish power in international trade and in the Ottoman Jewish community's relationship with state and society. As a class, collectors probably wielded more brute power than chief rabbis, community leaders, or doctors ever did. Both the legitimate merchant and the smuggler who hoped to thrive in Aleppo or Istanbul depended upon the customs collector not simply to expedite the movement of monies and goods, but also to turn his back on abuses and bribes. Such a man could do no better than hire a collector's brother, cousin, or coreligionist as his broker, translator, or factor. Such expedient hirings explain why the Englishman, Frenchman, or Venetian who despised and persecuted the Jew in his homeland often engaged the Jew in Aleppo, Alexandria, or Istanbul—despite the objections of state and company.[68] It was a matter of survival.

Jews, exploiting their administrative experience in other Ottoman port cities and their influence in Istanbul, also lodged themselves in such positions in Izmir. At first, this positioning worked well. European merchants flooding the port felt compelled to protect themselves with Jewish hirelings.[69] Before long, however, merchants began to realize that these positions did not dominate commerce as they had in older port towns. Venetians and Englishmen began appealing to brigands, notables, and local officials against the decisions of Jewish customs officials and ultimately even against the Sublime Porte. Therefore, the Jewish power network in Izmir was stillborn. Greeks and Armenians began to win positions as factors, brokers, even consuls for Venetians, Frenchmen, and finally English and Dutchmen. By the 1650s, Jews had lost their monopoly over customs. Armenians and others had replaced them.[70]

This erosion of Jewish influence in commerce began in Izmir and soon spread to other trading centers. Jewish brokers in Aleppo, Alexandria, and Istanbul found themselves without support in the customs sheds and divans of these cities, or discovered that the Jewish officials whom the sixteenth-century foreigners had so feared were now scoffed at and ignored. The severing of these threads between economic and political power in the Ottoman Empire exposed Jewish merchants to incursions from rivals, who rapidly displaced them as the middlemen of Levantine commerce.

In the late fifteenth and early sixteenth centuries, Jews instituted tremendous innovations in commerce between the Ottoman Empire and Europe. Their situations as bankers, industrialists, and especially Ottoman officials helped propel that empire beyond military dominance into economic distinction as well. Rather than continuing their practice of adjusting to a changing economic situation, the Ottoman Jewish community settled into the niches it already had carved out. Jewish merchants, middlemen, and officials became part of the Ottoman institutional framework. As the empire changed in the seventeenth century, as a novel relationship with Europe loomed, and as an innovative global commerce surfaced, new opportunities arose for Ottoman subjects. Those who profited from such opportunities, however, were not Jews. The Levantine culture that emerged was Italian, Armenian, and Greek. The Jewish community remained content within an economically outlying Ottoman world. Its horizons gradually shrank as Ottoman Jews became more marginalized within the Ottoman world and less linked to other worlds through their coreligionists and abilities to innovate.

CHAPTER 3

The Development of Community Organizational Structures

The Case of Izmir

Jacob Barnai

Around 1700 the French traveler Tournfort visited Izmir, leaving the following description of the city and its Jewish inhabitants:

> Smyrna is the finest Port at which one can enter into the Levant, built at the bottom of a Bay, capable of holding the biggest Navy in the World. . . . Smyrna is one of the largest and richest Cities of the Levant. The Goodness of the Port, so necessary for Trade, has preserved it, and caused it to be rebuilt several times, after it had been destroyed by Earth-quakes. 'Tis as it were the Rendezvous of Merchants from the four Parts of the World, and the Magazine of the Merchandize they produce. They reckon fifteen thousand Turks in this City, ten thousand Greeks, eighteen hundred Jews, two hundred Armenians, and as many Franks. The Turks have nineteen mosques, the Greeks two Churches, the Jews eight Synagogues, the Armenians one Church, and the Latins three Convents of Religious.
>
> The situation of Smyrna is admirable. The City extends itself all along the Shore, at the foot of a Hill which commands the Port. The Streets are there better enlightened, better paved, and the Houses better built than in other Cities upon the Continent. The Franks Street, which is the finest in Smyrna, runs all along the Port. It may be said it is one of the richest Magazines in the World: the City is placed in the Center of the trade of the Levant, eight days Journey from Constantinople by Land, and four hundred Miles by Water; five and twenty days Journey from Aleppo, by the

Caravans; There is no Bassa [pasha] in Smyrna, but only one Sadar [*serdar*, commander], who commands two thousand Janizaries, lodged in and about the City. Justice is administered there by a Cadi. The French in 1702 had about thirty Merchants there well settled, without reckoning many other Frenchmen, who drive a less considerable Trade. The English were as numerous, and their Trade flourishing.

At the time when we were in Smyrna, the Dutch were not above eighteen or twenty Merchants, well settled, and much esteemed. There were but two Genoese, who traded under the protection of France. There was a Consul from Venice, tho' there was not one Merchant of that Nation. . . . The whole Trade is carried on by the Interposition of Jews; one can buy or sell nothing but what must pass through their Hands. We may call them . . . miserable, but 'tis they [who] put all into motion. We must do them justice, and own they have better capacities than other Merchants; besides, they live at Smyrna well enough, and make a very handsome Appearance, which is very extraordinary among a People who study nothing but how to save.[1]

This description is clearly a faithful reflection of the central elements in the city's reality at various times: a port city with a heterogeneous population, economically flourishing and bustling with trade.

This article attempts to broadly delineate the organizational patterns of the Jewish community in Izmir during the Ottoman period, and the changes that took place in its society, community organization, and leadership.

The history of Izmir's Jewish community may be divided into four main periods:

1. From the establishment of the Jewish community in the flourishing port city in the late sixteenth century to the great earthquake of 1688—that is, most of the seventeenth century.

2. From the rebuilding of the city and its Jewish community in the early eighteenth century to the beginning of the economic and social crisis in the city and the community in the last quarter of that century—that is, most of the eighteenth century.

3. From the late eighteenth to the mid-nineteenth century. This is the period of economic decline and severe social crisis in the city and the Jewish community.

4. From the mid-nineteenth to the early twentieth century. This is the period of the *Tanzimat* (the Ottoman reforms), modernization, political up-heavals, and intergroup conflicts in Izmir.

The First Period: The Seventeenth Century

As is well-known, Izmir is an ancient city. When the Ottomans conquered it in 1424, it was an agriculturally based village and its port was scarcely func-tioning. Although Jews had lived in Izmir in the Hellenistic and Roman pe-riods, as far as we know there were no Jews there at the time of the Ottoman conquest. Even Jews exiled from Spain in 1492 did not settle there because of its poor condition.

In the late sixteenth century, Izmir began to develop as an economic and mercantile center for its region, and as a port city trading with Europe. The Levant companies of England, France, and Holland, with the encourage-ment of the Ottoman government, assisted in this process of development, turning it from a small village to the most important port city in the Levant.[2] Thus Izmir became the flourishing center described above in the excerpt from Tournfort.

As Izmir's economic importance grew, its population increased at an ac-celerated rate, with immigrants streaming in from all parts of the Ottoman Empire and from Europe: Muslims, Christians (mostly Greeks and Armeni-ans, but also some West Europeans), and many Jews. The first Jewish groups arrived in Izmir in the last quarter of the sixteenth century. These were Jews from nearby areas, from Anatolian communities, who came there for trade. They were followed by Jewish immigrants from Salonica, which had de-clined from the strong economic position it had held earlier in the century. These groups were then joined by Jews from Istanbul and many other Ana-tolian cities, and from the Balkans, the Mediterranean islands, and Pales-tine.[3] A significant group of Jewish immigrants arriving in Izmir in the seventeenth century were those called the "Portuguese Marranos," who re-turned to Judaism after they had left the Iberian peninsula. Many of them settled in western Europe, but they also established two congregations in Izmir, which were among the most important congregations in the city.[4] Seventeenth-century Izmir thus included two different groups of immigrants from the Iberian peninsula: not only the descendants of the exiles of 1492 but also former Marranos who had left the Iberian peninsula in the seventeenth century. The encounter between these two groups in Izmir and other parts of the Ottoman Empire is a fascinating episode that has yet to be thoroughly examined. In Izmir its expressions were felt in the city's economy, in the transformation of the Jewish society, and in Sabbateanism. Thus, for example, in 1644 the former Marranos established a society for marrying off orphans, similar to those in Portugese communities in western Europe at that time. They also maintained numerous ties with these European communities.

As soon as the Jews arrived in Izmir, they began to participate in its flourishing economy. Many Jews served as agents for European merchants, while others had their own businesses in the city's internal or international trade. The Izmir Jewish community thus grew and prospered at a time when the Ottoman Empire as a whole and many of its Jewish communities were suffering from a series of economic and social crises. The Jewish community of Safed, for example, which had prospered in the sixteenth century because of its flourishing textile industry and had become a significant spiritual center, collapsed entirely at the end of the sixteenth century. With its economy in ruins, the Jewish population of Safed sank into abject poverty, so that by the seventeenth century it no longer had any industry and it lost its place as a spiritual center as well.[5] Similarly, Salonica, which had also been an industrial center, suffered a severe crisis in the late sixteenth century, although there the Jewish community did not collapse entirely as in Safed.[6] In this respect, Izmir differed from other Jewish centers in the Ottoman Empire.

Izmir's economic prosperity was followed by a cultural and spiritual efflorescence. In 1658 a Hebrew printing house was founded in Izmir by the Gabbai family, which prior to immigrating to Izmir had operated a printing house in Livorno (Leghorn).[7] The waves of immigrants arriving in Izmir also included many rabbis and Torah scholars. As a result of economic prosperity, six Jewish congregations were established there in the early decades of the seventeenth century, increasing to nine congregations later in the century.[8] As early as the fifteenth century, the accepted practice among Jews immigrating to the Ottoman Empire was to establish congregations on the basis of the countries and even towns of their origin. This practice was adopted by the Iberian exiles who arrived at the end of the fifteenth century.[9] In Izmir, however, where the Jewish community was founded at a later date, only some of the congregations, mainly those of the Portuguese Marranos, were established according to this custom. The other congregations were almost certainly composed of a mixture of Jews from various cities in the Ottoman Empire. In this, as in many other areas, Izmir's seventeenth-century Jewish community was a reflection of Ottoman Jewry in general (especially its centers in Anatolia and the Balkans), as it developed during the course of the sixteenth century. Studying the Izmir community can therefore help in understanding the history of the Jews in the Ottoman Empire during the century following the exile from Spain. The encounters that took place in Izmir tell us something about the similarities and differences among Jews from various Ottoman cities.

The leadership and organization of the Izmir community during the seventeenth century developed according to the patterns established in the sixteenth century in the great Ottoman Jewish centers, especially those of Istanbul and Salonica. Above the individual congregations, each of which was headed by a rabbi, the community had a central leadership that took care of issues pertaining to all the Jews of the city. The chief rabbinate in Izmir generally consisted of a joint rabbinate held by two rabbis. The large Ottoman Jewish communities generally did not succeed in selecting a single chief rabbi because of conflicting interests among the various congregations. This was the situation in Izmir as well until the nineteenth century. The community's tax assessors, who determined the amount of tax each individual had to pay, also formed an important leadership group. Another influential figure was the community's representative to the Ottoman authorities, called the *kahya* or *kethüda*.[10]

Of several outstanding figures of the Izmir Jewish community in the seventeenth century, I present here brief descriptions of three: R. Joseph Escapa, R. Hayyim Benveniste, and Sabbatai Sevi (Shabbetai Tzevi).

R. Joseph Escapa[11] was one of the rabbis who had come to Izmir from Salonica in the early seventeenth century. Although born in Salonica, he lived for some time in Istanbul before arriving in Izmir, and the traditions of both these communities influenced him in both Torah and public matters. He may be rightly considered the founder of the community and its leadership. In particular, he was responsible for setting down the community's regulations in the seventeenth century in the areas of taxation and real estate and in matters pertaining to divorce. Whenever a new social organization emerges, the founding generation has a great influence on its structure and future; and R. Escapa was a particularly important member of this group in Izmir. The regulations that he had established while serving as chief rabbi, from the 1620s to the 1660s, became the foundation stones of all social, administrative, and economic issues that occupied the community for many generations.

R. Hayyim Benveniste[12] was an important Torah scholar and one of the greatest Ottoman rabbis of all time. He had extensive influence on the Izmir community in many different areas, but especially in halakhic decisions. Born in Istanbul in 1603 to a distinguished family (his grandfather was the grand vezir's physician, but was later convicted of spying and exiled to Rhodes[13]), R. Benveniste was in 1643 appointed rabbi of Tire, near Izmir. In 1658 he moved to Izmir and in 1662, after a series of bitter conflicts that divided the community, he was appointed one of the two chief rabbis of the city. In 1665, when Sabbatai Sevi returned to Izmir, his birthplace, as the messiah, R. Benveniste became his follower, after having opposed him at first. In return, Sabbatai Sevi appointed R. Benveniste as sole chief rabbi, deposing the co-rabbi. It is almost certain that R. Benveniste held this position until his death in 1673.

The third outstanding personality in seventeenth-century Izmir was Sabbatai Sevi himself, the "messiah," who was born there in 1626.[14] His father, an immigrant from Ottoman Greece, had served as an agent for an English merchant employed by the English Levant Company in Izmir. Sabbatai Sevi's biography, and the important influence he and his followers had on Jewish history, are well known, but some new details and perspectives are added here. Sabbatai Sevi's messianic activities in Izmir began in his youth and twice led to his expulsion from the city, in 1651 and 1661. His reappearance in the city, in 1665–66, led to intense messianic fervor, which did not end even after he had left the city and converted to Islam at the end of 1666. As in many other Jewish communities, in Izmir many continued to believe in Sabbatai Sevi until the mid-eighteenth century.[15] The Sabbatean movement also had a great impact on the types of rabbinic works written in the eighteenth century (a topic discussed in the next section).

Recent investigation of Sabbateanism, especially as it developed during Sabbatai Sevi's lifetime, has taken place in the shadow of Gershom Scholem's monumental work, especially his comprehensive book on this topic.[16] Scholem believed that the eruption of the Sabbatean movement originated in the spread of Lurianic Kabbalah in the generation prior to Sabbatai Sevi's appearance. Scholem forcefully rejected any other explanation for this phenomenon. This thesis, however, is only part of a more comprehensive view of the place of Jewish mysticism in Jewish history, in general, and of the historical continuity that Scholem perceived to have existed between the expulsion from Spain, the development and dissemination of Lurianic Kabbalah in the sixteenth and seventeenth centuries, Sabbateanism in the seventeenth and eighteenth centuries, and other movements that arose in the eighteenth century, such as Hassidism and even the Jewish Enlightenment. Although this is not the place for grappling with these weighty issues, I would like to discuss a few aspects relating to the origins of Sabbateanism.

A renewed investigation of the background and causes of the Sabbatean movement, in the light of both old and new sources, as well as progress in research on general and Jewish history in the seventeenth century, seems to me to lead to the conclusion that even if the influence of Lurianic Kabbalah on some of the founders and supporters of Sabbateanism (such as Nathan of Gaza) cannot be discounted, there were also other social and cultural factors that were clearly linked to this general outbreak of messianism among all the Jewish communities.[17] These factors include the pogroms of 1648–60 in Eastern Europe (which were not confined to the years 1648–49, as has been accepted in the general historiography and in the collective Jewish consciousness). The effects of these pogroms were felt even far away from the geographical region where they had occurred, and the sources representing the views of the Sabbatean movement leaders and others indicate a direct link between the pogroms and the emergence of Sabbateanism. Other factors that must be taken into account are the religious and political upheavals that occurred in the seventeenth century, especially in Europe, such as the Thirty Years War, Christian millenarianism, and the broad extent of mysticism among Jews, Christians, and Muslims in this period, including the mutual influences among the three religions.

Especially noteworthy is the link between the Christian millenarians and the kabbalists among the Portuguese Marranos in western Europe in the seventeenth century.[18] Not only did the Portuguese Marranos embrace the Sabbatean belief wherever they lived, but newly discovered documents show that they were among the founders of the movement in Izmir. In 1659 the classic messianic book by Menasseh ben Israel of Amsterdam, *Esperanca de Israel* (Israel's Hope), was printed in Izmir, in Spanish written in Latin characters, by Abraham Gabbai's press.[19] The Izmir edition of the book was brought to press by several Portuguese Marrano physicians in Izmir, who also added to it several poems. I believe that this book influenced Sabbatai Sevi and his close circle of followers in Izmir. The Portuguese Marranos of Izmir occupied a prominent place among Sabbatai Sevi's youthful friends, his principal supporters at the time of his appearance as the messiah, and in the list of "kings of the world" that he "appointed" in Izmir in 1666.[20]

Another noteworthy point in this context is the fact that the conflicts in Izmir between Sabbatai Sevi's followers and his opponents (characteristic of many Jewish communities during 1665–66) were based on deep rivalries that had existed in the Izmir community for some time before Sabbatai Sevi's appearance. Sabbatai Sevi took advantage of these tensions in order to gain control over the community.

As mentioned above, Izmir was a port city with a heterogeneous general and Jewish population. Its Jewish society was dynamic, as befits an immigrant society attempting to consolidate itself through economic growth. Thus it is not surprising that there were severe conflicts in seventeenth-century Izmir concerning the organization of religious and social life and the structure of the community's leadership. These internal conflicts were further exacerbated by contacts, mutual influences, and friction between the Jewish community and the surrounding non-Jewish society in various areas of life. The severe conflicts within the Jewish society and leadership stemmed mainly from differences among the immigrant groups in their customs and traditions, but also from economic conflicts of interest.[21]

In a cosmopolitan city like Izmir there were daily contacts between Jews and non-Jews, as well as ramified connections between the Izmir community and other Jewish communities in the Ottoman Empire and in Europe. These contacts were in both the economic and the social realms. They included trade relations and partnerships, and Jews served as agents, middlemen, interpreters, and doctors for the non-Jewish population of the city, including the European merchants. Most prominent among these Jews were those of Portuguese origin who had recently returned to Judaism. These varied contacts led to regular encounters among the various groups in the city, in the many cafes that were an accepted feature of Levantine cities of that period.[22]

In one of his books, R. Hayyim Benveniste complains about a custom that had become common among the Jews of Izmir, namely, frequenting the city's coffeehouses on the Sabbath and Jewish holidays. Here is an excerpt from his writings:

> Woe that in this city of ours a bad and bitter custom [has become established]—on the Sabbath people go to coffeehouses and drink coffee that was brewed for Jews on the Sabbath. . . . There is no doubt that if the Jews were not there, the cafe owners would not prepare half of what they do. . . . And this custom has become rooted among everyone; there is no one who does not drink . . . men, women and children, including most of the Torah scholars, . . . and the officers and their deputies take part in this more than the poor people.[23]

This phenomenon, which is described so harshly, teaches us something about the Izmir Jews' style of social encounter. We find this in other Ottoman cities as well, and not only in the seventeenth century.[24] It tells us about the relative openness of daily life in urban Ottoman society.

The Second Period: The Eighteenth Century

Before the Jewish community managed to recuperate from the blow it and its leadership had suffered during the Sabbatai Sevi episode—his appearance in Izmir, his conversion, the conversion of hundreds of his followers, and the founding of the Dönme sect[25]—another catastrophe befell the city. In 1688 a severe earthquake destroyed large parts of the city. Thousands of people were killed (20,000 according to one estimate), among them several hundred Jews (about 400).[26] The survivors fled the ruined city and sought refuge in surrounding towns and elsewhere. The harbor was almost totally paralyzed for nearly fifteen years. Eventually the Ottoman government, with the assistance of European countries and their Levant companies, which greatly needed the port for their international trade, decided to rebuild the harbor. It was restored to normal operation by the early eighteenth century, and Izmir began to flourish once again.[27]

The Izmir Jewish community also regrouped in the city at the beginning of the eighteenth century when it was rebuilt. In addition, many new settlers arrived from Anatolia, the Balkans, Palestine, and Europe. Among the new immigrants were Jewish merchants from Livorno (Leghorn) called "Francos." Most of these were of Portuguese extraction. They had begun to settle in the Levant cities in the late seventeenth century and had established merchant colonies and their own communities. Over time they became the harbingers of modernization for the Jewish communities of Anatolia and the Balkans.[28]

Although the history of the Izmir Jewish community in the eighteenth century has not yet been studied in depth by modern scholars, what we do know at present allows us to say that during that century there was some decline both in economic terms and in religious observance. From the organizational aspect, the community's patterns of leadership and structure continued as they had been formed in the seventeenth century by its founders, headed by R. Joseph Escapa. There was a joint chief rabbinate, generally consisting of two chief rabbis. The system of taxation also continued as it had been in the previous century.[29] The Hebrew printing presses continued to operate, and dozens of rabbinical works were printed in Izmir in the course of the century.[30]

Religious and social regulations established in 1725 by one of the city rabbis, R. Hayyim Abulafia, reveal a rather grim picture of social and religious conditions in the city. The Sabbath was not strictly observed, and the Jews would open their stores on Sabbath afternoons, undoubtedly due to economic competition from their non-Jewish neighbors. The regulations also prohibited the use of inaccurate scales, overcharging, and the oppression of the poor.[31] These phenomena should be seen as a further deterioration in the community's religious and social fabric beyond that displayed by the frequenting of coffeehouses on the Sabbath, which the rabbis had censured in the seventeenth century.

One salient characteristic of Jewish community life in eighteenth-century Izmir (as well as in other Ottoman Jewish communities) was the close relationship with the Jews of Palestine.[32] The Izmir community extended to Palestinian Jewry a considerable amount of financial assistance through the charitable organization known as the Istanbul Officials for Eretz Israel. Many Izmir Jews made pilgrimages to Palestine for the purpose of *ziyara,* visiting the holy places. For these trips, ships were chartered by the Istanbul Officials at the end of the summer, just before the Jewish high holidays, which the pilgrims spent in the Holy Land. Such a ship sailed each year from Izmir, Istanbul, Salonica, and sometimes also from Italy.

There were also quite a number of Jews, some of them rabbis and community leaders, who emigrated to Eretz Israel and settled there. For example, rabbis of the Abulafia, Almazi, Hazzan, Berav, and Ventura families moved there with their families. It is especially noteworthy that nearly the entire group of rabbis that edited and printed one of the most popular books in the Jewish world in the eighteenth century, *Hemdat Yamim* (Izmir, 1731–32), emigrated to Eretz Israel in the 1730s and 1740s.[33] This anthology (three volumes in the Izmir edition, four volumes in other editions) of moral essays, Kabbalah, poetry, and Midrash, arranged to correspond with the Jewish calendar, includes post-Sabbatean elements. The vast popularity of this book in the Jewish world and its publication in many editions[34] testify to a Sabbatean mood and to the great influence of the Sabbatean crisis on religious literary creativity within the Jewish world. The fact that this book was compiled, edited, and first printed in Izmir, the place where Sabbatai Sevi and his movement originated, is clearly significant. It attests to the spiritual upheaval that followed the failure of Sabbateanism and that extended into the eighteenth century.

As was mentioned above, the institution of the chief rabbinate in Izmir underwent severe strain and stress during the eighteenth century, reflecting the social upheaval within the community. In the first half of the eighteenth century, during the period when R. Hayyim Abulafia and R. Yitzhak Hacohen Rapaport were chief rabbis, these tensions relaxed somewhat although they did not disappear completely.[35] These two rabbis, both born in Palestine, retired there in their old age in the 1740s. In 1749, after their departure, an attempt was made to alter the system of electing chief rabbis in the city. Instead of having all taxpayers above a certain level participate in the election, as had been the case until then, the power to elect was given to a small group of community leaders. This change in the rules did not prove successful, and within two years (in 1751) the previous, more democratic system was restored. In the 1760s and 1770s, however, the election of the chief rabbis was once again in the hands of a limited group of leaders.[36] In the end none of these changes seems to have done any good; in the 1770s the conflicts surrounding the chief rabbinate intensified once more, becoming even more severe in the early nineteenth century (as will be discussed in the next section). It should nevertheless be mentioned that these problems affecting the Izmir leadership in the eighteenth century have not yet been thoroughly investigated, and so we should withhold final judgment.

The Third Period: From the Late Eighteenth Century to the *Tanzimat*

In the late eighteenth century there were signs of severe political and economic decline in the Ottoman Empire. The extended wars against European powers during that century, the loss of territory, and the internal disintegration affected every area. The Jews of Izmir also suffered greatly from the empire's economic decline. The Jewish community, which in the past had been an integral part of the city's flourishing trade, had become little more than a group of poor breadwinners. Many Jews who had previously dealt in international trade and brokerage were now compelled to engage in petty trade or hard physical labor, bringing in very little income. Many of the well-to-do lost their property in the early nineteenth century, and many of the middle class joined the ranks of the poor.[37]

At this time the European consuls had become more closely involved in Izmir's internal affairs, as was the case throughout the Ottoman Empire. This, too, had an adverse effect on the Jewish community. The Francos, who had become integrated into the international capitalist system in the early nineteenth century, increasingly tended to turn to the foreign consuls rather than to the legal institutions of the community whenever they became involved in disputes with other Jews in the community. The declining stature of its leadership led to increasing tensions among the various groups in the community. When British missionaries became active in Izmir in the early nineteenth century, some of the Jewish poor tried to put pressure on the community leadership by threatening to convert. In the course of the century, such events occurred with increasing frequency.

Another important cause of the upheavals at this time was the great fire that ravaged Izmir in 1772, burning down all the synagogues in the city. Like the earthquake of 1688, this fire led to changes in the social structure of the community. Because of the fire, the community was dispersed and no one was left to pay the heavy debts that it had incurred as a result of spiraling state taxes. Only thirty years later were the Jews able to receive permission from the central government to rebuild the synagogues (because, according to Islamic law, such permission had to be paid for). Until that time, they were forced to pray in private homes and temporary buildings, but meanwhile the social structure of the old congregations had disintegrated. Some of the old synagogues were replaced by new congregations, and new synagogues were formed according to occupation and associated with the various guilds in the community. Another sign of the crisis in Izmir was the fact that from 1767 until 1838 no Hebrew printing house operated in the city.

All these events led to a severe class struggle at the end of the eighteenth century between the poor and the lower middle classes, on the one hand, and the more well-to-do, on the other. The latter had constituted the community leadership for generations, so the anger of the other classes was directed mainly at them. The struggle centered mostly around the issues of tax assessments for both the community treasury and the government and controversy over the distribution of the payments for retiring the community debt. All these financial obligations were continuously rising and had become a heavy burden for the community. These severe class struggles were the most salient feature in the community's history in the last quarter of the eighteenth and the first half of the nineteenth century.

Another issue that caused controversy within the community at this time was the right for representation demanded by the Jewish guilds.[38] Most of the Jewish guilds in Izmir at that time consisted of workers employed in various types of manual labor, such as wool processing, fabric manufacturing, button making, glass-blowing, and other crafts. These poor laborers now demanded appropriate representation for the heads of their guilds at the community leadership institutions, which had long been in the hands of an established oligarchy. After severe struggles involving tax rebellions, the guilds succeeded in obtaining representation in the community's secular leadership. In addition to the twelve regular members of the leadership, four heads of guilds were appointed.

The sharp social divisions within the community during this period also involved the city's rabbis. Some of them supported the poor, while others continued to support the traditional oligarchy. Of the two chief rabbis at the turn of the century, for example, one, R. Joseph Hazzan, supported the demands of the poor, while the other, R. Yitzhak Mayo, supported the ruling establishment and the wealthy.

The Fourth Period: From the 1830s to World War I

Izmir was not exempt from the changes that transformed Ottoman Jewry in general in the second half of the nineteenth century and the early part of the twentieth century. However, while the Izmir community shared many characteristics with the rest of Ottoman Jewry, there also were some features that remained unique to that community. The following were the most salient causes of change at this period: (a) the *Tanzimat* (the Ottoman reforms); (b) the increasing penetration of the Western powers into the Ottoman Empire; (c) the West European Jews' growing interest in, and influence on, the Jewish communities in Islamic countries; and (d) Increasing conflicts between Jews and Christians.

In general, the *Tanzimat* brought about many changes, especially in the leadership structure of the Izmir community. The reforms paved the way for the replacement of the old system, under which the community was administered by a veteran oligarchy of rabbis and lay leaders and the chief rabbinate was held jointly by two rabbis, with a new and more modern type of leadership. This new leadership now included a new elite, the newly rich and young intellectuals. Moreover, as of the 1840s the government began appointing only one chief rabbi, thus ending the traditional joint character of the institution.[39] It seems that most other reform laws concerning the internal administration of the community were not carried out. Furthermore, the increased dependence of the new leadership on the government was a sign of the weakened autonomy of the Jewish communities throughout the Ottoman Empire.[40] The *Tanzimat* reforms did not create greater harmony in Izmir's social life, nor did they eliminate class conflict. The old disputes between traditional rival groupings within the leadership and the society were merely replaced by new factions and rival alliances that fought one another. The new conflicts were mainly of two sorts: between the newly rich and the poor, and between the young intellectuals and the veteran establishment.[41]

The most outstanding figure in the religious leadership of the Izmir community in the mid-nineteenth century was "the last of the giants," R. Hayyim Palagi.[42] He was rightly considered the greatest "Turkish" rabbi in the nineteenth century, a period in which there was a general decline in traditional Jewry and a lack of creativity in religious scholarship. R. Palagi was exceptionally productive, writing about seventy books on various religious topics. Although his work was not especially original or novel (and this too was a general characteristic of the decline of religious scholarship), his writings demonstrated great erudition and vast knowledge.

The increasing Western penetration of the Ottoman Empire left its mark on the Izmir Jewish community as well. For example, a Protestant mission was active among the Jews of the city, attempting to convert them. This mission was also active among the Eastern Christians, but it was not allowed to operate among the Muslims. Many Jews attended the modern European schools that were established in Izmir as of the 1830s. The Italian school appears to have been particularly popular.

The most important influence on the community's internal life during this period—as was the case with other Jewish communities of the Middle East and North Africa—was the increasing involvement of West European Jewry, especially in the areas of education and culture. It was the "Francos," hundreds of whom had settled in Izmir by the late seventeenth century, who introduced modernization and secular cultural activity to Izmir. Wealthy European Jews, such as Moses Montefiore and the Rothschilds, together with several Jewish organizations, provided assistance for the construction of modern medical facilities and schools in Izmir. Especially important were the educational activities of the Alliance Israélite Universelle, which established its first school in Izmir in 1873.[43] As of the 1840s, the first *maskilim* (members of the Jewish Enlightenment movement) in the city began publishing modern periodicals in Judeo-Spanish. They also published Judeo-Spanish translations of Western literary works.[44] By the second half of the nineteenth century there was a new generation comprising hundreds of young people who had acquired a modern Western education. They changed the community's landscape and social structure from one steeped in centuries-old traditions to a mixed community that included both the old and the new.

Another significant factor in Izmir at that time was the ongoing bitter strife between the various ethnoreligious communities. The Christian population (Greek and Armenian) became increasingly hostile towards the Ottoman regime and the Muslims as their national consciousness was awakened by their communities' struggle for independence. In this they were supported by European powers. The difficult economic conditions led to a persistent and merciless rivalry among the various groups in Izmir, and the economic conflict contributed to increasing interreligious tensions.[45]

The Jews of Izmir were caught in the cross fire. The Christian communities made use of both traditional-religious and modern-nationalistic forms of anti-Semitism to consolidate their religious and nationalist consciousness, as well as to achieve economic goals. The most notorious manifestation of Christian-Jewish tensions in the city was the Christians' blood libels against the Jews, which occurred with regularity throughout the nineteenth century.[46] Occasionally the Ottoman authorities were compelled to intervene. In these cases they generally took a stand in favor of the Jews. The regime's weakness, however, prevented it from bringing under control the intercommunal conflicts in Izmir.

◆ ◆ ◆

I have attempted, perhaps too boldly, to present in one article the outlines of the social history of one Jewish community in the Ottoman period as they emerge on the basis of our current knowledge. The history of the Izmir community exhibits a considerable degree of uniqueness, although for the most part it shares many common denominators with other centers of Jewish life in the Ottoman Empire and indeed with Jewish communities in the diaspora in general. In broad terms, these common characteristics are reflected in the tension between the influence of the surrounding environment, on the one hand, and both the overt and covert contacts with other Jewish communities, both near and far, on the other. The story told here is a variegated story of the Sephardic diaspora in one of its most important and energetic centers. Although this community was established about a hundred years after the expulsion from Spain, its history reflects most of the important elements characteristic of that diaspora.

CHAPTER 4

Rabbinic Literature in the Late Byzantine and Early Ottoman Periods

Israel Ta-Shma

The history of rabbinic literature and lore in the Ottoman Empire during the fifteenth century, before and after the conquest of Constantinople, is little known and its historical origins are obscure. I shall try to shed some light on the subject by adding to what is known about two rabbinic figures of this period. One of them, Rabbi Moses Capsali, chief rabbi of Istanbul, who lived for almost a hundred years (through most of the fifteenth century), is famous. The other, Rabbi Yohanan ben Reuven of Ohrid (Ochrida) in Macedonia, whose activity preceded that of Capsali by at least fifty years, is hardly known, and his name is not even mentioned in Bowman's history of the Jews of Byzantium.[1]

When Mehmed II captured Constantinople in 1453, he found there quite a large Jewish community—actually communities—headed by Rabbi Moses Capsali. This great man, born in Candia around 1410, was descended from a prominent Jewish family in Crete. In his youth he traveled to Germany to study under the famous Ashkenazi rabbis of the time. He probably settled in Constantinople sometime around 1445. In one of his very few extant letters, included in *Takkanot Kandia,* Capsali mentions his Candian teachers by name: his father Eliyahu, Rabbi Shemaryah, Rabbi Moses, and Rabbi Gershon.[2] Meir Benayahu, who summarized the available information on Moses Capsali in a small book on the sixteenth-century historian Eliyahu Capsali, identifies Rabbi Shemaryah with Shemaryah Delmedigo, whose signature is found on a community deed from the year 1400.[3] This identification seems to me most improbable. Since Capsali was born around the year 1410, Rabbi Shemaryah Delmedigo would have had to live, and be active as a *rosh yeshivah* (head of an academy), for almost thirty years after signing the said deed, up to around the year 1430, when Capsali would have come of age and possibly studied under him. In fact, Shemaryah Delmedigo is not mentioned on any document later than the year 1400. He is, however, mentioned on a much earlier document, from the year 1362.[4] We can therefore safely conclude that he was not Capsali's teacher.

In 1839, Eliakim Carmoly published in the *Israelitische Annalen* a few lines from a Paris manuscript, Orat. 110 (today Bibliothèque Nationale, no. 1005), to the effect that a certain Rabbi Yehudah, father of Rabbi Shemaryah, had come from Germany to the isle of Crete and that he had three sons.[5] The eldest was called Abba, and he became famous because of the synagogue that he had built there. The second son was Shemaryah, who became very famous for his great wisdom and was appointed a rabbi in Crete in the year 1412. This short but most informative list was used by A. Geiger,[6] who was the first to draw the Delmedigo family tree, and his conclusions were later adopted by Steinschneider in his comprehensive article on the Jews of Candia.[7] At present the Paris manuscript does not carry this information, but it is quite possible that Carmoly saw an opening or an end page that today is missing from the manuscript. In any case, the historical contents of Carmoly's unidentified source are nicely corroborated by Joseph Shelomoh Delmedigo's book, *Eilim:* "Our master and sage Shemaryah, a famous man in the world, the son of the prince and master of the Torah (*ha-sar ha-aluf*) Yehudah, who was the first who had come from Germany to live in Candia."[8] Joseph Shelomoh Delmedigo was a well-known scholar and rabbi in the seventeenth century, and he is apparently voicing a family tradition. According to him, this Shemaryah was the grandfather of the famous Eliyahu Del Medigo, author of *Behinat Hadat,*[9] who died in the year 1493, when he was barely forty years old. If I am not mistaken, he is the Rabbi Shemaryah ben Yehudah whose signature appears first among a line of dignitaries and rabbis who signed the edict of 1429.[10] We have, therefore, before us a great Cretan rabbi, well-known in his time, by the name of Shemaryah, whose father, Yehudah, the first known Jewish emigrant from Germany to Crete, had arrived in the island around the year 1360. Rabbi

Shemaryah was probably born in Crete around 1370, and his older brother, Abba, was the first to establish the Ashkenazi rite in the island, by building there the first Ashkenazi synagogue. In 1412, Shemaryah became a rabbi in Candia, and in 1429 he was still there to sign, as first among the dignitaries, a community document.

This, however, is not all that we know about Shemaryah. Manuscript Paris, Bibliothèque Nationale, Heb. 804, "Ma'arekhet ha-Elohut," an anonymous book of early Kabbalah literature, contains the information that it was copied by the scribe Moses ben Isaac Ibn Tibbon, in the year 1402, for "the wise man, the exilarch, who has the power and the dominance (*he-hakham rosh ha-golah, asher lo ha-oz ve-ha-memshalah)*, the honorable Rabbi Shemaryah ben Yehudah." The place of copying is not mentioned, although the handwriting is typical Judeo-Spanish. However, another manuscript—just one other manuscript—by the same scribe and of the same type of handwriting, has survived in the library of the Vatican, no. Or. 82, and it was copied in Candia in the year 1407. So there is really no doubt that our "Honorable Rabbi Shemaryah ben Yehudah" also lived in Candia, and it was for him that the said "Ma'arekhet ha-Elohut" was copied. Incidentally, the same Vatican manuscript also contains Rabbi Joseph Gikatila's famous *Ginnat Egoz* (first printed edition: Hanau, 1615) and the kabbalistic book, *Keter Shem Tov,*[11] by the German mystic Rabbi Shem-Tov ben Avraham Axelrod of Cologne, which were probably also copied for Rabbi Shemaryah ben Yehudah, together with "Ma'arekhet ha-Elohut," in the same volume. The title *rosh ha-golah* (the exilarch) fits perfectly well with the other outstanding honorific titles conferred on Rabbi Shemaryah, and it is clear that he was indeed a central rabbinic figure in Candia at the time.

I suggest that it was this Rabbi Shemaryah who around the year 1430 was the teacher of Rabbi Moses Capsali. It is also interesting to note that Rabbi Eliyahu Capsali, the father of Moses Capsali, was the first Candian rabbi known to have traveled in his youth to study in German *yeshivot*. Rabbi Eliyahu's formative years were around 1380, and his pioneering departure from Candia to study in Germany had probably something to do with the contemporary imported Ashkenazi influence of Rabbi Yehudah, the first Ashkenazi immigrant to Candia. And Moses Capsali, who was educated under a strong Ashkenazi influence, as can be easily seen from the few responsa known to us (included in *Takkanot Kandia*), learned from them both.

It also seems very probable to me that a few original pages by Rabbi Yehudah, our first German immigrant to Candia, have been preserved in the Cairo Genizah. In 1982, Naomi Goldfeld published twelve pages from the Cambridge Genizah, constituting a fragment of a large commentary on the Pentateuch.[12] In this fragment, the author mentions his name twice as Yehudah ben Shemaryah. He apparently was writing in a Greek-speaking country as is evident from two Greek *le'azim* (explanatory translations of Hebrew terms). He further states that he had originally come from Germany, and he mentions his earlier days: "When I was still in Germany, at the school of the great luminary, my teacher Rabbi Meir" (*be-odi be-Ashkenaz, be-midrash ha-maor ha-gadol mori ve-rabbi Meir zekher tzadik ve-kadosh li-vrakhah*). Goldfeld was convinced that the author was alluding here to the famous Rabbi Meir (Maharam) of Rothenburg; but I would rather argue that the reference here is to Rabbi Meir (Maharam) Segal of Fulda, who was the most important rabbi and head of an academy in Germany in the second half of the fourteenth century.

The name Rabbi Yehudah ben Shemaryah does not appear anywhere in our literature, except for a quizzical mention by Moses Botaril, who quotes him as the author of a kabbalistic book by the name of *Mikveh Israel*. Botaril, a late-fourteenth-century Provençal scholar, who lived in Avignon and wrote prolifically around the year 1400, has earned a questionable reputation as a literary forger of the first magnitude. In his writings, he quotes extensively from fictitious books, which he attributes to well-known rabbinic figures and to which he ascribes imaginary titles. Much has been written on this subject, summarized by Jacob Sussman, who dedicated a detailed study to Botaril's halakhic forgeries.[13]

Although the great majority of the unknown books quoted by Botaril were indeed fictitious, some of them can be proved to have actually existed and really studied by Botaril, such as the book *Mezukkak Shiv'ataim* by Rabbi Joseph ben Shaul, as demonstrated by Sussman in his article. It is quite possible therefore that the book *Mikveh Israel* by Rabbi Yehudah ben Shemaryah did indeed exist and was actually read by Botaril, who was Yehudah's younger contemporary. Furthermore, it is quite possible that these Genizah pages are actually a fragment of this book. The imaginary quotations attributed by Botaril to different sages were all invented by him to support his own opinions and decisions, and are all of limited scope and length, just enough to produce the desired effect. However, in this case, we have before us a lengthy fragment of seven leaves (fourteen pages), written according to the order of the weekly portions in the Pentateuch, and covering a rich variety of topics, undoubtedly representing a whole book, and that is of course a completely different matter. The fragment discusses astronomy and natural sciences, philosophy and Kabbalah, and the author, though well-versed in philosophy, opposes it vehemently, calling it *ha-filosofia ha-arura* (the accursed philosophy) and its followers *ha-filosofim ha-arurim* (the accursed philosophers).

As a student of the first Ashkenazi rabbi in Candia, and the son of the first Candian rabbi to attain a higher Talmudic education in Germany, it is not surprising that Moses Capsali too went to Germany and studied there under some of the foremost sages of the time. Among his teachers were Rabbi Jacob Landau, the father of Rabbi Moses Landau, author of the well-known halakhic composition *Sefer ha-Agur*,[14] and Rabbi Yehudah Mintz, who was his colleague and later conferred on him an Ashkenazi ordination. It should also be noted that the German-Ashkenazi influence on Capsali is evident in every line of the small but interesting literary remnant of his writings, saved for us by his distant relative, Rabbi Eliyahu Capsali, in his *Takkanot Kandia*. The *Takkanot* include four letters to the community of Candia, a quotation from a fifth letter, and a short mention of an oral halakhic decision, given by Capsali "when he came back from Germany." The first letter concerns a cantor who used force and the help of non-Jewish authorities to assume his position. Capsali quotes early and contemporary Ashkenazi rabbinic custom against such practice, reminisces on his own experiences in Germany, and finally declares a *herem* (excommunication) on the cantor if he does not step down. The second letter discusses the strict prohibition of abrogating ancient community customs, which is a classical Ashkenazi theme, and cites Ashkenazi sources, traditions, and lore. Two additional letters prohibit Jews from buying illegally-confiscated Jewish real estate or renting homes from which other Jews had been unjustly expelled.

These letters too follow, tacitly, well-known Franco-German precedents. The fifth letter concerns the correct technique, according to the Halakhah, enabling the use of gentile labor in Jewish vineyards, and it also follows strict Ashkenazi custom, going back as far as the eleventh century.

Rabbi Moses Capsali is not the only early Ottoman rabbinical authority known to us. Another rabbi of considerable stature, an older coeval of Rabbi Moses Capsali, was Rabbi Yohanan ben Reuven, who lived in Ohrid and was active there around the second quarter of the fourteenth century. He must have died before the year 1458, when the Berlin manuscript (Stadt Bibliothek, OR. OCT. 333) of his book was copied, blessing his memory. He is known to us only through this work, which is an extensive commentary on the famous eighth-century Babylonian Gaonic book of She'iltot by Rabbi Aha (Ahai) of Shabha. The commentary is extant in a few manuscripts and was printed for the first time by Samuel Mirsky on the margins of his critical edition of the She'iltot.[15] However, in his introduction, Mirsky never refers to Rabbi Yohanan's commentary, except for a short description of the defective Oxford manuscript (Neubauer, 542) that he used for his publication. In fact, Rabbi Yohanan's book was never analyzed by scholars, and it remains practically unknown.

In his commentary Rabbi Yohanan states that the people of his age could not dedicate time to the study of the Talmud itself, and they preferred to fulfill the positive commandment of Talmud Torah (the study of the Torah) by studying the more practical She'iltot. They therefore had asked him to write a running commentary on it. I must add that this piece of information is most valuable, and quite accurate too. Most, if not all, of the fragmentary commentaries on the book of She'iltot that are still extant in various manuscripts, and none of which have been analyzed by scholars, were written in Byzantium or the early Ottoman Empire. It is interesting to note that the majority of the full, or almost full, manuscripts of the She'iltot itself are Greek-Byzantine,[16] and the same holds true for the Genizah fragments. Rabbi Yohanan uses Greek words, and Greece itself is mentioned in his book twice. Fluent in Talmud, Halakhah, and rabbinic lore, he dwells mainly on the Talmudic material, adding to it much that is not quoted by the She'iltot, and commenting on the whole. Rabbi Yohanan bases himself mainly on Rashi, whom he frequently quotes verbatim, widely adding to it from the rich medieval rabbinic literature. His additions include many ethical issues and themes, and concrete moral instructions. He frequently relies on Rabbi Yonah Ghirondi's books and on kabbalistic material taken from the *Zohar*, which he quotes by name a dozen times, on halakhic and aggadic subjects. He also quotes from Rabbi Ya'akov ben Sheshet's *Meshiv Devarim Nekhohim*, of which he is one of the earliest users (Genesis, no. 18). As far as I know, Rabbi Yohanan is the first halakhist to make regular use of the *Zohar* in his work. His main authorities for deciding the Halakhah are Maimonides, who is mentioned on every page, and to a somewhat lesser extent Rabbi Ya'akov ben Asher's *Sefer ha-Turim*. Perhaps out of respect, he refers to the latter as his teacher, saying *"ve-ani Yohanan talmido,"* although it is unlikely that he could have studied under Rabbi Ya'akov in person, as the latter died sometime around 1345.

Rabbi Yohanan quotes extensively from other Franco-German books, although I am unable to discuss them here. I must, however, mention six Greek scholars quoted in his book:

Rabbi M. Kunzi, or *Kanzi,* an unknown person, mentioned by Rabbi Yohanan over fifty times, and serving, therefore, as one of the literary foundations for his entire book. It seems clear that the quotations are taken from Kunzi's commentary on the *She'iltot.*

Rabbi Shemaryah, whom I would take to be the famous Shemaryah ha-Ikriti, although there were at least six different sages with the same name living in the area between 1350 and 1450.

Rabbi Yishma'el, who is most probably the son of Rabbi Shemaryah ha-Ikriti, as we can see from the colophon to Rabbi Shemaryah ha-Ikriti's only extant commentary on a tractate from the Talmud, Tractate Megillah, the only one to survive out of a whole series of Talmud commentaries named *Elef ha-Magen*. According to the colophon, the copying of the manuscript, Cambridge, Mm 6.26.2(8), was completed in the year 1410 by "Shemaryah ben Yishma'el, [Shemaryah ha-Ikriti's] grandson," who copied it from his grandfather's book, *Elef ha-Magen.*[17] Rabbi Yishma'el must have died sometime around the year 1375.

Rabbi Hillel ben Eliakim, the most famous twelfth-century Byzantine commentator on the *Safra* and *Sifrei* and other *Midrashim* (homiletic interpretations of the Scriptures).[18]

Avraham Ze'ira, identical with the twelfth-century Rabbi Avraham Zutra of Thebes (Thebay), who was already quoted after his death by Rabbi Yeshayahu di Trani the first, and later by Rabbi Eliyahu Mizrahi.

Rabbi Menahem, probably identical with his namesake quoted by the said twelfth-century Rabbi Hillel.

Last, but not least, Rabbi Yohanan also cites the twelfth-century South Italian Rabbi Isaac ben Malkitzedek of Siponto and his Italian coeval Rabbi Shelomoh ben Avraham.

The latest personality mentioned in Rabbi Yohanan's work is, therefore, Rabbi Yishma'el, who died probably around 1375–80. He is mentioned in both manuscripts with the blessing for the dead, and although this cannot constitute final proof, it certainly indicates that Rabbi Yohanan wrote his book later than 1375, and probably around 1390–1400. If we are to take his self-designation as a "student" of Rabbi Ya'akov ben Asher in a literal sense, that would mean that he was born not later than 1320 and died about 1400. And there is indeed nothing to disprove these calculations.

Two other Greek scholars, contemporaries of Rabbi Yohanan, are mentioned by him. They are Rabbi Hayyim and Rabbi "Yitzhak Tzarfati," both of whom he had consulted orally on a halakhic problem. It is tempting to identify Rabbi "Yitzhak Tzarfati" with his famous namesake, who sent an open letter to the German Jewish communities, calling on them to leave their homes and settle in the developing Ottoman Balkans. The letter is probably from the year 1438, and Rabbi Yitzhak had been established in the Ottoman Empire for some time before writing it. This proposed identification had already been put forth by Steinschneider 130 years ago, and was more recently reinforced by my friend Joseph Hacker.[19] Hacker quotes Rabbi Mordekhai Comtino's preface to his commentary on Aristotle, written at the request of Rabbi Yitzhak Tzarfati, who is said there to have come from far away to teach Talmud in Byzantium. If this proves to be correct, we may have to fix a later date for Rabbi Yohanan's work, probably around 1430.

What is important for us to observe, in the immediate context of this article, is the considerable impact of Franco-German influence on Rabbi Yohanan's work. Besides Rabbi Ya'akov ben Asher, the central figure in the fourteenth-century Ashkenazi world of learning and tradition, Rabbi Yohanan made use of a rich gallery of Franco-German scholars of the thirteenth century. His book is almost equally balanced between the Spanish and the Franco-German schools. The Spanish tradition is mainly represented by Maimonides, who was accepted as an authority among the Ashkenazim as much as Rabbi Ya'akov ben Asher was accepted among the Sephardim. This cautious equilibrium, later adopted as a leading principle by Rabbi Yosef Caro in his classic *Beit Yosef,* clearly indicates the existence of a well-defined Ashkenazi influence in the Balkan area already in the mid-fourteenth century, an influence that developed into a spiritual hegemony in Constantinople by the mid-fifteenth century, on the eve of the Ottoman conquest.

CHAPTER 5

Jewish Contributions to Ottoman Medicine, 1450–1800

Rhoads Murphey

Jewish doctors were known in the East long before their expulsion from Spain. Their employment by the Byzantine emperor Manuel I in the twelfth century and by the Komneni of Trabzon in the fifteenth has been noted by specialists.[1] It is also known that Jewish doctors served at the Seljukid court in Konya,[2] as well as in the courts of the Turkish emirs of western Anatolia in the early fourteenth century.[3] From this evidence it seems clear that by the mid-fifteenth century, at the time when Jacopo (Iacopo) di Gaeta, known after his emigration to the Ottoman empire as Yakub Hekim (d. 1484), entered the service of Prince Mehmed, there already existed a long-standing tradition of Jewish doctors in the service of Eastern potentates. When his master Mehmed acceded to the throne as Mehmed II (1451–81), Yakub Hekim was singled out for particular favor and was promoted ultimately to a position as chief physician of the palace, or *hekimbaşı*.[4] It can thus be seen that Bayezid II's welcoming of the Spanish Jews after the expulsion was by no means an unprecedented step, nor would it be accurate to credit Bayezid with having shown exceptional tolerance; he was merely expanding the scope of already existing traditions.

A number of the standard accounts of Jewish life in Ottoman Turkey have fallen into the unfortunate habit of approaching their subject by the casting of heroes and villains on a regnal basis.[5] Accordingly, some sultans, like Bayezid II (1481–1512), are praised for their exceptional tolerance, and others, in particular Selim II (1566–74), are credited with exceptional political acumen for their willingness to place reliance on leading figures in the Jewish community such as Joseph Nasi, duke of Naxos (d. 1579). Because of the general adherence to this approach, the period after 1579 is frequently painted in the blackest of terms, as though Nasi's fall from favor and subsequent death was translated instantaneously into a degeneration of the condition of the Jewish community at large.

My account of the Jewish contribution to Ottoman medicine, while acknowledging the superior quality of work accomplished during the fifteenth and sixteenth centuries, will give equal weight to the continuing accomplishments of the seventeenth and eighteenth centuries. However, before beginning the three-part account of the successive phases in the development of Ottoman medicine from 1450 to 1600, from 1600 to 1700, and from 1700 to 1800, let me quote briefly from the work of one of the worst offenders among the old school historians who wrote on Ottoman Jewish affairs. Heinrich Graetz, who wrote at the end of the nineteenth century, justified his neglect of developments in the last three centuries of the Ottoman era by stating that "After the reign of Ahmed I [. . .] the empire sank into an enervation and each sultan became a sardanapalus. [. . .] The glory of the Turkish Jews was extinguished like a meteor, and plunged into utter darkness."[6] That no such steep decline in fortune or in the conditions of their professional life can be detected among Ottoman Jewish doctors will, I hope, become apparent from the account that follows.

The Role of Jewish Doctors during the First Phase of the Development of Ottoman Medicine: The Era of Institution Building, 1450–1600

It is imperative in writing an account of developments in Ottoman medicine of any period to strive not to exclude from consideration the activities of the less celebrated physicians who always made up the bulk of the profession. At any given time only one person could become *hekimbaşı* of the palace. What is perhaps most remarkable about the Jewish contribution to Ottoman medicine is not the periodic ability of the Jews to produce the exceptional scholar or administrator who succeeded in rising to the top ranks, but the fact of their sustained presence and numerical predominance in the profession as a whole. Over a prolonged period of time and in a variety of different economic and political climates, Jewish doctors maintained their place at the center of important developments.

In the second half of the fifteenth century, the demand for trained physicians increased dramatically: within the short space of one and a half decades, from 1470 to 1485, two major medical colleges were founded, the first by Mehmed the Conqueror in Istanbul and another soon after by his son and successor Bayezid II in Edirne. While precise data are lacking, it is clear that the recruiting for these newly opened positions was international in scope. It should not be supposed that the Jews supplied the only Western-trained doctors to serve in the Ottoman empire, and it is clear that Christian renegades also played an active role in this field.[7] However, by the mid-sixteenth century a combination of external and internal factors coincided to secure the ever-increasing dominance of the Jews in the Ottoman medical establishment. Externally the introduction of the Inquisition from Spain into Italy in 1542, the establishment of the Index of Prohibited Books in 1543, and the more or less unrelenting anti-Jewish atmosphere in Italy after the mid-sixteenth century drove increasing numbers of Jewish scholars to seek the largely unrestricted religious freedom of the Ottoman Empire. Thus it was both the negative push of repression, censorship, and religious intolerance in the West and the positive pull of a more favorable atmosphere for pursuing their professional careers in the Ottoman Empire that combined to give impetus to the sixteenth-century brain drain from West to East.

The career of João Rodrigues de Castelo Branco (1511–68), most often referred to by his adopted names of Habibi, Haviv, or Amatus Lusitanus, is illustrative of these trends. Amatus spent most of his distinguished career in the West. After leaving Portugal in the early 1530s, he arrived in Italy in 1540 via Antwerp and spent the next decade and a half in a variety of scholarly and professional activities, serving for a time as personal physician to Pope Julius III (1550–53) and to the pope's sister. By the time he fled Italy in reaction to the repressive anti-Jewish policies of Pope Paul IV (1555–59), his magnum opus, the *Curationum Medicinalium,* based on a study of 700 case histories published in seven volumes called the *centuriae,* was already well under way.[8] In fact, volumes one through six had already been completed by the time he settled in Salonica in the year 1559. Amatus was universally recognized for his scientific acumen,[9] and the fact that he wrote in Latin was certainly instrumental in securing his international reputation. However, of the many Jewish medical immigrants to the Ottoman Empire during the reign of Süleyman the Magnificent (1520–66), there were others who had more lasting influence.

By the mid-sixteenth century it becomes possible to discern two typical features connected with Jewish medical practice in the Ottoman Empire. One salient feature was the perpetuation of the craft within particular families, which led to the emergence of intergenerational dynasties of medical experts. A second feature was the proliferation of the skill within the Jewish community at large, which resulted in a steadily rising proportion of Jewish doctors within the ranks of the profession. Their presence is particularly noticeable in the palace corps of physicians, a group of some forty to sixty specialists forming part of the imperial household, and their predominance in those circles speaks of a general trust and respect for their qualifications among the Muslim populace at large.

The trend towards the establishment of medical dynasties can be seen most strikingly in the case of two sixteenth-century immigrant families, the Ben Yahya family of Salonica and the Hamons of Istanbul. Gedaliah ben Yahya, who served as the host of Amatus during his sojourn in Salonica between 1559 and 1568, was the patriarch of a medical family that produced a number of doctors who rose to prominence in the capital during the second half of the sixteenth century. Joseph ben Yahya remained in practice as an active physician throughout his life, while other relatives such as Moses ben Yahya and Tam ben Yahya devoted themselves in part to philanthropy and Hebrew letters as well.[10] A great many doctors in the premodern age resisted being confined to a narrow speciality or even to a single field of endeavor. Furthermore, a position as private body physician to a well-placed official or to the sultan himself provided a natural opportunity for the physician to act as his patron's adviser and representative in nonmedical matters. Due to their command of foreign languages, the employment of recently immigrated Jews as diplomatic envoys was both usual and expected. The Hamon family, starting with Joseph Hamon the Elder, who served under Selim I (1512–20), and followed by his son and successor Moses Hamon (d. 1554), author of a unique treatise on dentistry in Turkish,[11] provides an excellent example of the combination of medical and nonmedical talents. It is remarkable, however, that despite periodic retreats from the medical profession to pursue involvement in the affairs of the Jewish community in the Ottoman Empire or to serve as intermediaries of the sultan in international diplomacy,[12] the Hamon family continued for many successive generations, extending at least as far as the early eighteenth century, to produce doctors of the highest professional standing.[13] The example provided by these leading families of the Ottoman Jewish community gave encouragement to the trend toward a general proliferation of the medical profession among Jews.

The extent of Jewish participation in the medical profession can easily be gauged by the rising proportion of Jews in the palace corps of physicians. According to figures examined by Baron,[14] the sixteenth century witnessed a steep rise in the proportion of Jewish doctors in the palace service. While in 1536 they represented 5 out of 20 doctors or 25 percent, by 1548 their number had risen to 14 out of 30 or 47 percent. It may be presumed that this upward trend continued throughout the second half of the sixteenth century since Ayn-i Ali's figures from 1609 indicate that they then accounted for 41 out of 62 positions in the palace service, or a clear majority of 66 percent.[15] Examining the records of the sixty-man staff of the corps of palace physicians is not a very satisfactory way of trying to determine the role played by Jewish doctors in society at large, but the growth of their participation at court is surely indicative of broader trends and may be viewed as a barometer of increased general acceptance of their expertise in this field. As the sixteenth century drew to a close, we thus see little or no evidence of an erosion of either public or sultanic confidence in the skillful services provided by Jewish doctors. To the contrary, we witness in the subsequent two-century period from 1600 to 1800 a continued broadening of their role and a further consolidation of their position within the Ottoman medical establishment.

The Seventeenth Century: The Era of Continued Growth and Consolidation

The late Salo Baron, in assessing the post-sixteenth-century developments in Ottoman Jewish medicine and science in his summary volume on the Jews of the non-Western lands, stated his general conclusion in the following words: "With the cessation of the large-scale Jewish immigration from the Western lands and partial reversal to Jewish emigration from the empire in the seventeenth and eighteenth centuries, the contribution of Jewish physicians greatly diminished."[16] Whether or not and, if so, how close a connection can be drawn between migration patterns and the development of science is a complex question. The contention that the stream of immigration into the Ottoman Empire slowed appreciably during the seventeenth and eighteenth centuries is, I think, highly questionable. Much of the existing evidence seems to point in another direction. Uriel Heyd, in a study of the Istanbul community based on his detailed examination of tax census registers dating from 1623 and 1688, concluded that there was a "continuous immigration of Marranos" to the Ottoman Empire throughout the seventeenth century, which accounts in part for the doubling in the size of the Istanbul Sephardi community in the short span of sixty-five years.[17] The reasons for this are several. In the first place, far from abating in the seventeenth century, the religious tensions in Spain that had caused the first exodus of Jews in 1492 grew in intensity. The expulsion of the Moriscos in 1609 and the liquidation of the remaining Morisco communities of Spain during the years 1610–11[18] resulted in a reintensification of the search for crypto-Jews and, as Joseph Yerushalmi has shown in several of his studies, the flight of Marranos from the Iberian peninsula during the seventeenth century continued unchecked.[19] Secondly, it seems logical to conclude that the economic climate of the Ottoman Empire must have continued to offer attractive opportunities for immigrants, especially skilled professionals who settled in the empire's growing urban centers. That large numbers of these political, religious, and economic refugees continued to make their way east seems clear both from the contemporary evidence presented by Heyd and other indications from later centuries. A Turkish document dated 1839, published by Ahmed Refik, records that the Jewish community of Istanbul sought permission to add 20 *dönüm*s (approximately 5 acres) to the Jewish cemetery in Hasköy, a clear indication of the community's sustained numerical strength well into the nineteenth century.[20] The growing size of the indigenous Jewish community and the continued participation of new immigrants with medical expertise seem to point to the fact that there was no significant lessening of opportunity for Ottoman Jews during the seventeenth century.

The seventeenth century seems to have been a period of growth for Ottoman Jewish doctors at a variety of different levels. Jewish doctors such as the Cardoso brothers of Venice experienced no difficulty in transporting their skills across either shore of the Mediterranean. For example, Miguel Cardoso, who was born in Venice in 1630, practiced medicine in Venice and Livorno (Leghorn) before becoming private physician to the bey of Tripoli. After his banishment from Tripoli, he took up residence in Cairo, where he served as physician to the pasha of Egypt.[21] The case was by no means exceptional; indeed the reverse pattern, that of Eastern-born doctors traveling to the West to complete their education and training, was equally common. As an example, one might cite the case of Joseph Solomon del Medigo, also known as Joseph of Candia. Born in Crete in 1591 of German Jewish ancestry, he studied medicine in Padua and returned to Crete in 1613. He practiced medicine in a succession of Ottoman cities from Cairo to Istanbul, from whence he traveled to the Danubian Principalities. At the end of his career he returned to Europe, arriving in Amsterdam in 1627. He finally settled in Prague, where he died in 1655.[22] Such itinerant doctors traveling in either direction, from east to west and vice versa, helped to keep the channels of international scientific communication open.

Some modern specialists are conscious of a growing technological gap between the Ottoman Empire and the West starting in the seventeenth century.[23] There are indications, however, that at least so far as the medical field—together with other realms of the applied as opposed to the pure sciences—was concerned, a kind of international fraternity of health professionals emerged on an informal basis, and facilitated the timely exchange of new ideas and discoveries. As we saw in our account of the development of Ottoman medicine in the sixteenth century, doctors frequently doubled as diplomats, sultanic envoys, and even as commodity brokers or merchants. Their travels in a number of different capacities afforded them ample opportunity to renew and expand their medical education. An interesting Ottoman document found in the archives of Venice and datable to the year 1602 gives eloquent testimony to the mobility and versatility of Jewish doctors resident in the Ottoman Empire, as well their indispensability to their masters and patients. The letter addressed by a certain Mehmed Ali Pasha, a high-ranking Ottoman official holding at least the rank of *beylerbeyi* or governor, to Venice's resident diplomatic representative in Istanbul, the *bailo*, requests that the pasha's Jewish doctor, named in the document as Yakov Desakov, be granted a 5,000 *altunluk* (gold pieces) customs exemption.[24] This document serves as a clear indication that Jewish doctors residing in the Ottoman Empire continued to maintain close ties with the West, whether for commercial or scientific purposes. Of course, not all Ottoman Jewish doctors were so well connected as the likes of Desakov, but in general we do observe to an ever-increasing degree the internationalization of medicine in the seventeenth-century Ottoman Empire.

Certainly the Jews enjoyed no exclusive claim on the medical profession, but they continued to play a very active and increasingly prominent

Letter of Mehmed Ali Pasha regarding his Jewish physician dated ca. 1602. The document bears the signature (*pençe*) "Mehmed Ali al-Muzaffer," in gold ink, extending along the right-hand margin. The three *tuğs* (horse-tail crests) indicate that this official held at least the rank of *beylerbeyi*. This document is a facsimile from the state archives of Venice and reproduced with the permission of the Italian Ministry of Culture.

role. It is not possible here to elaborate fully or attempt to trace the careers of the many Jewish doctors who played a role in the development of Ottoman medicine in the late seventeenth century. Instead I have chosen three well-known figures whose biographies, I hope, will help to exemplify a variety of different trends. The first of our three subjects, Tobias Cohn (1652–1729), was a German Jew born in Metz; the second Daniel de Fonseca (1672–c. 1740), an Iberian Jew born in Portugal; and the last Mosheh ben Raphael Abravanel (d. 1738), a non–Muslim Ottoman subject, or *zimmi,* who con-verted to Islam, took the name Mustafa Feyzi, and adopted the profession-ally apt patronymic Hayatizade, or "son of the Lifegiver."

Tobias Cohn, a native of Metz, was orphaned during childhood and raised by relatives in Cracow. After completing his medical training at Frankfurt on the Oder and at Padua, he arrived in the Ottoman Empire as a young man.[25] In later life his main patron seems to have been Rami Mehmed Pasha, who in 1703 was elevated for a short term as grand vezir.[26] In particular, it appears that his ideas concerning the reform of the medical profession, which he elaborated in his written works,[27] struck a receptive chord among his Ottoman colleagues; and the spirit, if not the substance, of his remarks had an influence on the regulatory efforts initiated at the begin-ning of the eighteenth century.[28] Cohn ended his career in Jerusalem, where he died in 1729 at the age of seventy-seven, having spent his entire adult life, apart from a brief sojourn in Venice in 1709 to oversee the publication of his book, within the boundaries of the Ottoman Empire.

In contrast to Tobias Cohn, whose main contribution to Ottoman in-tellectual life was embodied in his scientific, administrative, and publishing activities, his close contemporary Daniel de Fonseca, like several of his six-teenth-century predecessors already mentioned, preferred to mix science with politics and diplomacy. Leaving Portugal at a young age, he received his medical education in Bordeaux and arrived in 1702 in Istanbul, where he ultimately acquired a position as personal physician to the baron Charles de Ferriol, France's ambassador to the Sublime Porte. Throughout the period from 1710 to 1730, when he fled to France following the deposition of Sul-tan Ahmed III, de Fonseca maintained very close connections with high government circles, and some sources maintain that he also served for a time as Sultan Ahmed's private physician.[29] As a consequence of the many distractions at the court and the grand vezir's council and his involvement as go-be-tween in intrigues at the various foreign embassies in the capital, he seems to have found little time for scholarly production and is not known to have left any published works. His political connections and considerable social prominence must thus be seen as a mixed blessing, since in his case, at least, they seem to have acted as a hindrance to scholarly productivity.

The last figure in our trio of seventeenth-century medical mentors is a convert from Judaism, Mustafa Feyzi. His enduring contribution was that, apart from his personal importance as the sultan's chief medical officer, or *hekimbaşı,* an office which he occupied for an unprecedented twenty-two-year term, from 1669 to 1691, he and his descendants succeeded, as had their sixteenth-century predecessors, the Hamons, in establishing a semidy-nastic control over that office, which lasted, with brief interruptions, for a period of eight decades. The hegemony of the Hayatizade clan over the *hekimbaşılık* really came to an end only with the dismissal of their associate, Said Mehmed Efendi, at the end of his second term in 1753.[30] In addition to Mustafa Feyzi's own prolific publication record,[31] each of his grandsons also made substantial contributions to the corpus of medical literature in Turk-ish. When we take into consideration the scholarly output of Hayatizade in-laws, such as Süleyman Efendi (d. 1715),[32] and of unrelated but closely af-filiated medical students, such as Mustafa ibn Mehmed,[33] the scale of their collective contribution is really quite impressive. From the few details pro-vided in the foregoing three biographies, ending with the life of the new dynast, Mustafa Feyzi (d. 1692), it can readily be seen that despite the gloomy prognostications made by scholars such as Baron concerning the vi-ability of Jewish intellectual life in the Ottoman Empire after the close of the golden age of the sixteenth century, as late as the turn of the eighteenth cen-tury Jewish doctors and philosophers were poised to make perhaps their greatest contributions to the advancement of Ottoman science.

The Eighteenth Century: The Era of Medical Reform

In assessing the scientific accomplishments of eighteenth-century Ottoman physicians, it is important to emphasize from the outset that little ground-breaking research was conducted, the bulk of the work being confined to

Turkish translations of contemporary and not-so-contemporary Western works written in Latin. The ideas expressed in the works of the sixteenth-century Swiss physician Paracelsus (1493?–1541) were hardly revolutionary by the time they were popularized in the Ottoman Empire through the efforts of early eighteenth-century codifiers, such as Ömer Shifai (d. 1742)[34] and his close successor Abbas Vesim (d. 1761).[35] Despite the many individual insights achieved in Europe during the era of the "scientific revolution," contemporary Western medicine itself did not achieve its most significant breakthroughs until after 1800. Prior to this time medicine's development was still inextricably linked with mysticism and philosophy, as can be seen in the career of the Austrian physician Mesmer (1733–1815), and it was not yet fully liberated from the influence of the church.[36]

While it remains important that we view with skepticism the vaunted "modernity" of eighteenth-century medicine, whether in the East or the West, and keep ever wary of the danger of falling into the trap of anachronistic assessments, in at least one area it seems apparent that some real progress was being made. From the very beginning of the eighteenth century, in the Ottoman Empire as well as in contemporary Europe, a new emphasis was being placed on defining and enforcing a standardized set of criteria for determining competence to practice medicine. In the Ottoman Empire we see that in this period the state began to play an increasingly intrusive role in the examining and licensing of physicians. These efforts did not prevent the admission of new doctors to the ranks of practicing physicians, but since it was the latter, in particular the top-ranking *hekimbaşı,* who decided what standards should be imposed, these changes served to consolidate the position of already practicing physicians. As I have already indicated, it appears that the views of Tobias Cohn—in particular, his aversion to charlatanism and medical fraud[37]—exerted a strong influence on his Ottoman contemporaries. As one would expect in any broad-based movement, the list of medical reformists active during the early eighteenth century contains the names of Jews, Jewish converts to Islam, second—and third-generation Muslims, and other Muslims in varying proportions. It seems clear that the eighteenth-century reform movement emerged not just from state initiative, but from a broad consensus within the ranks of the medical profession itself. It is nonetheless noteworthy that during the first half of the eighteenth century, when the movement was gathering momentum, the leadership provided from the office of the *hekimbaşı* was frequently in Jewish hands.[38]

The essence of the reform movement is summarized in the texts of two imperial *fermans*, the first issued in 1115 H/1703 and the second in 1142 H/1729. The texts of both edicts were published in Osman Şevki's work on Turkish medicine.[39] In the first edict the main goal seems to have been to secure the banishment of foreign doctors who without appropriate supervision or control had opened clinics in Ottoman cities, staffed sometimes by unqualified persons *(na-ehl)* posing as doctors. The regulation stipulated that all doctors operating clinics in the capitals Istanbul and Edirne would be subject to inspection by the *hekimbaşı* Nuh Efendi. Those who passed this inspection were to be issued permits *(temessük)* allowing them to operate their clinics. The regulation also explicitly forbade the sharing of practices or medical partnerships, requiring that each clinic be maintained by one licensed doctor served by a medical assistant or trainee *(şagird)*. The regulation of 1729 called for a renewal of the general inspections of physicians' credentials and recommended the establishment of a system limiting authorized clinics to a fixed number of licensed premises *(gedik)*. According to these regulations, upon the decease of a license holder the permit could pass only to one of five registered qualified alternate candidates, called *mülâzim*. These seemingly restrictive regulations, far from discouraging the development of the craft, served to instill high professional standards among medical practitioners while at the same time helping to restore the public's shaken confidence in the competence and reliability of doctors. There was an implicit danger in such legislation of fostering an excessive enclosure and isolation of the medical profession and sealing it hermetically from the stimulus provided by the uncontrolled influx of new practitioners and exposure to the new methods that these newcomers might conceivably have brought with them. But since, in theory at least, it was only the incompetent who were being excluded, it is difficult to see how the interest of either science or the public welfare would have been served by their inclusion.

It appears that two further factors helped to mitigate the effect of isolationist tendencies in eighteenth-century Ottoman medicine. One was the rise of a new phenomenon of nondiplomatic and noncommercial casual travel. This ensured that Ottoman men of science were more apt to be exposed to the fruits of their Western counterparts' discoveries through conversation and informal meetings with their peers and contemporaries from the West. These personal encounters added a new dimension to the dissemination of knowledge through the written word. Secondly, conditions were more favorable in the eighteenth century for Ottoman subjects—in particular, *zimmis*—to travel to the West, sometimes on a regular basis and for extended periods of time. By the terms of the Treaty of Passarowitz, signed in 1718, Ottoman Jews were given reciprocal rights to take up residence in Austrian cities, Vienna being the favorite choice. The primary purpose for permitting free travel to holders of Ottoman passports was the promotion of trade and commerce, but there is no reason to suppose that men of science did not equally avail themselves of the same right.[40] The extent to which such exchanges, whether touristic voyages and casual contact or residences of longer duration, affected the development of Ottoman medicine in the eighteenth century is difficult to gauge. There are, however, some telling indications that Jewish doctors maintained their position at the forefront of the profession in the Ottoman Empire.

In the late eighteenth and early nineteenth centuries, the Jews continued their role as physicians of choice for the Ottoman elite. We know most about their employment by officials of the highest rank and the provincial notables *(ayan),* but there is no reason to suppose that they would not have found equal favor among urban elites as well. Osman Pasha Pasvanoğlu (Pazvantoğlu), the rebel governor of Vidin in the late eighteenth century, employed a Jewish doctor from Salonica as his personal physician; and, when he decided to establish a medical center at Shumen (Shumla) he recruited another Jewish doctor from Edirne as its director.[41]

Despite various ups and downs in the political fortunes of the Jewish community in the Ottoman Empire in the 350-year period covered by this survey of Ottoman medicine between 1450 and 1800, the primacy of Jewish physicians within the medical profession remained unchallenged. Medicine, a skill in obvious and universal demand, served as the passport to social acceptance for large numbers of Ottoman Jews. Although the nineteenth century lies outside the scope of the present study, it is interesting to note that whereas the sixteenth century had produced the medical dynasty of the

Hamons and the seventeenth century gave rise to the Hayatizade clan, true to form it was another Jewish family, the de Castros, who emerged in the nineteenth century to play a leading role in the development of medicine.[42] In the medical sciences these Jewish families represented a pattern typical of many professions in the Ottoman Empire where knowledge, experience, etiquette, and practical lore tended to be passed on from father to son and from generation to generation. The Jewish doctors of the Ottoman Empire, however, achieved the unique quality of maintaining a high level of professional distinction over many centuries. In an unbroken chain of transmission starting with the time of their common ancestor Yakub Hekim in the mid-fifteenth century, the traditions of excellence in their craft were consistently maintained until the empire's end.

PART TWO

Modernization and Transformation
Nineteenth and Early Twentieth Centuries

Changing Patterns of Community Structures, with Special Reference to Ottoman Egypt

Jacob M. Landau

The organization of the Jewish community in the Ottoman Empire was not—and indeed could not be—monolithic, considering the dimensions of the empire and the length of Jewish life therein. Nevertheless, despite some variations in detail, until the early nineteenth century community structures followed the same general patterns throughout, and thus Jews traveling from one end of the empire to the other could feel themselves at home in any community they visited. The same institutions existed in most and perhaps all Jewish communities, although the personal impact of individual rabbis and officials lent some of these bodies more power than others.[1] Withal, institutional structures remained virtually identical at least until the beginning of Ottoman modernization and the concurrent increase in foreign influences. These influences affected many facets of daily life, not excluding the self-administration of minority communities, from the early nineteenth century to the disintegration of the Ottoman Empire soon after the First World War.

Of course, foreign impact and the ensuing Westernizing modernization of the empire varied in time, place, scope, and emphasis. In general, such developments were a function of a given area's proximity to European sea routes, the number and character of Western migrants, merchants, missionaries, and other visitors attracted to it, and the nature of the local population's relations with foreigners. Such relations generally involved members of the religious minorities to a much greater extent than the Muslim majority. Foreign influences impacted differently on various domains and seem to have been more evident in daily life, commercial contexts, and intellectual activity than in matters of community organization.[2] As far as the Jews were concerned, these influences varied from one community to another. This article, however, will focus on Egyptian Jewry in the nineteenth and early twentieth centuries as a case study, with some comparative notes on other communities. As these were times of change, the article will deal with both the traditional structures of community organization and some of the new institutions set up in response to changing circumstances.

The Changing Parameters of Autonomy

The crux of the matter involving community administration lies in the limits and nature of the autonomy granted by the Ottoman authorities to the community organization of the Jews—generally similar to that of other recognized religious minorities—and the use made thereof. In principle, self-administration was intended to be confined to the internal affairs of the community and to reciprocal relations among its own members. In practice, because Jewish communities could never be isolated from the neighboring non-Jewish population, a modus vivendi was continuously needed to determine mutual relations more precisely on both the institutional and personal levels. Much depended, of course, on the degree of influence of the central authority in Istanbul; the nature of the local government; the size, affluence, and relative importance of the Jewish community; as well as its relations with the powers-that-be. Within the parameters granted and the local conditions, each Jewish community developed its own institutions, patterned on those of the larger communities, but also subtly different in its own practical application.

The gradual modernization of the Ottoman polity, immigration into the Ottoman Empire of Jews from other lands, and, most importantly, a growing secularism all contributed to a weakening of traditional authority during the nineteenth and early twentieth centuries. Throughout the larger population centers of the Ottoman Empire, Jews moving out of their cramped quarters were a sign not only of demographic growth, but also of increased well-being among certain families. This was the case in Istanbul, Cairo, Alexandria, and elsewhere.³ Leaving what was called in the Arabic-speaking provinces *harat al-yahud* (the Jewish quarter) for other city areas entailed new administrative problems, often expressed in larger centers by the simultaneous activity of several Jewish communities in one and the same urban locality (a phenomenon known since the sixteenth century).

In the final decades of the nineteenth century in particular, younger groups in several Ottoman Jewish communities, as well as some of the immigrants from Europe, followed certain ideologies, such as *Haskalah* (Jewish Enlightenment), Zionism, socialism, and others. All were essentially characterized by a secular outlook and a secular way of life. The effect was increasingly palpable in such centers of immigration as Istanbul, the Balkans, Palestine, and Egypt. In the larger communities, conflict arose between the religious-minded and the secularists, sometimes creating seemingly complementary but, in fact, rival institutions in Istanbul, Cairo, Alexandria, and other centers. This duality could not but undermine the authority of the Jewish community's institutions.⁴

The Jewish traditional way of life was also affected by the rise of nationalism in various parts of the Ottoman Empire. In some areas these movements were explicitly or implicitly self-centered, struggling for the creation of homogeneous societies or, alternatively, for majority-led ones, in which one and all ought to conform to the same laws, government, and ideology. This was all the more relevant to the minority communities, because a relatively large number of their members were protégés of foreign states; at times this was true of entire communities, as we indicate below. Thus, rising nationalism militated against the autonomous administration of minority groups, while most of the nationalist movements were secularly inspired. The end of this process would be felt much later in the successor states of the Ottoman Empire. Secularization would be officially decreed in Turkey during the 1920s, whereas in Egypt this occurred only as late as 1956. While some authority would be left to the religious communities, their powers would be greatly reduced. The roots and dynamics of this process, affecting community organizational structures, may be observed in many parts of the Ottoman Empire during the nineteenth and twentieth centuries. In some ways Egypt, where foreign economic and cultural penetration played an ever-increasing role, culminating in the British occupation of 1882, is a prime example of these processes.

Traditional Community Institutions in Egypt

For the greater part of the nineteenth and early twentieth centuries, most traditional institutions of the Jewish communities in Egypt preserved their earlier characteristics as established under Ottoman domination. Only during the last generation of the empire were there marked changes, partly due to the British occupation of 1882. Formally, Egypt remained an Ottoman province, paying tribute to the sultan, its suzerain; an Ottoman commissioner resided in Egypt, pulling many strings there. However, for most practical purposes, the British held significant decision-making powers and implemented policies resulting therefrom. Several regulations concerning the minorities (such as special dress) were eliminated. Although the British were careful not to alter Ottoman laws and practices single-handedly, they were less than keen on strictly enforcing all those relating to the minorities. Further, as the latter felt more secure under British rule than previously, in such matters as taxation, judicial autonomy, and education, they guarded their religious structures jealously.[5]

The total number of Jews in Egypt increased from about 3,000 to 7,000 in the first half of the nineteenth century, then to 25,200 in 1897, 38,635 in 1907, and 59,581 in 1917 (according to the official censuses, which are also the source for the figures cited below[6]). Throughout the greater part of the nineteenth century, few Jews lived outside Cairo and Alexandria; only in its last third or quarter did more of them move to other localities—a result of both their growing number and Egypt's rapid economic development. Nonetheless, a decisive majority continued to reside in Cairo and Alexandria: respectively, 8,819 and 9,831 in 1897 (or together 74 percent of the total), 20,281 and 14,475 in 1907 (90 percent of the total), and 29,207 and 24,858 in 1917 (91 percent of the total). Some of the smaller localities had only a few families, and data on their organization, if any, are scarce. However, even those that had a community organization (Tanta, Mansura, Port Said, and, later, Suez) looked to the communities in Cairo and Alexandria for leadership and spiritual guidance. Consequently, much of the following discussion focuses on those two Jewish communities, albeit it applies to others in Egypt at that time and indeed to those of many other parts of the Ottoman Empire as well.

It seems that one implicit principle of Jewish community organization in Egypt (and other Ottoman centers) called for maintaining a delicate balance between religious leaders (mainly rabbis), on the one hand, and the local prominently wealthy Jews, on the other hand, for the common good of the entire Jewish community. This was reflected in the main community institutions, intended to provide a maximally self-sufficient administration, obviating the need for non-Jewish intervention in the community's internal affairs.

The Chief Rabbinate

In large urban centers, such as Cairo and Alexandria, the rabbi served not only as the supreme officer of the Jewish community and, ipso facto, as its head, but since the mid-nineteenth century he also enjoyed the status of chief rabbi, or *hahambaşı*. In practice, this meant that his authority extended beyond the city limits: the chief rabbi of Cairo settled many religious matters for the Jewish communities of Mansura, Port Said, Benha, and Miyyet Ghamr; his Alexandrian counterpart did the same for Tanta, Damanhur, and Kafr al-Zayyat. Although administrative and financial affairs were generally outside the chief rabbi's domain, in Cairo and Alexandria chief rabbis, both of whom were appointed from Istanbul, had an important say in directing the material affairs of their respective communities.[7] They thus continued a long-standing practice, frequently imposing their will forcefully, because they could usually rely on the backing of the Ottoman/Egyptian authorities. As these communities comprised Sephardim, Ashkenazim, and sometimes Karaites[8] as well, and were culturally and socioeconomically disparate, a strong hand was often needed to implement effective self-rule. However, these practices became less and less acceptable to the nontraditional elements in the Jewish communities of Cairo and Alexandria. From 1840 on, they tended to rebel against what they considered the excessive authority of the chief rabbis, and indeed against the system by which the *kahal* (or the com-

mittee managing the community, frequently referred to as *va'ad ha-commu-
nità*) was taking putatively authoritarian decisions. These elements did not
attempt to break down the community's structure but rather to reshape it in
a manner that would limit the chief rabbi's authority primarily to spiritual
and religious matters.[9]

The Committees

The changes in both Cairo and Alexandria were largely attained due to pressure for new regulations to reshape community organization (to be discussed
below). This pressure came mainly from wealthy and influential community
notables, who sought to play a central role in local Jewish affairs. In so doing,
they eroded the previous consensual balance of power between the various
spiritual and civic elements. In Cairo the Qattawi family, enjoying the support of the Mosseiris and others, led the Jewish community with little
meaningful opposition. In Alexandria, on the other hand, a coalition of
well-regarded families whose representatives joined together in a committee
(*va'ad*) attempted to lead the community consensually, but inevitably bick-
ered among themselves. Indeed, the conflict between the Aghions and the
de Menasces split the community in two for several years. Quarreling continued in the reunited Alexandria community until the early twentieth century. The committee, with its friends and associates, managed such matters
as tax collection, as well as educational, health, and welfare institutions.[10]

The Statutes of the Alexandria Community

In the nineteenth century, Alexandria was one of the most rapidly modernizing cities in the Ottoman Empire. Its relations with Europe were of long
standing; numerous Jews who arrived there from Europe during the second
half of that century settled in this port of entry. Many came from the far-
flung regions of the Austro-Hungarian Empire, then from the newly established Kingdom of Italy, and still later from eastern Europe. Some, at least,
were accustomed to institutionalized patterns of Jewish community affairs in
their home countries; their influence is perceptible in the statutes of the
Alexandria community, adopted in 1854 and then again in 1872.

The 1854 statutes were apparently drawn up by Albert Cohn, a French Jew involved in public affairs, who was then visiting Egypt.[11] The original version of the statutes, written in Arabic in Rashi script (an indication of the predominance of Arabic in the community at the time), seems to have been lost. A translation into French from this original was published later, however, in an Egyptian Jewish periodical.[12] These statutes, somewhat similar to those published by the Jewish *consistoires* in France, characteristically distinguished between the prerogatives of the community's rabbi and those relating to secular matters. The rabbi was expected to impose religious law on all Jews in matters of marriage and divorce, ritual slaughter, and chairing the court of law, or *beit din*. Here, however, an interesting innovation was introduced: the rabbi was to be elected by a majority vote of the community members. Most other matters were left to the decision of a five-member elected committee, including the committee's president, vice-president, and secretary. This committee was to control income and expenditure—collect taxes; supervise the administration and maintenance of the synagogues, schools, and cemeteries; administer welfare funds; and maintain relations with external factors.

The 1872 statutes were partly a result of serious rifts within the Alexandria community. During the 1860s the community had grown to comprise a fair number of Ashkenazi Jews. The Ashkenazim wished to obtain Austro-Hungarian protection for the entire community, following the example of the Cairo Ashkenazi community, set up in 1865 under Austro-Hungarian protection. The rift, which reflected Austrian-Italian rivalry, was finally bridged by 1871–1872, after Italy had emerged as an independent kingdom, with many protégés among the Jews in Alexandria. Not surprisingly, the 1872 statutes were printed in Italian,[13] the language of those Jews and of commerce in Egypt, although the community came under Austro-Hungarian protection. The 1872 statutes elaborated those of 1854 without basically altering the general conception. The changes included a declaration that all Jews residing continuously in Alexandria belonged to its community. The rabbi's rights and duties remained unchanged, but the committee was enlarged, reflecting the growth in Jewish population. It maintained the same powers it was accorded in 1854, with the additional right to determine relations between the rabbi and the community. Some of its decisions (e.g., sale or lease of the community's property) were subject to the approval of the general assembly of all members in good standing, as determined by tax records. This constitutes another instance of increased emphasis on decision making by majorities, rather than the rabbi and his officials, in all but strictly religious matters (while the rabbi himself was to be elected by a majority).

In practice, however, it seems that the rabbi's powers in the community were not immediately curtailed. Insofar as the religiously-minded members of the community were concerned, his word remained law. Although the rabbi's authority, already circumscribed by the activities of the mostly secular committee, diminished somewhat, his services were still needed in crucial areas of Jewish life, such as the performance of weddings, divorces, circumcisions, burials, and all other activities connected with Jewish religious observance in the synagogue. Although the purse strings were held by the committee, the rabbi and his staff usually succeeded well in carrying out their duties. After all, the supervision and administration of synagogues and cemeteries, in Egypt as elsewhere, were not only a liability but also a source of revenue. The community exacted a price for burial plots, according to the financial status of the deceased and his family.

Other Community Services

In the nineteenth and twentieth centuries, besides handling religious matters (including prayers and funerals as well as tax collection), Jewish communities in Egypt—as elsewhere—continued to deal with health, welfare, education, and judicial matters.

Health care was particularly needed in Egypt, which recorded several epidemics during this period, besides the endemic diseases (ophthalmia, bilharzia, tuberculosis, and intestinal disorders). The Jewish inhabitants of small localities with no hospitals or clinics of their own were often reluctant to use Christian missionary facilities. Instead, they traveled to Alexandria or Cairo, increasing the number of patients there requiring medical attention. A Jewish hospital was founded in Alexandria in 1872 and one in Cairo soon afterward. Both were free of charge for the needy, and so well regarded that non-Jews too sought their services. However, both hospitals were established and supported not so much by the community, but rather through the generosity of affluent Jewish families, such as the Mizrahis and the de Menasces.[14]

Welfare services, even more than health care, were supported by philanthropic contributions, frequently channeled via the community. Welfare services were particularly necessary in Egypt's largest cities, because of the sizable destitute population. On the other hand, the relative affluence of the few regular contributors made these activities possible. In late Ottoman Egypt (and elsewhere in the empire), charitable contributions could also be made through benevolent associations that specialized in a wide range of services, such as providing dowries to marry off indigent girls; constructing and maintaining hostels for poor Jewish visitors; disbursing financial help to beggars; providing food, clothes, and shoes for needy pupils; offering money, milk, and diapers to new mothers; and dispensing milk for the sick and convalescent. Some of these grants were earmarked for immigrants from specific places; thus, in 1913, an association to help Corfiotes was established in Alexandria. Only in the early twentieth century were literary or historical societies founded as well, primarily in Cairo, mostly financed by wealthy members of the community.[15]

Education was a matter of high priority in every Ottoman Jewish community, including that of Egypt. Official censuses indicate that the Jews were proportionately the most literate of the country's native groups. In 1907, 438 per thousand Jews could read and write, compared to 40 per thousand Muslims and 103 per thousand Copts. Only Europeans and some small Christian communities in Egypt surpassed the Jews, with 608 per thousand. The Jewish literacy rate, so much higher than that of Muslims and Copts, was undoubtedly achieved through persistent, continuous efforts at educating the young. Insofar as the communities in Ottoman Eygpt were concerned, this was a strictly primary religious education, dispensed in the heder and in the talmud torah, without any continuation. The effectiveness of the educational system depended to some extent on private financial contributions, either by foreigners, such as Adolphe Crémieux and the Rothschilds of Paris in the 1840s,[16] or by local wealthy Jews. In 1854 the newly formed Jewish community of Alexandria attempted to institutionalize Jewish religious education by setting up two community-supervised talmud torahs, one charging tuition fees and the other free. They were soon united into one, with 40 pupils, increasing to 78 in 1857. A girls' school, inaugurated in 1862, comprised 70 pupils. The Aghion family of Alexandria constructed another talmud torah, with a student body of 86 boys in 1884, 103 in 1897, and 140 in 1901.[17] All these schools catered to modest numbers, as did several others supervised by the Alexandria community and funded by the wealthy, such as the de Menasce family. The case was no different in Cairo, where, for example, four similar schools had a total of 155 pupils in 1872. Many children, however, remained without any Jewish schooling. Some Jewish families sent their children to Christian missionary schools. This prompted the Alliance Israélite Universelle, dedicated to advancing the education of Jews in Muslim countries, to open schools in both Cairo (1895) and Alexandria (1896), and then in Tanta (1905). These schools (separate for boys and girls) were, however, not a part of the Jewish communities' school network and were markedly secular, following the French educational philosophy of the day. Because of their competition, however, the community schools (chiefly those in Alexandria) had to introduce additional subjects into the curriculum, such as foreign languages.[18]

The Courts

The community's religious court, or *beit din,* was a major source of power and authority. According to the millet system in the empire, Muslim courts had the authority to administer justice to all Ottoman subjects, whatever their religion. Nevertheless, the community courts could and did rule on many matters, barring capital crimes and issues pertaining to religious endowments. In both theory and practice, they had far-reaching powers. In the nineteenth century, the Egyptian authorities empowered these courts to have exclusive authority over family matters of Ottoman Jewish subjects only. Following a judicial reform in 1883, however, only marital and inheritance issues remained the prerogative of the minorities' community courts. In the Jewish case, the courts in both Cairo and Alexandria preserved part of their autonomy, including the authority to impose fines, until the First World War; these courts were frequently consulted by smaller Jewish communities in Egypt's provincial towns. The chief rabbis of Cairo and Alexandria acted as judges, or *dayyanim,* in their respective courts, appointing additional *dayyanim* as needed. In the late nineteenth century, an era of decline of traditional Jewish community structures in general, there was also a certain erosion in the standing of these courts. An increasing number of secular-minded individuals turned, in the first instance, to noncommunity courts or, alternatively, appealed to the state courts to overrule the decisions of the rabbinical ones. This process was also known in other major centers of the Ottoman Empire.[19]

◆   ◆   ◆

The functioning of the Jewish community structures in Egypt in the nineteenth and early twentieth centuries depended largely on two factors. Their formal attributes depended on the powers allotted them by the state, and the day-to-day application of their role was affected by the balance between the community's spiritual mentors, the rabbis, and the lay leadership. Throughout the nineteenth century, encroachment by the state and by the secular leaders grew on both levels. In the latter part of the nineteenth century, the lay leaders legislated statutes increasing their own powers, as in Alexandria. A certain duality developed between the old and new structures, as reflected in similar, but not identical, developments elsewhere in the Ottoman Empire. In Egypt old and new structures often coexisted harmoniously, each focusing on its own domains of decision making.[20] But when this harmony fractured, the traditional community structures gradually lost their meaning, prefiguring their subsequent disappearance.

CHAPTER 7

The Changing Relationship between the Jews of the Arab Middle East and the Ottoman State in the Nineteenth Century

Daniel J. Schroeter

The Ottoman reforms of the nineteenth century (*Tanzimat*) created two opposing and essentially incompatible models of the relationship between religious groups and the state. One model, derived from European notions of a civil society, saw individuals, regardless of religion, as citizens of the nation-state—all having equal rights based on secular, universal principles. The opposing model, derived more from the theoretical construct of the Islamic polity than from Western principles, formalized the new relationship between the state and the non–Muslim communities by reifying the separate, group identity through the *millet* (the self-governing non–Muslim religious community recognized by the Ottoman state).

The contradictory principles embodied in the *Tanzimat* reflected the efforts of the Ottoman state to legitimize the continued existence of the empire. The reforms aimed at increasing the power and resources of the state in response to foreign pressures and threats. Central to these reforms was changing the legal status of the non-Muslim minorities, a cause advocated by the foreign powers but also seen as necessary by the Ottoman reformers themselves. The *Tanzimat* conceptually undermined the Islamic polity, replacing it with Western, civil notions that granted all religions theoretical equality. But such concepts had little meaning for most Jews and non-Jews (especially outside the major urban centers of the empire), since they were not accompanied by the kind of social transformation from which such con-

88

cepts had sprung in Europe. This conceptual shift at the center to accommodate external pressures for change was in many ways incompatible with the existing structure of the empire, and even with the internal objectives of reform.

It has been argued that the *Tanzimat* weakened the religious and ethnic communities by removing some of their former privileges and making them more subordinate to the state. This premise assumes that the transition from a traditional, Islamic government to a secular, bureaucratic state entailed also the undermining of the relatively autonomous nature of the religious communities. But greater subordination to the state did not necessarily mean the weakening of the culturally and institutionally embedded communal attachments or the development of a civil society. Furthermore, when the state granted all religions equal rights in the nineteenth century, the corporate religious status of the Jewish community was in some ways reinforced.

There was tremendous regional variation between different Jewish communities in the ways their relationship to the state evolved. Despite the immense differences, there is a tendency to look at the reforms promulgated from the center with surprising inattention to the meaning of these reforms for local communities.[1] This article will focus on several Arab provinces under direct Ottoman rule in the nineteenth century, on which research has been done, especially Syria and Palestine, Iraq, and Libya.

Dhimmi and Millet

The notion of *dhimmi* (*zimmi* in Turkish, literally a "protected person") was formulated in early Islam as a kind of contract between the ruler and the non-Muslim communities. Non-Muslims were guaranteed protection and freedom to practice their religions in exchange for an inferior status that included humiliating disabilities and payment of an annual capitation tax (*jizya* in Arabic, *cizye* in Turkish). This status of the non-Muslim subjects was essentially incorporated by the Ottoman state, as described in Gibb and Bowen's monumental study.[2] But in addition to the Islamic concept of contract between non-Muslims and the state (*dhimma* or *zimmet* in Turkish), in the nineteenth century the Ottomans also superimposed a more formalized and hierarchical structure, commonly known as the *millet*. The basic assumption of Gibb and Bowen is that with the conquest of Constantinople, "the Jews were tacitly recognized as forming another millet."[3] In the opinion of Gibb and Bowen, the Ottomans appointed a chief rabbi (*hahambaşı*) with authority over all Jews in the empire much like the Orthodox Patriarch governed his community.[4] This essential unity had been maintained since the fifteenth century, despite the various internal ethnic and religious divisions among the Jewish communities themselves.

This model has been challenged by more recent studies, which convincingly demonstrate that the *millet* system, anachronistically described by Gibb and Bowen, was a nineteenth-century development linked to the process of institutional reform. The non-Muslim communities themselves invented myths of their own foundation in the empire (e.g., the notion of a patriarchate or *hahambaşı* in the earlier periods) and these myths, previously ignored by the Ottoman state, were accepted to justify their subsequent policy.[5] Prior to the nineteenth century, Jews living in predominantly Muslim parts of the Ottoman Empire were defined essentially by the parameters of Islamic law.[6] The nineteenth-century *millet* system assumed a kind of hierarchical relationship between the Jewish community and the Ottoman state, in contrast to the concept of the Islamic polity, where the state negotiated its relationship (i.e., payment of *cizye*) with individual, regional communities.

The idea that one can actually speak in a generalized and undifferentiated manner about the *millet* system and its transformation in the nineteenth-century Ottoman Empire needs to be reassessed. For instance, distinctions between the Balkans, with a predominately Christian population, and the Middle East need to be made.[7] Kemal H. Karpat has argued that the relationship of the state to non-Muslims, though in theory based on Islamic concepts embodied in the idea of the *dhimmi*, was in practice determined by the relationship of the individual to the state. To support this hypothesis, Karpat has shown how service to the state rather than religion determined the individual's payment of taxes and social ranking; various individuals were tax-exempt because of their service to the state. This, in effect, challenged the very ideological conception of the *millet,* theoretically based on the Islamic polity, which required all non-Muslims to pay *cizye*. However, these examples are drawn from the Balkans, where there was not a Muslim majority. It is doubtful that this would apply to the Middle East, and it certainly is not relevant for discussing the Jewish *millet*.

Karpat also suggests that *dhimmi* status was applied to non-Muslims mainly as a result of nineteenth-century reforms that undermined the *millet* system. In his opinion, as corporate privileges were undermined, the population became divided between majorities and minorities, based on religion.[8] Karpat is attempting to establish the relationship between the Ottoman reforms and emerging nationalism. Although this analysis may in some ways be useful for regions where non-Muslims were a majority, it makes little sense for understanding the Jewish communities. For the Jews, there was no specific sense of territoriality (nor even language, for that matter), and therefore the link between a weakened millet system and emergent nationalism is absent.

Even more importantly, and in contrast to Karpat's analysis, the *millet* "system" itself was a development quite distinct from the notion of the *dhimmi*. In other words, the *millet* system was formulated in the nineteenth century specifically as a result of the reforms, and on a conceptual level came to replace the *dhimmi* system. The *Tanzimat* reforms and the articulation of the Jewish *millet* strengthened the formal corporate status of the Jews in the Ottoman Empire, a development fundamentally different from the aim of developing a civil society.

Tanzimat: Civil Notions, Corporate Structures

The *Tanzimat* reforms, initiated by the *Hatt-ı Şerif* of Gülhane in 1839, came as a response to foreign pressures and the need to strengthen the power of the state at a time when the empire was losing more and more European territory. It is in this edict that the notion of being an Ottoman subject, regardless of religion or language, began, though Ottoman nationality was more explicitly defined in the Nationality Law of 1869.[9] *The Hatt-ı Şerif* of Gülhane expresses the ideology of a civil society, employing the rhetoric of the Declaration of the Rights of Man of the French Revolution. It was inspired by Westernizing reformers who also hoped to win European and especially British approval, because Ottoman territory was being threatened by the ruler of Egypt, Muhammad Ali. Beginning with the edict of 1839 principles were established that would define, at least in theory, the individual's rights and obligations vis-à-vis the state, transcending religious and ethnic affiliation. It has been inferred from this that the autonomy of the *millet* was undermined.[10] Yet this view presumes that the development of a civil ideology by the reformers at the center was translated into an institutional reality throughout the empire. Quite the contrary was often the case, because the *Tanzimat* began a process of defining and formalizing the corporate structure of the *millets*. Paradoxically, this process developed at the same time that the individual was redefined as being a subject of the state, regardless of religious affiliation.

The *Hatt-ı Hümayun* of 1856, a result of the continued pressure of those Western powers that saw themselves as guarantors of the territorial integrity of the empire in the Crimean War with Russia, formally did away with the notion of *dhimma*. The *cizye,* the most important symbol of subordination of non-Muslims to the dominant religion of the state, was banned, though a new tax, the *bedel-i askeri* (military substitution tax), which required non-Muslims to pay the tax in lieu of military service, was implemented and has been seen by many as a kind of continuation of the *cizye*. It was only in the twentieth century, with the Committee of Union and Progress in power, that Jews were conscripted into the Ottoman military, and this policy seems to have been generally applied wherever direct Ottoman rule still existed: Syria, Iraq, Libya, etc.[11]

The Ottoman reforms can be seen as creating a new kind of formalized, hierarchical superstructure for the Jewish community that affected in an uneven way the authority of the traditional leadership in local communities. Too much emphasis, however, has been placed on the theoretical implications of the edicts of the *Tanzimat,* and the formal reform of the Jewish *millet.* A distinction therefore needs to be made not only between *millet* and *dhimma,* but also between the concept of the Jewish *millet,* which can be defined as the formal, bureaucratic relationship of the Jews to the state as it was elaborated in the nineteenth century, and the local, relatively autonomous Jewish *community* that negotiated its relationship to the *millet* superstructure. In other words, millet and community represent different but interrelated concepts.

Already well before the *Hatt-ı Hümayun* of 1856, efforts were under way to reform the Jewish *millet* through the official appointment of a chief rabbi (*hahambaşı*) in 1835. The Jewish community, as a consequence, became part of the general movement of reforms initiated by Sultan Mahmud II. Some scholars have maintained that the Jews of Istanbul themselves sought the appointment of a chief rabbi so that they could attain an influential position in the Ottoman court along with the Greek and Armenian patriarchs,[12] but evidence suggests that the government, recognizing the usefulness of the Jewish community, took the initiative to strengthen it with this appointment.[13] The idea of a chief rabbi established by the state seems to have been drawn from the French system, where rabbis were on the state payroll.

The theoretical position of the *hahambaşı*, as it was elaborated in subsequent years, was as chief representative of the Jews of the empire, serving as the intermediary between the community and the state. He was, in theory, responsible for the civil administration of the community, collecting taxes, and enforcing the law of the state. The *hahambaşı* was also in charge of the various institutions of self-government, and as chief religious leader in the empire, he was considered head of the Jewish court system and the other rabbinical authorities were subordinate to him. Appointments and dismissals of the provincial or city *hahambaşı* were dependent on the approval of the chief rabbi.[14]

It was therefore hoped that the reform of the rabbinate, through the patronage of the Ottoman state, would strengthen the Jewish community's institutions of self-government. At the same time, authority and leadership would be associated with the state. The *hahambaşı* himself was under the supervision of government authority, and he in turn became dependent on imperial orders to specify his areas of competence within the Jewish community. Although such an arrangement—with the Jews of the empire subordinate to a chief rabbinate and a lay and rabbinical council in the capital—bore certain resemblances to the French consistorial system, the reality was quite different; for in France the consistory served as agents of assimilation and secularization of Jewish society, in which the hierarchical authority over the Jewish community was facilitated because membership in civil society eroded the communal institutions of self-government. The aim of creating a hierarchical, secular, and bureaucratized rabbinate in the Ottoman Empire was incompatible with a religious culture that recognized no such hierarchy. The lives of individuals were ordered by a kind of universal *Halakhah,* mediated at a local, community level. The religious leadership itself continued to be either indifferent or openly hostile towards formal efforts at secularization, such as the introduction of secular education through state or foreign schools, or adjudication in the new, modern law courts. Furthermore, the elaboration of the *millet* system during the *Tanzimat* served to reinforce the notion of communal self-government—paradoxically, at the same time that Western secular civil notions, which assumed a reciprocal relationship between the individual and the state, were formulated. In the absence of a more general secularization of society, these contradictions were the source of continued conflict until the end of the Ottoman Empire.

Besides introducing the notion of civil equality, the *Hatt-ı Hümayun* also stipulated that the *millets* should embark on a program of reform. In theory, all *millets* were to be equal. The decree, in fact, led to the expansion of the *millet* system by creating new *millets* for various religious denominations. In these reforms the *millets* were made more subordinate to the central government in a variety of ways; and to a certain degree (especially with regard to Christian *millets*), their authority was restricted more to religious matters. Thus, in some ways ecclesiastical authority was undermined by the *Tanzimat* reforms.

But for the Jewish authorities, whose traditional authority was not derived from any sort of ecclesiastical hierarchy, greater subordination to the central government did not necessarily weaken Jewish corporate identity. For Christian *millets*, civil reforms may have undermined the traditional leadership (since some of their old privileges were removed), without instilling a new political sense of Ottomanism. For the Jews, the strengthening of the Ottoman state at times had the reverse effect—Jewish communities often saw their corporate status strengthened as a result of reforms.

The Jewish community did not immediately implement the reform of their *millet* as stipulated by the *Hatt-ı Hümayun*. The assumption was made that such a reform would emanate from the Jewish community of Istanbul and the rest of the empire's Jewish communities would be subordinated to the Jewish leadership of the capital. The community's inaction was due in part to a dispute between wealthy lay notables and rabbis over the curriculum in a Jewish school. In 1860 the Ottoman grand vezir, Fuad Pasha, intervened, and a commission of lay and rabbinical leaders was convened to establish a constitution for the Jewish community. The Organic Statute for the Ottoman Jewish community was formulated in Istanbul by the lay and religious body in 1864, and the following year it was approved by the sultan.[15] The constitution stipulated that the *hahambaşı*, who would receive a fixed salary, would continue as temporal head of the *millet* (i.e., throughout the empire) and spiritual head of the Istanbul region. The *hahambaşı*'s own position would be limited by a lay council (*meclis-i cismâni*) and a religious council (*meclis-i ruhâni*), which together would form an assembly responsible for electing the chief rabbi. At the same time, individual Jewish communities were to be governed by committees of notables, including rabbis and lay members (reproducing in the provinces the pattern set up for Istanbul). Some eight rabbinical districts in addition to Istanbul were created, each of them requiring a *hahambaşı* to be appointed, and this number increased during the nineteenth century.[16]

The reform at the center proved to be ineffective in the long run, and ultimately the specific stipulations of the constitution fell in abeyance, both in the capital and the provinces. Between 1863 and 1909 there were no formal appointments of *hahambaşı*s in Istanbul, instead, acting chief rabbis filled the position. The idea of communal councils also met with failure; there were long periods in which no such bodies were constituted.[17] Again, the tone of the reform was clearly inspired by Western, especially French, influence among the lay elite with their more extensive connections abroad. Perhaps they hoped that they could succeed, along the lines of the French consistory, to impose a kind of secular authority over Jews throughout the empire.

As for the provinces, the very notion that a single rabbinical authority could have some kind of "civil" jurisdiction over the Jewish *millet* as a whole had little meaning—what that authority would entail was not clear. Among other things, the absence of a clerical hierarchy in Judaism limited the symbolic authority of the chief rabbi. Although the autonomous jurisdiction of the local rabbinical courts was partially undermined by some of the legal reforms (individual Jews could have recourse to secular courts), a self-contained, corporate type of *culture* remained in ways that cannot be defined only in terms of formal laws and structures. The Jews for the most part did not come to identify with some type of Ottomanism, nor did many identify with Jewish nationalism. Adherence to the community in its universal and local sense defined the identity of the majority of Jews. For some, affinity to the community did diminish, but the new identity that developed among the reforming elite was directed less towards Ottomanism, which remained the preserve of a very few, and more towards a European civil culture, quite detached from the reality of the Ottoman order of things.[18]

Istanbul and the Provinces: The *Tanzimat* Applied

The *Tanzimat* affected the Jews unevenly. All the Jews of the empire were theoretically to become part of a hierarchical system similar to the Greek or Armenian *millets*. The reforms introduced a more Western notion of a "rabbinate," which to a degree became secularized. The chief rabbinate of Istanbul, closely connected with the Ottoman bureaucracy, was able to implement the *Tanzimat,* and as a consequence reduced the competence of the Jewish courts. With the development of the secular institutions of the state, such as schools and law courts, and the expansion of foreign schools, especially those of the Alliance Israélite Universelle, the authority of the religious leadership was greatly limited, while the power of the lay notables grew.[19] But even in early twentieth-century Istanbul under the leadership of a very reformist-minded chief rabbi, Haim Nahum, the ability to transform the Jewish community through modern reforms had its limitations.[20]

The effectiveness of the *Tanzimat* outside the capital was much more uneven. The relationship between the chief rabbi in Istanbul and the various *hahambaşıs* throughout the empire was not clearly defined. The reception of the government-appointed *hahambaşıs* was often controversial, and sometimes resisted by local communities. Though some were highly respected religious figures, others were simply unqualified cronies of provincial governors.[21] The degree to which appointments of the provincial *hahambaşıs* were supervised by the chief *hahambaşı* of Istanbul depended on a variety of circumstances. In theory, the *hahambaşı* of Istanbul recommended the appointments and this was stated in the *berat*s (diplomas) investing the provincial *hahambaşıs.* Depending on the relationship of the central government to the periphery, the provincial *hahambaşı* was at times directly appointed and sent from Istanbul without consultation with the local community. Provincial protests against government appointments were therefore often directed to the *hahambaşıs* of Istanbul.[22]

It seems likely, however, that just as too much centralized control made provincial government ineffective, greater control of appointments of the local *hahambaşı* devolved to the provincial level. This was reflected more generally in changes in Ottoman provincial government. In a series of regulations in the 1850s, and with the provincial law of 1864 and its subsequent modifications, much greater administrative authority was given to the provincial governors at the time when the different parts of the empire were administratively reorganized as *vilayets* (districts).[23] The tension between center and periphery, though acted out in a number of ways, was particularly conspicuous in the relationship of the Ottoman state to the Jewish communities of the provinces.

Syria and Palestine

In the early nineteenth century, Jews in Palestine and Syria numbered about 25,000, although the number of Jews in Palestine increased greatly from the 1840s on.[24] The change in status of some Jews in Syria and Palestine predated the *Tanzimat* reforms, and was the result of the growing interest of Europe in trade in this region. Jews, together with Christians in Aleppo and Damascus, were crucial intermediaries between native and European traders. As elsewhere in the Middle East and North Africa, Livornese Jews settled in Syria. These Jews especially were beneficiaries of extraterritorial privileges guaranteed by the Capitulations, because they carried passports from a number of European states.[25] Accordingly, the consulates rather than the Ottoman state had jurisdiction over them. In the nineteenth century a Livornese Jewish family controlled many of the consular positions in Aleppo and consequently extended protection to other Jews.[26] In Palestine as well, growing numbers of Ashkenazi settlers from the late eighteenth century came to acquire the protection of the consulates.[27] The number of Jewish protégés expanded considerably in the 1830s and 1840s when European consulates were opened in Jerusalem because of growing foreign interests.[28] The British especially extended their protection to the growing number of Russian Jews arriving in Palestine in the nineteenth century.[29]

In Palestine and Syria secular institutions of government were established prior to the *Tanzimat* during the Egyptian occupation under Ibrahim's rule. Local councils *(meclis),* including representatives from non-Muslim communities, were set up in all the towns to advise on matters of administration, trade, and finance and to act as civil courts. After the Egyptian withdrawal in 1840, this *meclis* system seemed to form the basis for the new Ottoman councils in which non-Muslims were also represented. The *hahambaşıs*, who were first appointed in Syria and Palestine after the Egyptian withdrawal, served on the provincial councils. In Jerusalem, for example, the head Sephardi rabbi *(ha-rav ha-kolel,* referred to as *rishon le-tziyyon),* Abraham Hayyim Gagin, was formally appointed as *hahambaşı.*[30] The Ottoman councils, however, allowed little representation to non-Muslims. Although the authority of the councils themselves was strengthened, they were largely controlled by prominent members of the *ulema* and wealthy Muslim notables. Efforts in the 1840s to reduce the power of the councils and to enlarge the representation of Christians, Jews, and broader Muslim social classes met with failure because of the entrenched interests of the powerful oligarchy in control.[31]

At the time of the Egyptian withdrawal from Syria and Palestine, Sultan Abdülmecid issued a *ferman* (edict) denouncing the blood libel that developed into the so-called Damascus Affair. The *ferman* guaranteed the protection of the Jewish community, as stipulated in the *Hatt-ı Şerif* of Gülhane. Further elaboration on the protection of Jews and the right of Jewish participation in the Ottoman council came in the following year.[32]

The reaction of the Muslim population at large to the progressive dismantling of the Islamic definition of the *dhimmi,* especially through the *Hatt-ı Şerif* of Gülhane and the *Hatt-ı Hümayun,* was hostile. The relationship of the state to non-Muslims was seen as a reflection of the superiority of Islam; with the growing external menace, the granting of equality to non-Muslims was viewed as underlying the weakness from within. In some respects, therefore, aspects of the former inferior status were reinforced, despite the rhetoric of equality (though in the case of Syria, the position of

Jews was somewhat better than that of the Christians, who took a greater share of the growing hostility). For example, restrictions on the ownership of land and slaves were imposed;[33] and as elsewhere in the empire, the abolition of the *cizye* did not spell the end to discriminatory taxation. Non-Muslims paid the *bedel* tax—the Jews for the most part preferred the tax to military service, but many Christians protested.[34]

The formalization of a rabbinate through government appointment of *hahambaşıs* was intended to bring the Jewish community under greater central control. The *hahambaşıs* were closely tied to the governors; consequently, appointments were often politically motivated and led to clashes with the traditional leadership of the Jewish community. Conflicts over appointments of *hahambaşıs* were reported, for example, in Aleppo and Saida.[35] *Hahambaşıs*, as well as members of the rabbinic courts, were ordinarily selected locally by committees of lay and religious leaders, though the state would sometimes intervene to resolve controversies over the appointments.[36] It seems that at times direct appointments of *hahambaşıs* were made through the supervision of the chief rabbi in Istanbul, but this could cause discontent in the local community. In the 1840s an attempt was made to appoint a chief rabbi for Jerusalem direct from Istanbul, which would have left the already-serving head rabbi *(ha-rav ha-kolel)* with only spiritual authority. It seems, however, that opposition on the part of the Jews of Jerusalem forced the state to abandon the idea.[37] In 1909, when a controversy erupted over the conduct of the *hahambaşı* of Beirut, a sector of the Jewish community petitioned the chief rabbi of Istanbul for his removal from office.[38] It should be pointed out, however, that from 1840 until the end of the Ottoman Empire, only three out of the thirteen head Sephardi rabbis of Jerusalem received official *fermans* investing them as *hahambaşıs*.[39]

The *hahambaşıs'* authority was much more limited than has often been suggested. Although it was commonly believed that the appointment of the chief Sephardi rabbi of Jerusalem by the Ottomans gave him authority throughout Palestine, he did not have formal powers outside the district of Jerusalem, and certainly not in the towns of the Galilee that were under the authority of the *vilâyet* of Damascus. His authority at times was more extensive, but this had more to do with his status and prestige as a spiritual leader and his abilities at halakhic discourse.[40]

In Syria and Palestine, the Jews for the most part constituted a self-governing community until the end of the Ottoman era. The appointment of *hahambaşı*s may have politicized rabbinical authority, leading to disputes over local versus centralized authority, but it also gave greater legitimacy to the self-governing community. Jews, with the exception of the Zionist settlers in Palestine, continued to adhere to Halakhah as their primary, unifying source of authority. It was rabbinical authority, and not so much the formal sanction of the *hahambaşı,* that continued to have considerable influence over the communities. The rabbinical courts still had wide-ranging jurisdiction in the community until the end of the Ottoman era.[41] In early twentieth-century Aleppo, for example, the rabbis were still exercising their control by pronouncing bans over desecrators of the Sabbath.[42]

Palestine presents a more of an anomalous situation, because its Jewish population was so fragmented, often separated into contentious and opposing communities. The Ashkenazim were divided into numerous *kolels*, corporate groups associated to countries of origins, and the Sephardi Jews as well were divided into a number of ethnic components. Furthermore, the so-called New Yishuv (settlement) of Zionist settlers was growing. The majority of Jews in Palestine were either protégés or subjects of foreign powers, since there were so many Zionist and non-Zionist settlers from foreign countries. As Jewish settlement increased, the authority of the Ottoman Jewish establishment was weakened. The *hahambaşı,* though formally invested with extensive powers by the Ottomans, in reality represented only a minority of the Jews of Palestine. The various Jewish communities, therefore, independently negotiated their relationship with the Ottoman authorities.[43] By the end of the Ottoman period, as the strength of the Zionists increased, a kind of civil society began to emerge in Palestine, but this was the result of foreign implantation rather than an organic development from within.

Iraq

Iraq contained the largest Jewish community in the East (about 65,000 in 1880),[44] with the community of Baghdad growing rapidly in the nineteenth century. The reforms of the *Tanzimat* were unevenly applied in Iraq in the first half of the century, when direct Ottoman rule proved to be impossible. Greater centralized control was restored in 1869, when Midhat Pasha, the leading advocate of Ottoman reform, was appointed governor. It was during his tenure as governor (1869–1872) that the civil principles of the *Tanzimat* were introduced in Iraq and the position of the Jewish community began to change. Jews used their newly acquired civil status to protect their rights against violations by the Muslim population.[45]

With the provincial reforms of 1864, implemented in Baghdad during the administration of Midhat Pasha, Jews began to participate in political life by serving as representatives in the administrative councils of the *vilayets*. The Ottoman Constitution inaugurated in 1876 provided for the representation of Jews and other *millets* in the Parliament.[46] A Jewish representative from Iraq served in the short-lived parliament of 1877–78 (there were also Jewish representatives from Istanbul, Salonica, and Bosnia-Herzegovina).[47] This rather tentative political activity was not very consequential and certainly did not indicate a rising civil consciousness among the majority of Iraqi Jewry. Here it should be emphasized again that despite the proclamation of equality for all, Muslims and non-Muslims, the *millet* system that divided the empire into different groups remained.[48]

For the Jewish community, the appointment of *hahambaşis* was an important dimension of the reforms. In 1849, a *hahambaşı* was appointed for Baghdad. Formerly, the chief authority in the Iraqi communities was a lay leader called a *nasi*, whose position was ensured by his financial links to the Muslim governor. Not only Baghdad but also other communities appointed *nasis* as the chief intermediaries between the community and the government. The *nasi* collected taxes from the Jewish community and was partly responsible for making appointments to religious posts in the community. With the appointment of the *hahambaşı*, who assumed the religious as well as lay leadership of the community, the authority of the *nasi* seems to have ceased. The aim of the Ottoman authorities was presumably to weaken the regional authority of the lay leadership in an effort to centralize state authority. The effect was the greater formalization of the religious leadership, as an increasingly influential body of religious sages entered into the political arena.[49]

The appointment of *hahambaşis* became a source of increasing tension and controversy in Baghdad. At the time of the first appointment, the community became divided between supporters of two rival sages.[50] It seems that at this stage appointments were being made not solely on the basis of power and status within the community. They were now influenced by a relatively large group of religious and lay notables (although the joint rabbinical and lay assembly that was to select the hahambaşı according to the statute of 1865 was considerably smaller than intended).[51] Sometimes the appointed hahambaşı was foreign to the community and lacked social status. His close relationship to the Ottoman authorities and his responsibility to collect taxes, especially the bedel-i askeri, often led to accusations of corruption and high-handedness. Consequently, and perhaps in part as a result of the greater implementation of the Tanzimat beginning with the period under Midhat Pasha, appointments were often contested and there was much turnover. In 1879, members of the community, together with the two leading sages, signed a petition to the governor of Baghdad to remove from office the hahambaşı, Sason b. Elijah Smooha. Although he was removed, Smooha was able to obtain the intervention of the hahambaşı of Istanbul, and the provincial council in Baghdad reinstated him in office. Further protests on the part of the community finally led to his replacement by the authorities in Istanbul. However, the strife continued regarding his successor.[52] In 1884, a petition was signed by some four hundred community members in protest of an appointment.[53]

As Shlomo Deshen has argued, the reforms strengthened the position of the religious authorities vis-à-vis the lay notables because the leading authority in community affairs was now a rabbi. The community was governed by a committee for secular and another for religious affairs, but the head of the joint committee was the hahambaşı. The authority of the hahambaşı was increasingly contested not by the lay leadership whose power had been undermined by the disappearance of the nasi, but rather by the noted rabbis from the wealthy families of Baghdad, who often enjoyed a higher status within the community than the hahambaşı.[54] The hahambaşı, who supported himself through a tax on kosher meat and income from endowments and, as mentioned earlier, was also responsible for collecting the bedel-i askeri tax, was essentially regarded as representing the government. His responsibilities often led to clashes with the local rabbinical authorities and junior rabbis, whose former tax-exempt status was now threatened. These conflicts also reflected the newly invigorated position of the religious authorities in the community. By strengthening the religious leadership, the corporate status of the Jewish community was reinforced. Despite the ostensible equality granted to all individuals in the Ottoman state, the community became further consolidated. In the case of Baghdad, whose population was growing rapidly in the nineteenth century, a variety of new community institutions developed, such as talmudic academies and benevolent funds. The community itself continued to collect taxes internally and to raise funds to support its institutions. The introduction of civil notions in Iraq did not, therefore, undermine the communal identity of Iraqi Jewry.

Libya

Since 1711 effective control of Libya (to the degree that the state was able to extend its authority into the hinterland) was in the hands of the local Qaramanli dynasty, who were members of the military elite (the *qulughliya,* offspring of Janissaries and local women). In 1835 a rebellion against the Qaramanli ruler broke out. The Ottomans, fearing intervention by either Muhammad Ali of Egypt, the Husaynids of Tunisia, or the French or British, sent a force to occupy the country, and the period of direct Ottoman rule began.[55]

Little is known about the position of the Jews during most of the Qaramanli period. It is clear that Jews were intricately involved in urban life in Tripoli, and there were also scattered communities in the smaller towns and villages of the hinterland in Tripolitania. The status of Jews was defined by the Islamic concept of *dhimma,* but its application varied from place to place. After the Ottoman reoccupation, the position of Jews was legally transformed by the same edicts affecting the rest of the Ottoman Empire. The disabilities specifically related to *dhimmis* were theoretically abolished, but what this change in legal status meant outside of Tripoli, especially in the provinces where Ottoman rule was often challenged by rural rebellion, is much more difficult to measure.[56] Evidence suggests that in parts of the hinterland the *Tanzimat* reforms had little if any immediate effect on Jewish life. There are still references to Jews paying the poll tax, and indications of opposition to granting Jews the right to build new synagogues, as in the case of the Jews in the mountains of Gharyan.[57]

In the tribal areas of the interior, such as in the Western Mountains (Jabal Nafusa), Jews were vital intermediaries and under normal circumstances lived tranquilly. During periods of unrest, however, especially in the 1840s and 1850s, Jews suffered oppression. Jews were also caught sometimes between the Turks, who were trying to consolidate their control in the countryside, and the rebels who resisted the Turkish penetration. Such was the case, as one tradition relates, of the Jews of Yefren (Yafrin), who in 1840 were accused by the Turks of manufacturing weapons and serving as traders for the tribal leader and rebel Ghuma al-Mahmudi (though the intervention of well-placed Jews prevented the Turks from taking action). A decade later, Ghuma returned from exile and, as the tradition goes, extended his protection to the Jews, allowing them to wear red hats instead of their normal black ones. Again Jews became closely aligned with him, manufacturing arms for the tribal leader. The tradition recounts, however, that the Jews continued secretly to send their taxes to the Turkish governor in Tripoli. Again, after the Turks reasserted control over the area, the Jewish communities were plundered and it was only due to the intervention of some prominent Jews in Tripoli that a local Jewish leader was saved from being shot.[58]

With the appointment of Ali Pasha as governor in 1862, the Ottomans managed to consolidate their control of the countryside, and Jews in the provinces began to enjoy greater security.[59] In 1867, when a synagogue in Zliten (Zlitin) was burned down, the Ottoman authorities arrested local leaders and sponsored its rebuilding.[60] What this incident suggests is that provincial government in Libya was beginning to adhere to the *Tanzimat* reforms and, more importantly, that law and order were beginning to take hold in the towns and countryside. Furthermore, Jews who served important functions as traders and intermediaries for both Europeans and Turks began to benefit from Ottoman development initiatives. Thus, for example, the government allocated property to Jews who came to establish a market in the coastal town of Misrata.[61] In Tripoli itself, the position of Jews seemed favorable. New synagogues were built by the Turks, and although Jews were concentrated in a Jewish quarter *(hara)*, they were free to reside elsewhere in the city.[62]

In addition, efforts were made to incorporate Jews into the new administrative and legal system stemming from the *Tanzimat*. The reforms led to the establishment of a provincial council whose role was to advise the government on a variety of political and legal matters.[63] In 1847 the head of the Jewish community was appointed to serve on the Ottoman court in Tripoli, and by 1867 there were two Jewish representatives in this body.[64] Jews also served in the local branches of the administrative council, such as in Benghazi and Yefren.[65] After the establishment of the first municipality in Tripoli in 1870,[66] Jews began to serve on the municipal council. Furthermore, in Tripoli, Jews were appointed to the new secular courts: the civil and criminal court, the appeals court, and the commercial tribunal established in 1863. Jews, on the whole, continued to litigate primarily in the rabbinical court (*beit din*) of their community, though it can be surmised that for some matters state courts replaced certain functions of the rabbinical courts (e.g., civil and commercial matters).[67]

The increasing institutionalization of the *millet* system in the latter half of the nineteenth century led to changes in the relationship between the Jewish community and the Ottoman government. Traditionally, the chief Jewish intermediary between the government and the community, the *qa'id,* exercised considerable control over the community because of his link with authority. The *qa'id* was generally a lay leader from the influential urban elite of Tripoli. He had power to imprison those Jews who refused to adhere to the decisions of the *beit din,* or who refused to pay the *cizye.*[68] The reimposition of direct Ottoman rule led to a limitation on the authority of the *qa'id.* This was probably a reflection of the fact that the Ottoman authorities generally preferred to confer leadership positions on religious figures instead of lay notables.[69] The prominent rabbis in Libya had little formal relationship with the state, but in 1874 a *hahambaşı* was appointed to Tripolitania from Istanbul. He also was a member of the urban council that advised the pasha in Tripoli. As a consequence, the role of the *qa'id* diminished, and the *hahambaşı* became the principal intermediary between the Jewish community and the government.[70]

From the 1870s on, growing foreign—and especially Italian—influence in Libyan affairs began to affect the relationship between the Jews and the authorities. Many of the wealthier Jews became either Italian nationals or protégés. The governor Ahmed Rasım Pasha (1882–1896) made efforts to curtail the growing number of natives acquiring foreign nationalities.[71] Not only did this cause tensions with the Ottoman authorities, but it also led to divisions within the Jewish community, between those with Italian or Western leanings and the more traditional Jews.[72] A reflection of these tensions within the community and with the authorities was the departure of Hizkiyyah Shabbetai, the last *hahambaşı* to serve in Tripoli, without a replacement being sent.[73]

The transformation of Libyan society engendered by Ottoman reforms and European penetration gradually had an effect on the relationship between Jews and the native Muslim population. Foreign observers reported a growing Muslim hostility towards the Jews, in part because of the general unrest of the period, but also because Jews were often identified with European political aims. The increased hostility towards the Jews reflected a wider Islamic reaction to European imperialism. The narrowing legal distinction between Jews and Muslims was seen as a symbol of the growing weakness of the Islamic polity.[74] In principle, the central Ottoman authorities in Tripoli arbitrated incidents that occurred between Muslims and Jews, admitting Jewish testimony in Muslim courts and taking action against the perpetrators of crimes. But increasingly, Jewish leaders complained that the Libyan governors and local officials did little to ensure justice for Jews.[75]

◆   ◆   ◆

With the revolution of the Young Turks, tensions increased between the local populations and the Jewish communities throughout the Arab Middle East. Growing foreign intervention, of which Jews were often the beneficiaries, was certainly one cause. It might be argued, as well, that the efforts to superimpose a civil society from above disrupted the traditional patterns of relationships at the local level, without leading to the development of a common civil consciousness in the society as a whole.

The enthusiastic support for the reforms of the Committee of Union and Progress by significant numbers of Jews in the Ottoman Empire, and the participation of Jews in parliament during this period,[76] might be seen as a significant step in the direction of the development of a civil consciousness on the one hand, and a diminishing corporate identity on the other. Quite the opposite occurred. Many Jews had seen their own corporate status strengthened as a result of the reforms, though their position as a whole had often deteriorated under Abdülhamid II. In the Arab provinces, relatively few Jews identified with the nascent nationalist movements, but rather saw a brighter future in the consolidation of Ottoman power that the Young Turks promised to achieve. The support, or suspected support, of the Jews for the Young Turks aroused the hostility of the Arab population.[77]

Although the Jewish communities were profoundly affected by the process of modernization—the result of both foreign influences and internal reforms—Jewish identity continued to center on the local community. To the degree that Jews participated in public Ottoman life, their participation was directly linked to the centralized state. No kind of autonomous, non-state, civil culture developed to which Jews could adhere.[78] The result was a pattern of modernization significantly different from that of Western Jewry. It allowed the Jews of the Arab world to accommodate themselves to modernity without the massive severing of community bonds and the erosion of attachments to the religious culture of Judaism.

CHAPTER 8

Changing Relations between Jews, Muslims, and Christians during the Nineteenth Century, with Special Reference to Ottoman Syria and Palestine

Moshe Ma'oz

The Pre-Reform Era

The Jewish population in the Ottoman Empire numbered, by the early nineteenth century, only about 150,000, out of a total population of some 35 million. Some 70,000 resided in the various Balkan provinces and the rest in Turkey, Iraq, and Egypt, as well as in Syria and Palestine, where they totaled about 25,000.[1] Most of the Ottoman Jews were Sephardim—descendants of Iberian Jewry expelled in 1492 and later—who had found refuge in various Ottoman provinces and had become Ottoman subjects. Other Ottoman Jewish subjects were descendants of ancient Jewish inhabitants in Iraq, Yemen, and Syria who, over the centuries, had become "Arabized" in their language and habits. In contrast, small communities of Ashkenazim—Jews of Central and East European origin who had gradually settled since the sixteenth century mainly in Palestine (and subsequently also in Egypt and elsewhere)—mostly continued to adhere to their former nationality.

Most Ottoman Jews lived in cities and towns (although Jews in Kurdistan and Yemen were partly rural), and a noticeable number of them held senior positions in commerce and finance as merchants, bankers, and treasury officials. Jews periodically also served as physicians, interpreters and advisers in the courts of sultans and provincial governors (*valis*).[2] For example, in the late eighteenth and early nineteenth centuries, members of the Farhi family were heavily involved in the financial administration of the *eyalet* (province) of Damascus. They managed accounts, engaged in banking and money lending, and even partly financed the annual *hajj* (pilgrimage) caravans to Mecca.[3]

In addition to good economic conditions (and personal achievements), for centuries Jews enjoyed a considerable degree of communal autonomy (during the nineteenth century this was formalized as part of the reforms in the *millet* system) in matters of religious worship, jurisdiction in issues relating to personal status, the levying of certain taxes, and managing educational and welfare institutions. Jewish rabbis exercised authority in administering their communities and enjoyed official status in the Ottoman state.

In contrast, however, like the Ottoman Christians, the Jews were also officially inferior subjects in the state, which had been founded on—and practiced—the principles of Muslim superiority. They had to pay the *jizya* (poll tax) as a symbol of their inferiority and for their protection (*dhimma*) by the state. They were by and large discriminated against in the Muslim religious courts (*mahkama*), were not admitted to senior government positions (as opposed to administrative ones), and were not allowed to carry arms or to serve in the military. Periodically Jews, as well as Christians, were forbidden to build or repair places of worship, to wear dress in colors reserved for Muslims (green), or to ride horses in towns. They were also occasionally subjected to oppression, extortion, and violence by both the local authorities and segments of the Muslim population.[4]

These precarious—and indeed uncertain—conditions of Ottoman Jews and Christians can be illustrated, for example, by the testimony of Burckhardt, the perceptive Swiss traveler, who noted in 1811: "There is scarcely an instance in the modern history of Syria of a Christian or Jew having long enjoyed the power or riches which he may have acquired. These persons are always taken off in the last moment of their greatest apparent glory."[5]

One such instance was the case of Hayyim Farhi, the Jewish treasury manager and senior administrator in the *eyalet* or *pashalik* of Sidon (with its headquarters in Acre) during the late eighteenth and early nineteenth centuries. Initially, like his family members in Damascus, Hayyim Farhi had been able to amass a great deal of power and influence, to the extent that a contemporary Christian historian wrote, with apparent bias: "Hayim the

Jew has been holding all reins of government and has been doing whatever he wishes. It is said that a Jewish person dominates the Muslims and Christians, the great and the small, the near and the far, without any restrictions."[6]

Yet, under the rule of Abdallah Pasha in Acre (1819–1831), Farhi was executed in 1820 and his property confiscated.[7] It is true that Muslims in various Ottoman provinces were also periodically oppressed and squeezed, occasionally also killed by tyrannical rulers and greedy soldiers. For, as it happened, according to Gibb and Bowen, during the pre-reform era the "Ottoman regime was essentially a system of exploitation, injurious to the social and eocnomic welfare of the subjects. . . . It . . . lacked any guarantees for life and property against the violence, cupidity and caprice of the soldiery."[8] Nevertheless, many Muslims were able to protect themselves against their oppressors either through influential Muslim religious notables or by placing themselves under the protection of powerful local leaders and military groups. From time to time Muslim masses would also rebel against their oppressive rulers and expel or even kill them.[9] Jews and Christians would not dare—and did not possess the arms—to oppose their Muslim oppressors; in order to acquire security they had to regularly pay "protection" money to powerful local Muslim leaders or enlist the help of European consuls.

Nevertheless, during long periods of time Jews had been less molested than Christians by their Muslim neighbors and particularly by the Ottoman authorities; indeed, by and large Muslims preferred Jews to Christians (while the two minority communities had been engaged in fierce economic competition and religious hostility) and not only because they were economically productive and did not compete with Muslims. As a tiny community, loyal to the Ottoman Empire and free from any attachments to Europe, Jews could be better trusted than the more numerous Christians, who were suspected by many Muslims of harboring treasonable sympathies toward European Christendom—the major enemy of the Ottomans.[10]

Muslim-Jewish-Christian Relations during the Reform Period

This pattern of intercommunal relations further developed and crystallized during the nineteenth century, notably under the impact of the Ottoman reforms, which *inter alia* officially granted Christian and Jewish subjects equality with their Muslim fellow countrymen. The Ottoman reforms, which had been influenced largely by the West and aimed at strengthening the Ottoman Empire and the fabric of its society, were first introduced on a large scale by Sultan Mahmud II (1808–1839). Although his measures were directed primarily toward building a new army and asserting his control over the provinces, Mahmud also declared that all his subjects, regardless of their religion, should be equal.[11] But whereas Mahmud II did not issue any official decrees to that effect, his son and successor, Sultan Abdul Mejid (1839–1861) promulgated two sets of royal *fermans*, in 1839 and in 1856, which granted equality to all Ottoman subjects regardless of their religion. The 1856 *ferman* in principle provided full equality to the non-Muslim communities in the judicial system, taxation, and military service. The equal status of all Ottoman subjects regardless of their religion was reconfirmed in the first Ottoman constitution (1876), which was subsequently suspended (1877) by Sultan Abdul Hamid but reinstated in 1908 under the pressure of the Young Turks.[12]

Yet, this series of decrees and declarations notwithstanding, equality between Christians, Jews, and Muslims was in fact only partially implemented during the nineteenth century. And, as it happened, the new reforms largely aggravated intercommunal relations between Muslims and Christians, as well as between Christians and Jews, particularly in the Syrian provinces. Indeed, during the Ottoman *Tanzimat* period, Muslim traditional attitudes of contempt and suspicion toward Christians turned into deep hatred and were periodically manifested by great violence, notably in the 1860 Damascus massacre.[13] Similarly, Christian-Jewish economic competition and religious hostility also sharpened, and Christians periodically accused Jews of committing ritual murder around the Jewish feast of Passover. Such accusations, particularly the 1840 Damascus Blood Libel, provoked anti-Jewish feelings and violence, and led Jews to take vengeance against Christians, especially in times of Muslim-Christian hostilities. Muslims, while continuing to look down on Jews, sided with them, by and large, in their rivalries with Christians. In other words, in the prolonged Christian-Jewish competition for Muslim backing, Jews gained an upper hand in large parts of the Ottoman Empire, excluding Egypt, throughout the nineteenth century, with the exception of two phases in the modern history of Ottoman Syria: the era of

Egyptian rule (1831–1840) and during the emergence of Arab nationalism at the end of the nineteenth century and the beginning of the twentieth century.[14]

Muslim–Christian Antagonism

It would appear that the deepest and most persistent motive for Muslim animosity and violence toward Christians in various parts of the Ottoman Empire was the suspicion and fear that local Christians were sympathetic to, or supportive of, the hostile European powers, and were likely to help them to "overset" the Muslim state.[15]

Already in 1799, when Napoleon's French troops invaded Palestine from Egypt, Muslims in Damascus rioted against their Christian neighbors.[16] In 1821, when the Greek revolt broke out, apparently with Russian inspiration, Christians were again attacked by Muslims in various parts of Syria[17] (while the Greek patriarch in Istanbul was executed by order of Mahmud II). During the second half of the nineteenth century, anti-Christian outbursts by Syrian Muslims occurred more frequently in reaction to events such as the Russian-Ottoman military conflicts of the Crimean War (1853–55) and the 1876–77 war. During the latter war, for example, Syrian Muslims alleged that their Christian neighbors "caused the war," while other Muslims "insisted on having from the mufti a *fetva* [religious opinion] declaring it lawful to kill Christians."[18]

It should be pointed out that Syrian Muslims, while attacking their Christian fellow countrymen, made no distinctions between those protected by Russia and those supported by other European powers. Syrian Muslims did not trust France and Britain either, in spite of the fact that these powers had been traditional allies of the Ottoman Empire. Indeed, in the eyes of Muslims, the Western powers also adversely affected the integrity and character of the Muslim state by military action and conquest and through diplomatic pressure and intervention in favor of the local Christian communities. For example, British and French warships occasionally patrolled the Syrian coast at the time of anti-Christian activities; and during the 1860 Druze-Maronite civil war, French troops landed in Lebanon in order to help their Maronite allies, thus triggering anti-Christian acts by

Muslims in neighboring areas.[19] Similarly, hostile feelings and actions against Syrian Christians were manifested by Muslims after the British occupied Egypt in 1882.[20]

Other crucial causes for Muslim hostility and aggression toward Christians were related to the new policies of the Ottoman government and to new modes of behavior on the part of many Christians. Indeed, the *Tanzimat* reforms, which were introduced in part to satisfy the expectations and demands of Britain and France and which granted non-Muslims greater equality, evoked among many Muslims feelings of frustration and despair as well as anger and hostility toward the Ottoman government, the European powers, and especially the Christian population. In many parts of the Ottoman Empire such feelings were expressed particularly strongly following the formal abolition of the *jizya* in 1855 and the proclamation of the 1856 *İslahat Fermanı*. A typical reaction of many Ottoman Muslims was described by the Ottoman historian Ahmed Cevdet: "Today we have lost our sacred national rights which our ancestors gained with their blood; while the nation used to be the ruling nation it is now bereft of this sacred right. This is a day of tears and mourning for the Muslim brethren." [21]

In the Syrian provinces similar feelings had been expressed by Muslims already during the 1830s under the Egyptian occupation, which had imposed full equality between non-Muslims and Muslims. A consular report clearly stated: "The Mussulmans . . . deeply deplored the loss of that sort of superiority which they all and individually exercised over and against the other sects." [22] Muslims were likewise reported to have said to each other: "O my brother, the state [or government] has become a state of Christians, the Islamic state has ended (*ya akhi, al-dawla sarat dawlat nasara, khalasat dawlat al-Islam*)." [23]

These severe religio-political grievances of Muslims against Christians were also enforced by crucial socioeconomic factors, namely, the growing economic prosperity of Christians, on the one hand, and the impoverishment of the Muslim middle and lower classes, on the other. Thus, for example, the expansion of Syrian foreign trade—notably, imports from Europe following the Egyptian occupation—contributed to the enrichment of local Christian merchants who acted as agents and brokers for European firms. In contrast, the great influx of European goods, which were sold cheaply, undermined the livelihood of many Muslim craftsmen, artisans, and traders— the backbone of the Muslim urban middle class.[24] Consequently, not a few Muslims were concerned lest the Christians "should take advantage of the power which their financial resources give them to encompass the destruction of the Moslem either by corrupting or impoverishing him."[25] And if all these economic and political factors were not sufficient to kindle "fires of fanatical hatred" among Muslims, the more assertive behavior of Christians, at least as perceived by Muslims, was regarded as highly provocative and led to further anti-Christian riots. A consular report from Damascus in 1860 states: "The splendid houses built by the rich classes of Christians excited jealousy and their general prosperity tended to create in the Mussulmans feelings of envy."[26] And an earlier report from Beirut similarly relates: "The Greek Catholic Patriarch Maximus is accused of having excited the ill will of the Mussulmans by a sort of triumphant entry which he made not long ago into Aleppo with much pomp and great display of costly church ornaments."[27]

No wonder, then, that such behavior contributed to the eruption of anti-Christian riots in Aleppo in 1850 and in Damascus in 1860, constituting the high-water mark in Muslim-Christian hostility in the Syrian provinces.

Muslim-Jewish Relations

Significantly, Jews in the Syrian provinces were not hurt at all during those anti-Christian riots, even though they were also officially granted equality with Muslims, and several Jewish families—notably in Damascus and Aleppo—enjoyed economic prosperity and had established contacts with European countries. It is true that Jews in Syria, as well as in other Ottoman provinces, continued to be treated by Muslims with traditional contempt and from time to time were subject to intimidation, blackmail, and general maltreatment. On some rare occasions Jews were even murdered by Muslims who were motivated by economic envy and/or religious fanaticism. But by and large there was no intense hostility between Muslims and Jews as there was between Muslims and Christians, mainly because Jews did not pose a security threat to the Muslim state and they continued to behave as a submissive religious community, devoid of any political ambitions. This behavior of Ottoman Jews vis-à-vis both the authorities and the Muslim masses was described by a contemporary author as follows:

> This tranquility under Ottoman rule so opposite to the agitations and con-
> vulsions of other raias [non-Muslims] . . . is explained partly by the peace-
> able habits and disposition of the Jews, which cause no umbrage to the
> Porte. . . . Patient, industrious, and resigned to their fate, they wear with-
> out apparent sense of humiliation the coloured benish (Jehoudane) [cloak]
> which the ancient sumptuary laws of the empire enjoined as a mark to dis-
> tinguish them from the Mussulman.[28]

Syrian Jews, unlike their Christian fellow countrymen, also refrained from publicly displaying those new liberties that could offend Muslim sensibilities, such as opening wine shops in the markets, wearing green clothes, or conducting religious worship in public view. Jews behaved in accordance with the advice that a Syrian Christian intellectual gave in vain to his own brethren:"It is necessary for them [the Christians] to know that the grandees of the land, . . its government and ministers, and the army, and all its senior people are Muslims. . . . They ought to show the utmost respect to the Muslims and complete obedience to the ruler."[29] Furthermore, unlike many Christians, Jews demonstrated their loyalty and gratitude to the Ottoman state, particularly during hard times for the Ottomans. For example, Jews supported and contributed to the Ottoman war effort during the Crimean War and the First World War, and in 1892 they celebrated with gratitude the fourth centennial of the settlement in the Ottoman Empire of the Jewish exiles from Spain.[30]

In addition, Jews would occasionally go out of their way to assist Muslims in their violent attacks on Christians. Such events occurred, for example, in 1821, when a Jewish mob mutilated the corpse of the Greek patriarch who had been executed by the Ottoman authorities for his alleged link to the Greek revolt, and in 1822, when Jews from Salonica volunteered for the Ottoman army in order to put down the Greek rebellion.[31] Similarly, in the Syrian provinces Jews joined Muslims in assaulting Christians upon the return of Ottoman rule in 1840,[32] as well as during the Crimean War; and in the 1860 anti-Christian massacre, Jews in Damascus allegedly "put at the gates of their houses sugared ice water to give the rioters to drink."[33]

Jewish–Christian Antagonism

Anti-Christian actions by Syrian Jews were not only intended to demonstrate Jewish allegiance to the Ottoman state or to win the good will of local Muslims. These deeds also occurred in reaction to Christians' hostility and their attempts to demonize Jews, especially by means of "blood libels," which had emerged as a new weapon in the Christian-Jewish rivalry during the nineteenth century.

Indeed, as was already mentioned, there had been intense economic rivalry, colored by religious antagonism, for generations between Christians and Jews for positions in commerce and in government service in the Syrian provinces, as elsewhere in the Ottoman Empire. Prior to the nineteenth century, Jewish and Christian families would employ political influence, lobbying, bribery, and the like, in order to gain Muslim support to undermine the economic positions of their rivals. In Syrian towns Jewish families, notably the Farhi family in Damascus (and Acre), had gained, until the early nineteenth century, the upper hand in their competition with Christian families, notably the Greek Catholic Bahri family, in part due to the support of an influential Jewish network in Istanbul. However, during the Egyptian occupation of Palestine and Syria (1831–1840), Christians, led by the Bahris, occupied senior positions in the newly established administration, partly at the expense of Jews. The success of the Christians was due not only to their familiarity with modern administrative methods and to their effective network in Cairo, but also to the attempts of Muhammad Ali, Egypt's ruler, to please France, the protector of Christian Catholics in the region.

It would appear that Syrian Christians, notably in Damascus, did not content themselves with their preferential position vis-à-vis Jews in the economy and in government bureaucracy. Since they encountered at that period deep Muslim hostility because of their new predominant positions and provocative behavior, Christians presumably wished to divert this animosity toward a new common enemy and scapegoat—the Jews. By accusing Jews of committing ritual murder—notably the 1840 Damascus Blood

Libel—Christians aimed at dehumanizing Jews and justifying their destruction. The political circumstances surrounding the Damascus Blood Libel were also suitable: a pro-Christian Egyptian administration and a sympathetic French consul in Damascus, Ratti Menton, both actively backed the anti-Jewish accusation. Consequently Jewish leaders, including Raphael Farhi, were arrested and tortured, while other Jews were maltreated by both Christians and Muslims; subsequently Jews continued to be associated with the blood libel and were occasionally accused of committing this crime by both Christians and Muslims.[34]

Nevertheless, the Damascus Blood Libel, like subsequent accusations, was refuted by the Ottoman authorities who resumed their rule of Syria and Palestine in 1840–41, and who tended by and large to side again with Jews in their renewed rivalry with Christians.[35] Jews took advantage of the new conditions to regain their former economic and administrative positions and to retaliate against their Christian enemies. For example, in 1841 the British consul in Damascus reported with some bias:

> Maalem Raffael Farchi, who in consequence of holding an old Berrat as Banker of the Pachas of this city in the former government of the Porte, has assumed—concerting and acting with those [Muslim] members [of the new provincial council] an undivided control in measures and appointments under the present government—an enmity and fanatical feelings towards the Christians and an opposition to the appointment of Christians in the offices of the government. . . . He employs wholly Jews in the different departments . . . [and] discharged all the Christians and replaced them by Jews.[36]

Although Farhi's influence subsequently diminished under the newly introduced *Tanzimat* reforms, Syrian Jews continued for several decades to occupy important positions in the treasury as well as in commerce and finance.[37]

Conclusion: Intercommunal Alliances

Jews in Syria (less so in Palestine) enjoyed better relations than Christians with Muslim notables because in spite of the reforms, they continued to conduct their lives as a small religious minority devoid of political ambitions. As was already noted, Jews occasionally sided with Muslims at times of anti-Christian riots, notably during the 1860 Damascus massacre, in order to avenge the 1840 Damascus Blood Libel and also to forge a Muslim-Jewish alliance against the Christians. In 1860 a Christian from Aleppo wrote with some frustration: "As for the evildoings of the Jews and their hatred toward the Christians—this is not surprising. But the surprise is that the Muslims prefer the Jews to the Christians." [38]

Indeed, in the preceding year (1859), a Jewish observer had depicted with apparent exaggeration the new configuration of intercommunal relations: "The Ishmaelites [Muslims] and the Jews do not hate each other; on the contrary, they love each other, but toward the uncircumcised [Christians] the Muslims are filled with hate." [39]

Yet this form of triangular intercommunal relations, which continued for several decades in various parts of the Ottoman Empire, underwent a gradual change since the end of the nineteenth century, particularly in Palestine, with both the appearance of Zionism and the emergence of Arab nationalism among Christian and Muslim intellectuals. Christian intellectuals already in the 1860s and 1870s had established various cultural clubs and literary journals in an attempt to spread ideas of common Syrian patriotism and Arab cultural affinity among Muslims and Christians. But it was particularly the Zionist venture in Palestine that enabled Christian Arabs to start forging a new Christian-Muslim alliance against the emerging Jewish nationalist challenge and potential threat. [40] The impact of this nascent alliance was observed already in 1911 by David Yellin, a Jewish leader and member of the Ottoman General Council in Jerusalem: "Fifteen years ago the Muslims hated the Christians while their attitude to the Jews was one of contempt. Now their attitude to the Christians has changed for the better and to the Jews—for the worse." [41]

CHAPTER 9

A Tale of Two Women

Facets of Jewish Life in Nineteenth-Century Jerusalem as Seen through the Muslim Court Records

Amnon Cohen

The nineteenth-century records (Arabic: *sijill;* Turkish: *sicil*) of the Jerusalem Muslim court differ from those of the previous three centuries in both form and content. The processes of modernization in the Ottoman Empire, accompanied by the introduction and gradual entrenchment of new, secular legal systems in various parts of the empire, had divested the religious courts of many of their former spheres of activity, especially by the 1860s. Matters pertaining to political, administrative, military, and many social and economic issues have disappeared from the Muslim court records when these areas came under the jurisdiction of other judicial authorities. Henceforth the bulk of the Muslim court proceedings would deal primarily with matters relating to issues of personal status (marriage, divorce, inheritance) and real estate transactions, the latter especially as they concerned religious endowments (*waqf*).

In spite of these cautionary remarks, however, students of Jewish history, who have come to rely on the rich and highly variegated information that the court records of earlier centuries have provided with respect to Jewish life, need not despair. Because Jews resorted to the Muslim court for the most part to resolve issues that remained under its jurisdiction, the nineteenth-century records still contain thousands of cases involving Jewish litigants. I have chosen to discuss here just one such case to illustrate the

119

continuing importance of this source into the second half of the nineteenth century, as well as to shed new light on yet another aspect of Jewish life in Ottoman Jerusalem.

Pages 14 to 16 of volume 350 of the Jerusalem court records deal with an unusually detailed case—and hence the document is considerably longer than usual—that the *kadi* of Jerusalem decided on 5 July, 1865. The parties in this lawsuit were the Jewish community's endowment (*waqf*), on the one hand, and two Jewish women, on the other hand. The details of this case are known only from the records of the Muslim court, where the names of the two women are given as "Hefter [perhaps a corruption of Esther] daughter of (*bint*) Menahem" and "Rahel daughter of Leyzer."

The document opens with an account of an earlier stage in the lawsuit—a court decision reached six years earlier. At that time the Jewish women had requested permission to reconstruct a ruined building that constituted part of the Jewish community's endowment in Jerusalem. After the facts had been verified by the parties concerned, the chief rabbi (*hakham bashi* or *hahambaşı*) of Jerusalem, Hayyim Abulafia, in his capacity as trustee (*mutawalli*) of the endowment, granted the women a written authorization. The gist of that document was that whereas the Jewish *waqf* lacked the financial means to repair various pieces of property under its jurisdiction, it would permit the women to invest whatever funds were necessary to rehabilitate the building in question. In return, the women would be granted rights equal to full ownership (*raqaba*) of the building. However, since under Muslim law the title to *waqf* property had to remain inalienable and could not be transferred, the building would technically continue to be regarded as part of the Jewish *waqf.* In such cases, however, it was common to use the legal artifice of *istihkar,* namely, long-term tenancy,[1] and it was under the terms of this arrangement that the women received the rights to the building. In return for their lease, they were required to make a large down payment of 60,000 kurush, "for the full payment of the debts incurred by the *waqf.*" Thereafter they would continue to pay installments of 50 kurush per year as "proper rent."

The reconstruction of the building was conducted on a large scale and lasted six years, from 1859 to 1865. In 1865, when the case was again brought before the court, the *kadi* appointed a committee of inquiry that visited the site and prepared for the court a detailed report on the building and its reconstruction. A close study of this report would yield rich architectural and linguistic information, since it describes in great detail the structure itself, the various components that were either repaired or newly constructed, the tools and materials used, and so on. For our purpose, however, a summary will suffice. The end result of the construction was a structure three stories high. Most of the ground floor consisted of new construction: two vaulted sitting rooms, two kitchens, three toilets, a large barn, and a refurbished water cistern. The second floor had several rooms, a toilet, a new kitchen, and a new stone staircase. New windows of varying shapes and sizes were cut into the walls of the third floor, as was the case, though to a lesser degree, with the second floor. A stone staircase with an iron banister was built, connecting the two upper floors. All the rooms were fitted with wooden doors; the floors, including that of an open balcony, were all paved, and glass panes held by metal frames were installed in the windows.

The committee of inquiry appointed by the *kadi* consisted of Jews and Muslims, including the chief architect *(mimar bashi)* of Jerusalem. Its detailed report confirmed an earlier statement made by the women that over and above the aforementioned down payment, they had spent 1,000 Austro-Hungarian gold coins on the entire reconstruction project. All of this was stated in court, and the judge confirmed that it constituted sufficient grounds to entitle the tenants to the quasi-ownership rights to the property, in accordance with the original agreement. The court reasoned that since the Jewish *waqf* authorities had been unable to secure income to repay their debts from any other source, and since the sums paid by the women constituted a substantial contribution to the endowment as a whole, all the money spent by the women would be regarded as a loan made to the endowment. Until this loan was repaid, the tenants would retain ownership rights *(raqaba)* to the property.

Although the entire transaction was conducted within a totally Jewish context and all the parties concerned were Jews, in actual fact they all used Muslim legal formulations and terminology and maneuvered within the Muslim legal system. The question presented before the Muslim court had to do, first and foremost, with the establishment of the facts on which the entire case rested. In 1861, when Hayyim Abulafia died, David Hazzan succeeded him as chief rabbi, and he was prompted to declare that the women-tenants had no right to the property. The chief rabbi's representatives asked the court to declare the women's claim null and void because, they alleged, the house had never been in ruins. Therefore, Abulafia, the former chief rabbi, had not been in a position to grant a long-term lease on the building, nor to authorize repairs and alterations. In other words, the women could not have acquired any rights to the house, and the court was asked to have them evicted. In response, the representative of the two women submitted the original lease contract that attested to the veracity of his clients' claim factually and legally. He further contended that the substantial sums spent by the women on the renovations should be regarded as exceeding any "appropriate rent" and that the entire undertaking proved to be most beneficial to the Jewish endowment. At the *kadi*'s request, the women's representative introduced several Jewish and two Muslim witnesses who substantiated his arguments. Thus the case for the women proved well grounded factually and legally, and the *kadi* ruled unequivocally in their favor.

Having discussed the factual and legal aspects of the case, it would now seem appropriate to investigate some of its broader historical implications. The question presents itself, To what extent was this seemingly straightforward legal case related to more general issues of nineteenth-century Jerusalem? As we have amply shown elsewhere, there was a close, almost intimate, relationship between the Jewish community and the Muslim court.[2] Suffice it to say here that this relationship does not seem to have significantly diminished during the early *Tanzimat* period. If anything, it may even have become stronger as a result of increased Jewish activity in Jerusalem at the time.

The reconstruction of the ruined building described here was not in itself exceptional. During the second half of the nineteenth century, a steady increase of Jerusalem's Jewish population brought about a greater demand for appropriate housing (sixteenth-century Jerusalem had experienced a similar trend in the growth of the Jewish population, but it had been reversed toward the end of the century[3]). During the economic boom of the late 1850s, rents skyrocketed. A report from Jerusalem that appeared in *Ha-Levanon,* the Hebrew weekly, although exaggerated, described the prevailing conditions as follows: "The price of an apartment has risen seven-fold. . . . Things [in Jerusalem] are twice as expensive as they are in Paris."[4] Faced with these realities, the Jewish leadership in Jerusalem became increasingly concerned with the community's mounting debts, and it intensified its overseas fund-raising activities.[5]

In 1857–58 a more effective solution was sought to alleviate the housing shortage generated by the rising demographic pressures. An Austro-Hungarian Jew purchased a relatively large plot of land with the intention of building a new housing complex called Batei Mahseh. This plan was actually carried out in the early sixties by the Jewish Dutch-German *kolel* (community and collective fund).[6] The architectural style introduced by the builders of the Batei Mahseh complex was conspicuously new and modern. The apartments were large and more sanitary, full of air and light, and each was equipped with its own separate kitchen.[7] There appears to be a striking resemblance in style between the Batei Mahseh apartments and the building constructed by the two women. Although the terminology used in the Muslim court documents is traditional, it suggests a new, almost modern, architectural approach: the relatively large number of toilets and kitchens; the introduction of windows on all floors, allowing for more light, air, and healthier living conditions; and especially the use of glass window panes, a modern improvement that would render the rooms more comfortable in both winter and summer.

So the question arises, Why did the new chief rabbi try so hard to undo the agreement reached by his predecessor only a few years before? Ignorance of the facts must be ruled out because the rabbi could easily have ascertained the truth within the Jewish community. Intentional disregard of his predecessor's decisions or opposition to them are difficult to establish, although they might have had some weight. Simple greed and perhaps the growing burden of community debts could also have been factors. The deplorable state of the Jewish endowment was not significantly alleviated by the contribution of the two women. The sums that they had paid in the days of Chief Rabbi Abulafia were regarded as very considerable at the time, but insufficient some six years later. Moreover, because Chief Rabbi Hazzan himself had lived in the newly built Mishkenot Sha'ananim complex for some time, he personally was in an excellent position to appreciate the financial potential of the renovated building, in the event that its current tenants/owners could be forced out. He was also personally involved in fund-raising activities overseas for the Batei Mahseh[8] and knew that the modern architectural style of the project, intended to house both Ashkenazi and Sephardi families, was highly prized. Thus, when the chief rabbi's representative, Shirizli, argued in court that the annual rent paid for the refurbished house was not commensurate with the property's true value, he was very likely correct: in 1865 the building was worth much more than in 1859.

There was, however, an additional dimension to Rabbi Hazzan's intransigence. It should be remembered that for more than a century the Ashkenazi community in Jerusalem had not been officially recognized by the Ottoman authorities. Unable to pay their community's debts, in the early eighteenth century all the members of the Ashkenazi community were forced either to leave the town or to conceal their ethnic identity. Those who stayed behind or arrived in Jerusalem later had to wear Sephardi clothing so that the authorities would not recognize their origins. Ashkenazi Jews did in fact continue to settle in Jerusalem, and with time they were more tolerated by the authorities; still, the lack of official recognition led to some severe limitations on their community. For example, they were not entitled to have their meat prepared by their own ritual slaughterers. As slaughtering (shehitah) was an important source of income and not only Jews but also Muslims used to purchase their meat only from Sephardi butchers, it is not difficult to understand why the Sephardi slaughterers did everything to discourage Ashkenazi competition.[9]

In the early 1860s, however, there was increased Ashkenazi activity and influence in Jerusalem, and the building of Batei Mahseh was just one of its facets. In August 1864 the Hebrew language press reported extensively on the progress made in building an Ashkenazi hospital, and towards the end of the same year it described the completion of the impressive Hurvah synagogue.[10] At about the same time, the Ashkenazi community attempted to enlist the influence of Sir Moses Montefiore to convince the authorities to permit also Ashkenazi slaughtering.[11] Chief Rabbi Hazzan used to be head slaughterer of the Sephardi community in his native town of Izmir, and he was fully aware of the economic and other ramifications of the Ashkenazi drive in this respect.

The attempt to prevent the Ashkenazim from undermining Sephardi privileges is understandable, but in the changing reality of Jerusalem it was doomed to failure. At about the same time as this case went to court, or perhaps slightly later, the Ashkenazim had won the right to conduct their own slaughtering.[12] The conflict, however, bred antagonism and animosity, leading to an open breach between the Sephardi Rabbi Hazzan and his Ashkenazi colleagues. The latter were merciless in their public denunciations of his position on slaughtering, as well as on other current issues. Together with the North African rabbis of Jerusalem, they accused Hazzan of high-handed behavior, unjust treatment of his fellow Jews, and of imposing exceedingly high taxes on all Jews.[13] In April 1863, Rabbi Hazzan was promoted to the rank of *hakham bashi* of all the sultan's Jewish subjects in Palestine. The Ashkenazi Jews, however, continued to accuse him of favoring the Sephardi community.[14]

The dispute described in the Muslim court records had taken place at a time when internal tensions among the Jews of Jerusalem were at their peak. Returning now to the names of the two women leads us to an obvious conclusion: Hefter (Esther?) daughter of Menahem could well be an Ashkenazi name; but Rahel daughter of Leyzer is definitely an Ashkenazi name. The Hebrew name Eli'ezer appears quite often in the court registers, in either Arabic or Turkish documents, and it may equally apply to Sephardim or Ashkenazim. Leyzer, a variant of Eli'ezer, appears only—and fairly frequently—in reference to Ashkenazi Jews. In other words: When Chief Rabbi Hazzan disputed the women's right to the property in question, he was once more pitting himself against further Ashkenazi inroads in Jerusalem. It is reasonable to assume that monetary and personal considerations formed an equally important, if not greater, motive for his actions. However, in view of the general atmosphere in Jewish Jerusalem at the time, and particularly in the case of Rabbi Hazzan, one cannot dismiss ethnic bias as playing a role in this episode.

Nevertheless, justice did prevail. Once again, it was the Muslim judge who defended the weaker party, the two women, against the attempt to abuse their rights, even though this involved clipping the wings of the influential *hakham bashi*. The Muslim court thus continued its traditional role as fair adjudicator of disputes. Furthermore, the case described here offers clear evidence that, although the *Tanzimat* reforms may have narrowed the scope of the Muslim court's activities, they did nothing to undermine its active support of the weaker elements in Jerusalem's society, regardless of religious or ethnic origins.

Jewish Female Education in the Ottoman Empire, 1840–1914

Rachel Simon

Jewish women in the Ottoman Empire did not receive a formal education until the nineteenth century. This was due to several factors. Until the Ottoman reform period *(Tanzimat)* that began in 1839, the state did not offer public education for males or females. Education was essentially controlled by religious authorities—Muslim, Christian, and Jewish. In traditional Jewish society schooling was seen as necessary for preparing a person to participate in community life, mainly in the synagogue service. Because women had no part in the synagogue service, they did not need a formal education. It is true that girls did receive some instruction at home from family members or tutors, but this was usually rudimentary and brief. Their training focused primarily on the acquisition of household skills. Although there were some women who gained renown as scholars, they were exceptions to the rule.

General Educational Conditions in the Ottoman Empire

Until the *Tanzimat* the state provided training only for its military and administrators. The population at large could study in institutions administered by Muslim religious endowments *(waqfs),* by the non-Muslim reli-

See also appendixes A–C for data about Jewish girls' schools and mixed schools.

gious communities, and by private teachers.[1] Very little private education
was available for Muslim females, and that mainly in the mosque schools in
the cities. In these schools girls could study in the same classes with boys
until they reached puberty. The curriculum consisted of learning the
Qur'an, reading, writing, and arithmetic as well as some history and geography. Poor and rural girls rarely attended school at all.[2]

The state started to become involved in education in the nineteenth
century as part of the reforms, and girls' schools were eventually established.
Female education was addressed in the Public Education Regulations
(*Maarif-i Umumiye Nizamnamesi*) of 1869. These stated that girls aged six
through ten should be in school and study religious principles, Ottoman
Turkish, Arabic and Persian language and literature, history, geography,
arithmetic, household skills, embroidery, drawing, and music (not all the
subjects were, however, mandatory). Women were preferred as teachers in
girls' schools, but when there were not sufficient numbers of qualified female teachers, it was permissible to have old gentlemen in these positions.[3]

In 1863–64, there were 14,377 elementary schools in the empire with
493,885 students; of these, 279 schools were in Istanbul, with 16,757 students, including 6,782 girls.[4] The first *rüşdiye* (upper elementary) school for
girls was opened in Istanbul in 1858–59, twenty years after the establishment
of the first *rüşdiye* for boys. By 1869–70, similar schools were established in
some of the main centers of the empire.[5] In 1887–88, there were 477 *rüşdiyes*
in the empire; of them, 31 were in Istanbul, including ten for girls, and 25 in
Edirne, with three for girls.[6] In some places, boys and girls studied in the
same school building, although not at the same time.[7]

As called for by the Public Education Regulations, a female teachers
training college (*Darülmuallimat*) was opened in 1869–70 in Istanbul. The
curriculum was similar to that of the male teachers training college, with additional "feminine" subjects (embroidery, household skills, etc.).[8] The first
idadi (preparatory secondary school, above *rüşdiye*) school for girls was established in Istanbul in 1911. In 1913 it was renamed İstanbul İnas Sultanısı and
it became the first *lise* (upper secondary school, or high school, above *idadi*)
for girls. In contrast to the boys' high school, it offered no logic, philosophy,
Persian, or Arabic; instead, home economics, needlework, drawing, etc.
were added.[9] The first Ottoman vocational schools for girls were established

in 1865 in Rusçuk and in 1870 in Istanbul. In these schools girls studied vocations (mainly needlework) and some academic subjects (mainly reading, Qur'an, and arithmetic).[10] In 1898, apparently reacting to the rapid spread of missionary schools, the government issued new regulations regarding education in Anatolia, including the imposition of stricter supervision on Protestant schools, with particular attention to girls' schools.[11] Toward the end of the period, observers praised the cultural level of Turkish women, especially the Istanbulis.[12]

In Syria, Lebanon, and Palestine, changes had started to occur earlier as a result of the Egyptian occupation (1831–1840), when Egyptian *nizami* (government) schools were introduced.[13] The first modern Ottoman government schools, *rüşdiyes,* were established in Aleppo in the late 1850s, in Damascus in the early 1860s, and in Jerusalem in 1891. But it was only in 1891 that a Muslim *elementary* school for girls opened in Jerusalem.[14]

In Egypt, too, traditional Muslim education had some provisions for girls. They were admitted to the *kuttabs* (primary religious schools), but apparently only a few took advantage of it. Some were taught by private female tutors (*shaykhahs*) or old males (*shaykhs*). They usually learned to memorize the prayers and certain parts of the Qur'an, but were not taught to read or write. Few women learned the Qur'an by heart to become a *fiqiyah* (female reciter of the Qur'an) or a *shaykhah*. Some attended recitations of the Qur'an by other women or listened to lectures by *shaykhs* from behind a curtain. Girls of the middle and upper classes learned embroidery and artistic needlework from a *mu'allimah* (female instructor), while poorer women learned to use the spindle.[15]

Modern education in Egypt for girls started under Muhammad Ali through vocational training. A midwifery school was established in 1831–32 by the French physician Clot Bey in the school of medicine in Cairo. The first students were Abyssinian and Sudanese female slaves purchased for that purpose, as well as eunuchs and orphan girls. They first studied Arabic and then a wide range of practical subjects. After its reorganization in 1838, the course of studies was established at five years. During the period 1831–83, the number of students fluctuated between 20 and 44.[16]

It took almost another forty years to start public academic education for girls in Egypt. In 1867 a special committee drew up a plan to establish a girls' school, but it was only in 1873 that such a school was opened in Cairo under the patronage of and at the expense of Cheshmat Hanum, the third wife of Khedive Ismail, the viceroy of Egypt. Students were at first recruited from white slaves belonging to families related to the ruler and from families of officials. In 1875, the school had 298 pupils studying under a Syrian directress, Rose Najjar, five male teachers (in charge of teaching the Qur'an, Turkish, and drawing), and eight female instructors (teaching needlework, piano, and laundry). At the same time, the *waqf* administration opened a girls' school with 147 students under Cécile Najjar, with four male teachers instructing the Qur'an and five women teaching needlework and laundry. When Khedive Ismail was deposed in 1879, his wife had to withdraw her support, and both institutions were combined under the administration of the *waqf*.[17]

In Egypt, Copts and Greek Orthodox at first usually went to their own schools, but later also went to missionary ones.[18] In addition, there were also private schools in Egypt, which provided a primarily European education and vocational or business training. Of these, twelve institutions were established in Cairo in the years 1867–77 (four were for girls only and six were of mixed gender), nine in Alexandria in 1866–1877 (three were for girls and five were mixed gender), two in Port Said in 1875 (one was for girls), and two mixed-gender schools in Ramle 1876.[19]

Missionary Schools

Christian missionary penetration of the Ottoman Empire accelerated during the nineteenth century. The missionaries soon realized that as a Muslim state the Ottoman Empire strongly opposed any Christian missionary activity among its Muslim population. As a result, missionaries focused on Eastern Christians and Jews and to a lesser extent on other minorities (e.g., Druze). Although many missionaries directed their activities toward the minorities at large, some missionary societies specifically targeted the Jews. The lack of educational opportunities for girls was one of the main reasons that prompted missionaries to invest particularly in female education, believing that women interested in education would attend their schools and would become exposed to their teachings.

Jews were aware of the proselytizing goals of the missionaries and were generally careful to avoid their institutions. At times, rabbis proclaimed a *herem* (excommunication) on those Jews who availed themselves of missionary services. Nevertheless, some Jews did make use of missionary institutions, and female education was a case in point. Since neither the state nor the Jewish community provided any formal education for girls, those Jews who wanted their daughters to be literate sent them to missionary schools. In order to attract Jews, these schools often refrained from overt proselytizing, and indeed, in most places, hardly any conversions took place. Even so, the Jewish leadership remained opposed to the missionaries.

Among the missionary societies most active in the Ottoman Empire were the London Society for Promoting Christianity amongst the Jews, commonly known as the London Jews Society (LJS, established in London in 1809), and the Female Society for Promoting Christianity among the Jews (established in Boston in 1816), both of which, as their names suggest, aimed their activities particularly at Jews. Other missionary organizations active in the Ottoman Empire included the American Board of Commissioners for Foreign Missions (ABCFM), the Church Missionary Society (CMS), and the Orthodox Palestine Society (Russian, active mainly among the Greek Orthodox in Palestine, Syria, and Lebanon). Missionaries' wives and female missionaries focused on local women, and in many places they were the first to establish girls' schools.[20]

Since the official traditional leadership of the Jewish communities usually did not approve of any kind of formal female education, they generally did not bother to establish institutions that would compete with those of the missionaries. As a result, it fell to local and foreign Jewish individuals and organizations to try to establish alternatives to missionary female education. Thus, the constant challenge of missionary education served as a major impetus for the establishment of modern Jewish girls' schools and the gradual advancement of the services that they offered the Jewish community. Nonetheless, in many places some Jews continued to send their daughters to missionary schools even after the establishment of modern Jewish schools, because they believed that some subjects, especially languages, were better taught at missionary schools; and, in addition, the latter generally offered free tuition, food, and clothing.

Development of Jewish Female Education

Until the nineteenth century, the Jewish communities in the Ottoman Empire provided most of the cultural and social services for their members. But, as we have seen, this generally did not include formal education for girls. Nonetheless, in most places there were some institutions, mainly private, that educated women. Thus, in several regions, girls were sent to private teachers, with whom they studied together with boys until they were eight or nine years old. The study focused on reading the Torah and on prayers.[21] Another institution that existed in some places can hardly be considered educational: female toddlers would be sent to the *maestra,* whose main responsibility was to keep them quiet; the *maestra* neither taught the girls nor played with them.[22] Despite these conditions, some women became renowned for their scholarship. Such was the case of Rabbanit Osnat of Mosul (16th c.), who headed the yeshivah of her late husband,[23] and the nine daughters of R. Abdallah Yosef Farraj of Basra (19th c.), who were well versed in the Bible, Mishnah, and the Zohar.[24] These, however, were exceptional cases. (On a more popular level, female oral poetry was well developed in various regions as a unique genre. Expressed in the local dialects, it focused on women and family issues as well as on the adoration of the Torah and saints.[25])

In the 1850s, as we have seen, public education started to spread. Missionary activities were also on the increase, with a large effort directed toward the education of girls. At the same time, private Jewish educational initiatives started to take hold. These were not only in response to the missionary threat, but also in order to advance the community and improve its cultural and economic conditions. Although cultural advancement was very important to Western Jewish philanthropists, economic considerations were often of prime interest to the local Jews, whose communities were afflicted with severe poverty. Thus, while in the past it was rare for Jewish women to engage in work for wages, during the nineteenth century this increasingly became a necessity. Many families realized the opportunities that Western schools offered in this respect. For their part, the educational institutions promoted their own interests by responding to these economic needs. Consequently, most schools offered some vocational training, usually related to needlework, which provided girls with a chance to obtain profitable jobs and to improve their economic condition. General literacy and knowledge of languages and arithmetic were also considered important in themselves, as well as a requirement for upward social mobility. Even if at first families focused more on the immediate economic benefits of a modern education—food, clothing, and a monetary subvention—they soon came to realize its intrinsic long-term importance.

The first Western Jewish attempt to establish modern female education in the Ottoman Empire took place in Egypt following the visit of Adolphe Crémieux in 1840, as a result of which the "Crémieux schools" were established in Cairo and Alexandria. Crémieux obtained French Jewish financial support for these schools, and he was also involved in setting their curricula, which emphasized handicrafts. At first, the Jewish community and the Egyptian authorities were pleased with the schools, and parents started to send their children there. In Alexandria some parents objected to the non-Jewish subjects that were taught. The school apparently ceased to exist after 1842 due to financial difficulties and the fact that wealthy Jews preferred to send their children to Christian schools. The school in Cairo continued to operate, although with some interruptions and a change of administration.[26]

In Jerusalem the beginning of female education was linked to missionary activity. "Miss Cooper's Institution" was established in 1848 by an Englishwoman, a close friend of the wife of the British consul, James Finn. This was a workshop that focused on training girls and women in sewing, knitting, embroidery, spinning, weaving, and some academic subjects. Its main attraction was that it held out practical benefits during a period of severe economic crisis, which worsened during the Crimean War. In 1854 the institution had 160 trainees. After Miss Cooper's death, the school was transferred to the LJS, and was referred to as the "Jewesses' Institute."[27]

Two important Jewish enterprises were launched in Jerusalem in the mid-1850s. The first, which continues to the present, was started in 1854 by the Rothschilds and became known as the Evelina de Rothschild School. Starting under a strong French influence, it came under English tutelage following its takeover by the Anglo-Jewish Association (AJA) as of 1892. In 1901 the language of instruction was changed from French to English. In the beginning, emphasis was placed on Judaic subjects, prayers in Hebrew, and handicrafts. Later, the curriculum broadened to include reading, writing, arithmetic, geography, history, and foreign languages as well as handi-crafts. In order to attract girls to the school, it was necessary at first to pay and feed them (the food program continued into the 1880s), and many students received free tuition. Among the personalities connected with this school were Fortuna Behar (its first directress, appointed in 1889), Devorah Ben-Yehudah, who taught Hebrew and tried to make it the girls' spoken lan-guage, and Annie Landau (directress, 1899–1945), whose long tenure left its mark on the character of the school.[28]

In 1855, the Montefiore school was established in Jerusalem, named after Sir Moses Montefiore (1784–1885), the well-known Anglo-Jewish financier and philanthropist. The school emphasized reading, prayers, sewing, embroidery, and household skills taught by local female teachers. In mid-1857, the Committee of the Holy Land Appeal Fund decided to close the school, ostensibly because of financial constraints. While this was the of-ficial reason given for the closure, it seems that the strong opposition to the school by the local Ashkenazi rabbis and Montefiore's desire not to antago-nize them contributed to the decision.[29]

The 1860s witnessed the beginnings of the activities of L'Alliance Is-raélite Universelle (AIU), which gradually spread throughout the Ottoman Empire. Indeed, the next decades were characterized by the growing role of the AIU in Jewish female education. At the same time some attempts were made in this field also by local communities and organizations as well as in-dividual philanthropists, although the role of the last was on the decline.

In Egypt from the 1860s onwards, the role of the community leadership and various philanthropists became important in developing modern educa-tion, including girls' schools. Thus, in 1862 the community in Alexandria established a girls' school with 70 students.[30] In 1897 the Karaites in Cairo established a school, but it was closed in 1907; after that, only evening sewing classes were offered for poor Karaite women.[31] In Cairo, once the Crémieux schools came under the management of the community in 1860, the girls' school was closed. Classes for girls were renewed only in 1875 as a result of a donation by the Egyptian-Jewish banker and philanthropist David Aghion and the involvement of Moïse Cattaui, banker and president of the Cairo Jewish community. At the time the school had 225 students of both sexes. The curriculum included Hebrew, Arabic, French, and Italian as well as general studies. Instruction was usually conducted in French, and the school's academic standards were considered to be good. The schools benefited from the support of the community's council and some wealthy individuals (e.g., the Cattaui, Aghion, and Mousseri families). At the beginning of the twentieth century, the number of girls at the school approximately equaled that of the boys.[32] The initiative of Baron Jacob de Menasce resulted in the establishment of the girls' school Shadai Ya'azor in 1892 in Alexandria.[33] The AIU schools in Egypt were established only later, after community and private Jewish schools already operated. An AIU school was opened in Cairo in 1896, in Alexandria in 1897, and in Tanta in 1905.[34]

In most cases, the AIU established schools after it had received a request from the local community and after the founding of a local AIU committee that assumed responsibility for supporting the school. Unless the mixed-gender schools are taken into consideration, the general pattern is that schools providing education for boys preceded by quite a number of years those providing education for girls.[35] The requests for opening AIU schools usually came from places that did not have any other modern, or Jewish modern, schools. At times requests were made specifically in order to counter missionary activities (e.g., Tanta). In some cases, the community already had Jewish schools, but nonetheless wanted to have AIU institutions as well (e.g., Cairo and Alexandria). The AIU generally expected that the community would pay for the upkeep of the school, but this was not always possible. Thus, whereas the communities in Tanta and Mosul paid for the school building as well as the costs of tuition, in many places only a small number of students paid tuition fees, which in any event usually were very low.

All in all, the AIU established more than 45 schools for girls, including vocational and mixed institutions, in the Ottoman Empire, most of them during the last twenty years of the period. Many of these were located in what is today Turkey, although gradually most big cities with a sizable Jewish population witnessed the establishment of an AIU girls' school. All these schools operated under identical guidelines and generally according to the same curriculum, although modifications were often introduced to meet local conditions and needs. Thus, English was the main language in the Basra school; Hebrew became the dominant language in the schools in

Palestine; and the school in Galata had a special bilingual class (French and German) for girls from Russia and Romania. Most of the teachers were graduates of the AIU's teachers training college, the Ecole Normale Israélite Orientale (ENIO), in Paris. But those who taught Hebrew and Jewish subjects usually were local rabbis who had not undergone any specific pedagogical training. The regular AIU teachers and school directors often complained about the rabbis' poor performance. These rabbis and directors of the AIU boys' schools usually provided the only male teachers for the AIU girls' schools. The girls' schools were generally managed by directresses who often were the wives of the directors of the local AIU boys' schools.

Another organization that made an important contribution to Jewish female education was the Hilfsverein der deutschen Juden (HV), which had objectives somewhat similar to those of the AIU but emphasized German culture. In contrast to the widely spread activities of the AIU, the HV operated mainly in Palestine and Turkey. The organization started its activities in Palestine in 1904 and established girls' schools in Jerusalem (1905) and Jaffa (1913). In addition, it supported a number of other schools and kindergartens in Palestine with a mixed student body. An important contribution of the HV was the establishment of teachers training colleges in Palestine, first for male schoolteachers (Jerusalem, 1904) and then for female kindergarten teachers (Jerusalem, 1909). The existence of these colleges prompted the local Hebrew teachers to establish teachers colleges of their own, including one for women in Jaffa (1908).[36]

The role of Italy in advancing Jewish female education in the Ottoman Empire was confined to Libya. It began after Jewish merchants in Tripoli requested Italian Jews to help them develop modern education. The Jewish interest was soon backed by Italian political ambitions to colonize Libya, which in the nineteenth century were expressed through peaceful cultural and economic penetration. Thus, while the first steps were taken by Jews, the Italian educational network in Libya soon became one of the major means of Italian state intervention in that Ottoman province.

The first secular Italian school in Libya was a boys' school established in Tripoli in 1876. A year later a girls' school was founded, also in Tripoli, and it was directed by a Jewish woman from Livorno, Carolina Nunes-Vais. In 1911 the school had 348 students. By that time, the Italian educational network in Libya had twelve schools, including three for girls—one each in Tripoli, Benghazi (with 160 students), and Khoms. At first, most of the teachers came from Italy, but gradually they were augmented by local women, some of whom were themselves graduates of the Italian schools in Libya. Emphasis was placed on the study of the Italian language, literature, and culture, in addition to general studies. Due to the growing competition with the AIU girls' school in Tripoli from the mid-1890s onwards, new subjects were added, such as French, English, history, geography, and Jewish studies, as well as sewing and embroidery. The two latter subjects were taught primarily for recreation.

Most of the students in the Italian schools came from mercantile, upper-middle-class Jewish families possessing Italian citizenship. These families were already influenced by European culture through their commercial and financial activities, and the schools further advanced their Italianization and imitation of European customs. In the late 1890s, political pressure was added to the social and cultural attraction of the Italian schools when the Italian consulate in Tripoli required all Italian citizens to send their children to Italian schools. Other attractive features of the Italian schools were the completely free education that they offered and their modern facilities and equipment.[37]

At the turn of the century, Zionist influence became particularly strong in the new Jewish schools in Palestine, especially in the elementary schools in the new colonies (*moshavot)* and Jaffa, in the Hebrew gymnasiums of Jaffa (founded 1905) and Jerusalem (1909), and in the Betzalel College of Arts and Crafts in Jerusalem (1906). This was due to the strong impact of the Hebrew language teachers who spread Zionist ideas even to the schools of the AIU and HV, organizations that were non-Zionist and at times even anti-Zionist. The latter organizations were forced to employ Zionist teachers because they lacked faculty qualified to teach Hebrew and Jewish subjects. The schools under direct Zionist influence engaged in various innovative pedagogical experiments, such as coeducation, the teaching of Hebrew in Hebrew, and the use of the Sephardi pronunciation of Hebrew as the language of instruction. In the Jaffa Gymnasium, the critical study of the Bible was also introduced.

Zionist influence outside Palestine was felt in Jewish schools in Cairo and Damascus, although in both places this was of very short duration. In 1900, Max Mushli and Y. Hornstein opened in Cairo what became known as the "Zionist School" because of the founders' involvement in the Zionist organization and the financial support that the school received from that organization. Starting with 100 students of both sexes, it soon grew to 290, mostly Ashkenazim. The curriculum was similar to that of Egyptian state schools (with the addition of Hebrew), and tuition was free. Despite Zionist support, however, financial difficulties quickly mounted. In 1903 the school had only 40 pupils, and when it had to close down, many moved to the local AIU school and even to missionary schools.[38] In Damascus during World War I, some 1,200 students of both sexes studied in a Zionist Hebrew school that also included a kindergarten. The institution was operated by Jews deported from Palestine. The school also offered evening classes for male and female youths.[39]

During this period most of the schools provided only elementary education. In part, this was a choice grounded in ideology. In Palestine the AIU made it known that it did not want to educate scholars, but only good workers, farmers, housewives, and mothers. The HV, too, did not want to make the students overly learned, fearing that they would then seek higher education and better jobs abroad and leave their towns and villages in Palestine. Nonetheless, both organizations felt the need for some sort of higher education. The AIU provided it mainly through its teachers college (ENIO) in Paris, which had sections for both sexes; otherwise, its secondary education was limited to male vocational and agricultural training institutions. The HV, by providing teachers' training in Palestine and also participating in the establishment of a technical college in Haifa, was instrumental in developing higher education in Palestine for men as well as women. Other initiatives, launched by private individuals, led to the establishment of the Hebrew Gymnasiums in Jaffa and Jerusalem and the Betzalel College of Arts and Crafts in Jerusalem. All three institutions were coeducational from the beginning (although Betzalel had some special crafts classes for girls only) and advocated Hebrew language revival. The gymnasiums were in fact planned as twelve-year schools, and as such they usually attracted students from better-off families interested in providing a more well-rounded education for their children.

Attitudes toward Female Education

The principles upon which the AIU and other Western-based organizations and individuals had constructed their educational policies were influenced by those common in Europe at the time. Female education did not result from changes in the definitions of the role of women in society and the family structure. The main purpose remained as it had been in the past: to prepare women to be better wives, mothers, and homemakers. The curricula in the girls' schools were somewhat different from those in the boys' schools: the former included sewing, embroidery, knitting, etc., and only towards the end of the nineteenth century did the curricula of girls' and boys' schools become similar. These changes took place especially after a growing number of schools, mainly in Palestine, became coeducational, with the same curriculum for all students.[40]

The attitudes of Westerners who wanted to introduce female education were not uniform. Montefiore, for example, advocated a cautious approach because of the chasm existing between modernizers and traditionalists. He suggested a rudimentary course of study for girls that would include elementary reading, writing, and arithmetic, knowledge of the local and European languages, as well as prayers and reading of the Scriptures.[41] In order to discourage early marriages, which were common, the Evelina de Rothschild school in Jerusalem offered a prize of 200 francs to girls who attended the school for three years and reached the age of fifteen before being married. But only a few received the prize.[42]

The AIU had formulated special instructions regarding female education in order to raise the position of women without, however, making them less feminine. Thus, a strong emphasis was placed on moral education, handicrafts, and household skills. The AIU maintained that education would free women from their abasement. Emphasizing the role of girls as the mothers of the next generation and as those responsible for the children's early education and for shaping their character, the AIU directors hoped that the moral principles instilled in the girls at school would become the basis for future character building.[43] For that reason, the organization regarded it as imperative not only to educate young women, but also to reform their manners and views.[44] At times, the AIU was quite explicit in its purpose, stating that its goal was "to inculcate habits of orderliness and diligence in those who had been sluggish and untidy."[45] With regard to women of low socioeconomic status, the AIU believed that its goal should be to transform them into productive working women, intelligent and efficient, of decent behavior, capable of understanding their situation and of helping their children. At the same time, however, the organization maintained that such "advancement" need not go too far.[46] In Jaffa the AIU made it clear to the directress of the girls' school that it did not intend to make the girls too learned in Hebrew or French, but rather wanted them to be expert in running the house and in handicrafts, so that they could earn a living and be of benefit at home. For that reason, the AIU opposed the opening of higher grades or expanding the curriculum.[47] The organization believed that it could utilize the example of the Bible, where women are glorified, to facilitate the introduction of female education into traditional society and change the customs of Middle Eastern Jews.[48]

In some of the main Ottoman Jewish centers (e.g., Istanbul, Edirne, Salonica), opposition to female education was often related to power struggles between the traditional religious leadership and modernizing personalities who often had commercial relations with the West. Similarly, in Tripoli, Libya, the local community leaders were opposed to modern education, but the chief rabbis, who were brought in by the authorities from other parts of the empire, as well as many local Jews, both rich and poor, supported female education (though many of the poor boys continued to frequent the traditional community schools). In Iraq those who received a modern education or were exposed to external cultural, social, or economic influences usually favored female education. But there were also rabbis who supported it, and many wanted Jewish girls' schools as a means to fight missionary influence.

The fact that Jews have been divided into different "ethnic" communities (known in Hebrew as *edah,* sing.; *edot,* pl.), such as Ashkenazim and Sephardim, had some influence on attitudes toward female education and how it was implemented. These attitudes varied from one region to another and were based not only on the community's character, but also on more general local circumstances.

In Palestine there was a double division: one between the Old Yishuv (the pre-Zionist community) and the New Yishuv, and another between

Sephardim and Ashkenazim, especially within the Old Yishuv. Although the New Yishuv generally accepted modern and female education, this was not always the case with the Old Yishuv. Within the latter, the Ashkenazim were staunchly opposed to modern education, including that of girls, so as to preserve their traditional institutions and way of life. This opposition was in part based on Ashkenazi experiences in Europe, where modernity often led to secularism and assimilation. In fact, the Ashkenazi traditionalists in Palestine emerged as the most adamant opponents of modern and female education, and their rabbis excommunicated all those connected with the Montefiore and Rothschild schools in Jerusalem as well as the girls' school in Safed. They maintained that women should not be educated because they are not required to study the Torah and they are also known to be frivolous (*nashim da'atan kalah*).[49] The Sephardim in Palestine, however, were more dependent for their livelihood on economic and social interaction with the majority, non-Jewish society. They quickly realized the advantages of acquiring a modern education, especially languages, arithmetic, and the sciences, as well as modern occupations. Consequently they were not opposed to female education, and indeed, many of the early students in the modern schools were Sephardi girls. Even before Jewish schools were established, Sephardi families had sent their daughters to missionary schools to acquire a modern education.[50]

In Egypt the division between Sephardim and Ashkenazim had a different manifestation. Although the opposition to modern education had weakened among both groups due, apparently, to the earlier onset of the modernization process in Egypt, quite a few Ashkenazi immigrants preferred to send their daughters to missionary schools rather than to Jewish ones, because in the former Yiddish was used by Jewish converts as a language of instruction.[51]

In their reports the AIU representatives often complained about the attitude of Jews of Islamic countries to modern education, including female education. The AIU reiterated the idea that the "Orientals" wanted their women to be proficient only in household skills and it was irrelevant to them if the women were otherwise ignorant. What mattered to them most was that the husband be a pious Jew. On the whole, the AIU claimed, the "Orientals" resisted any modern ideas regarded as endangering the status

quo.[52] The AIU also believed that it should not rush to establish female educational institutions after opening boys' schools, because of the negative attitudes such a move could generate in the traditional communities.[53] In fact,
however, some traditional Sephardi religious leaders strongly advocated female education: when the AIU decided to open a boys' school in Mosul, R.
Eliyahu Sayig of this town asked the organization to open a girls' school as
well, and he labored to collect the necessary funding for this purpose. The
AIU's position in this instance, as reflected in its actions and in the advice offered by the director of the boys' school, Maurice Sidi, was to postpone the
establishment of a girls' school until the traditional community of Mosul
were deemed ready for it, in spite of the fact that the local rabbi had urged
the AIU to go ahead.[54] On the other hand, in some communities scholarship among women—and even literacy itself—was derided.[55]

Vocational Training

Most advocates of female education also emphasized vocational training,
and at times this overshadowed academic studies. In some places female education actually started with vocational workshops, to which some academic studies were later added.[56] In most other institutions (e.g., the
Montefiore and Rothschild schools in Jerusalem), handicrafts and household skills were an important part of the curriculum from the very beginning.[57] This approach was taken because of several reasons: first, the need to
convince poor families who had to send their daughters to work that their
chances for better-paying jobs would improve with the acquisition of modern skills; second, the widespread belief among the founders of these schools
that proficiency in crafts and household skills were central to a woman's life,
and in order to advance the community, women should know how to function properly; and third, by attracting girls to school through vocational
training, it was hoped that they would become exposed to academic studies,
and thus to Western civilization, ideas, and customs.

This approach was quite evident in the AIU schools, although some of
the later organizations (e.g., HV, the Italians in Libya, and the Hebrew
teachers in Palestine) placed a greater emphasis on the academic aspects of
the girls' curricula. Vocational training was at times provided by the com-

munity, even when it did not have regular academic education for girls. Thus, in 1903 the Karaite community of Cairo operated a workshop to train poor girls in sewing. The workshop had 93 trainees, of whom 48 paid tuition fees.[58]

Preschool Education

As we have seen, before the arrival of modern education, it was common in some communities (e.g., Jerusalem, Izmir, Cairo) to send little girls to the maestra (who did not have any educational qualifications) for a few hours of supervision.[59] This institution was primarily intended for girls, because boys, even at a tender age, were sent to a primary religious school (the heder or its equivalent).

With the introduction of modern Western education, the need for kindergartens was recognized. Some of the early ones became, in fact, schools for little children. But later, in most places, modern educational ideas regarding toddlers were taken into account, and teachers had to be trained in special institutions in Europe (usually in those of the Pestalozzi-Fröbel school) or in other kindergartens, and later in a special college in Palestine. Most kindergartens were coeducational. The first modern kindergarten in Palestine was established in 1892 in Zikhron Ya'akov, after a local woman returned from her studies in Paris. Teaching was at first in French. In 1986 the Evelina de Rothschild girls' school in Jerusalem opened its kindergarten, where the language of instruction was at first French and then English.[60] The first Hebrew kindergarten was opened in Rishon le-Tziyon in 1897 by David Yudelevitz, and others were soon to follow.[61] In 1902, Hebrew kindergartens were opened in several moshavot (Rehovot, Nes Tziyonah, Petah Tikvah) and in Jaffa, and children talked their parents into speaking Hebrew at home.[62] The first Hebrew kindergarten in Jerusalem opened in 1903, with branches opening in 1904 in Me'ah She'arim and in 1906 in Yemin Mosheh, all supported by the HV.[63] In 1908 a Hebrew kindergarten (Menahem Daniel) was opened in Baghdad with six Hebrew teachers and 234 pupils. But after a short while, because of the opposition of the rabbis, it became a regular school.[64] The kindergarten of the AIU in Galata served for training AIU kindergarten teachers in Turkey and Bulgaria.[65] The HV advanced preschool education in two ways. It established and supported several kindergartens in Palestine and elsewhere (Beirut, Kolomea, Salonica, and Istanbul),[66] and it also opened a college in Jerusalem in 1909 with a two-year program for training kindergarten teachers.[67]

Women and Teaching

The introduction of Jewish women into teaching in the Ottoman Empire made a great change in their status. Previously, when women had to work for wages, it was mainly in low-status manual occupations. Their employment in educational and cultural positions marked their entrance into a realm that until then had been reserved for men. The need for female teachers was due to several reasons: first, the wish of parents and the community to keep girls within a primarily female environment; second, the need to teach "feminine" subjects (e.g., needlework), which men did not know or were reluctant to do; and finally, the notion that women were better suited to teach girls and toddlers.

The entrance of women into teaching required the establishment of appropriate teachers colleges and at first these, too, were gender-based. Many teachers were trained outside the Ottoman Empire. Most of the AIU teachers received their education in the organization's college in Paris (ENIO),[68] and the HV's teachers were trained mainly in Germany. Late in the period appropriate institutions were opened in Palestine by the HV and local teachers. The Kindergarten-Teachers College of the HV was opened 16 August 1909, in Jerusalem, with a two-year program.[69] The Lewinsky Teachers College of Hovevei Tziyon was established in Jaffa in 1908.[70] In addition, some kindergartens served as "workshops" for training kindergarten teachers. Many of the female teachers of the AIU in the Middle East and North Africa were themselves from the Ottoman Empire, and thus education paved the way for them to reach out of their own environment. Some of the teachers and directresses became quite well known and influential, as, for example, Fortuna Behar, Devorah Ben-Yehudah, and Annie Landau (all connected with the Evelina de Rothschild school in Jerusalem); Flora Randegger-Friedenberg from Trieste, who came to Jerusalem to direct a girls' school; and Carolina Nunes-Vais, directress of the Italian school in Tripoli.

Despite their entrance into the field of teaching, women's participation in the managerial levels of the profession was slow to follow, as was the improvement of their status. Women usually directed only girls' schools and kindergartens, and they rarely taught older boys. In addition, the salary of the kindergarten teachers, who were women, was lower than that of schoolteachers, most of whom were men.[71] Women were also little represented in teachers' organizations. When the Hebrew Teachers Assembly in Palestine was established in 1892, not one woman was among its fifteen founders, and women did not participate in the twelve formal meetings of this body in the years 1892–96.[72] Later, however, when the Teachers' Association in Palestine was established in 1903, there were already eleven women among its forty-seven founders. A five-member Central Committee was chosen, including one woman, but as she was elected in absentia, Annie Landau, the directress of the Evelina de Rothschild school in Jerusalem, informed the Association that she wanted neither to join the organization nor to represent it. At the Association's second meeting, in 1904, thirty-nine teachers participated, three of them women.[73] By 1913 the Association already had 350 members, but they included only a few women, apparently because most of them were young and worked as teachers' assistants, or they taught lower grades and in kindergartens; there were, nonetheless, also some women teaching in high school.[74] All in all, the number of female teachers in Palestine was not large, and most of the Association's female members were not active in its central governing bodies. The first women to be chosen to these positions were directresses of girls' schools and kindergartens.[75] It is possible that fewer women were involved in the Association's activities because of the appointment of unqualified female teachers, although not all male teachers were adequately qualified either. It was rumored, however, that female friends of Baron Rothschild's administrators (pekidim) in the moshavot benefited from special considerations and were appointed as teachers—and even as directresses in some cases—without appropriate qualifications. It should also be pointed out that many male teachers were opposed to the appointment of women as directresses of schools that included male teachers and students.[76]

The teachers associations in Palestine hardly ever dealt with issues related to female education and teaching. The topic came up for discussion at the sixth meeting of the Hebrew Teachers Assembly, but was postponed until the eighth meeting (1896), when it was decided not to discuss it, because, as was stated, the issue was "out of our hands."[77] At the tenth Zionist Congress in 1911, it was suggested that women be involved in the organization's activities in order to provide Zionist education, because women played a major role in shaping the character of the young generation. This broad and vague proposal was accepted without any discussion.[78]

The Language Issue

The opportunity to acquire European languages was a major attraction of the Western-based schools in the Ottoman Empire. Certain languages were associated with specific schools. Thus, French was identified with the AIU schools, German with the HV schools, and Italian with the Italian schools. However, because the schools were in competition with one another, most of them offered more than one European language.[79] Moreover, as a result of local conditions and needs, some schools changed the language of instruction. Thus, English became the language of instruction in the AIU school in Basra in 1913,[80] and Hebrew became the dominant language in the AIU schools in Palestine following the so-called Language War of 1913 (see below).[81] In 1901, English replaced French at the Evelina de Rothschild school in Jerusalem after the takeover of the school by the AJA.[82] In some schools the local dialect was used in the lower grades but not in the higher ones. When the Montefiore and Rothschild schools were opened in Jerusalem in the mid-1850s, they had separate sections for the Sephardi and Ashkenazi girls, each using their own language of instruction: Judeo-Spanish and Arabic in the former and Yiddish and German in the latter.[83] In 1897, Judeo-Spanish was used in the AIU schools in Salonica[84] and in the lower grades of the school at Galata, but it was forbidden in the higher grades of the latter school.[85] Most schools also taught one or more of the following languages: Hebrew, Arabic, and Turkish.

The choice of one language over another had political implications, and these were particularly strong in Palestine, where they precipitated the "Language War." The Hebrew teachers opposed the HV's preference for German as the main language of instruction, especially in the planned Technikum in Haifa. As a result, local Hebrew teachers resigned from HV schools and established new schools and a teachers college. HV girls' schools and kinder-gartens were also affected, although in most of them Hebrew had already been established as the main language of instruction before 1913. The cam-paign to strengthen the position of Hebrew was waged more for political reasons than for educational ones. As a result of this campaign, Hebrew gained strength also in the AIU schools.[86]

Related to the issue of making Hebrew the language of instruction in the *moshavot* and in the Hovevei Tziyon schools in Palestine was the Hebrew teachers' decision to use the Sephardi pronunciation of Hebrew as the dom-inant one, despite the fact that most of the population served by these schools was Ashkenazi. This decision not only reflected the teachers' belief that the Sephardi pronunciation was more accurate, but apparently also ex-pressed a desire to establish closer relations with the Sephardim and to sever the ties with the "shtetl culture" of East Europe.[87] This decision by a small number of teachers had a lasting impact on the character of the modern He-brew language and culture in Israel and in Jewish communities around the world.

The revival of the Hebrew language had indeed acquired a central place in the Jewish national revival, and the important role of female education in this process was clearly expressed by those who initiated it: "We wanted that our daughters, the mothers of the next generation, would speak Hebrew, and as a result the children and the youth would also be compelled to use this language."[88] In other words, they believed that if babies were to hear their mothers speak Hebrew fluently and naturally, they too would acquire a free and fluent command of the language.

Jewish Intercommunity Relations

In some cases, the early schools were segregated along Jewish community (*edah*) lines. Thus, the Sephardi and Ashkenazi girls in the Rothschild and Montefiore schools in Jerusalem in the mid-1850s had separate classes and teachers belonging to their respective communities: the language of instruc-tion, the special customs, and some textbooks also reflected this division.[89] In the AIU school in Galata, a special class was opened for Russian and Ro-manian Jewish girls, with German as the language of instruction. But the school also tried to teach all students the dialect of the other community, and used French as a "neutral" language.[90] Some schools became more attractive to one community or another because of their orientation. In the HV schools in Jerusalem, for example, the Ashkenazim had been the majority, and their percentage increased from 66.5 percent in 1909 to 81.1 percent in 1913.[91]

In Palestine some educators and politicians believed that the schools should serve the purpose of nation building. Some were quite explicit about the fact that the schools should be a means for ethnic integration and inter-community marriages. They suggested that the main reason why Ashkenazi men refused to marry Sephardi women in Palestine was because these women were uneducated. They further argued that such marriages were highly desirable for the future of the Jewish people, because Sephardi women were hardworking, healthy, and very honest.[92] The process of national integration was undoubtedly facilitated by the decision of the Hebrew teachers to use Hebrew in the Sephardi pronunciation in all schools.[93]

Coeducation

Although not very common, coeducation existed in several forms and was due to a variety of factors. In those regions where little girls received traditional education, they often shared the classroom with boys until the age of eight or nine. Then the girls usually ended their schooling, while the boys continued on to more advanced studies.[94] Coeducation was also prevalent in most of the new kindergartens.

Most modern educational institutions were at first gender-based, although some of the later schools established around the turn of the century were coeducational from the beginning. At times, only some courses were coeducational: in Baghdad, for example, boys and girls attended English classes together in the school year 1905–1906.[95] In small communities, co-education resulted for the most part out of necessity: the community simply could not bear the burden of two separate schools and twice as many teachers. In fact, some communities could afford only one teacher and a one-class school.[96] In some places, although one school building accommodated both sexes, boys and girls studied in different sections or floors of the same building, or they studied at different times.[97] In quite a few cases, especially in Palestine, coeducation was driven by ideology intended to promote notions of equality between the genders.[98] Even where boys and girls studied separately in schools under the auspices of the AIU or the HV, in time a growing number of mixed-gender activities took place.

Interreligious Relations

Missionary schools provided the first locale where Jewish girls became exposed to contacts with members of other faiths, mainly Christians. As we have seen, while the official leadership of the Jewish community opposed missionary education, mainly because of fear of conversion, quite a few Jewish families opted to send their daughters to those schools for the benefits that they offered. This was true for all social classes within the community, but especially the poor.[99] In some institutions missionaries made a special effort to accommodate the particular needs of their Jewish students (e.g., kosher food) and at the same time to present Christian values in a Jewish guise.[100]

Interreligious contacts also occurred at the modern Jewish schools. Turks, Arabs, Ottoman Christians, and Westerners quite often sought admission to AIU schools. The new Hebrew schools in Palestine also attracted gentile students, apparently due to their high standards and the fact that they were the only modern schools available.[101] In these instances, there was no fear of conversion, and Jews could come into contact with gentiles in ways that were impossible within the traditional community setting. At a later period such contacts from school would become a growing channel of external influence on Jewish women.

Education and Social Class

In general, many students in the modern educational institutions at first came from the poorer classes, for whom a modern occupation and a general education were seen as a means for survival and a chance for upward mobility. Thus, poor girls and women were the first to attend the vocational workshops established by missionaries and the AIU.[102] Nonetheless, despite the obvious advantages of attending school, these institutions were often compelled to lure students by offering material benefits. This trend increased as the competition among the various institutions intensified and as Jewish interests began exerting pressure on parents to transfer their daughters from missionary to Jewish schools. As a result, until the end of the period, many schoolgirls were exempt from tuition fees.[103]

Contrary to the general trend, in Iraq well-off girls were the first to attend modern schools and only later did the poor join them in the AIU schools.[104] In Jerusalem one teacher observed that the students in the Evelina de Rothschild school represented all the Jewish communities and many of them were poor, whereas those at the Hebrew Gymnasium in Jaffa came from better-off families.[105] The students who attended the girls' school in Jaffa around 1899 came from the lower middle class and included poor girls, as is evident from the occupational background of their families.[106] In Alexandria wealthy parents were often reluctant to send their children to the AIU school because it was frequented by many poor and lower-middle-class children. Instead, the wealthy preferred to send their children to missionary schools or to hire AIU teachers as private tutors for their children in order to avoid what they regarded as undesirable contacts.[107] In Tripoli most of the students in the Italian schools were of the more Westernized, mercantile, and wealthier Jewish families, while many of the lower middle class and the poor went to the AIU school. Still, wealthier girls sometimes went to the AIU school after graduating from the Italian school in order to learn French or needlework for recreation. They were quite surprised to be in close contact with the poor, who sometimes surpassed them academically.[108] In the *moshavot* in Palestine, the economic background of the students was quite similar—most came from poor farming families, while some belonged to the service sector. Thus, it would appear that in many schools the economic position of the students reflected that of the general population in the area, while wealthier families tended at times to send their children to what were considered to be better schools. The latter category included some missionary schools and those that had a high school.

Adult and Extracurricular Programs

Educational and extracurricular activities in which women participated or which were intended for women only took place in several regions, especially in Palestine from the late nineteenth century on. At first the schools themselves initiated these activities, but later on they were organized by local societies as well. The participation of women in these activities was a sign of—as well as a means for—growing social and cultural openness, and they became as frequent and public as the general openness of the community allowed. In an increasing number of places, women felt free to pursue activities of intellectual enrichment and cultural entertainment. These included evening courses for school graduates who wanted some sort of continuing education.[109] In Palestine, Hebrew evening courses were offered for new immigrant women who did not know the language.[110] In Jerusalem in 1902, the Society of Young Women of Jerusalem (*Agudat Tze'irot Yerushalayim*) was established with the purpose of organizing evening cultural activities. This followed the formation of a similar society by a group of men. The women's society planned to mount lectures on Jewish history, literature, and current affairs as well as to offer instruction in the Hebrew language—all free of charge. Within a short time the society grew from 80 to 109 members aged fifteen and above. Some 40 students regularly attended the Hebrew evening classes that it offered.[111]

Some institutions, like the Betzalel College of Arts and Crafts in Jerusalem, conducted cultural activities open to the entire public.[112] Participation in a choir was a popular activity. In Jerusalem in 1910 a mixed choir was formed with girls from the HV school and boys from the Lämel school.[113] Some schools staged plays, recitals, and gymnastic performances—all open to the public, which in addition to family members often included state and town officials and members of the consular corps. The participation of girls in these activities was considered a novelty.[114]

◆　　◆　　◆

In the course of the nineteenth century, a combination of economic factors, various Western initiatives, and the emergence of an increasingly supportive environment paved the way for the rise of modern Jewish female education. To be sure, the number of educated women still lagged behind that of men. However, because traditional society for the most part did not provide for formal female education, in the new circumstances women became the only segment of the community whose formal education was entirely modern.

Female education was both a product of, and a major contributor to, the modernization of Jewish society. Within that society it paved the way for closer relations among classes and various Jewish groups, and it generated greater openness between the genders. On the whole, education improved the economic position of women and enabled some to reach out beyond the boundaries of their community. In spite of this, however, the social and political status of women was slow to change.

CHAPTER 11

The Siege of Edirne (1912–1913) as Seen by a Jewish Eyewitness

Social, Political, and Cultural Perspectives

Avigdor Levy

M uch has been published on the Balkan Wars (1912–1913) in general, and on the siege of Edirne (Adrianople) in particular, by journalists, diarists, historians, and others.[1] The Balkan Wars, it will be recalled, had the distinction of being the first twentieth-century international conflict on European soil, complete with the use of aircraft. The siege of Edirne by the Bulgarian and Serb armies, which lasted more than five months, was one of the war's most dramatic events, and it elicited much public interest in Europe and elsewhere. However, in spite of the considerable literature describing the military operations around Edirne, the number of accounts written by civilians who actually experienced the siege from within the city itself remains very limited.

The two best-known sources in this category are the journals of Paul Christoff[2] and Gustave Cirilli.[3] Both were published in several editions during 1913 and 1914, immediately following the war. These journals received wide circulation in the West and served as primary sources for a number of later studies. Christoff was a Catholic missionary, a member of the Augustine Order of the Assumption, employed at the French Catholic school Saint Basil at Karaağaç, a suburb of Edirne. Cirilli was a correspondent for the Paris newspaper *Le Matin* and the London Reuter (now Reuters) news agency. He had arrived in Edirne a short time before the beginning of the siege to report on the war.

More recently was published the journal of the Turkish *imam* (prayer leader, religious official) Hafız Rakım Ertür.[4] Ertür was descended from a family long established in Edirne, which produced several religious scholars and officials. He received a primarily religious education and in 1911 was appointed as "second imam" (*ikinci imam*), or assistant *imam*, at the Old Mosque (Eski Cami) in Edirne.

These three journals, while very valuable as the only published sources that present a picture of civilian life in besieged Edirne, also have their limitations. In 1912, Edirne was a relatively large city with several widely spread suburbs. Its population of over 100,000 consisted of Turks, Greeks, Jews, Bulgarians, Armenians, and various European nationals. For the most part this heterogeneous population tended to live in their own quarters and neighborhoods. Christoff and Cirilli spoke only European languages. Although both had access to Ottoman officials (Cirilli apparently more than Christoff), they moved about primarily among Europeans and local Westernized circles with whom they could communicate. Furthermore, Christoff's reports suggest that for the most part, he was limited to his institution at Karaağaç, which during the siege served as a field hospital, and most of his information appears to be secondhand. Ertür, on the other hand, spoke only Turkish, and his observations were limited to the Turkish-Muslim population and to the conduct of the military and civil officials with whom he was familiar.

For these reasons and others, the unpublished journal of Angèle Guéron, the director of the Alliance Israélite Universelle (hereafter: Alliance) school for girls in Edirne, which is located at the Alliance archives in Paris,[5] is important as a source that fills many gaps and complements the accounts presented by the three published journals mentioned earlier. Guéron, whose maiden name was Cohen, was born in 1886 in Istanbul, where she received an Alliance education. She continued her studies in Paris at the Alliance teachers college, known as l'Ecole Normale Israélite Orientale. After graduation, she was appointed as an instructor at the Alliance school in Tunis (1905) and later in Istanbul. In 1907 she became director of the Alliance school for girls at Haifa, and in 1909 she was transferred to Edirne as director of the girls' school in that city.[6]

As one raised and educated within the Ottoman milieu, Guéron was familiar with the local society, customs, and languages; and, of course, she also was a member of that urban, heterogeneous, Westernized Ottoman cultural elite. Her journal indicates that as a school director, Guéron had established a wide network of contacts in Edirne within the Jewish community, as well as with the local Ottoman authorities, foreign institutions, and leaders of other ethnic groups. Of the four diarists, Guéron was possibly the only one who could comfortably move among Edirne's heterogeneous population. She was at home with Europeans and the local Westernized elite, and at the same time she understood, with much sensitivity and compassion, the problems facing the poor Muslim masses. For this reason Guéron's observations are often more comprehensive and accurate than those of the other authors.

Guéron's journal also adds to the story of the siege the perspective of a woman. While the other three diarists tend to pay considerable attention to military operations, Guéron's main focus is on the human condition. Her journal tends to be more detailed and descriptive when dealing with subjects such as hunger, disease, and human suffering and uprootedness.

Finally, there is the Jewish perspective. The journals of Cirilli and Ertür hardly mention the presence of Jews in Edirne. Christoff, on the other hand, does write in an anecdotal fashion about individual Jews quite frequently. However, as we shall see below, his attitude toward Jews is generally so hostile and derogatory (and he makes no attempt to hide it), that it is difficult to take his information seriously, at least with regard to issues pertaining to the Jewish population.

Since the journals of Christoff and Cirilli, used as "primary sources" by a number of studies, refer to Jews marginally, anecdotally, or in negative stereotypes, it is not surprising that the historical literature that deals with the siege of Edirne contains hardly any references to the sizable Jewish population in the city and to their rather unique fate. The Carnegie report,[7] for example, discusses the Turkish, Greek, and Bulgarian populations in Edirne, but it almost completely fails to mention the Jewish population, in spite of the fact that the Jews were more numerous than the Bulgarians and they were about equal in numbers to the Greeks. In general, reading the Carnegie report, one has the impression that there were hardly any Jews in the Balkans. Guéron's journal is, therefore, a source that fills this gap, presenting much valuable and interesting information on the condition of the Jewish community during the siege.

Edirne and Its Jewish Community on the Eve of the Balkan Wars

In 1912, Edirne was the capital and administrative center of a large and central Ottoman province (*vilayet*) by the same name, comprising an area of 42,500 square kilometers and a population of almost 1,500,000.[8] The city of Edirne and its suburbs had a population of more than 100,000,[9] and according to one source, in 1912 the population consisted of approximately 55,000 Turks, 20,000 Greeks, close to 20,000 Jews, 10,000 Bulgarians, 6,000 Armenians, and an unspecified number of foreign nationals of various European states.[10]

Edirne was an important crossroads and a major Ottoman military, commercial, and economic center in the eastern Balkans. From a historical and cultural perspective, Ottomans regarded Edirne, a former imperial capital, as second only to the current capital, Istanbul. The political and economic importance of Edirne was underscored by the fact that Austria, Britain, France, Russia, and Bulgaria all maintained consulates in the city. In addition, the city had foreign schools, hospitals, and various religious institutions under the protection of Austria, France, and Italy.[11]

The Jewish community of Edirne was historically one of the oldest and most important in the Ottoman Empire. It was probably the largest and most important Ottoman Jewish center in the period between the Ottoman conquest of the city in 1361 and its transformation into the Ottoman capital and the conquest of Constantinople (Istanbul) in 1453 and the transfer of the capital to the latter city. In subsequent years other Jewish communities—especially those of Istanbul, Salonica, and Izmir—surpassed the community of Edirne in their size and importance. Nevertheless, until the end of the Ottoman era, Edirne was known as a vibrant and important Jewish cultural center.[12]

Following a period of decline in the eighteenth and early nineteenth centuries, the community became stabilized in the mid-nineteenth century and began flourishing anew. At the end of the nineteenth century, the numbers of the Jewish population increased from approximately 4,000–5,000 in

1870 to some 15,000 by the beginning of the twentieth century. The Jews constituted then approximately 17 percent of the city's total population that numbered 87,000, and they were the third largest group after the Turks and the Greeks.[13] This growth was due to some extent to Jewish emigration from eastern Europe and the Balkan countries, especially from areas that the Ottoman Empire had lost to the Balkan states following the 1877–1878 Ottoman-Russian war.[14] The Jewish population continued to increase in the first decade of the twentieth century, and in 1911 it numbered some 17,000.[15]

The community of Edirne was for centuries an important center of Jewish scholarship that produced a significant number of renowned rabbis, some of whom went on to serve as leaders of other Jewish communities.[16] As of the mid-nineteenth century, Edirne became a minor center of the Jewish Enlightenment *(Haskalah)* movement that sought to introduce modern values and education into Jewish life. Among the well-known figures active in Edirne were the linguist Joseph Halevi (1827–1917), the author Barukh Mitrani (1847–1919), and the educator Abraham Danon (1857–1925). In 1891, Danon founded in Edirne a modern seminary for the training of rabbis, which in 1898 moved to Istanbul. These leaders attracted circles of "seekers of enlightenment" *(maskilim)*, as they were known, who engaged in a variety of cultural and social activities.[17] Through the initiative and cooperation of these *maskilim*, the Alliance established in Edirne modern educational institutions, a school for boys in 1867 and a school for girls in 1870. Unlike in some other Jewish communities, from their early beginnings the Alliance schools in Edirne met with great success. By 1911 a total of 1,704 students were enrolled in these two schools, 1,077 at the boys' school and 627 at the girls' school. Approximately half of all the Jewish school-age children in town attended the Alliance schools.[18] In spite of the historical importance of the Jewish community of Edirne, little has been published about its recent historic past,[19] and this further enhances the value of Guéron's journal.

Why Guéron Wrote Her Journal

The journal's first entry is dated 30 October 1912, that is, three days after the Bulgarian army cut off the Edirne-Istanbul railroad line and with it the postal service with the outside world. Addressing the first entry (and the entire journal) to the president of the Alliance in Paris,[20] Guéron explains:

> *30 October 1912*
>
> My [previous] letter departed with the last train to Istanbul[21] and since then we are unable to communicate with the outside [world]. It is my intention to prepare for you a journal of political and academic developments . . . in order to send it to you with the first mail. When? This is just what everyone keeps asking himself anxiously. (1r)

The author makes it clear that she does not intend to write a personal journal, but rather an account of her official activities and those of the school during the siege. Indeed, the journal contains very little personal information about the author and her private life. On two occasions she indirectly mentions the fact that she has an infant boy, without giving his name or age. On one occasion she indirectly mentions her husband, again without disclosing his name.

While the journal gives us little information about its author's personal life, Guéron uses it extensively to express her views and opinions on a wide range of subjects: the war and the hardships of life under siege, the nature of the Ottoman state and society, the enemy and his conduct, and the Jewish community and its leadership. The journal devotes little attention to military operations, but it does describe their impact on the life of the civilian population in the city.

It would appear, however, that the journal had at least two additional objectives, not explicitly stated, the first self-understood and the other not. In the first place, the Alliance required its school directors to provide the organization's headquarters in Paris with regular, detailed reports not only on the operation of the schools, but also on the Jewish communities that they served. By writing the journal, Guéron fulfilled this basic obligation. In addition, however, it seems that the journal had the purpose of preserving its author's reputation. Several of Guéron's actions caused controversy within the Jewish community and met with opposition on the part of its leadership. It appears, therefore, that the journal was intended to document and defend its author's actions and positions. For this reason, one should, perhaps, treat with caution certain passages in the journal that deal with Guéron's conflict with Edirne's chief rabbi, Hayyim Moshe Bejerano (Becerano)[22] and other community leaders. In spite of this reservation, the journal has great value as a document that reveals much unknown information on life in Edirne during the siege, the condition of the Jewish community, and the activities of the Alliance school.

The image of the author that emerges from the journal's entries is that of a highly literate, young woman (Guéron was only twenty-six years old when the war broke out), energetic, independent, and strong-willed, with a taste for self-promotion. She is uninhibited in freely expressing her views and is not easily deterred from confrontation, even with her seniors. She considers herself an Ottoman patriot, fully dedicated to serving her country. Unlike many Western writers who at this period make no distinction between the terms *Turk* and *Ottoman,* Guéron generally uses these terms advisedly and accurately: Turks are a well-defined ethnic group; Ottomans are members of various ethnic and religious groups who consider the Ottoman state their homeland. In spite of her unquestionable dedication to her country, she observes the realities of her society with a critical eye.

Her devotion to the Ottoman homeland does not appear to come into conflict with her self-image as a representative (she even refers to herself as a missionary) of the Alliance, since the doctrine of that organization was to help Jews become useful, loyal, and well-integrated members of their societies. However, her role as representing the Alliance and her loyalty to that organization often bring her into conflict with the local Jewish leadership. Reading the journal, one senses that Guéron lives in a state of continuous tension between a sense of belonging and a feeling of alienation that exists on two levels. First, as a patriotic Ottoman, she usually identifies with that larger society. However, as a member of a small minority group, during periods of crisis and great frustration she sees herself as standing somewhat apart from that society. On another level, tension pervades her relations with the Jewish community. On the one hand, she is, of course, not merely an ordinary member of that community but one who occupies a rather significant leadership position within it. On the other hand, her loyalty to the Alliance and her conflicts with the community leadership often result in a sense of alienation from the community. On such occasions she sees the community, and especially its leadership, as petty, provincial, and opposed to progress, whereas the Alliance is an important international organization with a high-minded civilizing mission.

The following discussion of the journal's contents is arranged chronologically in sections, according to the different stages of the siege, each of which had its own characteristics. Although this article does not discuss the political and military aspects of the Balkan Wars, each section begins with a brief summary of the main political and military events relevant to that stage of the siege in order to place the events described in the journal within their historical context.

The Coming of the War and the Beginning of the Siege (1 October–21 November 1912)

Following months of growing tensions between the allied Balkan states (Bulgaria, Serbia, Greece, and Montenegro) on the one hand, and the Ottoman Empire on the other, and after it appeared that war was unavoidable, on 1 October 1912, the military commander of Edirne received orders to declare a state of alert and to begin mobilizing the reserves. On 8 October, Montenegro attacked Ottoman Albania and declared war on the Ottoman Empire. The following day, 9 October, both the Bulgarians and the Ottomans ordered a general mobilization, and martial law was established in Edirne. Government and foreign schools were closed and were prepared to serve as hospitals. Meanwhile on the Ottoman-Bulgarian front, clashes occurred between Bulgarian irregulars and the Ottoman army. On 18 October, Bulgaria formally declared war and its forces launched an offensive. On 22 October the Bulgarians defeated the Ottoman army at Kırklareli (known then as Kırkkilise), and Bulgarian forces reached the outlying suburbs of Edirne on 23 October. In battles that lasted from 28 October to 3 November, the Bulgarians again defeated the Ottomans at Lüleburgaz and their forces advanced to the Çatalca line, the last Ottoman defence line before Istanbul, while Edirne remained under siege behind the Bulgarian lines. Before the war the Ottomans had completed an elaborate system of defences around Edirne. Thus was created around the city a fairly sizable Ottoman pocket resembling a rectangle approximately fourteen kilometers long and ten kilometers wide, which included, in addition to the city of Edirne, several villages and farms.[23]

A Mass Exodus

The easy victories of the Bulgarians and their allies were primarily due to inadequate Ottoman preparedness for war in the Balkans. Since September 1911 the Ottoman Empire had been embroiled in a war with Italy, which first attacked Ottoman Libya and later extended the war to the Dodecanese Islands. The Ottoman-Italian war was concluded only on 18 October 1912, just as the Balkan states launched their offensive. For these reasons the Ottoman general staff had decided in advance of the war to adopt in the Balkans a defensive posture until the arrival of reinforcements from the empire's Asiatic provinces. Because of Edirne's proximity to the Bulgarian frontier, the Ottoman command anticipated the possibility that the city would come under direct Bulgarian attack. Consequently, the Ottomans prepared for a siege that they expected would last forty to fifty days, until the arrival of fresh reinforcements from the east. In order to alleviate anticipated shortages of supplies, in the beginning of October the Ottoman military command in Edirne issued instructions to evacuate from the city toward Istanbul women, children, and those unfit for military service.[24] These instructions resulted in a mass exodus of population from the city even before the beginning of the war. This was the first significant development related to the siege that affected the city's population. Because the evacuation is described somewhat differently in each of the four journals mentioned (Christoff, Cirilli, Ertür, and Guéron), it is possible for us to assess their accuracy and their authors' awareness of developments in the city.

According to Ertür, Muslim families of military and civil officials, among them Ertür's mother and other family members, began leaving the city early in October, following military instructions. Within a few days, by 5 October, the exodus of the Muslim population sharply increased and assumed the character of a mass flight.[25] Cirilli reports on 9 October, possibly on the basis of his contacts with Europeans and minority groups, that "the population is calm; but some wealthy families have left for Istanbul."[26] Following the first military operations and the mass exodus of the Muslims, unease in the city had increased. On 11 October, Cirilli reports on rising anxiety among the civilian population and a growing exodus,[27] and on 16 October he writes that "a very large number of Greek, Jewish, and European families have left Karaağaç and Edirne."[28] He does not mention Muslims. At this point it appears that mass flight had begun to affect also the minority communities, and among those who left the city were members of all the religious and ethnic groups represented in Edirne.

Christoff reports only on 19 October on a great exodus from the city and adds:"The rich Jews of Karaağaç were, naturally, the first ones to escape."[29] On 27 October he returns to this subject:"Not one rich Jew remains in Karaağaç and very few [Jews] remain in the city."[30] Christoff's reporting is, of course, far from reflecting the facts, at least on this subject. Among those who had left the city there were indeed many Jewish families and individuals, including Guéron's mother and sister (31r). According to Moïse Mitrani, director of the Alliance school for boys, "more than 500 Jewish families," mostly well-to-do, had found shelter in Istanbul.[31] In other words, perhaps 2,500–3,000 individuals, or approximately 15 percent of Edirne's total Jewish population, had left the city. Guéron's journal and Mitrani's letters make it abundantly clear that the great majority of the Jewish population remained in the city. In fact, it would appear that the ratio of Jews leaving the city was about the same as that of the general population, or perhaps even somewhat smaller. Guéron in her first entry, dated 30 October, summarizes this subject as follows:

> The first cannon shots [on 23 October] . . . caused the population to become agitated and increased the emigration [from the city]. . . . Turkish women, women and children . . . of government officials, were the first to leave on the day following the announcement of general mobilization. For days we could see on the road to Karaağaç only endless columns of vehicles, transporting passengers and luggage. . . . At the railroad station . . . the refugees waited, without complaint, . . . for hours, sometimes 12 to 15 hours, for the trains to depart. . . . They all left behind loved ones, not knowing whether they will ever see them again. (1r-v)

Guéron is the only memorialist who recalls that among the refugees there were many for whom this was not their first uprooting. Following the disastrous Ottoman losses in the 1876–77 war with Russia and the establishment of independent Balkan states, many Muslims, and among them some Jews, fled from the new states to the remaining Ottoman territories. Guéron continues with a great deal of empathy:

> In the frightened look of the old women it was possible to read memories of previous migrations, of previous uprootings, as if tacitly accepting this cruel law that 20, 30, 40 years earlier had driven them out of their homes and their lands, where the Crescent had protected them and from where the new masters forced them to leave under pressure.
>
> These scenes were repeated until Sunday, the 27th [of October], when the last train departed for Istanbul, carrying with it the last refugees and a sad procession of wounded. (1v)

Estimates of the total number of Edirne residents who left the city for Istanbul vary from 15,000 to 20,000,[32] or about 15 to 20 percent of the city's total civilian population.

Arrival of Refugees in Edirne

While many of Edirne's residents were still departing the city, as of 19 October, a growing number of refugees, fleeing before the advancing Bulgarians, began arriving in Edirne and its vicinity. Most of these refugees were Muslim, but there were among them also Jews and Greek villagers.[33] It is not known how many refugees found shelter in Edirne and the neighboring villages. Estimates vary from 20,000[34] to 40,000[35] and even 50,000.[36] (I am inclined to believe that the first estimate, 20,000, is closer to reality than the others.) Therefore, depending on the numbers of incoming refugees that one accepts, estimates of the total number of civilians in Edirne during the siege vary from 100,000 to 120,000, and even higher. According to official Ottoman sources, there were in Edirne during the siege about 106,000 civilians. (This estimate assumes that the number of incoming refugees was more or less equal to that of those who had left the city.[37]) In addition, the city had a military garrison of some 53,000 men.[38] It should be pointed out that more than a quarter of the Edirne garrison consisted of minorities—

Greeks, Bulgarians, and Jews—who numbered some 14,000 men. It was the first time in Ottoman history that the government drafted large numbers of minorities in accordance with the recent military reorganization and universal conscription laws.[39]

All sources are unanimous in describing the poverty and misery of the refugee villagers. However, the villagers brought with them their livestock and because of insufficient pasture, they began selling them for meat at low prices. During almost the entire siege, in spite of growing shortages in basic foodstuffs, Edirne had plenty of cheap meat. However, the meat's quality gradually declined due to the lack of pasture and the deteriorating condition of the animals. In describing these circumstances, Guéron again expresses her sensitivity to the plight of the villagers: "Poor peasant, his heart breaks when he departs from his beloved animals, which are all he has." (4r)

Guéron pays considerable attention to the destruction caused by the war. She foresees—and her apprehensions proved prophetic—that the war would devastate the area for many years to come:

30 October
There is destruction without mercy. As he advances, the enemy burns the Turkish villages; the Turks burn the Bulgarian villages. (2r)

17 January 1913
When the tens of thousands of refugees who found shelter in our city return to their villages, they will probably find their granaries burned, . . . their fruit trees cut, and their fields devastated. . . . Without the help of the young men who fell in battle and without their livestock, . . . how can they begin a new life? . . . Whatever may be the outcome of the war, our region, which is primarily agricultural, will have to go through many years of hardship before it can return to normal. It is necessary to see with one's own eyes the impact of the war in order to understand the full horror. (17r)

A Spy Scare

As soon as hostilities broke out, the Ottoman authorities in Edirne arrested several leaders of the Bulgarian community and executed a number of Bulgarians accused of spying for the enemy.[40] The city was rife with rumors that Bulgarian and Greek youths from the city and its vicinity had run away and joined the Bulgarian and Greek armies, respectively. There were also numerous reports that Bulgarians and Greeks serving in the Ottoman army had deserted and gone over to the enemy.[41] Indeed, as we will later see, the Bulgarian army succeeded in maintaining regular contacts with the Bulgarian community in the city. During the entire siege the city's population was gripped by fear that spies were regularly providing the enemy with vital information.[42] Guéron expresses these feelings:

30 October
The intelligence that the Bulgarians possess within the country strengthens them. They need not exert themselves in order to conquer. The Bulgarian and Greek peasants welcome them with open arms and rally to their cause. . . . The enemies' situation would have been different had they not been aided by spies in such a cowardly manner. (2r)

In spite of the fear of spies, during the entire siege the city did not witness any unrest or violence against minorities. Guéron traveled extensively throughout the city without any fear. Christoff writes that "the [foreign] consuls present at Edirne are unanimous in praising the correct attitude of the soldiers and the authorities" toward the Christian population.[43] Cirilli also notes that the "explosion of fanaticism" that some had expected never materialized and that "non-Muslims and especially foreigners feel as much secure [in Edirne] as in the best-policed cities of Europe."[44]

Isolation and Lack of Reliable Information

A subject that Guéron repeatedly brings up is the sense that prevailed in the city of complete isolation and lack of reliable information on the progress of the war. The railroad and telegraph lines that connected Edirne to the outside world had been cut off. Thus the population was prevented from receiving newspapers, letters, or telegrams. Edirne also possessed a wireless telegraph, but that was used only by the military. The authorities made periodic announcements by means of placards and handbills. These announcements, however, proved to be, time and again, unreliable. Consequently the population fed on rumors. Some examples:

5 November

The situation has decidedly become alarming. It seems that we are entirely besieged. I say "it seems," because we are lost in guesses. No certain news, nothing confirmed. . . . Siege. (3v)

19 December

The population is depressed, nervous, and thirsting for news. Some staff officers seem weary and sad. One of them . . . lets us clearly understand that we have been defeated. . . . Contradictory news circulates all the time. . . . This lack of knowledge of [what will happen] tomorrow, this uncertainty are intolerable. (13v)

6 January

An official announcement that appeared today congratulates the population and the garrison of Edirne for the courage, sacrifice, and dedication that they have demonstrated, . . . which will contribute to the improvement of the terms of the peace which, one hopes, is near. Unfortunately we know the value of these promises. (15r-v)

The Alliance School and the Jewish Community

After Edirne first heard the sound of cannon on 23 October, Guéron decided to close the girls' school, and she herself moved to Karaağaç. This suburb, situated about four kilometers from the center of Edirne, was believed less likely to be bombarded by the Bulgarians because of the European nationals and foreign institutions that abounded there. While Guéron was at Karaağaç, the chief rabbi assembled at the school the teachers and students of the two upper grades in an attempt to set up a sewing workshop to serve the needs of the army. Because this was done without Guéron's prior knowledge, it caused her much consternation. She records:

3 November

I think that [the chief rabbi] should have informed me in advance. Seeing that he was not obtaining any results, in spite of the supervision conducted by his son and daughters who had become transformed—I don't know how?—into inspectors of my school, he had me sought out at Karaağaç and asked me to come and put things in order at the workshop. I would have refused to respond to this invitation, *but I did not want it said that the school of the Alliance, at the time when the country needs its services, obeys any other sentiment except that of being useful.* (2v–3r; italics added)

This paragraph reflects issues that are repeated throughout the journal: first, the question of to what extent the Alliance school was under the authority of the community leadership; second, the need to demonstrate loyalty to the state.

In essence, the Alliance schools operated under a kind of dual control. While there were some local variations, in general, the Alliance administration in Paris was responsible for curriculum development and the training and appointment of school directors and teachers. The local community contributed toward the school's financial support and had some influence on its management and activities through a local school committee, known as *comité scolaire.* The journal makes it abundantly clear that Guéron, like most Alliance school directors, considered herself first and foremost as the representative of the Alliance and its interests, and her willingness to accept orders from the community leadership was generally limited. This attitude quite frequently led to tension and conflict. In any event, Guéron set up at the school a sewing workshop with seventeen sewing machines, including eight borrowed from the local agency of the Singer Sewing-Machine Company. The workshop manufactured and mended sheets, blankets, robes, and dressing for the wounded. The workshop served several hospitals, especially a small hospital established by the British consul, Samson (3r–v).

At the beginning of November, together with Rosa Avigdor, the director of the Alliance school for girls at Kırklareli,[45] who had found refuge in Edirne, Guéron organized a collection of gifts for wounded and sick soldiers. Within a few days they collected some 50 kilograms of preserves, some cloth, and 40 francs, with which they purchased tobacco. They sent it all directly to the governor *(vali)*, Halil Bey, with a note stating that this was the contribution of "several Jewish families who would have liked to be more wealthy in order to be more generous" (4v). They also used the note to report on the activities of the school's workshop and to express their complete dedication to the state, as well as their confidence in the final victory. The governor sent them back a letter of reply, thanking them for their efforts and praising the "true Ottoman patriotism" of all those who had taken part in the collection [5v–6r; 10 Nov.] The governor, however, sent his reply through ordinary channels, that is, by way of the chief rabbi. Even this insignificant incident became a matter of disagreement between Guéron and the chief rabbi. She records:

> *10 November*
> The chief rabbi found it necessary to express to me his displeasure that my initiative had not passed through his channel. I responded that *within my means as representing the Alliance, I had to give the government proof of [the Alliance's] sympathy for our country.* (6r; italics added)

Following an initial period of disruption, the city adjusted to the siege, and several schools reopened. On 12 November the Jewish community council (in the journal *Conseil Général;* in Turkish, *Meclis-i Umumi*) decided to renew classes in the Jewish schools in town immediately. The following day the chief rabbi sent Guéron a formal letter, instructing her to reopen the school. Guéron was opposed to that and presented her objections to the school committee. She argued that there were not enough teachers and instructional materials and that water, wood for heating, and money were lacking. On 13 November she writes: "At the same time I pointed out the improper manner of reaching a decision that primarily concerned me without consulting with me" (6v). The committee promised to take care of all the school's needs, and on 17 November the school reopened.

Within a few days, however, the school had to close again. On the evening of 21 November, the Bulgarians began a massive bombardment of the city's center and residential areas that lasted, with few pauses, until 4 December. On 22 November, the day after the beginning of the bombardment, four teachers and ten students showed up at school. Guéron cancelled classes and released the teachers and students. On that very day, she bitterly records in her journal: "The community that took upon itself the responsibility to reopen the school does not bother to find out what we are doing there" (9v).

The skirmishing between Guéron and the community leadership continued unabated. On 13 November Guéron records that "at the official request" of the director of the Sultaniye government hospital, she opened at the hospital a "branch" of the school's sewing workshop. Eight students, under the supervision of two teachers, worked at the hospital, sewing garments, underwear, and dressing for the wounded. A Jewish soldier was posted to guard the students and teachers (6r–7v). However, only a week later, on 20 November, Guéron reports that the establishment of the workshop at the Sultaniye hospital met with opposition on the part of the community leadership. It appears that the opposition was headed by the rabbinic council; and although this is nowhere explicitly stated, reading between the lines suggests that the objection was motivated by apprehension over the safety and moral well-being of Jewish girls employed in a military hospital populated for the most part by non-Jewish men. Without directly mentioning the argument, Guéron forcefully rejects it. She points to the fact that the girls never have the opportunity to come into contact with the patients: the workshop is located on the hospital's ground floor, whereas the patients are housed on the second floor; the students come to the hospital and depart only as a group, and they always are under the supervision of their teachers and the Jewish soldier. She also states that the girls working at the hospital were selected by her from the most respected families in town at the request of their parents, who "asked that their daughters be given the honor to serve their homeland in their own way" (8r). She further asserts that the workshop "brings honor both to the Alliance and to the community" (7v).

Guéron attributes the opposition to the workshop to envy of her success and of "the official marks of satisfaction" that she had received from the authorities (7r). The opposition also stems from the "fanaticism" of the rabbinic council, whereas "the chief rabbi follows it willingly or unwillingly. . . . But no one finds any fault that the chief rabbi's daughters attend to the wounded at the British hospital" (8r-v).

The chief rabbi, through one of the community's leaders, Joseph Bar-ishac (Bar-Yitzhak),[46] tried to convince Guéron to end the workshop's activity at the hospital. However, neither the rabbi nor any other member of the community's leadership was prepared to assume direct responsibility for such an act, which under the circumstances of the siege could have been interpreted as unpatriotic. Guéron, who understood the chief rabbi's dilemma, informed the leadership that she was prepared to close the hospital workshop provided she received formal instructions to that effect, *in writing*. But since no one was prepared to issue a written instruction, the hospital workshop continued to operate. Guéron records in her journal:

20 November
I suffer more [from this meanness] than from the isolation, privations, worries, and dangers that the siege reserves for us. But what is important is that the difficulties from which I suffer [still] permit me to be useful and *they provide me with the opportunity to demonstrate that I am a respectable missionary of the Alliance.* (8v; italics added)

However, the operation of the hospital workshop did not last very long. The Bulgarian bombardment that began on the evening of 21 November forced its closure. The following day, 22 November, Guéron went to the hospital and took the students that worked there back to their homes (9r). It would appear, however, that the workshop located at the school itself continued to operate a few more days, until 26 November, when the Bulgarian bombardment was particularly savage. Guéron records in her journal:

2 December
Since the panic of last Tuesday the girls do not go to the workshop anymore; I do not dare to take upon myself the responsibility to send them there. (11v)

The Bombardment of the Inner City
(21 November–4 December, 1912)

The bombardment that began on 21 November marked a new phase in the siege of Edirne. Until that date the Bulgarians had limited their attacks to military targets mainly on the perimeter of the Edirne enclave, well outside the city limits. On 17 and 18 November, the Bulgarians had launched a major offensive against the Çatalca line, but were repulsed with heavy losses. Consequently the Bulgarian command became determined to increase the pressure on Edirne. Strengthened by Serbian forces and new long-range heavy artillery, as of the evening of 21 November, the besieging forces began an indiscriminate bombardment of the city. The shelling continued with some pauses until 4 December (in spite of an internationally mediated agreement that called for an armistice on 3 December), and civilian life in Edirne was almost entirely paralyzed.[47] Here are some illustrative passages from Guéron's journal:

22 November
The situation has decidedly become serious. The Bulgarians have succeeded in installing several heavy cannons in a position . . . from which they can bombard the city. The enemy fires on Sultan Selim [mosque] where the wireless telegraph is located in order to deprive us of this last means of communication with the outside. . . . Since yesterday about one hundred shells exploded in the neighborhoods of Kıyık and Sultan Selim. . . . The bombardment and shooting continue without interruption. (8v–9r)

24 November
We expect to read official announcements of reassurance. But we hear nothing, and this is not a case where one can say, "no news is good news." Everyone prudently stays at home, trembling. . . . The bombardment of the inner city continues unabated day and night. . . . They are cowards, the Bulgarians, for thus attacking a peaceful population and mercilessly hitting women and children. (9v–10r)

26 November
The bombardment continues endlessly, and I begin to feel that my energy weakens and my infant, whom I breastfeed, begins to feel the consequences. . . . What will happen to us? . . . I am afraid of dying. I am afraid, it's true. . . . And our poor country, what will become of it in the face of so many united enemies while Europe is indifferent? . . . They would like to

tear our country to pieces, like another Poland, while Europe keeps quiet and considers all this as just, because she quietly whispers to herself: There will also be something in it for me. (10r-v)

2 December
Last Tuesday [26 November] the city's bombardment continued without mercy and in all quarters. Shells and bombs fell ceaselessly. Shrapnel exploded exactly over my head. Miraculously I was not hurt. My fear was indescribable. Even more fortunately, a few minutes after leaving the school's courtyard it was hit by shrapnel . . . that caused a large breach in the wall. (11r)

At this stage of the siege, most of Edirne's civilian population was concerned with two basic existential problems that only became more acute as time went on: first, to secure a shelter safe from the bombs; and second, to obtain food and fuel for cooking and heating. From this period on, the journal repeatedly describes growing shortages in basic commodities. Here is one example:

2 December
Food supplies are becoming smaller. So far we lack kerosene, sugar, salt, alcohol, and charcoal. Now it is necessary to besiege the bakery in order to obtain a loaf of bread. . . . Fortunately we had stocked some flour and we knead our bread at home. . . . The [foreign] consuls have placed their nationals in solidly constructed buildings where the cellars could provide relative safety from the bombs. The [Alliance] school for boys, which is built from stone, is completely packed, with two or three Jewish families sharing the same room. (11v–12r)

The Armistice Period (4 December 1912–3 February 1913)

Through the mediation of the Great Powers, Bulgaria and Serbia, but not Greece, agreed to an armistice with the Ottoman Empire as a preliminary for peace negotiations. The armistice was supposed to begin on 3 December and to last for one month. (It was later extended for another month, until 3

February 1913.) At the Edirne front the agreement was implemented one day later, on 4 December.

On 16 December the combatants began peace negotiations in London, but these quickly reached a stalemate. One of the main obstacles was the fate of Edirne, whose annexation the Bulgarians demanded, but the Ottomans refused to give the city up. In January, however, the position of the Ottoman government, headed by Kâmil Pasha, softened, and it was prepared to compromise. This, however, resulted in opposition in Istanbul. The Committee of Union and Progress, which was then in opposition and which rejected giving up Edirne, on 23 January staged a successful coup under the leadership of Enver Bey. The new Ottoman government, headed by the military leader Mahmud Şevket Pasha, was convinced that the Ottoman army still had a fighting chance; thus it was not prepared to give up Edirne and eastern Thrace. The negotiations in London broke down, and on 3 February the war was resumed anew at the Edirne front.

The first news about the armistice resulted in much joy, and hope, among Edirne's population. Guéron records:

> *4 December*
>
> Yesterday, Tuesday, the news regarding the armistice surprised us like a ray of sun after coming out from a long, entirely dark tunnel. Our joy is immense. This situation that we thought was insoluble will finally come to an end and we will again be able to see our distant parents who may think that we were forever lost. We were miraculously saved from death and we hope to start a new life. . . . A dispatch—true, from an official source—that quickly circulated through the city, announces a great victory of our armies. . . . This is a brilliant achievement for our country. It is said that the Bulgarians are encircled from all sides and that they are starving. (12r-v)

However, the joy and enthusiasm did not last long. The bombardments did indeed stop, but Edirne remained isolated and starving. The armistice agreement did not permit the Ottomans to reprovision the city. On the other hand, the Bulgarians could use the railroad line that passed through the Edirne enclave and the station at Karaağaç to resupply their forces in eastern Thrace.

The Beginning of Hunger and Epidemics

During this stage of the siege—and, in fact, until its very end—the journal increasingly deals with the following issues: severe shortages of foodstuffs, medicines, and other essential supplies; the spread of disease and epidemics and a general deterioration of health conditions; a growing demoralization of both civilians and the military; and a concomitant loss of confidence in the leadership abilities of the Ottoman administration. Here are a few illustrative passages:

> *18 December*
> The cost of living has increased since the beginning of the siege and it continues to rise with every passing day. Basic necessities cost more that what [even] people of means can afford to pay. . . . The price of bread and flour has doubled; that of vegetables, eggs, and pasta tripled. Meat, which used to be in abundance at the beginning of the siege, is becoming more expensive every day. Misery is becoming more cruel day by day. . . . Salt water [used to preserve] cheese has replaced salt in baking bread and cooking vegetables. This salt water that was normally thrown out now sells at food stores for one franc per okka.[48] In addition, the poor must often stand in line for hours before they can buy a limited quantity [of groceries]. . . . Sanitary conditions leave much to be desired. Scarlet fever, cholera, and dysentery have broken out. Our children drink water from the Arda river which is contaminated with corpses. (13r-v)

And again on food shortages one month later:

> *19 January*
> As time passes, stocks in the food stores decline. Beans, peas, rice, pasta, potatoes, and whatever else could replace bread command the price of gold. At the bottom of the warehouses were discovered rotten beans and dried-up peas dating from years ago. They were snapped up within a few

days and now no longer can be found. . . . The poor suffer terribly. The financially privileged still have some salt manufactured chemically and sold for the price of pharmaceutical products. (18v)

Growing bread shortages forced the authorities to post guards near the bakeries in order to maintain order:

19 January
Around the bakeries, which are guarded by soldiers, there is always a crowded mass of people that patiently wait for hours before obtaining a tiny loaf of black and bitter-tasting bread, half-baked and full of bits of straw.[49] The flour used for baking this bread contains a miniscule quantity of grain. Only the millers know what else it contains. (18v)

Bulgarian Supply Trains

Given the growing famine, the sight of Bulgarian supply trains travelling through Edirne greatly demoralized the city's population. Ottoman sources set the number of trains that passed through Edirne during the armistice period at 120, consisting of 3,600 freight cars.[50] Here are some examples of Guéron's reaction:

19 December
We are beginning to doubt [the possibility of attaining] victory. The road that is closed to us is open for provisioning the enemy's armies. Trains full of provisions pass through Edirne without stopping. (13v)

1 January
While we are rationing our flour and eat bread without salt, . . . hundreds of Bulgarian train-cars full with provisions cross our station [at Karaağaç] and the very proud engine-drivers grant us a patronizing salute. (15r)

However, the Bulgarian trains did not cross Edirne without leaving something behind. The Bulgarians would surreptitiously drop packages of Bulgarian and French newspapers in order to inform the population of the

Ottoman Empire's hopeless situation.[51] Guéron's journal reveals that this is how the besieged population learned about the London peace negotiations [13v, dated 19 Dec.; 19v, dated 22 Jan.], the Ottoman defeats on the various fronts [15r, dated 1 Jan.], and the change of government in Istanbul. To the last piece of news Guéron reacts with the following comments:

26 January
One blow after another. We hear about the assassination of Nazım Pasha, the fall of Kâmil Pasha's cabinet, and the return to power of the Young Turks. We are gripped with anxiety, because we know that the party in power is very warlike. (19v)

Toward the end of the armistice period, Guéron's journal reflects increasing desperation and a complete lack of trust in the authorities:[52]

17 January
Exactly three months ago hostilities began; we have been under siege here more than two and a half months, and more than one and a half months ago the armistice was signed. . . . Every day they announced to us the imminent arrival of a supply train from Istanbul, and every day the facts have crushed our hopes. We no longer believe anything, except what we see with our own eyes. And what we see is, alas, pitiful. . . . The pastures that were green until some fifteen days ago have disappeared under the cover of snow. The few animals left alive no longer have the strength to scratch the ground [with their hooves] in order to reach the grass. . . . On the frozen road . . . we see fallen cattle that died of starvation. Will this be soon [our] fate? (16r–v)

The School and the Jewish Community

The armistice made it possible to reopen the girls' school for a short period of time.[53] Guéron reports the resumption of classes with a total lack of enthusiasm:

15 December

The school committee asks me to reopen the school. Without personnel, without students (380 children out of 900 arrive at school), without water (the water pipes have been destroyed by the Bulgarians), without wood for heat, and without materials, I reopen the school and request that every effort be made to pay our teachers a partial payment of their salaries. (12v)

It appears that during this period the school's sewing workshop resumed its activities, since Guéron records on 18 December that "the workshop continues to operate in the service of the wounded" (13v). However, due to the deteriorating sanitary conditions in the city, on 25 December the Ottoman authorities ordered the closure of all schools, and Guéron readily complied. (14r)

The payment of salary to the school staff was another recurrent issue that placed further strains on Guéron's relations with the community leadership. On 2 December she writes:

In the midst of this misery, our poor teachers still wait to receive their salaries that are already three and four months late. *In spite of my repugnance to approach that which at this moment constitutes the community,* I have returned ten times to request a little money for them, and I only received . . . promises. (12r; italics added)

On 18 December she again returns to the same subject:

For four days they have promised me 50 [Ottoman] pounds out of 500 that the Alliance, the Hilfsverein,[54] and B'nai B'rith cared to send to our community by means of the wireless telegraph. So far I have not received a penny. The misery of our teachers is horrible. I lend them money and sink into debt. (13r)

The hardships of the school's staff and the inability—or as Guéron saw it, the lack of interest—on the part of the community leaders to help, became common themes during this phase of the siege. On 17 January she records that the chief rabbi's office requested, "in the name of the teachers," a supply of salt from the director of the Ottoman Public Debt Administration[55] in Edirne. The latter sent a dozen kilograms of salt intended "for the staff of the Jewish schools." According to Guéron, four kilograms were distributed to rabbis closely associated with the chief rabbi. Joseph Barishac, a member of the school committees of both Alliance schools, received one and a half kilograms, "and the rest disappeared; and neither my teachers nor the teachers of the boys' school have received one gram" (18r-v).

In contrast to Guéron's poor relationship with the Jewish leadership, the journal describes several instances of assistance and cooperation across community lines:

21 January

My teachers are suffering from hunger. Some of them have been eating for many days [only] boiled corn and one has not eaten a thing for an entire day. I was able to bring their suffering to the attention of Mrs. [V. L.] Fundukliyan, the wife of the principal shareholder of the flour mills company,[56] who did the impossible and sent me four sacks of flour. . . . I immediately caused the flour to be distributed under my own eyes, in your name [Mr. President], confident of your approval. (19r-v)

Fundukliyan is an Armenian name. The journal leaves no room for doubt that this was an act of charity and not a business deal. In the circumstances of siege and hunger that characterized Edirne in the latter part of January 1913, this was indeed a very generous gesture. It would appear that Guéron also received some flour from the French consul, Marcel Cuinet, but her efforts to obtain help from the Austrian consul were unsuccessful at this time (29v, dated 13 Feb.). The journal makes reference to the fact that the foreign consuls were in contact with the Ottoman authorities to secure the needs of their nationals.

The Last Phase of the Siege (3 February–24 March 1913)

By the end of January the peace negotiations in London had collapsed and hostilities resumed on 3 February. The foreign consuls made a last attempt to secure within Edirne a neutral zone that would not be bombed, or alternatively, to permit foreign nationals to leave the city. These attempts, however, failed.[57] From the third to the eighth of February, the Bulgarians and Serbs unleashed a heavy and continuous bombardment of the civilian quarters of Edirne. The shelling was directed for the most part at the Turkish quarters, although it did not spare the other parts of town. It caused many casualties and much destruction of property. Among the buildings hit at this time were both Alliance schools.

On 5 and 6 February, Bulgarian planes flew over Edirne and dropped leaflets describing the defense of Edirne as hopeless and futile.[58] Among other things, the leaflets revealed considerable knowledge of conditions within the city. One leaflet declared: "Officers and citizens of Edirne! They promised you trains with flour, sugar, rice, and baklava, . . . but nothing arrived except war. They promised you that the Turkish army would arrive within a few days, but the Turkish army remains impotent, corrupt, disintegrated" (22v). The leaflets urged soldiers and citizens to surrender. Guéron surmised that the bombardment combined with the dropping of leaflets was intended to break the spirit of the city's defenders (24v).

Just before the renewal of hostilities on 3 February, Edirne witnessed uncommon activity as its population, already experienced in the horrors of bombardment, scurried to find shelter in solidly built stone structures. The old khans at the city's center were considered among the most secure shelters. Here in some two hundred dark and damp rooms that normally served as offices, shops, and storerooms were crowded, according to Guéron, some four hundred families, including many Jews. Every room—used for cooking, dining, and sleeping—sheltered between ten and twenty persons. The Catholic schools and the Alliance boys' school that was located on Istanbul Yolu, Edirne's main street, were also desirable shelters (20r, 25r). Following a visit to the latter school, Guéron recorded:

13 February
The office of Mr. Mitrani [the school director], the teachers' lounge, the classrooms, the basement rooms have all been invaded. All settled down as best they could in one corner of a classroom, barricading themselves with benches. . . . The basement that was first used only during periods of bombardment, also became crowded with families. . . . It is difficult to

imagine a sight more distressing than this basement, smelling like a damp and cold tomb. . . . When I entered it the dampness and an acrid odor of tobacco choked me. (29r).

According to Mitrani, over five hundred Jewish families had found shelter at the school since the first bombardments. The building received two direct hits and it was damaged, but no one was hurt. Mitrani proudly writes that in spite of the very crowded conditions and the epidemics that were common in the city, there was not one case of an epidemic disease among those who had found refuge at his school "thanks to very strict preventative measures that were maintained until the end of the siege." During the months of the siege, three elderly persons died of "natural causes" and were "replaced" by the birth of three infants.[59]

This time the bombardment did not spare Karaağaç, and thus, on 7 February, Guéron and her husband decided to leave their home and find a more secure shelter in one of the large stone buildings. Guéron records on 12 February that after a frantic search they were able to find refuge, with the help of the Austrian consul Hertsfeld,[60] at a school for girls administered by the convent of the Sisters of Agram of Saint Mary of Lourdes. The convent and school were under Austrian protection. At the time of their arrival, the school already provided shelter to some 150 persons, including European nationals and local Jews, Armenians, and "even Turks."[61] In this disparate crowd, writes Guéron, "hostilities are born and friendships are formed" (28v). The Guéron family settled into the corner of a large classroom populated already by four other families. They stayed there for almost six weeks, until 24 March.

The heavy shelling of civilian quarters between 3 and 8 February led the foreign consuls in Edirne to telegraph to their embassies in Istanbul protest notes, and it would appear that these proved helpful. As of 9 February the shelling was directed primarily against military targets. Civilian neighborhoods still continued to come under fire, but less intensely and with the object of causing more harassment than damage.

During this period, shortages in foodstuffs, medicines, fuel, and other vital supplies grew more acute day by day and prices of essential goods sharply increased. Forests and orchards around Edirne gradually disappeared as their wood was used for cooking and heating. Toward the end of February, the army began slaughtering its horses, offering their meat to the population (30v, dated 24 Feb.). Hunger became more widespread, affecting most severely the refugees and lower classes. At the end of January, the authorities began searching shops, storehouses, and private homes for hidden stores of food and vital supplies.[62] These searches continued until the fall of the city, and from time to time large quantities of food were discovered and confiscated. These searches resulted in the complete disappearance from the open market of all basic commodities with the exception of meat and cheese. A black market flourished in basic foodstuffs, especially in flour, salt, sugar, and legumes.[63] Amid the hunger and misery emerged a new class of war profiteers, who reportedly amassed fortunes at the expense of the public's misfortune (35v–36r, dated 9 Mar.).

The authorities attempted to secure for the poorer classes, and especially the refugees, a basic daily food allowance. In early March this consisted of 200 grams of bread—"something shapeless, black, and clammy that through habit is still called bread" (32r, dated 1 Mar.)—and miniscule quantities of cheese and meat. On the same date Guéron reports that the authorities had decided to increase the volume of flour by adding to it ten percent sand. The local medical council protested, declaring the bread to be unfit for human consumption (32v).

On 9 March, Guéron reports that the bread rations have been further reduced to 100–150 grams and that starvation has already claimed the lives of "hundreds" of victims (35r-v). In the fields that had just begun to become green again, "humans compete with animals over the new grasses that inflame their intestines and make them forget their hunger" (35v).

As hunger became more and more widespread, public order and safety declined. At the bakeries the public no longer waited patiently for hours. Instead, mobs began storming the stores, desperately struggling with the military guards before obtaining a "microscopic loaf of bread." Also, the number of burglaries, especially of uninhabited houses, greatly increased. The police admitted to its inability to prevent the break-ins and advised the public to post their own guards (35r, dated 7 Mar.).

In spite of the widespread misery and signs of deteriorating public order, the population remained generally quiet and disciplined. "A dull exasperation has seized the hungry people, but they always remain calm and apprehensive. Discontentment does not dare to express itself publicly" (32r, dated 1 Mar.). Guéron attributes this phenomenon to the "very heterogeneous" nature of the Ottoman urban population. At the end of February a public demonstration of several hundred women and children marched on the governor's mansion demanding bread, but it dispersed quietly. A larger demonstration was subsequently planned, but it never materialized. Guéron ascribes this to the passivity and lack of initiative that characterize Ottoman society (32v, dated 1 Mar.).

During this period Guéron's journal entries reveal extreme changes of mood. Hope is quickly replaced by utter desperation. Guéron's harshest criticism of the Ottoman system is expressed at this time:

7 February

The unhealthy atmosphere that spreads from the head to the limbs, from the government to the army, from the capital to the provinces has been the principal cause for the Turks' defeat. People wonder through what miracle Edirne and the Ottoman Empire still hold out with a government whose patriotism is lacking, an army that is poorly trained and poorly provisioned [and led by] officers who are inferior to their adversaries as far as training and dedication. . . . Officers bring prostitutes to their tents, even during combat. . . . The commandant of Edirne must maintain [the army] . . . in a constant state of alert in order to prevent officers from frequenting places of debauchery.[64] The military commissariat that was aware of the probable siege has nevertheless refused to grant merchants authorization to import [to Edirne] stocks of salt, sugar, and kerosene . . . because the officers had not received sufficient bribes. With the complicity of the authorities who had an interest in the matter, the flour mills continued to sell flour [privately] at exorbitant prices. . . . While the poor die of starvation and the bread is rationed and often is entirely unavailable, highly placed people gather at banquets. (26v–27r)

Toward the end of the siege, however, as the bombardment continued and misery and privations reached their peak, Guéron was at times overcome by defiance, pride, and patriotic feelings:

3 March
Our siege will be remembered for a long time to come. The memory of our suffering . . . will remain engraved on our hearts. We stand proud and strong in front of the enemy's shells. . . . Dear Bulgarians, what right do you have to strike at us indiscriminately, to mutilate women and children, and to burn our homes without mercy? . . . Do you think to frighten us and thereby reduce our resistance? Certainly not. . . . Do you think that we are not as valiant [as you] and that because of a few [civilian] victims killed indiscriminately, while so many brave [soldiers] fell in battle, we will surrender our beautiful and dear city Edirne? The strident shrieks of your shells . . . do not impress us any more. . . . We ridicule those [shells] that so often miss their mark. (33v–34r).

The Jewish Community

While Guéron at times writes disparagingly of the Ottoman administration, her most severe criticism and anger are reserved for the leadership of the Jewish community. When Guéron visited the numerous Jewish families who had found shelter in the khans at the center of town, she was dismayed to find out that the population there passed their time gambling, playing with dice and various games of cards. Men, women, young and old were engaged in this activity during most hours of the day and night:

7 February
It is truly heartrending to see the best of our youth and those who lead our community thus waste their time, which they could have used more productively and effectively to help the poor among our coreligionists. (25v)

Guéron fully realizes that the circumstances of bombardment and confinement leave room for few activities with which to pass the time. She also knows, however, that among those who gamble there are many poor—even those who live on charity—who can hardly afford to risk funds needed for their very survival and that of their families. This leads her to accuse the Jewish leaders, and principally the chief rabbi, of negligence, selfishness, and lack of leadership. She argues that they have not done what they could for the community poor, thereby contributing to a deplorable situation (25r–26v, dated 7 Feb.). She reports that international Jewish organizations have sent the Jewish community, through the wireless telegraph, 1,500 Ottoman pounds (*lira,* sing.) in three installments of 500 pounds each.[65] The money was intended for the community poor. Guéron maintains that through the Circle of Charity (*La Cercle de la Bienfaisance)*[66] she has urged the leadership to purchase foodstuffs with the money and to distribute flour to the needy instead of cash. Her intention was to assure that the aid would help families and not be squandered on gambling or otherwise wasted:

7 February

When the second and third installments of 500 pounds each arrived, there was still enough time to procure bread for our needy coreligionists from members of our community who still possessed important stocks of cereals that had not yet been confiscated. But nothing was done. Due to personal interests, stupidity, or to avoid the inconvenience of purchasing the flour and distributing it, we allowed ourselves to be convinced that the siege is about to be over. At the same time, the Christian communities quietly provided their members with food for weeks and months. The chief rabbi, whose duty it was to protect the poor and to rally and encourage all people of good will to organize aid, devolved his responsibility on a committee whose uncontested leader became Joseph Barishac and which was satisfied with the distribution of the money that came from the outside, perhaps honestly?

Relying on the bourgeoisie and knowing how to flatter influential persons, the chief rabbi sacrifices the true interests of the needy, whom he should protect, in order to gain marks of honor from the authorities and cause them to praise him at even higher places. This chief rabbi has no true dignity. He is kind to the rich and harsh toward the poor. . . . Our community is in need of a man of courage to help it struggle against the destructive influences of the environment. In spite of the efforts of the Alliance, we are still not adequately progressive and we are in need of a truly superior man capable of guiding us at this critical time, awakening and channeling our generous sentiments. (26r-v)

It seems that the issue of help for the poor had become a subject of controversy within the Jewish community. Moïse Mitrani also addresses this subject and writes—perhaps in response to Guéron's accusations—that the Jewish leadership had indeed intended to stock provisions in order to help poor families during the siege. However, according to Mitrani, the community did not have adequate financial resources. With the help of private contributions collected within the community, sufficient resources were gathered to help the poor for one month only. However, by the beginning of November 1912, the community had exhausted its resources, and it was at that time that financial assistance began arriving from the outside. Mitrani admits that the Greek and Armenian communities were able to organize a more effective system of assistance for their poor than did the Jewish community. According to Mitrani, the great majority of the Jewish population, like their Muslim neighbors, were forced to eat the poor-quality bread produced in the bakeries under the supervision of the military authorities. Those who ate that bread subsequently became ill and some had died.[67]

The Fall of Edirne (26 March 1913)

Toward the middle of March, the bombardment of the city subsided, and it came to a complete halt around the twentieth of the month, although on the front lines the fighting continued to rage. In view of the peaceful conditions in the residential areas, on 24 March the Guéron family left the Catholic school and returned to their home in Karaağaç at the urging of the head of the convent. Two days earlier, on 22 March, Guéron recorded in her diary:

> The enemy has not bombarded the city for the last two or three days. Nevertheless, we have reason to believe that some decisive event is about to take place. From a source that is ordinarily well-informed, *we hear that the Bulgarian community [in town] have received a letter from the commander of the besieging forces, informing them that the final assault would take place on Wednesday, 26 March.* We refuse to believe that the capture of Edirne is possible, having become accustomed to consider the city as impregnable. (37v–38r; italics added)

Indeed, on the night of 24 March, the Bulgarian and Serb forces launched a massive bombardment of Edirne and its defences, followed by an all-out ground assault that lasted until the early morning hours of 26 March, when the city finally surrendered.[68]

The First Balkan War formally ended with the Treaty of London (30 May 1913) that ceded Edirne and other territories to Bulgaria. On 29 June 1913 the Second Balkan War began, pitting Greece and Serbia against Bulgaria. Rumania and the Ottoman Empire also declared war on Bulgaria, and the Ottoman army reentered Edirne without opposition on 21 July. The Peace Treaty of Constantinople (Istanbul) of 29 September 1913 confirmed the return of Edirne and much of eastern Thrace to Ottoman control.[69]

Conflicting Reports about Brutality during the Balkan Wars

As a truly twentieth-century conflict, the Balkan Wars were characterized by a great deal of cruelty and brutality committed against combatants as well as civilians. Mass murder, torture, rape, wholesale looting and destruction, and the expulsion of civilian populations from their homes (what we know today as "ethnic cleansing") were quite common and received wide coverage in the international press. The combatants accused one another of serious war crimes. Reports by journalists and other observers tended to be partisan. Edirne's conquest and occupation by the Bulgarian army for a period of almost four months also became the subject of serious recriminations on the part of the Ottoman and Greek governments, as well as journalists and other observers. The report prepared by the Carnegie Endowment for International Peace, published as a book that with its appendixes is more than 400 pages long, studies this subject in some detail. It can still be considered, in spite of its lacunae, as the most comprehensive and objective study available.[70] It should be pointed out, however, that the authors of the report collected testimony from Turkish, Bulgarian, and Greek eyewitnesses and spokesmen, but, as far as is known, not from Jews.

With respect to Edirne's occupation by the Bulgarian army, the Carnegie report determines that there were two principal charges made against the Bulgarians: first, that they behaved with great cruelty and brutality toward the Ottoman prisoners of war; second, the Bulgarian authorities permitted the pillaging of the property of Edirne's Turkish population for three days after the city's surrender.

With regard to the first charge, the report strongly affirms that "when all . . . admissions have been made, there remains as a fact not to be denied, the cruel indifference in general to the life of the prisoners."[71] The report and its appendixes contain graphic descriptions of how, during severe winter weather, wounded, sick, and starving Turkish soldiers were kept for days in the open, without shelter, without medical care, and either without any food or without adequate food. As a result, many Turkish soldiers died from cold, starvation, and disease after the city's surrender. Moreover, the report clearly determines that Bulgarian soldiers killed prisoners of war after their surrender.[72] One incident recurs in several accounts. It describes the killing of a Turkish officer holding the rank of captain, Ismail Yüzbaşı on the street in Edirne, in front of many eyewitnesses, during the first day of the occupation. The officer, who was too weak to march, was mercilessly beaten by a Bulgarian soldier with the butt of his rifle. A Jewish passerby named Salomon Behmi tried to help the Turkish officer, but both were killed by the Bulgarians.[73] The journals written by Christoff and Cirilli also contain many details describing the murder and abuse of prisoners.[74]

The second principal charge concerning the pillaging of Turkish property is more problematic. According to Christoff, even before the Bulgarian army entered the city, while the Turkish troops were disarming themselves, Greek residents of Edirne "began to pillage with a frenzy. . . . The Turks let them carry everything away without saying a word."[75] Further on, Christoff adds that the entry of the Bulgarian army to Edirne was

a signal for murder, theft, and pillage [committed on the Turkish population] by the Greeks, Bulgarians, Armenians, and Jews. Not one Turkish home was respected and we must add that not only material property was violated. Many Bulgarian and Serb soldiers widely participated in the disorders.[76]

Cirilli describes the entry of the Bulgarian and Serb forces into Edirne on 26 March as orderly. The conquering troops were met "with indescribable enthusiasm . . . by Greeks, Jews, and Armenians."[77] However, what followed the first day of occupation he describes thus:

On the following day, what a terrible awakening! . . . During three consecutive days the city is being sacked. The Turkish homes in particular are delivered to the pillage of a brutal soldiery, thirsting for vengeance. . . . [They] rape, kill, and plunder whatever falls into their hands . . . and crush to pieces furniture that cannot be carried away. [They] are aided by Jews, Armenians, but mostly Greeks . . . who take their share of the profits.[78]

The Carnegie report concludes that there was indeed extensive pillage, but that these acts were carried out mainly by the civilian population of Edirne itself, "to some extent [by] the Jews and Armenians, but mainly [by] the Greeks who simply fell upon the undefended property of the Turks."[79] The report generally lauds the efforts of the Bulgarian army to establish order in the city, and it determines that this was the policy of the Bulgarian military command, although here and there Bulgarian soldiers were "induced by their Greek hosts to take part in pillage." The report concludes that by the third day after the occupation, the Bulgarians were generally successful in establishing order in the city.[80]

The Carnegie report relies heavily on an early edition of Christoff's book, published in Edirne shortly after the siege.[81] However, in view of the Jewish public's decidedly pro-Ottoman sentiments, the affirmation that Jews (and Armenians, for that matter)[82] participated in the plunder of Turkish homes appears strange. Christoff's negative attitude toward Jews is an established fact. Is it possible that the Carnegie report, which relies heavily on Christoff, simply repeats his assertions? Still, we also have Cirilli's account, unless he, too, is merely following Christoff, whose book was published first.

Those who drafted the final version of the Carnegie report evidently chose to ignore one aspect of one of the report's appendixes. This is an official account by the former Bulgarian military magistrate at Edirne, Topaldjicov, who writes:

It is true that a certain number of Turkish and Jewish houses were pillaged, but not by our soldiers. The local Greek population alone are to be blamed for these crimes. I was able to see this and to verify it personally many times. . . . When order was reestablished in the city, numerous complaints of offences committed by the Greeks, such as the looting of houses, incendiarism, pillage and so on, were addressed to me.[83]

In another appendix, a report first published in the London *Daily Telegraph* on 20 August 1913, the journalist Machkov writes that almost all "the better Mussulman houses" were pillaged. But this fate was not limited to Turkish homes. "Those belonging to Greeks and Israelites suffered in the same way." Machkov, however, attributes these acts to Bulgarian soldiers and officers. He specifically mentions the plunder of the homes of three wealthy and well-known Jewish families in Edirne—Rodrigues, Benaroya, and Moses Behmoiras.[84]

The general picture that emerges from these conflicting accounts is that during the transition from Ottoman to Bulgarian rule and the disorder that accompanied it, especially in the early days, many families, possibly representing all the ethnic groups in Edirne, suffered from some sort of abuse. However, systematic pillage and plunder were directed primarily against the Turks and the Jews, while the main persecutors were Greek residents of Edirne and Bulgarian soldiers who joined them. The Greeks were the largest community in Edirne after the Turks, and their ambition was to see Edirne annexed to Greece.[85]

Guéron's journal confirms this conclusion. In her last entry, dated 27 March, one day after Edirne's surrender, she writes:

> This morning several Jewish families have witnessed their homes pil-
> laged by Greeks and Bulgarian soldiers. A dozen of the culprits were
> caught in the act and imprisoned. What is most troubling is that only Jew-
> ish homes have been pillaged, not only with an intent to steal, but with
> motives of hatred and vengeance. The furniture that the pillagers could not
> carry away they have destroyed and broken into pieces.
>
> A rumor is spreading, disseminated by the Greeks, that we, Jews, had
> sustained Ottoman resistance through our efforts and our money, and that,
> were it not for us, Edirne would have fallen a long time ago. Even if it were
> true, should it not have added to the victors' joy for having been able to

conquer a population capable . . . of demonstrating energy and patriotism? But how can one reason with anti-Semitism? (40r-v)

It should be remembered that Guéron's last entries are from the day of Edirne's surrender and the following day (26 and 27 March). Moreover, it would appear that during these two days, due to the uncertainties of the occupation, Guéron did not dare to leave the area of her residence in Karaağaç that, as has been pointed out earlier, was a well-to-do suburb where foreign institutions and European nationals abounded. It is reasonable to assume, therefore, that public safety at Karaağaç was better than what could be expected in other quarters of Edirne; and yet Jewish homes were looted even at Karaağaç.

In her final entries Guéron describes an orderly transition from Ottoman to Bulgarian rule. The Bulgarian soldiers in her neighborhood are friendly: "They generously distribute sugar and salt and ask for flowers in return" (39r, dated 26 Mar.). Her first impressions of the Bulgarian army are positive, and she expresses admiration "for the Bulgarian talent that was capable of making such a great effort . . . and winning so decisively" (40r, dated 27 Mar.). Still, the dominant feelings expressed in the journal during these final days are those of pain and apprehension:

26 March

I knew that this misfortune was inevitable; I knew that our Edirne that so valiantly defended herself would one day fall prey to the enemy. Still, when it actually happened, when [I saw] our soldiers disarmed and the Bulgarian soldiers laughing, triumphant, filling the air with their rough Slavic language, I felt deep anguish. I was particularly incensed by the noise and cruel happiness of the [local] Greeks and Bulgarians who rushed to meet the victors. One should not laugh in front of those who cry. When so many Ottoman hearts were bleeding it was not necessary to demonstrate so much joy. . . .

Turkey succumbs today due to the obscurantism of Abdul-Hamid's regime. [Turkey] could obtain cannons, but she did not have schools, and here lies her great misfortune. May she learn from this cruel trial a useful lesson for the future and may she soon put into practice that beautiful slogan, "Union and Progress." (38v–39v) [86]

27 March

This page in history approaches its end with ominous signs. The Bulgarians will undoubtedly give us beautiful cities and magnificent edifices. They will give us a foretaste of Europe. But we, Jews, have much to be thankful for to this Ottoman society that is so far from progress—this is true—and yet, it is so humane. Who knows after how many days of suffering we will lament the [ruling] hand of the Turks that was so gentle toward the Jewish population. (40v)

New Perspectives from Guéron's Journal

Above and beyond the information, much of it new, that Guéron's journal provides on the siege of Edirne—and especially on its Jewish community, a subject that had been entirely ignored—in a wider sense this document portrays the final days of Ottoman society, corrupt and disintegrating and yet rich in its tolerance and human diversity. As is known, a major feature of Ottoman society was its plural character. Within the Ottoman Empire coexisted numerous ethnic and religious groups. Edirne could be said to have been a microcosm of Ottoman society as a whole: half its population was Muslim-Turkish and the other half consisted of "minorities"—Greeks, Jews, Bulgarians, Armenians, and others. Guéron's journal describes the daily functioning of this plural society during a period of great trial, when the city's Christian population, who comprised one-third of all residents, were torn between their duty to their state and their sentiments toward their national groups, which were at war with their state. And although it could not be said that this society functioned very successfully or effectively, it passed this trial without persecution or oppression, without massacres or bloodshed, while on the whole maintaining public order and personal security and a large measure of basic human decency that cut across religious and ethnic lines.

By the outbreak of the Balkan Wars, the Ottoman Empire had been in a state of disintegration for some time. However, the Balkan Wars, which resulted in the Ottoman Empire's loss of most of its European territories and the concomitant rise of victorious and strong Balkan national states that laid claim to the loyalties of the empire's Christian minorities, delivered the final blow to the possibility of Ottoman plural coexistence and foreshadowed the empire's complete demise. Indeed, within one decade from the end of the Balkan Wars, the remnants of the empire would be transformed into a national state in which the great majority of its population would follow one religion (Islam) and speak one language (Turkish). And these processes were fully reflected in the fate of Edirne.

According to Turkey's official census of 1935, Edirne's total population was 36,121, including 31,731 Muslims, or Turks (88 percent of the total), 4,020 Jews (11 percent), and 368 Christians (1 percent).[87] What is striking about these figures is the almost total disappearance of the Christians (who were more than 30 percent of the population in 1912) due to migration and population exchange and the decline of the Jews (17–18 percent in 1912) in both absolute numbers and relative terms. But perhaps even more surprising is the numerical decline of the Muslims (55,000 in 1912). In fact, between 1912 and the post-World War I era, Edirne lost about two-thirds of its population and did not begin to recover until the 1960s.[88]

The reason for Edirne's decline is well known. The city that until the Balkan Wars had been a major administrative, military, economic, and commercial center had essentially become an isolated border town, cut off from its commercial and economic hinterland. The Balkan Wars, as Guéron had predicted, also caused extensive destruction throughout eastern Thrace, further undermining Edirne's economy. The outcome was a rapid flight of population and commercial and economic enterprises from Edirne.[89]

The fate of the Jews of Edirne was in some ways unique. Unlike the Christians, they did not disappear en masse, but instead, they faded away gradually. The Jews whose main economic activities were in commerce and crafts were particularly adversely affected by Edirne's economic decline. In addition, the Jews of Edirne, like those of other towns in eastern Thrace, felt pressured by antiminority sentiments that were particularly strong in a region whose population suffered a great deal during the war.[90]

Immediately following the Balkan Wars, Edirne's Jewish population increased, and in 1914 it reached 28,000. But this was a temporary rise that was due to the arrival of many Jewish refugees from Balkan countries.[91] During World War I and following it, thousands of Jews left Edirne. Immediately after World War I, Edirne still had a Jewish population of about 13,000.[92] But in 1927 only 5,712 Jews were counted in Edirne;[93] in 1935, 4,020;[94] in 1945, approximately 2,000;[95] in 1960, 438;[96] and in 1965, 298.[97] It appears that by the 1980s an organized Jewish community ceased to exist in Edirne. According to the Turkish-Jewish newspaper *Şalom (Shalom),* only a few Jews lived in Edirne in the 1990s.[98]

CHAPTER 12

The Industrial Working Class of Salonica, 1850–1912

Donald Quataert

> Salonica . . . is a paradise for Jews. When you are rowed ashore there, your
> boatman is an Israelite masquerading in Turkish fez and trousers. On
> landing, you are hustled by porters in turbans and red shoes; but they are
> Jews. You enter the Customs-house: the mobs of officers, with their
> continuous gabble, are Jews. Jews in turbans and Jews out of turbans; Jews
> as builders of houses and Jews as barbers—the children of Israel are
> everywhere, in every kind of work.[1]
>
> —Samuel S. Cox, *Diversions of a Diplomat in Turkey*

The Transport Sector

In 1912, at the end of its life as an Ottoman city, Salonica was flourishing
as a major industrial and transportation center. Railroads that first
reached Salonica in the early 1870s, as well as the telegraph linkages that
came in the next decade, played crucial roles in the growth of the city. Before the end of the century, railroad lines connected Salonica to the Ottoman capital, Istanbul, as well as to the Serbian network and thus to
Europe. Salonica boomed as the railhead of three lines that redirected the
import-export trade of the southern Balkans through the city. As a result,
ship tonnage at the port of Salonica doubled to two million tons by 1912. At
this time Salonica was tied with Beirut as the third-largest Ottoman port,
surpassed only by the much larger ports of Istanbul and Izmir.

Despite these huge increases in sea-borne commerce, improvements in Salonica's port facilities came very slowly. Financed by European capital and carried out by Western corporations, construction of more modern facilities was retarded by two quite different forces. The first was the Ottoman state itself, concerned that Western development of ports would lead to increased foreign control of the Ottoman economy and, perhaps, as in China, to extraterritorial port zones. In addition, merchants' efforts to streamline operations were checked by the Salonica porters' guilds. These workers, who were overwhelmingly Jewish, saw modernization neither as a blessing nor as progress, but rather as a threat to their jobs of manually hauling freight. As in other Ottoman ports, the porters' guilds at Salonica prevented real improvements until the end of the century. Finally, in 1897, the Ottoman state yielded to foreign pressure and granted a concession to a French firm. The expansion of the port was completed by 1904. A few years later, the porters' guilds were curbed further. In 1909 the Salonica Quay Company, the Oriental Railways Company, and the Salonica-Constantinople Junction Railway Company signed an agreement making it possible for trains to run all the way onto the quays, directly discharging to vessels in the port. Previously the trains had stopped at the railway station, where porters picked up the goods and manually carried them over one kilometer of bad road to the port. The new arrangement certainly did make handling more efficient. But the porters who had hauled the goods over that bad road now lost their jobs.

Transport Workers: The Jewish Porters of Salonica

Thanks to a series of interviews conducted in the 1960s with an aging population of former Salonica porters (*hamallar*) who had emigrated to Israel, we have an unusually detailed picture of these workers near the end of the Ottoman period.[2] Each porter belonged to a group (*taife*) that kept account books but had no formal hierarchical structure. At the end of the workday, members of the particular group met for sunset prayers, changed clothes, and gathered at a pub for raki and discussion of the day's work. On payday, Thursday, the employer paid the money owed to a representative of the entire group. From this amount a small sum was set aside in a communal chest and for charitable purposes. This sum also paid for the raki drunk communally and, according to the informants, for one bottle for each porter's home consumption during the coming week. Then the balance was divided among the members of the group.

A porter received a range of benefits from his participation in the group. When sick, even if for an indefinite time, he would receive his normal share of the group's profits, less the amount paid to a temporary replacement that the group hired. The group provided a physician, medicines, and aides to attend to the sick during the night. On the death of a member, the group paid for his grave marker and other funeral expenses. Sons automatically had the right to replace their deceased fathers. The widow of a porter without male heirs had two options: she could hire a permanent substitute and retain the difference between the amount paid to this person and the average wages of her deceased husband, or she could sell the right to her husband's position and pocket the entire amount.

Some of the porters of Salonica were casual laborers who waited on the streets or at shops for hire, usually to bring charcoal to homes for heating and cooking. Generally, however, the porters were organized by location of the work or the kind of commodity carried, and they were both well-disciplined and tightly structured (in an informal fashion, as we have seen). Seven major groups were remembered by the old workers. Thus, one group, *hamal del sivi,* monopolized the movement of goods of the commercial center (*sivi*): dried fruit, olives, salted fish, oranges, limes, and cheese. The porters of *los jurikus* (two small streams flowing through a nearby mosque) monopolized the handling of leathers, fats, soap, and butter. The hundreds of porters of the *istira,* the central commercial district of the city with large warehouses, carried bulk goods such as wheat, barley, and flour. These porters were divided into groups, each dealing with a particular merchant, of fewer than ten workers. The porters *de la köşe Malta,* the Malta corner that was the banking and textile sales center, were both porters and packagers of goods sent to Macedonia, Serbia, and Albania. The Akhbarim family provided all the porters of the mice group (*los ratones*), so-called after a nickname of their synagogue. These workers handled metal furniture, large machinery, and other heavy goods. Porters of the train station consisted of two groups, one from the Levy family and the other, the sons of Nehama

Romano. The Levy group originally consisted of seven brothers who passed their positions down to their children over the generations. The Levy family group handled the freight cars while the Romano family group carried passengers' luggage.

The famed porters of the port area, who played a critical role in enforcing the 1908–1909 boycott against Austria-Hungary, were split into many groups, each with a particular monopoly. The sons of Molkho handled flour; those of Tzhimino, sugar; while the Filuda (shaved heads) group transported goods from large ships to the shore. There also were separate groups that handled opium *(taife afyon)* and silk cocoons *(taife kokoyo)*.

The Industrial Sector

The industrial infrastructure of Salonica—including both factories and workshops—probably was the largest in the Ottoman Empire, thanks to a phenomenal boom that began in the late 1870s and continued until the end of the Ottoman period.[3] In just five years, from 1878 to 1883, some thirty new factories and workshops opened in the city and its hinterland. These differed radically in size and degree of technological sophistication. The newly founded establishments included a distillery, six soap factories, a brick factory, another factory making nails from imported wire, a factory making iron bedsteads, four workshops producing handmade chairs, three macaroni factories, ten flour mills, and two cotton spinning mills. Virtually all of these establishments, as well as those opened later on (with the notable exception of the tobacco industry), served to promote the autonomy of the city's economy, because most of the new industries served the local market, replacing foreign-made products with Salonica-made goods in the homes of city and area residents.

Textile production at Salonica—the famed wool cloth industry as well as cotton cloth weaving—had been in sharp decline when compared to the eighteenth and earlier centuries. Overall, the surviving manufacturing was low-technology and had become dispersed in the countryside, where the labor costs were low.[4] This pattern of decline was reversed, beginning in the early 1880s, when several large workshops opened in the city, producing knitted goods and flannel shirts. In addition, and of greater significance, local production of coarse wool cloth started to increase sharply. As local weavers' demands for raw materials mounted, once-significant exports of raw wool from Salonica fell off sharply and were redirected to meet the local needs. In fact, the city even began to import raw wool for the weavers who produced cloth for the Ottoman army and, secondarily, for the civilian population. The number of wool-weaving factories increased dramatically in the early twentieth century, although at first these establishments were filled with hand looms. A cottage industry supplied various wool cloths, using French and German wool yarn. Typically, such a business had several looms and very simple presses.[5]

Mechanization came very late to the wool industry. In 1908 several small mechanized factories opened. A small mill was established with five looms from Bielefeld, making a high-quality dyed and finished wool cloth for the Ottoman government. In 1911 a second mechanized mill, a joint stock company financed by Salonica Jews, opened with thirty looms. The enterprise, however, quickly went under. Salonica also held a jute-weaving mill that the Torres, Misrachi, and Fernandez families established in 1906. This factory burned down two years later, an event said to be advantageous to the owners. It later reopened in 1909, with sixty looms and more modern equipment that made sacks for the tobacco industry. A fez factory opened in 1908 and shared the fate of the jute mill, burning down almost immediately. Unlike the jute factory, however, the fez factory was not rebuilt.[6]

The expansion in wool cloth production at Salonica late in the nineteenth century was paralleled by rising cotton textile output. At the turn of the century, the city contained numerous (although their exact number is unknown) small weaving workshops, holding just two or three looms and making cotton socks as well as wool shirts and shawls. The mounting production of locally made and very cheap socks, an imitation of French goods, substantially reduced the level of imports. In the early twentieth century, the women's ready-made garment industry significantly expanded output, employing hundreds of female workers.[7]

Late in the nineteenth century, the Salonica area also enjoyed substantial increases in cotton yarn production thanks to the formation of a network of mechanized cotton mills. By about 1900 the city and the Macedonian interior came to possess the densest concentration of mechanized cotton-spinning mills in the Ottoman world. The oldest of these mills, located at Niausta, dated back to the 1870s, while five others were founded after 1900. On the eve of World War I, there were ten such mills in Macedonia overall. Three of these were in Salonica itself, containing a full one-third of the 60,000 spindles in the ten mills. Two of the Salonica yarn-making factories opened in 1878 and 1885. The first was built by a group including Schalon (Shalom), Sayas, and Ripote; it was later taken over by I. Sydes and Company. Torres, Misrachi and Company opened the second spinning mill, to be later succeeded by the Société Anonyme Ottomane Nouvelle Filature de Salonique. Both used English equipment exclusively. By 1909 a third steam-powered mill had opened in the city, but it was not Jewish-operated. These factories received Ottoman governmental tax exemptions to help improve their competitive position. The Torres-Misrachi mill was enlarged in 1886 and again in 1890 and, a decade later, reportedly possessed the very newest equipment of English origin. In 1905 the firm became a joint stock company. In contrast to Jewish domination of the city-based spinning industry, Ottoman Greeks owned all of the mills outside Salonica. These were located in Niausta, Karaferia, and Wodena. None of these spinning mills was owned by a single party; instead, multiple owners spread the risks. Members of the owners' families often worked in the mills, sometimes in managerial posts but also on the production line.[8]

Quite late in the period, about 1913, six of the seven Greek-owned cotton-spinning mills of the interior formed a syndicate in order to gain control of the market. It is likely that the effort was part of the mounting interethnic warfare ravaging the Ottoman lands—in this case, a Greek drive to eliminate Jewish competition. The proliferation of spinning mills promoted a vast expansion in cotton cultivation in Macedonia, an upsurge noticeable by the mid-1880s. The Salonica mills produced for an extensive market and successfully competed against Italian and English yarn of certain qualities, especially the coarser threads. At the turn of the century, these mills provided about one-quarter of all cotton yarn consumed in the Salonica region (the balance came from England, Italy, and Austria). About one-third of their output went to Macedonia and Albania, and the balance was shipped to Serbia, Anatolia, the Aegean islands, and Bulgaria—a market lost when Bulgaria became independent of Ottoman control after 1908. As early as 1885, the Anatolian Aegean port of Izmir was importing 650 bales of cotton yarn spun at Salonica.[9]

The Salonica mills generally found it difficult to compete with factories in the Macedonian interior. In fact, about 1900, the mill owned by Sayas and partners that was still operating with its original equipment closed down for a time, some say for as long as seven years. Production costs of the Salonica mills were higher because they used coal to run their steam engines; their Macedonian competitors, by contrast, used water power, which was less reliable but cheaper. Some of these water-powered mills added turbine engines, while the steam mills at Salonica did not modernize but continued to work with worn-out and outdated equipment. Also, land values in the city were higher than in the countryside, further raising overhead costs. The booming tobacco industry also hurt the spinning industry, by drawing off the cheap female labor on which the yarn factories depended. More generally, Salonica workers during the post-1885 boom had a variety of employment options, unlike workers in the interior, who had few other wage-earning alternatives to yarn factory labor. In addition, as we shall see, Salonica workers were better organized than their Macedonian counterparts. As a result of all these factors, the wages of Salonica yarn factory workers in 1913 were as much as three times those of Macedonian girls working in the Karaferia, Niausta, and Wodena mills.[10]

The long-standing Salonica silk reeling industry had faded in importance and essentially disappeared during the late-nineteenth-century boom in the Salonica economy. Among Ottoman silk producers, those at Salonica had been the first, back in 1829, to adopt Western technology for making silk thread that European factories could use in weaving cloth. By the late 1840s, Salonica contained some thirty modern spinning mills with several hundred reeling machines, employing perhaps 1,000 reelers. While the old-style mills had been controlled exclusively by Jews, Italians played a key role in introducing this new Western-derived technology. Although the new mills were very successful, Salonica residents complained about the air pollution they caused, prompting the local authorities to restrict traditional factory construction to areas outside the city walls. Thus, by the early 1860s, the number of filatures in the city had declined to nineteen with 791 reels while surrounding villages held nearly as many, approximately fifteen additional reeling factories. Most of the latter were owned or rented by foreigners and no longer by local Jews.[11]

Just when the residents of the city and its environs had become familiar with mechanized silk reeling, the silk industry at Salonica and in the rest of the Ottoman Empire was beset by a series of crises. Diseases affecting silkworms spread from France to the Middle East at the same time that East Asia began exporting massive quantities of silk to Europe. Salonica's raw silk production, and that of the Ottoman Empire in general, collapsed for several decades and then recovered thanks to the discoveries of Louis Pasteur that made it possible to control the silkworm disease, as well as to strong international demand. Two rather large silk factories at Salonica and six smaller ones in nearby villages had survived into the late 1880s. As Salonica entered its period of unprecedented industrial growth with the proliferation of so many different kinds of factories, the Ottoman Public Debt Administration founded a silk-reeling factory at nearby Gevgeli as a model for local capitalists and would-be entrepreneurs to follow. This silk-spinning mill, leased to the Parisian firm of Boutet Frères, was comparatively large and contained the most modern equipment. Despite these efforts, however, and contrary to the generally favorable business climate, silk reeling in the Salonica region and in the city virtually disappeared.[12]

It would seem that this apparent paradox derives from the nature of the silk-reeling industry as well as the booming Salonica economy of the late nineteenth century. More than in most enterprises, capitalists in silk reeling relied on cheap wages to remain competitive. Silk reelers were the worst paid of all Ottoman textile workers, who in turn received the lowest wages of Ottoman industrial workers in general. As we will see in more detail in the section on workers, the late-nineteenth-century factory proliferation in Salonica pushed wages upwards to the point where local silk reeling became uncompetitive. That is, the general prosperity and increased number of local factories doomed any revival of the Salonica silk industry, even when well-capitalized. For example, the Ottoman Public Debt Administration reeling mill at Gevgeli was undermined by the higher wages that a nearby tobacco factory paid to its six hundred workers.[13]

While silk reeling declined, tobacco production and processing acquired major significance. In the early twentieth century, the Ottoman provinces in Europe accounted for one-half to two-thirds of the substantial tobacco exports from the empire as a whole. During the late Ottoman period, tobacco exports skyrocketed, thanks largely to the seemingly insatiable demands of the American Tobacco Company. Between 1892 and 1909, for example, tobacco exports from the Ottoman European areas rose a full 250 percent! The center of the industry was outside Salonica proper, in the Kavalla district, which accounted for the vast majority of tobacco exports. Salonica, however, supplied about one-fifth of the processed tobacco, and it contained one of the most important cigarette-making factories in the empire. In 1883 the factory of the tobacco monopoly in Salonica was daily producing 100,000 machine-made cigarettes; thereafter, its annual cigarette output grew steadily.[14]

Some of the new factories in Salonica produced durable goods. During the late 1880s a group of skilled blacksmiths worked in the city; these were mainly Armenians and Greeks who had learned the craft in English shops or railroad yards in Ottoman Istanbul. In 1900 a local stock company was formed to modernize the existing iron foundries, repair, and sheet metal shops. Founded by local Jews, the company hand-produced substantial quantities of cheap sheet metal articles, such as tin cans and lamp stands. Copper working was far more important, and shops in the city annually used approximately 100,000 tons of the metal. In 1887 a Frenchman was brought in to establish a copper foundry, but he failed in the effort. On the other hand, towards the end of the period, the city possessed a successful brass foundry. At about the same time, an Armenian opened a workshop that manufactured machinery replacement parts, including motors, transmissions, and agricultural machinery. By 1907 the city had three smelters. Thus, the Salonica economy began achieving some measure of independence from imports to maintain its industrial infrastructure.[15]

From about 1883, a factory owned by the rich and powerful Allatini family (see below) produced common building bricks and good quality roof tiles, supplying European Turkey as well as the archipelago. In 1905 the factory, using clay drawn from a site several kilometers outside the city, doubled its output but was still unable to meet the soaring demand. At that time the city also had a second brickworks, making hand-pressed bricks slightly below the quality of the Allatini factory. Within two years, however, four large factories in the city were producing handmade bricks.

Many factories focused on the production of foods and beverages. Overall, the output of the various comestibles increased sharply in the early twentieth century, particularly after 1906. The Allatini flour mill was usually singled out as the most important of the food-processing factories. Originally founded in 1857, it was later taken over by the Allatini group in conjunction with the French company Grand Moulin de Corbeil. It had been expanded and modernized after a fire in 1898, so that its new facilities were considered exemplary. In 1902 the mill produced a reported 28,000 tons of flour and found buyers mainly in the city and its hinterlands, but also as far away as Beirut. In addition, two small mills produced an inferior flour. The Allatini mill expanded again in 1906, now operating a 650-horsepower steam engine from Italy, and it annually produced 49,000 tons of flour, up sharply from the levels just four years earlier. Although the mill possessed up-to-date equipment, it suffered from a poor location—away from rail lines and the port. Construction of a small pier and a silo with an elevator helped, but locational disadvantages remained. More seriously, the mill suffered from the general underdevelopment of the Ottoman Empire. In common with flour mills in other cities, such as Istanbul, the Allatini mill could use domestic wheat only with some risk: Ottoman cultivators did not clean the grain sufficiently for proper use in the modern equipment of these flour mills. Thus, the Allatini and other mills usually preferred to buy foreign grain, losing thereby the advantage of relative proximity to the Macedonian grain fields.[16]

Two macaroni factories opened in the city in 1906; of these one was steam-powered and produced a high-quality product. Just before World War I, the firm of Modiano, Fernandez and Company that initially had opened the Olympos brewery incorporated as the Société Anonyme Brasserie Olympos, now run by the firm of Misrachi, Fernandez and Company. In the early twentieth century, the brewery mainly supplied local buyers, but it was also exporting to Istanbul and Izmir. This brewery, in common with the Allatini flour mill, considerably increased its productive capacity; it often used Zonguldak coal to fire its modern steam engine and, after 1908, added a central electric capability. A second Salonica brewery opened between 1909 and 1913. It was financed by four Greek partners who sought to use nationalist appeals to attract coreligionist customers away from the Jewish-run Olympos brewery. The Olympos brewery also contained a section that produced ice. In 1900 the ice factory section of operations daily produced ten tons of ice, partly sold to ships in port. By 1906 two Salonica workshops were producing iceboxes, a comparative luxury good at the time.

A new soap factory opened in about 1901, replacing the lesser quality soaps imported from Marseilles, Mytilene, and Crete. A year later, local perfume factories were recapitalized and began underpricing imported extracts, powders, and soaps. These manufacturers sold their wares in Salonica, as well as in Istanbul, Izmir, and Beirut. In 1907, Salonica had seven soap-making firms with daily production estimated at approximately 160,000 kilograms.

During the early 1880s some Greeks and Maltese opened workshops to make chairs that formerly had been imported. In 1905 the city also possessed a very busy furniture factory, which expanded operations in subsequent years, employing some 50–70 workers. By 1907 there were three such workshops. In addition, a woodworking factory employed 70 persons. There were two tanneries in the city until 1907, when Nouchia Fils and eight partners opened a third. Four years later, in 1911, the city firm of Calderon and Arvesti opened the only shoe factory in the European provinces of the empire. Working solely for military contracts, the factory's 75 machines produced up to 600 pairs of boots daily.

To this inventory, we need to add the five book printers that operated about 1906, all using good equipment and producing school books in Ottoman Turkish, Greek, and Bulgarian, as well as newspapers in Ottoman Turkish, Greek, French, and Hebrew. Workshops in the city, about 1906, also produced sun and rain umbrellas, artificial flowers, wagons, cement, raki, cognac, and rum. In addition, the city had two soda water factories and three large and modern candy-making plants that often sold their products in the Macedonian interior.[17]

Salonica was unique in the Ottoman Empire in the sense that the majority of its factory founders were Jewish. The Allatini family, important for their activities in flour and silk, was surely the best known and most influential industrial entrepreneurial group in the European provinces of the empire. The Allatinis' fortune was based on agricultural exports. Using their wealth, the family moved first into steam-powered flour-milling and then into brick manufacture. The Allatini family earlier had monopolized the export of tobacco from most Macedonian districts to Salonica, handling the greatest part of the business. From the middle of the 1880s, foreign merchants—Hungarian, American, and others—became more assertive and started displacing local houses. In 1895 the Allatini house responded by founding the Commercial Company of Salonica, Ltd., to finance its tobacco trade. With this new tool, the family remained the second-largest house in the tobacco industry, after the Hungarian firm of Herzog and Company.[18]

Jewish merchants of Salonica—Capandji, Jahiel (Yehiel), and Bensussan—were the primary backers of a large cloth factory founded in 1911 in Niausta as a joint stock company. Other prominent Jewish families, notably the Misrachi, Fernandez, and Torres families, also were important in Salonica factory formation. The Allatini family allied itself first with the Fernandez and Misrachi families and later created marriage alliances with the Torres. Their factories almost always involved several partners, although they became more involved in stock companies after 1908.[19]

The Industrial Workers

Thanks to its broad manufacturing base, Salonica possessed an unusually dense concentration of industrial workers. In the early twentieth century, according to one estimate, some 20,000 workers were employed in manufacturing, four times the number of workers in the transportation sector. Altogether, this accounted for perhaps 17 percent of the total population of Salonica—women, men, and children—at the time.

We know surprisingly little about the workers and their working conditions. Guilds remained a visible part of workers' lives in the industrial sector through the midpoint of the century. In the 1860s, over one hundred guilds legally operated in the city with many in the transport sectors. Only about one-quarter of these were of mixed religious membership. This is a low proportion when compared with other Ottoman cities, but it seems consistent with the fact that Jews formed a majority among the workers. Joseph Nehama, the chronicler of Jewish life in Salonica, draws a portrait of workers' organizations that is more of an ideal type than a description of working-class reality. (In this case he is basing his account on an earlier nineteenth-century source.) All artisans, Nehama implies, were grouped into guilds, the most powerful of which were those of the Albanian tanners and the Jewish porters (*charretiers*), whom he includes in the artisanal category. Each guild had a steward, or *kahya* (a term that Nehama inaccurately translates as chairman), who arbitrated disputes, imposed fines, closed shops that he considered superfluous, and handled the relations between his guild and other guilds and with the authorities. Probity among workers of all ranks and in all professions was absolute, Nehama asserts; weighing, measuring, and all other transactions were carried out with complete honesty.[20]

In some Ottoman cities craft guilds remained active and important until the end of the empire, and this may have been the case also at Salonica. However, considering the kinds of industries that had been expanding after 1850 and the female labor that they often employed, it is more likely that the importance of craft guilds at Salonica declined sharply during the later nineteenth century, although, as seen above, transporters' guilds in the city continued to retain considerable importance.

Many of the factory directors and managers were foreigners, imported by the entrepreneurs. Thus, in the cotton-spinning mills during the 1880s and 1890s, the managers were from England and they were provided with lodging and comparatively high salaries. Similarly, a British subject managed the tobacco monopoly factory in the early 1890s. At the Allatini brickworks Italian nationals directed operations. Earlier in the century, similarly, Italians had often managed the silk-reeling mills.[21]

Most workers, however, were drawn from the local population. Female labor played a very important role overall and, because it was cheaper, was used whenever possible. The various textile workshops employed eight to twenty female workers each. During the 1880s, in the cotton-spinning mills within the city, all of the 800 workers were Jews, while elsewhere in the region they were Greek, except for the Bulgarian workers at the Wodena mill. Three-quarters of these Salonica mill workers were girls, twelve to eighteen years of age, and they received starting wages that were a full fifty percent less than those for the boys who worked in these factories. The workday was from dawn until dusk, year-round. Thus, spinners worked for fifteen hours in the summer and ten hours in the winter. They received a thirty-five minute break for dinner but no time for breakfast. Sometimes the girls quit factory work after accumulating a cash dowry, but usually they labored in the mills until marriage; for Jewish Salonica girls, this meant until about the age of fifteen.[22]

The Allatini brick factory, including the clay quarry, employed about two hundred workers; youths daily received 10 piasters in about 1912, while others received 16–18 piasters, a living wage at the time. The factory employed mostly Greeks and Bulgarians. Their employment is worth noting, since some observers of the Middle Eastern economy have argued that entrepreneurs of a particular ethnic or religious group hired only workers from that same group. There were real advantages to following this custom, notably, a certain assured access to labor. But, as we see here, the practice was not always observed. In the case of this Jewish-owned brick factory, the management chose to employ workers of a different religion. There was a similar pattern at the Jewish-owned Olympos brewery that, in 1912, employed about eighty workers. The workers in the machine departments were usually Greeks, while Bulgarians toiled in the malting and brewing operations and ran the taverns as well.[23] These Jewish entrepreneurs reportedly employed Christian workers because the factories needed to run continuously, without interruptions. Since the Jewish workers of Salonica refused to work on the Sabbath, industrial entrepreneurs preferred non-Jewish labor when confronted with technological demands that conflicted with religious practices.[24] Jews and Bulgarians, however, dominated the bottling tasks. In 1889, the silk factories of Salonica employed 450 workers. The shoe factory that opened in 1911 employed some sixty workers of unknown gender and ethnicity. The Allatini milling operations in its various phases employed one hundred persons, twenty of them actually inside the mill in 1912.[25]

Tobacco handling and processing was easily the largest single source of employment at Salonica. Some 4,000 to 5,000 persons (as compared to at least 15,000 workers in the Kavalla district and another 5,000 in the Xanthi district) sorted and packaged tobacco. Employed in numerous workshops, they broke apart the baled tobacco shipped by the cultivators and then re-sorted and repackaged it by color and quality. In some districts, such as Xanthi, mostly men were employed, while at Kavalla tobacco manipulators were almost evenly divided by gender. In the Salonica sorting shops, however, women were the overwhelming majority. Besides the sorters and packagers, there were the factory-based cigarette makers, who numbered 250 in 1883, most of them Jews. In 1891, there were fifteen foremen supervising 300 such workers, of whom two-thirds were female and 270 Jewish. Sixty Greeks and Bulgarians, 83 percent female, also worked in the factory, along with five Turkish guards. The workday was nine hours long, and the women received 50 percent or less in wages than the men. Altogether, there were 335 workers, 90 percent of them Jewish.[26]

In the late nineteenth and early twentieth centuries, a unique cluster of factors came together that pushed up wages and created a labor militancy and degree of labor organization unparalleled in the Ottoman Empire. Salonica's workers, without question, formed the most politically aware working-class group in the Ottoman Empire. Wages for Salonica's workers began rising late in the nineteenth century, after about 1896. In part, they improved because of a general increase in Ottoman prices and the consequent, more sluggish, rise in wages following the end of the worldwide price depression of 1873–1896. But wages at Salonica rose more than elsewhere in the Ottoman Empire because of particular local conditions. In 1906 daily wages had already risen to 5–8 piasters for unskilled male workers and to 15 piasters for skilled male labor; women and girls, however, received only 3–8 piasters. Workers hurt by inflation struck in the factories of the tobacco monopoly in 1904; similarly, shoemakers also struck in that same year, while textile workers walked out in 1905, followed by Allatini brickworkers in 1906. The rapid rise in the number of factories of all kinds placed a premium on workers, and employers soon found themselves bidding up wages in an effort to obtain labor. Details are lacking, but it is clear that workers moved from one factory to another in response to better wage opportunities. As international demand and prices for Ottoman tobacco soared at the end of the century, the local tobacco industry could afford to pay wages that were much higher than those offered by other factories. Thus, both the cotton-spinning mills and the silk-reeling mills in Salonica fell into decline, unable to pay the higher wage levels necessary to attract and retain workers. The sharp rises in tobacco production and export played a decisive role in the mounting militancy of Salonica workers.

The Young Turk Revolution of 1908 and the new constitutional government promised new opportunities and freedoms to Ottoman workers. The following weeks were filled with hundreds of strikes for higher wages (but successful labor actions quickly led to repressive countermeasures by the Ottoman government). Virtually every category of labor in the empire was involved in the agitation: textile workers, waiters, barbers, railroad workers, pharmacists, department store clerks, and stevedores—the list goes on—demanded and received higher wages. Pay for unskilled workers at the Olympos brewery had been 7–8 piasters, but following the strikes it rose to 11 and later 12 piasters. In 1909, after a two-week lockout, workers in the Allatini flour mill obtained impressive wage increases, from 10–11 piasters to about 15 piasters. By 1913 the average wage for female labor in Salonica was not less than 7 piasters, more than twice the minimum levels of 1906.[27]

The situation of Salonica's workers was further improved by the emigration of Ottoman subjects, another major trend of the late nineteenth and early twentieth centuries. In part, this migration corresponded to a general pattern in the Mediterranean basin, as Sicilians, other Italians, and Greeks flooded to the New World. But in the Ottoman lands, this migration was given new impetus by the conscription laws of the Young Turk administration that, for the first time, really, made Ottoman Christians and Jews subject to military service. In response, vast numbers of Ottoman Christians (Greeks, Armenians, Lebanese) and Jews fled from the opportunity to serve and from the empire. Real labor shortages now emerged, a trend exacerbated by labor demands in the booming tobacco sector.

Thus Salonica's workers were in an exceptionally strong bargaining position. In a movement that had begun before the 1908 revolution and thereafter acquired exceptional momentum, many workers in Salonica formed labor unions and syndicates to articulate their grievances. By 1910 the important unions at Salonica included those of the tobacco workers, cotton spinners, porters, and workers on the Salonica-Monastir (Manastır, Bitola) railway, while those of the joiners, jute spinners, waiters, shoemakers, and cigarette paper workers were said to be in a state of formation.[28]

Many workers' organizations were not class-based. Thus, for example, the Jewish woodworkers were led by the owners of the ateliers, while a doctor led the Greek tailors' union. National antagonisms, it is clear, fatally flawed the actions of most groups, blocking unity by class and preventing worker solidarity. For the Ottoman Greeks, national questions consistently took precedence over labor and socialist considerations.[29]

But Salonica became the center of the most successful efforts in the Ottoman world to overcome national differences, and it was remarkable for the strength of its socialist organizations. The comparatively high degree of union organization among Salonica's workers and the precocious development of socialism among them certainly derives in part from the unusually favorable local conditions: high wages triggered by the boom in tobacco, combining with shortages of workers caused by general industrial growth and emigration. The character of the Salonica labor movement also owed much to the comparatively high levels of literacy that derived from the programs of the Ottoman state, as well as those of the various religious communities and the Alliance Israélite Universelle. The particular form of labor militancy owed a great deal to the location of the city and its role as a transportation center, with links to western Europe and the various Balkan states. Its proximity and excellent rail links promoted the flow of ideas from Bulgaria, which had a rich social-democratic tradition, as well as from Austria-Hungary, Germany, and points further north and west. Salonica led the way in introducing progressive ideologies into the Ottoman Empire.

A vital core of socialist activity that gave Salonica's socialism its unique quality rested with the Jewish tobacco workers of the city. The tobacco workers had formed a syndicate that was one of the earliest class-based workers' organizations. In August 1908 it had some 3,200 members at Gevgeli, Kukush, and Salonica. Of these, 63 percent were Jews, while Greeks, Turks, and Bulgarians made up the balance. These tobacco workers provided the bulk of support for perhaps the most notable of the socialist organizations in the city, La Fédération Socialiste Ouvrière de Salonique, founded in May–June 1909. The founding members were a group of militant Sephardic Jews, including A. Benaroya, A. J. Arditti, D. Recanati, and J. Hazan, as well as a number of Bulgarians and Macedonians, notably A. Tomov and D. Vlahov. Only months after its founding, a German visited the Club des Ouvriers in Salonica that had just published the second issue of its newspaper, *Journal del Laborador/Amele Gazetesi,* that briefly appeared in four languages. At the time, the Club had 100 members, who reportedly were well versed in German social democracy.

The federation became the most important socialist organization in the Ottoman Empire until the Greek conquest of Salonica in November 1912. By 1910 the federation comprised fourteen syndicates. Its strength is suggested by the fact that in 1912 it could mobilize some 8,000 workers to take part in its various demonstrations. It was a multiethnic, multireligious organization that drew its main strength from the Jewish workers of the tobacco-handling sheds. Some workers, notably Bulgarians, believed that the federation was a mere tool of the Young Turks and did not represent the working class. They might have drawn this conclusion because Salonica's Jews strongly opposed separation from the Ottoman Empire and thus the federation that they dominated adopted an Ottomanist and federalist position. The federation's position, however, can be seen as an effort to remain above nationalist politics and appeal to the working-class identity of its members.[30]

CHAPTER 13

The Special Relationship

The Committee of Union and Progress
and the Ottoman Jewish Political Elite, 1908–1918

Feroz Ahmad

In 1978, in a paper entitled "Unionist Relations with the Greek, Armenian, and Jewish Communities of the Ottoman Empire, 1908–1914," I wrote that the Ottoman Jewish community "was totally untouched by political Zionism. . . . Thus when Zionist propagandists sought support for their movement amongst Ottoman Jews, they found their coreligionists unresponsive. Ottoman Jewry seemed too well integrated to seek a separate identity."[1] At the time when I was researching that paper, the important revisionist research of scholars like Esther Benbassa and Aron Rodrigue was not available and one was forced to rely on the prolific writings of Abraham Galanté, in which, as Rodrigue notes, "the subject of the Zionist movement in Turkey was treated only very tangentially."[2]

Rodrigue's book (and especially the chapter "The Alliance and the Emergence of Zionism in Turkey") paints a radically different picture of the situation after the restoration of the constitution in 1908. He provides a detailed account of political infighting in the community over the question of Zionism and concludes that "developments after 1908 in Istanbul indicate that the degree of local support for the [Zionist] movement was much more significant than hitherto believed."[3]

Such a conclusion is now difficult to refute. But it raises questions about the nature of what Rodrigue describes as "Turkish Zionism." If there was such a thing as "Turkish Zionism," how political was it? Was it political in the sense that Ottoman Jews were willing to emigrate to the Holy Land? Rodrigue found "little evidence to suggest that Turkish Zionists were very concerned in [sic] the emigration to Palestine."[4] Indeed, the statistics of Jewish immigration to Palestine speak for themselves. Up to the year 1931 only 1,339 Jews left Turkey,[5] a remarkably low figure given the turbulent times in the late Ottoman Empire and especially when compared with the far more substantial emigration to Europe and America during the same period. According to the writings of Chaim Weizmann, David Ben-Gurion, and other prominent Zionists, the return to Palestine was the hallmark of Zionism. But at the time this interpretation of Zionism was shared by only a minority of Jews around the world, including Turkey. It seems that Turkish Zionism tended to be more cultural than political. It was a search for a "national" identity at a time when other religious communities in the empire were asserting their own national identities. It was also a manifestation of a social struggle whose aim was to break the hold of the community's notables who were closely associated with the Alliance Israélite Universelle.[6] Rodrigue emphasizes these social tensions, noting that "sections of the mass following of Zionism in Istanbul were composed of individuals that had hardly been touched by the educational activities of the Alliance. Often poor and uneducated, many gravitated toward an anti-establishment movement that promised change in communal affairs and the imminent dawn of better days."[7] Here he almost describes the social base of the Unionist movement, which opposed its own notables. That might also explain the affinity between Turks and Jews, especially as the latter showed no separatist tendencies.

These developments in the Jewish community of Istanbul found no echo in the Turkish writings of the period. The Turkish political classes were aware of European Zionism, and, given the role played by people like Ahmet Ağaoğlu and Celâl Nuri in the propaganda activities of the Zionist organization in Istanbul, they knew of these developments in the Jewish community as well. Still, perhaps because Turkish political activists were too preoccupied with bigger and graver problems, or because they did not consider the Zionism in the local Jewish community as a threat to the empire, the subject was largely ignored.[8]

The flowering of Zionism in the Jewish community seems to have had no ramifications for Ottoman political life after the 1908 revolution. This was so despite the hopes that the Zionist organization entertained, as expressed, for example, in a letter written by Chaim Weizmann on 10 August 1910. The restoration of the 1876 constitution and the establishment of parliamentary government were expected to bring about positive changes in official Ottoman attitudes toward Zionism. "Of special significance," wrote Weizmann, "were the anticipated changes in the administration of the Provinces, perhaps presaging an easing of restrictions in Palestine."[9] Some, like the young David Ben-Gurion, hoped that a Zionist lobby would emerge in the Ottoman assembly. According to Ben-Gurion's biographer, Shabtai Teveth, he was of the opinion that

> Jews in all walks of life, in all parts of the Ottoman state, had to create and take part in a national, political organization that would be empowered to demand in the Ottoman imperial parliament and from the central government their civil, political, and national rights and to defend their economic and cultural interests, together with all other Jewish communities in the Ottoman Empire, to become Ottoman subjects and to unite in one autonomous political body that would have the right to elect its own representatives to parliament. He wanted to study law to groom himself for the election to the Turkish parliament; he said that his plan was not only to be a member of parliament, but to be a minister in the sultan's government, "so that I shall be able to defend Zionism."[10]

But Ottoman Zionists played no role in the elections for the Ottoman assemblies. They were not as well organized as the other major non-Muslim communities, the Greeks and the Armenians. The Greeks coalesced around their patriarch and presented a virtually monolithic bloc, which the Unionists found difficult to penetrate. The Armenians, though divided, were organized in three groups: the notables around the patriarchate, the nationalists in the Dashnak party, and the socialists in the Hunchak party. The Unionists were able to find acceptable accommodations with both the Dashnak and the Hunchak, though they preferred the nationalists whose ideology was close to their own.

The Jewish community presented no such problems for the Unionists.

The Committee of Union and Progress (CUP) established good relations with the Jewish elite once Haim Nahum Efendi replaced Mosheh Halevi as the acting chief rabbi after the fall of the Hamidian regime. Mosheh Halevi had been closely associated with the old regime; Nahum, on the other hand, was a liberal with close links to the Alliance Israélite, an institution much respected by the Young Turks. Talât Bey, who became grand vezir and pasha in February 1917 and was one of the most influential and powerful Unionists, "had taught Turkish in the Alliance school in Edirne and had been instructed in French by the daughter of the school director there."[11] Nahum's election to the grand rabbinate on 24 January 1909 placed the Jewish leadership's relationship with the CUP on firm ground and Nahum's ties with Talât remained very close until the end of the Ottoman Empire.

Although the Unionists struck bargains with Greek and Armenian organizations prior to elections, they allotted seats to the Jewish community, knowing that its representatives had important contributions to make to the Ottoman cause. It is worth remembering that just after the 1908 revolution, relations between the various religious-ethnic communities were still based on mutual respect and trust forged by a common hostility to the Hamidian autocracy and a shared desire to start afresh. That was particularly true for Turks and Armenians, and Turks and Jews; the Greeks, who were still very much under the sway of their patriarch and looked to Athens for inspiration, were viewed by the Turks with suspicion.

There was another reason why the Unionists sought a rapprochement with the non-Muslims. They hoped to use the expertise of these better educated and more developed groups to further their own program of reform and progress. That is why the social radicalism of the Armenian Dashnaks appealed to them. The non-Muslim deputies in the assembly were expected to play a vital role in the introduction and passage of legislation designed to bring about the modernization and economic revival of the empire. In a sense, given the social composition of the 1908 assembly (and the 1912 and 1914 assemblies were not very different), the Unionists were the ideological captives of the deputies from the so-called minorities. (Incidentally, the use of the term "minorities" is anachronistic, for at the time such groups were described in the empire as *anasır*, "elements," a neutral word that had a connotation very different from "minorities.")

Non-Muslim deputies tended to be better educated and more open to the ideas of change and modernization than Muslim deputies. Many of them were professionally qualified (engineers, agronomists, etc.) and were expected to provide expert opinion when matters related to their professions were discussed in the Chamber. A rough breakdown of the 1908 Assembly according to profession shows that of the 220-odd deputies about whom we have some information, 35 percent were *ulema* or *sarıkh* (Muslim religious scholars), another 29 percent came from the landed classes, 20 percent were state officials, only 10 percent were from the liberal professions and business, and 5 percent were designated "other." [12] The essentially conservative character of the Chamber increased the importance of the non-Muslim deputies in the eyes of the Turkish reformers.

Unfortunately, the information we have on the Jewish deputies is rather limited, but that is true for most other deputies of this period. More research will have to be undertaken before we can arrive at more definitive conclusions. Still, the four Jewish deputies who were elected to the 1908 Assembly more or less fit the profile of the 10 percent of the representatives who came from the professions and business.

Vitali Faraci (Farraggi), who was elected from Istanbul in 1908 and again in 1912, was a leading lawyer in the capital. He also worked as the legal counselor at the Régie des Tabacs, the Ottoman tobacco monopoly. His portrait reveals a cultivated, cosmopolitan gentleman of about fifty-five, dressed in a European suit, who would be completely at home in a European setting. He died in 1912. [13]

Emmanuel Karasu (Carasso) was also a lawyer. He was elected from Salonica in 1908 and 1912, and moved to Istanbul when Salonica was captured by Greece during the Balkan Wars. He represented the capital in the 1914 Assembly. Karasu joined the secret organization of the CUP before 1908 and was able to further its activities in his capacity as the Grand Master of the Macedonia Risorta Lodge of Freemasons, though Galanté writes that he merely served as a courier for the Unionists. Though he was never a member of the CUP's central committee, he was part of the inner circle and a confidant of Talât and his faction. During World War I he was put in charge of food distribution and is reported to have amassed a fortune of two million liras. This, he told an unsympathetic correspondent of The *Times* (London), was "all honestly made out of my commission on purchase." During the armistice, half of this fortune was confiscated by the Damad Ferid Pasha government, and Karasu fled to Italy, where he died in June 1934.[14]

Nissim Mazliyah (Masliah), described as Manisalı Nissim Mazliyah Efendi in the Izmir press, represented Izmir in the three assemblies. Apart from his legal training, he also had commercial interests. Before 1908 he was in Salonica, where he became active in the CUP. According to Friedman (who cites contemporary Zionist reports as his source of information), Mazliyah belonged to "the small group [of Jews?] that funded the C.U.P." Galanté describes him as a member of the Commercial Tribunal of Salonica who was appointed Professor of Administrative Law and Capitulations at the Police Academy. Hüseyin Hilmi Pasha, who was the Inspector-General of the provinces of Salonica, Kosovo, and Manastır before the revolution, used Mazliyah's legal expertise, especially when he had to deal with problems related to international law. That may explain why Mazliyah thought Hilmi Pasha could be "swayed" in favor of Zionism.[15]

Mazliyah was a committed Unionist, much respected in the CUP. This fact, rather than his Jewishness, accounted for his election from Izmir, for, according to the yearbook (salnâme) for the province of Aydın, the Jewish community in the district (sancak) of Izmir was not large enough to elect its own deputy. There were only 25,002 Jews out of a population of 627,850, and 25,000 males over twenty-five were required for each deputy.[16] Mazliyah was an eloquent Turkish speaker, and the CUP used his talents during election campaigns. He wrote for the Unionist press and founded in Istanbul the paper İttihad, which had a life of nine months.[17]

Mazliyah served as Secretary to the Chamber in 1908–1909. During the counterrevolution of April 1909, he spoke in the Assembly, explaining to the counterrevolutionaries that their demands for the return of the Şeri'at were incompatible with the constitution, thereby rallying the Unionists. In November 1912 he was arrested by Kâmil Pasha's government as part of its anti-Unionist purge and was released after the Unionist coup of January 1913. He was chosen to represent the government at the Stockholm conference in 1917, and he maintained contact with Talât Pasha until the latter's assassination in Berlin in 1921. Galanté tells us that he wrote Le Parliament Ottoman (n.d., n.p.) and published the political daily Hür Adam in 1930.[18] It is a pity that he did not leave behind any memoirs about his fascinating and eventful life.

Hasgayl Sason (Ezekiel Sasoon) was deputy for Baghdad in the three assemblies. He came from a prominent family and was described as a businessman, at one time director of the Ottoman Steamship Company. After his election, the CUP had him appointed Undersecretary of State at the Ministry of Commerce. This was part of the Unionist strategy to penetrate the state structure and influence policy making, something they could not as yet control directly through their own ministers.[19] Friedman writes that "Jacobson could hardly rely on Sasoon . . . whom he termed an 'Arab patriot.' "[20]

In contrast to the Jewish intelligentsia, the Armenian intelligentsia seems to have been more attracted to professions like engineering and agronomy, though it too provided its share of legal experts for the Ottoman bureaucracy. Karakin Pastırmacıyan (deputy for Erzurum), for example, was a graduate of the Ecole des Mines in Nancy; Dr. Nazaret Dagvaryan (deputy for Sivas) studied agriculture in Paris; and İhsan Onnik (deputy for Izmir) was an agronomist who wrote extensively on the subject. It is not surprising that Armenians, who were engaged in farming throughout Anatolia, should take an interest in scientific agriculture. Ottoman Jews, especially in the Salonica community, also studied scientific farming. Galanté mentions Vitali Stroumsa, who graduated from the school of agriculture in Montpellier and later became director of the Ecole Pratique in Salonica, Inspector of Agriculture in Salonica and Kosovo, and Secretary-General of the Financial Commission of the three provinces of Salonica, Kosovo, and Manastır. After he moved to Istanbul in 1908, he seems to have abandoned totally his interest in agriculture. He was appointed to the Supreme Council for Financial Reform, and during World War I he was placed in charge of supervising the printing of Turkish currency in Berlin.[21]

If the list of electors of the second degree in Izmir is an indicator of educational and professional trends among Ottoman Jews, then medicine came high on the list. Three of the four electors were doctors—Amado, İshak, and İshak Abuaf. The fourth, Mordechai Levy, is not identified by profession.[22] Generally speaking, the Jewish community (including the women) participated in the expanding modern commercial sector of the economy in cities like Izmir and Istanbul. Writing in the March 1914 issue of *Kadınlar Mecmuası,* a Rhodie Tully, who described herself as "one of their [Ottoman women's] sincerest admirers," noted: "There are many large companies and institutions in Istanbul that would be [only] too willing to employ women clerks could they but find good and accurate workers, but at present demand is far greater than the supply, and the field is almost entirely held by Israelites."

While Greeks and Armenians were willing to play a role in the economic revival of the empire, they were not keen to see the creation of a strong, centralized state. This was the principal concern of the CUP, a concern shared by the Jewish political elite, the only non-Muslim, non-Turkish group to do so. Apart from the few members of the elite who have already been mentioned, there were many others whose identities remain hidden but who were active in the various arms of the bureaucracy. Two more names come to mind: Nissim Russo and Samuel Israel (the latter adopted the family name İzisel after 1934). Both men came from Salonica, where they were active members of the CUP, and both moved to Istanbul after the revolution. Russo, who had served under Hüseyin Hilmi Pasha in Macedonia, worked closely with Mehmed Cavid when he was minister of finance. I do not know much more about him, though I am sure there is a great deal more to learn. It would be most useful to have a book for the Jewish community like Çark's compendium for the Armenian community.[23]

A little more is known about Samuel Israel because he was active also in the Republic. He too had a legal education and served on a number of tribunals in Macedonia, remaining in Rumelia after the revolution. He was serving as a judge in Serez when the counterrevolution broke out in the capital in April 1909. Thereupon he joined Mahmud Şevket Pasha's Action Army and came to Istanbul. He was appointed chief of police of the port and began climbing up the ladder until he became the deputy chief of the political section of the capital's police force. This appointment was of some significance at a time when political intrigue was rife and government unstable. The activities of people like Samuel Israel are by their very nature secretive and secret. But we are told that he accompanied Enver Bey on the fateful day when he carried out the coup of 23 January 1913, leading to Kâmil Pasha's overthrow and Mahmud Şevket Pasha's brief grand vezirate. After the latter was assassinated along Divanyolu on 11 June 1913, Samuel Israel was himself shot and wounded while leading a detachment of special police against the assassins. The wound left him with a limp, but he was decorated for bravery and valor in the line of duty by the Unionist government.

Samuel Israel served the Unionist regime throughout World War I but was relieved of his post during the armistice period. When the Kemalists came to power, he was restored to his former post and remained in the police force until his retirement in 1947. After his retirement he taught law and French at the Police Academy in Ankara. He died in 1949, at the age of seventy, in Paris, where he had been sent for medical treatment. As late as December 1971 he was remembered affectionately by his comrades as "Kemal Ağabey." They described him as a brave and conscientious officer who had played an important role in the service of the Turkish secret police organization.[24]

The close working relationship between the CUP and members of the Jewish elite was apparent to observers of the contemporary political scene, especially to members of the intelligence communities of the Great Powers. The British embassy (and the *Times*), which after July 1908 supported the liberal faction of the Young Turks, came to regard the Unionist movement as a Jewish-Freemason conspiracy and went so far as to describe the CUP as the "Jew Committee of Union and Progress."[25] Such a notion of politics reflected two European attitudes prevalent at the time: firstly, anti-Semitism and the theory of a Jewish conspiracy to control the world; and secondly, the conviction that a non-Western people like the Turks were incapable of modern government and required guidance from a European hand. Thus Sir Gerard Lowther, Britain's ambassador in Istanbul, informed the Foreign Office:

> The Turk, devoid of real business instincts, has come under the almost exclusive economic and financial domination of the Jew . . . and as Turkey happens to contain the places sacred to Israel, it is natural that the Jew should strive to maintain a position of exclusive influence and utilize it for the furtherance of his ideals, viz. the ultimate creation of an autonomous Jewish state in Palestine or Babylonia. . . . In return for "unrestricted immigration" of foreign Jews he has offered the Young Turks . . . to take over the whole of the Turkish National Debt.

Moreover, the Jew hates Russia and its Government, and the fact that England is now friendly with Russia has the effect of making the Jews to a certain extent anti-British in Turkey and Persia—a consideration to which the Germans are . . . alive. The Jew can help the Young Turk with brains, business enterprise, his enormous influence in the press of Europe, and money in return for economic advantages and the realization of the ideals of Israel, while the Young Turk wants to regain and assert his national independence and get rid of the tutelage of Europe, as part of a general Asiatic revival.[26]

Lowther's analysis makes no distinction between the Zionist representatives in Istanbul, who held out the hope of bailing out the Ottoman state from its foreign debt, and the local Jewish elite, which had neither the resources nor the pretentions to make such offers. His analysis justified in his mind the embassy's support for the liberals and the subversion of the CUP. But Ottoman conservatives and liberals, as well as the deputies from Syria, used the Jewish-Freemason accusation in another way—as a stick with which to beat the Unionists, claiming that the alliance with the Jews undermined the Islamic foundations of society. This campaign had its effect on the CUP, especially after the abortive counterrevolution of April 1909. The Unionists became more cautious with regard to their radical program and took care not to offend the sensibilities of conservatives. The counterrevolution had been a close call for the CUP, leaving its members badly shaken and beholden to Mahmud Şevket Pasha and the military High Command. The sympathetic attitude toward Zionism was abandoned in order to meet the criticism of Arab deputies and their allies. About the same time, there was a change in the attitude of the Jewish elite as well. Friedman writes that the Francophile Alliance Israélite Universelle

became progressively more vociferous in criticising Zionist ideology. It culminated in a speech made by Narcisse Leven, the Alliance's President, during a reception given to the Ottoman parliamentary delegation in Paris in the summer of 1909. The Turkish press picked up the theme, and consequently some of the Ottoman Jewish leaders damped down their earlier enthusiasm. Those involved were closely linked with the Alliance, like Chief Rabbi Nahoum.[27]

When Victor Jacobson, the Zionist representative in Istanbul, returned to the capital early in 1910, he noted the change and found that Unionists who had been supportive of Zionist aspirations were now cool and guarded. Dr. Nâzım, who was very prominent in the inner circles of the CUP,

> told him that he still favoured Jewish immigration into Turkey but evinced no sympathy towards Zionist aspirations, which, he implied, were "separatist"; they could undermine the hitherto harmonious relations with the Jewish community. This he would regret since the Jews were "a very valuable element.". . . Chief Rabbi Nahoum confirmed that in the ruling circles in Constantinople hostility towards Zionism was increasing. In consequence Ottoman Jewish leaders became reserved. Jacobson could hardly rely on Ezechiel Sasson, . . . but even Carasso [Karasu], Matzliach, and Russo remained aloof. David Fresco, the editor of *El Tiempo,* the Judeo-Spanish periodical, . . . turned against the Zionists and . . . accused them of disloyalty to Turkey.[28]

The Jewish elite acted as intermediaries between the Unionists and the Zionists, interpreting the one to the other. They, like the Unionists, could not support the separatism implied in Zionist ideology despite assurances to the contrary given by leaders like Jacobson. Soon after the restoration of the constitution, Haim Nahum, who was then deputy chief rabbi, "confirmed that the new regime viewed Jewish settlement in Palestine with favour, though they would not allow Palestine to become autonomous. . . . Nahoum was ready to support the Zionists provided they adhered to a moderate programme." As to Ottoman Jewry, Nahum described it as "largely materialistic and indifferent [to Zionism]."[29]

It is a pity that Nahum did not spell out what he meant by a "moderate programme." For Unionists such a program could have meant nothing less than Zionist willingness to remain Jewish while becoming fully integrated Ottoman citizens in the new commonwealth that the CUP was struggling to create. For Max Nordau this was nothing short of assimilation, which he rejected, claiming: "If we wished to assimilate we have a closer and easier way of doing it at home."[30] Wolffsohn had already spelled out Zionist goals at the Ninth Congress on 26 December 1909: "We aspire to build within the framework of the Ottoman Empire a nationality like other nationalities in the Ottoman realm. Our ambition is to earn the reputation of being the most loyal, trustworthy, and useful nation among the national groups, but a Jewish nation."[31]

Isaiah Friedman concludes that the Turks were not impressed with Zionist protestations or assurances. "With their bitter experience in the Balkans fresh in their minds, they could not risk creating a new nationality, however trustworthy. With the regime of Capitulations still in force and the majority of Jewish settlers in Palestine reluctant to adopt Ottoman nationality, the Porte had reason to be suspicious."[32]

The hegemony that the Great Powers exercised through the regime of the Capitulations was perhaps the principal concern of all Young Turks, especially the Unionists. Of all the non-Muslim communities, the Jews shared this concern with the Turks since neither benefited from the protégé status and protection that the Great Powers provided to some of the sultan's Christian subjects. Both Turks and Jews stood to gain from the abolition of these unequal treaties, because it would restore the autonomy of the Ottoman state, create a level playing field, and allow for fair economic competition among all groups. One has only to examine the *Lloyd's Register of British and Foreign Shipping, 1912–13,* to grasp the extent of Europe's economic hold over the Ottoman Empire. Among the companies represented in the capital, there was no Turkish company apart from the Chirket Haire (*Şirket-i Hayriye).* There is not a single Jewish name, though Greek and Armenian names (Atyehides & Vahratoğlu, Pandelis Frères, Petzalis & Dounias, Seropian, Carnich & Sons) are prominent. They are as prominent as the Levantine names, such as Foscola Mango & Co., La Fontaine, Edwards & Sons, and Sir J. W. Whittall & Co., described as "Merchants, Bankers, Shipping & Insurance Agents, Lloyd's Agents." Of all the listings, only in Izmir was there a Jewish concern founded in 1911: Efraim Cohen, "Agents P&O, S.N. Co., Khedival Maritime Line & Marine Insurance Co., General Import and Export Merchants."

No great political insight was required to understand that Europe's hold on the empire's finances (partly maintained by the Capitulations and the system of loans) strangled the economy and rendered reform and revival impossible. Israel Helphand, better known as Parvus, the socialist who resided in Istanbul during the years 1910 and 1914, understood this problem well. His major work on Turkey was a serious analysis of the problem with proposals for solutions.[33] His influence on the Unionists was considerable, especially on ideologues like Moïse Cohen (better known as Munis Tekinalp) and the nationalists who published the journal *Türk Yurdu*.[34] But the Greek and Armenian deputies, even if they were socialists, did not show the same concern about this problem as did the Turks (and Jews). That is how it appears in the Assembly debates. Thus, when the issue of modernizing the economy and creating industry was raised, there was paradox in the positions adopted by socialists and pro-capitalist Young Turks. The socialists argued that foreign capital investment had to be encouraged in order to develop the economy; the Turks argued that that would only tighten the hold of Europe over the empire. The socialist Dimitri Vlahof, deputy for Salonica, retorted that "in all countries, industry had been created by foreign capital. In England industry was set up by Dutch capital, in America by English capital, in Germany and Austria by French capital, and in Russia by foreign capital."[35]

Vlahof called for an open-door policy to attract more foreign capital. The Turks answered that thanks to the Capitulations the door was already wide open and one of their goals was to shut it so as to regain fiscal autonomy and political sovereignty. They failed to understand the argument of the Christian deputies, and even a liberal like Lütfi Fikri, deputy for Dersim, concluded that such people were not sufficiently "Ottoman" or patriotic.[36]

An understanding between the Christian and Muslim deputies over the question of the Capitulations was impossible to reach. The Christians were convinced that their situation would be impossible if the Capitulations were removed; the Muslims felt that their removal was vital for any progress. When the Capitulations were finally abrogated unilaterally in September 1914, the Turkish and Jewish communities welcomed the decision as deliverance from foreign control; the Christians mourned, uncertain as to their future.

◆   ◆   ◆

There is another feature of the Turkish-Jewish relationship which deserves comment: the question of military service. Until the revolution, non-Muslims (and some Muslims from the elite) were able to pay the exemption tax, the *bedel-i askeri,* in lieu of military service. But the new regime introduced conscription as a measure to create equality between all citizens. In practice, there were loopholes in the law, and many still bought their way out. The constitutional regime was too much in need of cash to allow this source of revenue to disappear. Nevertheless, members of the non-Muslim communities, especially those not rich enough to pay the tax, were conscripted into the Ottoman army.

This topic needs to be researched, and all I can say for the moment is conjectural and based on the reading of rather limited sources. But it seems as though Ottoman Jews took the question of military service more seriously than the other non-Muslim communities. I suspect they did so because they identified with the Ottoman state and the new regime more fully than others. Unlike the Greeks and Armenians, they had nowhere else to look. As evidence for my speculation, I shall quote from the diary of a Turkish officer kept during the Balkan Wars as the Ottomans suffered defeat and retreated towards the capital. The officer, a Cemal Bey, wrote about desertions from the ranks and noted the differences in attitude between Greeks and Armenians from Anatolia and those from Rumelia. In his diary entry of 29 December 1912, he wrote:

> Until today not a single Christian has deserted from our battalion to the enemy; in our company there were even two Bulgarian privates who went into every battle and fired off shots. One of them was Manastırlı Dimo. Because we treated all soldiers equally in our battalion, and because we never said a bad word about their nationality *(milliyet)* and religion, we had great confidence in the Christians. We thought that they also had affection for us. But today these ideas have brought about unfortunate consequences. Yes, we thought that because of our well-intentioned management and treatment and the effect of our brotherly words the

Christian soldiers in our battalion would not desert like the Christians in other battalions. . . . However, this was naive; they were only waiting for us to advance further [before deserting]. . . .

The desertion of Armenians hurt even more because of the affection we had developed for them. We had looked upon them with genuine trust and affection. Now we no longer have confidence in any Christian other than the Greeks and Armenians of Anatolia. These people, the Greeks and Armenians of Anatolia, were sad that their coreligionists had deserted. They cursed them and felt ashamed.

Finally, Cemal Bey turns his attention to the Jewish soldier and pays him the highest compliment he can think of. He writes:

A Jewish soldier if he is a regular, properly trained, serves like a Mussulman. The effort and bravery of Sergeant Mişon from Mustafa Paşa in the Third Company really did his officers proud. Even though Sergeant Mişon is the son of a rich Jew, he did not pay the exemption tax. He commanded his troops at the most dreadful phase of the battle. He commanded a detachment.[37]

Not only could the Ottoman state depend on Jewish troops to fight with valor, in some areas it also armed the Jewish population so as to resist a Greek invasion of the Aegean coast. On 4 April 1913, Consul-General Barnham reported from Izmir

that arms have recently been distributed to a considerable number of the Mahammedan and Jewish subjects of the Porte in such districts as Tourbali, Sokia, Menemen, Phokia, and Magnesia, all of which are in comparative proximity to the sea.

My informants stated that arms were distributed to most Moslem and Jewish males, whether in small townships or villages, and with the Martinis 100 rounds of ammunition were given out.[38]

It is worth noting that the Porte did not arm the Armenian population of the region; one may conclude that the Armenians of the region were not trusted to resist a Greek invasion. There is general agreement that the Armenians of Anatolia remained loyal to the Ottoman state during the Balkan Wars. Richard G. Hovanissian notes, however, that "In 1912 Balkan Armenians responded by forming a volunteer unit to assist Bulgaria against Turkey, while the Armenians of Transcaucasia again agitated for Russian involvement in Ottoman affairs." [39]

After the Balkan Wars the bond between the CUP and the Jewish elite grew closer and tighter. Many Jews left Salonica and settled in Izmir, Edirne, and Istanbul, where they played an important role in filling the vacuum left in the economic life by Greeks who were forced to leave. After Turkey's entrance into World War I in November 1914 and the catastrophic defeats it suffered at the hand of the Tsarist army in the Caucasus, the loyalty of Armenians in the empire became suspect. Of the non-Muslim, non-Turkish elements that had given the Ottoman Empire its cosmopolitan character, only Christian Arabs like the Bustanis, Levantines like the Whittalls and Girauds, and members of the Jewish elite like Nahum and Karasu remained loyal to the Ottoman ideal.

Despite the growing influence of Zionism during these years, the Jews of Anatolia remained committed to Ottomanism. Mandel defines three groups who were opposed to Zionism:

> First, there were the followers of the city's Hahambaşı [Nahum], who appears to have feared the Zionists might compromise the position of Jews in the Empire at large. Then, there were the graduates of schools run by the Alliance Israélite Universelle, which was resolutely anti-Zionist during this period. And finally, there were members of the Club des Intimes, a Jewish society which supported the Government's Ottomanisation policy. They had made Dr. Nazım Bey of the CUP's Central Committee an honorary member of the club. [40]

Turkey's special relationship with the leaders of its Jewish community proved to be a great asset in the propaganda war, which commenced as soon as hostilities broke out in Europe in August 1914. Arnold Toynbee, one of the architects of the British propaganda campaign against the Turks, wrote that Britain was greatly embarrassed by her Russian ally's treatment of the Jews, knowing what an adverse effect that was having in the United States.

That is why the British government decided to exploit the Armenian question in order to neutralize the German campaign against Russia and the Triple Entente by exposing the alleged misdeeds of Germany's ally, the Ottoman Empire.[41] But the campaign had little effect because the Armenian community in America was not, as yet, visible or well organized. At the same time, Jewish opinion in America continued to favor Germany, which remained the center of Zionist activity. Berlin was able to exercise its influence in Istanbul so as to prevent the large-scale deportations of Russian Jews from Palestine to Egypt. As a result of Berlin's influence, of the 50,000 or so Jews with Russian citizenship in Palestine, only about 11,000 left the country.

But Cemal Pasha's evacuation of the Jewish population of Jaffa in March–April 1917 proved a blessing for Britain's anti-Turkish propaganda, and Berlin and Istanbul had their work cut out for them to counteract it.[42] The Istanbul press issued indignant denials about the persecution of Jews and emphasized Ottoman Jewry's opposition to Zionism. Two articles representative of the sentiment in the capital are worth quoting. On 27 August 1917, the respected Turkish journalist Ahmed Emin (Yalman) wrote:

> The spreading of news about supposed Turkish atrocities is not the only means that our enemies use to incite the Jews against us. Another way is exaggerated promises of territory, such as have been made to Italy, Serbia, Montenegro, and Greece. They try to create the belief among the Jews that the aim of a part of their people, namely an independent Jewish kingdom in Palestine, will now be fulfilled. . . . It is said that the former American ambassador in Istanbul [a reference to Henry Morgenthau] is to be sent to London for this purpose. *The New York Tribune* denies this fact in its issue of 20 June. . . . There is therefore no question whatever of the establishment of an independent Jewish state. . . . What the Turkish Jews think about these efforts and how faithful they are to Turkey can be seen from the Note that the grand rabbi has sent to the government, as well as from the declaration of the Jewish associations attached to the Note.[43]

An editorial in *Tasvir-i Efkâr* written after the Balfour Declaration also accused England of "patronizing the Zionist movement so as to stir up the Jews everywhere against the Turks." It went on to say:

During the war Turkey has never persecuted the Jews and rumors to the contrary are false. Turkey has protected and provided shelter for Jews oppressed in other countries and is proud of its record. The majority of Jews in the Ottoman Empire remain loyal and grateful. Talât Pasha also promises refuge to all Jewish immigrants who share this sentiment. But Zionism implies the separation of a part of the empire and it is therefore repugnant to Turks, and naturally those who propagate it do more harm than good to the cause of the Jews.

In conclusion, the editorial noted:

> The Entente powers are currying favor with the Jews. But the Jews in Turkey remain loyal and others are welcome to join them when they come with the idea of becoming good patriots. Naturally we do not want elements hostile to our country. . . . No country wants to be partitioned and therefore we cannot encourage Zionism. But as Jews in the Ottoman Empire have always been loyal to the state, there has never been a Jewish question in our empire.[44]

If Nahum's views are any guide, the following quotations undoubtedly expressed the opinions shared by many of the Ottoman Jewish elite, and that is why the "special relationship" had such strong foundations. In February 1917, Nahum, in his capacity as grand rabbi, informed the German ambassador in a private conversation "that Ottoman Jews regarded Zionism as 'a foreign importation,' which was chiefly supported by Germany and America." He continued:

> The vocal and determined manner of the Zionist propaganda gave a false impression of their real influence among the Jews, but those in Turkey regarded it as an undesirable movement that endangered their interests. . . . The Jewish people, thousands of years after the destruction of their political existence, had no cause to revive a Jewish state. The Jews should unconditionally and with no ulterior motives consider themselves as nationals of the states in which they are domiciled and endeavor to identify themselves with their countries' interests. This was the basic principle of Ottoman-Jewish policy. The Jews had always been on good terms with

their state and had no intention of sacrificing this good relationship to any fantastic foreign ideas.[45]

Given this conformity of views, members of the Jewish elite represented Unionist policy at home and abroad and were entrusted with sensitive missions. Thus in January 1915, Leon Taranto, a relation of Isaac Taranto, legal counselor at the Foreign Ministry, was sent to neutral Greece to make contact with the British to explore the possibility of a separate peace. Emmanuel Karasu's advice was also sought in matters of foreign relations. In 1912 he was sent on a secret mission to Rome to discuss the end of Ottoman-Italian hostilities. In July 1918, Karasu, along with Nahum and Mazliyah and three prominent Unionists (Midhat Şükrü, Ziya Gökalp, and Dr. Nâzım) formed a commission to negotiate an Ottoman "Balfour Declaration" with German Zionists.[46] In the last months of the war, Nahum went to the Netherlands and Sweden "to persuade his co-religionists throughout the world to back Turkey and the integrity of the Empire."[47]

By August 1918 it was too late to maintain the integrity of the empire; in fact the very survival of a Turkish state was in doubt. Even in these circumstances the Jewish elite did not desert the sinking ship. Nahum continued to speak for the Turks even after defeat; Nissim Mazliyah maintained relations with Talât Pasha in Berlin so as to better inform the public about the situation in Turkey.[48]

The Jewish political elite was never monolithic, and the conflicting commitments to Ottomanism and Zionism would have been a matter for the individual conscience. Nahum's attitude may have been guided by his religious role as grand rabbi, while Karasu (in his own words) had "to reconcile his duty as a Turkish patriot with that of a nationalist Jew."[49] Others, like Tekinalp, traveled beyond Ottomanism and supported the ideas of Turkification, ideas that at the time only a minority held, even within the CUP. Those who want to learn more about Tekinalp have only to turn to Jacob Landau's excellent monograph.[50] Suffice it to say here that Tekinalp, though never a ranking member of the Jewish elite, became one of the most important ideological voices among the Turkish nationalists and led the way for the integration of the Jewish community into the new republic.

PART THREE

Aspects of Turkish-Jewish Relations in the Twentieth Century

CHAPTER 14

German Jewish Emigrés in Turkey

Frank Tachau

In 1933 a remarkable historical coincidence linked political developments in Germany and Turkey. Both countries were in the throes of profound change, though the character of that change in the two countries was very different. The Nazi revolution in Germany was essentially destructive in nature, transforming the political system, crippling educational, scientific, and cultural institutions, and culminating in an orgy of aggressive expansion that plunged the world into the bloodiest war in history. The Turkish revolution, in contrast, was constructive in nature and intent. Its prime objective was to build a modern European-style society and culture on the ruins of the corrupt and discredited Ottoman Empire. It had no expansionist or aggressive ambitions externally, seeking instead to establish a society that would live at peace with its neighbors.

Both of these movements experienced important turning points in 1933. Early that year, Adolf Hitler became chancellor of Germany, effectively putting an end to the wildly unstable politics of the Weimar Republic and inaugurating an exceptionally brutal dictatorship. In Turkey, on the other hand, the old Darülfünun, Istanbul's institution of higher learning, was abolished on July 31; in its place, the modern University of Istanbul (İstanbul Üniversitesi) was founded on August 1. These two developments were emblematic of the differences between the changes occurring in Germany and Turkey. The Nazi seizure of power in Germany sounded the death knell for free science, scholarship, and intellectual activity. Intellectuals who opposed the Nazis or were likely targets of Nazi repression and those who valued their academic and professional integrity were obliged to flee. Jews, of course, regardless of profession, were doomed from the outset; the only question for them was whether they had the resources to flee, and if they did, how quickly they could prepare themselves psychologically and physically for flight.

The Turkish university reform had precisely the opposite effect: it offered an opening for the very types of persons who were fleeing Germany. The coincidence in the timing of these developments created a highly unusual situation. It provided a unique opportunity to ameliorate a major tragedy. Given the propensity of large organizations, especially public bureaucracies, to miss such opportunities, it is remarkable that this one was successfully exploited.

Turkish University Reform

Reform of Turkish higher education was a natural culmination of Kemal Atatürk's nationalist program. The Istanbul Darülfünun was itself a relatively new institution, having been established as recently as 1900, but it was destined to have a short and unstable existence. Despite reforms in the wake of the 1908 Young Turk Revolution, the Darülfünum was the object of severe criticism in a government report prepared in 1919. Its faculty was a heterogeneous group, most of whose members depended on nonuniversity careers for their livelihoods. Hence there was a singular lack of that scholarly collegiality which might have provided a clear sense of purpose and direction to the institution. Its academic reputation was poor, and many of the faculty opposed Atatürk's ideas and policies. In short, the institution was hardly likely to be harnessed to the effort to produce competent young Turks capable of carrying forward the nationalist reform program. Indeed, it constituted an important symbolic and institutional obstacle to the Atatürk reform plan.[1]

The University reform was foreshadowed by a device that had been utilized a number of times in the course of the modernization of the Ottoman Empire and republican Turkey: the preparation of a report by a foreign expert. In this case the expert was Albert Malche, a respected professor of pedagogy and former rector of the University of Geneva. He undertook a thorough examination of the Darülfünun and, in late May of 1932, submitted a formal report to the Turkish government. His report was highly critical of the institution as it then stood and recommended far-reaching reform. This report was favorably received, and Malche was invited back to Turkey early in 1933 to advise the government on the implementation of the reform. To overcome opposition from among the faculty of the Darülfünun, Reşit Galip, the education minister who sponsored and energetically pursued the reform and who had invited Malche to become a key adviser, stressed the notion that the projected university marked an entirely new beginning and that it was in no way to be a continuation of the old institution. This point was emphasized by the fact that less than half the faculty of the defunct institution were invited to join the new university. The rest of the new teaching staff was to be made up of Turkish graduates of European universities, and foreign (i.e., European) professors. The sharp break with tradition was further highlighted by the wholesale adoption of a new set of terms to describe the institution, its staff, and its program. Thus, the Darülfünun became a *üniversite,* the *reis* became a *rektör,* the *müderris* a *profesör,* etc. Overnight, a koranic inscription gracing the entryway to the campus was replaced with the stark words: "İstanbul Üniversitesi." [2]

Malche stressed the importance of inviting European professors to replace the traditional method of instruction with rigorous training in the scientific method. Initially, this would require massive translation of European texts into Turkish. Ultimately, the goal was to train a Turkish cadre to staff not only the University of Istanbul, but other institutions yet to be established elsewhere in the country. Given the dearth of reliable and appropriately trained Turkish personnel at the time, the role of European academics assumed critical importance. In May of 1933, however, less than three months before the inauguration of the new university, no invitations had yet been extended to foreign academics.

The Emergency Union of Exiled German Scholars to the Rescue

Meanwhile, an exodus of scholars from Germany had begun. A small group of these individuals gravitated to Zurich, Switzerland, a German-speaking center beyond the reach of the Nazis. This group quickly agreed on the need to organize in order to save as many talented scholars as possible in a rational manner, avoiding panic. They published a notice in the Zurich press announcing the formation of an advisory office and inviting inquiries. A flood of queries descended upon them, resulting in the formation of a list of available scholars, by 1936 totaling 1,652 names, which was published in London under the heading "List of Displaced German Scholars." Dr. Philipp Schwartz, the informal leader of the group, testified that thanks to the great need and critical contributions from compassionate Swiss citizens, the fledgling organization, now styling itself as the Emergency Union of Exiled German Scholars, had garnered sufficient material resources and personnel to maintain a complete list of "prospective scholar-victims of racist madness" and to keep up contact with these individuals.[3]

In late May of 1933, Dr. Schwartz and his colleagues in Zurich received a postcard informing them of the reform efforts underway in Istanbul. This postcard initiated a feverish series of activities that produced concrete results in a matter of weeks. Upon receipt of the postcard, Schwartz immediately contacted Professor Malche in Turkey. An exchange of letters led Schwartz to travel to Istanbul, where he arrived on 5 July, 1933; almost without pause, he continued his journey to Ankara. By two o'clock in the afternoon of the next day, Schwartz was received in the national capital by the minister of education and about twenty members of his staff. The Turks wasted no time. They asked Schwartz to recommend potential faculty in a particular field. Schwartz had brought with him enough of the file of the Emergency Union to be able immediately to suggest three persons and to provide their basic resumés. He was even able to add his own personal impressions of two of these individuals, whom he had met in Zurich. This turned out to be merely an opening bid; requests for thirty additional recommendations quickly followed. Schwartz might well have been emotionally overcome as he wrote:

> I, and probably all those present forgot time, complications, and obstacles. I knew that in these hours the disgraceful expulsion from Germany had achieved a positive result. I had discovered a wonderful country, untouched by the Western plague! The establishment and development of the Emergency Union was fully justified; it had proven itself to be historically significant.[4]

Before this remarkable meeting ended, the text of a contractual agreement was formally signed. Education Minister Reşit Galip marked the occasion with these words:

> This is an extraordinary day on which we were able to accomplish an unprecedented act. When Constantinople fell almost 500 years ago, Byzantine scholars decided to leave the country. There was no holding them back. Many went to Italy, resulting in the Renaissance there. Today we have prepared the ground to receive a return gift from Europe. We hope for an enrichment, yes, a renewal of our nation. Bring us your knowledge and your methods, show our youth the road to progress. We offer you our gratitude and honor.[5]

The seven-hour meeting ended at nine o'clock in the evening. Schwartz promptly cabled Zurich: "Not 3, but 30!" Before Schwartz's departure, Reşit Galip spoke to him again about the urgency of the situation from the Turkish point of view, given the designation of 1 August, 1933 as the founding day for the new university. In addition to asking Schwartz to make a second trip within a matter of weeks, he offered to intercede on behalf of any scholars who were under detention in prison or concentration camps and to provide them with legal contracts and the diplomatic protection of the Turkish government. (Indeed, this offer was soon followed by action.[6]) Schwartz also met with the health minister, Refik Saydam, who requested personnel to help staff the Nümune Hospital, then under construction in Ankara, as well as the Central Institute of Health (*Hıfzısıha*).[7]

Less than three weeks later, Dr. Schwartz returned to Istanbul, accompanied by Dr. Rudolf Nissen, a former professor of surgery at the University of Berlin, to carry forward the task of recruiting displaced academics for the new University of Istanbul.[8] A temporary setback occurred when Reşit Galip suffered a serious accident in mid-August, leading to his resignation from the post of minister of education, and shortly thereafter, to his untimely death. Although the official Turkish commitments were confirmed, this misfortune created an air of uncertainty that did not dissipate until the appointment of Hikmet Bayur, then a relatively youthful historian of the Turkish War of Independence, as the new minister of education. Bayur was fully committed to the university reform program and to fulfilling the plans to recruit the displaced scholars.

By late October some 150 persons had arrived in Istanbul, including not only the scholars, but also their families, siblings, mothers, mothers-in-law, and even professional assistants. Schwartz was among them, having himself accepted an appointment as professor of pathology and director of the Institute of Pathology at the University of Istanbul. He gave this impression of the new arrivals:

> They were seen . . . everywhere, in Taksim Square, on Istiklal Caddesi, in the mosques, the museums, on the ferryboats, on the islands, and above all at the beaches. They came straight from Germany, persecuted and despised, often having left patrician homes behind; or they came from modest boarding houses in England, or from cheap and overcrowded *pensions* in Paris where they had sojourned as hard-pressed emigrants. Now they have found themselves, exhilerated, among a hospitable people, living as free and honored—indeed spoiled—immigrants.[9]

Early in November the new education minister presided at the official opening ceremonies of the new university. He took pains to introduce each of the newly arrived professors individually, as well as their newly appointed Turkish colleagues. Instruction began immediately afterwards, often amidst the dust of new construction or reconstruction, in many cases with makeshift classroom furniture, and in the case of the immigrant faculty, invariably with interpreters at their side, translating from German into Turkish word for word. Schwartz seemed genuinely surprised to note that this great experiment worked. He describes a sense of mutual appreciation, on the part of the faculty for the opportunity to continue with their calling, and on the part of the students for the extensive learning and expertise that the faculty represented. "They understood us!" he exclaimed. "We became friends!"[10]

A later arrival, Professor Friedrich Reimann, commented that "this university [the University of Istanbul] . . . was the best German university of its time."[11] This evaluation was confirmed by Dr. Erich Uhlmann, who, together with Dr. Friedrich Dessauer, was involved in the establishment of a radiological clinic in Istanbul. According to Uhlmann, Atatürk himself took a close personal interest in the development of the clinic, insisting that it be a state-of-the-art facility. And so it was—although incongruously, much of the equipment had to be transported from the port by horse cart.[12]

It is worth noting, however, that mutual appreciation did not go so far as to give the foreign scholars a completely free ride. Each of them was offered a contract, but it included certain stipulations that could prove burdensome. These contracts typically prohibited pursuit of other occupations or income-earning activities outside the university; required preparation of Turkish-language textbooks and study guides; specified that the immigrants would attain a reading knowledge of Turkish within three to five years; required that, on request of the Turkish government, they complete their professional training without salary; and required that they actively participate in adult education and extension activities. Since many of the professors were eminent scholars who had held tenured positions at internationally renowned universities in Germany and Austria, one can imagine that under normal circumstances they might have hesitated to commit themselves to provisions such as these.[13]

Life in Turkey

The characteristics of the emigrés are worth reviewing. Table 14.1 provides a summary of the fields of specialization of 144 emigrés and the location of their places of employment in Turkey. Widmann provides detailed data on 80 of these individuals, showing that 65 percent were mature scholars (i.e., between the ages of 40 and 59), 35 percent were senior (i.e., over the age of 50), and only 10 percent were junior (i.e., under the age of 35). In other words, Turkish institutions benefited from an influx of highly experienced and in some cases very accomplished individuals. Nearly 75 percent of them arrived in Turkey before 1937, and half of those came in the year 1933 alone. Approximately half of the sample of 80 remained in Turkey 10 years or less (and this group was about evenly divided between those who remained 5 years or less, and those who remained 5 to 10 years). About 30 percent remained more than 16 years, while nearly 25 percent retired and/or died in Turkey.[14]

Table 14.1
Fields of Specialization and Location of Emigrés

Field	Istanbul	Ankara
Medicine	46	8
Natural Science	21	4
Humanities and Social Science	21	8
Law	10	
Performing Arts	5	21
Totals	103	41

Source: Widmann, pp. 131-32, 167.

Not all the immigrants were Jewish. A number of them were political opponents of the Nazis who were fully as vulnerable as the Jews—perhaps even more so in the early days of the regime. A prime example was Alexander Rüstow, philosopher, sociologist, and economist, who had been active in the German labor movement through much of the 1920s. In 1933, Rüstow was involved in a "last-minute . . . desperate anti-Hitler coalition"; indeed, his name was included on an abortive cabinet list as minister of economy.[15] Others were marked not by their "non-Aryan" identity, but by the fact that they were married to Jews. Regardless of religious status in Germany, however, they all shared a common antipathy to the Nazi regime.[16] This created a curious situation for them in their new Turkish environment. Under normal circumstances, one would have expected them to seek to maintain as much contact with their homeland as possible. In Turkey, this would have been quite feasible, since there was an active German community, stemming partly from the traditional friendship that had existed between the two countries at least since the late nineteenth century. But, of course, these were not normal circumstances. The Nazi regime soon preempted the embassy, consulate, and other official and cultural organizations in Turkey. Accordingly, the emigrant group was effectively cut off from participation in official activities. Even had they attempted an approach, they would certainly not have been welcome. Given the conditions under which they had left Germany, however, they were in no mood to mix socially with those who represented their tormentors. Nor, given the recency of their arrival and the absence of sufficient opportunity to prepare for the cultural transition, could the new arrivals assimilate easily to the Turkish social scene. As a result, they were thrown back upon their own resources, giving rise to a self-contained community. Thus, two distinct German social circles developed in Istanbul and Ankara, one tied to the official institutions of the Nazi regime, the other consisting of the anti-Nazi, predominantly Jewish, emigrés.

The position of the emigré group was thus highly ambiguous. Although they had deep roots in German culture and society, which involved strong emotional ties (in many cases with family members who remained behind), they bore a natural antipathy toward the Nazi regime and its supporters. The feeling was reciprocated; indeed, the regime actively tried to interfere in the relationship between the emigrés and their Turkish hosts. The uncertainty spawned by this complex situation was underlined as the emigrés' German passports expired. Since renewal of these passports was not possible, the result was that these individuals became stateless, remaining in Turkey only by the good graces of the Turkish government.[17]

One case in particular illustrates the complexities of the situation. This individual had a Jewish father who converted as an adult; his mother was non-Jewish, and he himself was baptized as a child. By Nazi reckoning, nevertheless, he could be treated as a Jew. Within days after the appointment of Adolf Hitler as Imperial Chancellor, this person was denied a position at a prominent public institution for which he was eminently qualified, even though there was not yet a legal regulation in effect—nor even a settled policy—regarding employment of those who might possibly be "non-Aryan." Because of his particular expertise, this scholar was then invited to join a German archaeological expedition in Turkey. Subsequently he was appointed by the Turkish government as a professor at the newly established Faculty of Language, History, and Geography in Ankara, where he established a department in his field. Some years later he married a Jewish woman, herself the daughter of one of the emigré professors in Istanbul. The marriage was performed by a German consular official in Istanbul, since both bride and groom were German citizens. Under Nazi law, however, now that this German citizen was espoused to a "non-Aryan," he acquired the definite status of non-Aryan himself; accordingly, the letter *J* was promptly stamped in his passport. Some time after the marriage, the Nazis enacted a law that invalidated *J* passports. As World War II began to wind down and the defeat of Nazi Germany seemed imminent, Turkey broke off diplomatic relations with Berlin. This development affected the status of German citizens residing in Turkey: they were offered the choice of leaving or facing internment. Our protagonist was able to avoid these stark alternatives, since his passport had become invalid due to the *J* imprint added after his marriage, and he was therefore no longer a German citizen![18] This case highlights the absurd consequences that may ensue from extremist racist chauvinism.

The Nazi regime was not satisfied with merely expelling innocent German nationals—highly talented ones at that—and depriving them of their citizenship. It went so far as to hound the exiles in their places of refuge. For example, in May 1938 the German diplomatic missions in Ankara and Istanbul sent questionnaires to the emigrés requiring them to attest to their status as Aryans (and the status of their spouses as well), and inquiring as to whether they had been affected by a 1933 law designed to rid the German civil service of non-Aryans and other politically unreliable officials. In the spring of 1939, the Nazi government dispatched one of its officials, Herbert Scurla, on a mission to report on the political reliability (from the Nazi perspective) of the German emigrés in Turkey. Scurla filed a report that went into great detail regarding the official status of each of the emigré academics, including an evaluation of their loyalty and political reliability. The Scurla mission, which included a number of meetings with Turkish officials, was undoubtedly designed to persuade the Turkish government to cancel, or at least not renew, the contracts of persons singled out by the Nazis. If that was indeed the purpose, the project was apparently a failure.[19]

Nazi officiousness was not, however, the only source of uncertainty for the emigré scholars. Although the Turkish government was hospitable and supportive, this positive attitude was not necessarily shared by all of the emigrés' Turkish colleagues or others with whom they came into contact. The massive dismissal of Turkish faculty members of the Istanbul Darülfünun in

1933 and the awarding of contracts of limited duration to the emigrés indicated that their own tenure in the new institutions might become rather unstable if circumstances changed. Indeed, several individuals were forced to leave Turkey rather abruptly precisely because their contracts were not renewed, or because they experienced serious problems in relationships with Turkish colleagues, including survivors of the change from the Darülfünun to the university.[20]

There were other problems as well. Working conditions in the newly formed Turkish institutions were hardly conducive to the pursuit of pure scientific research. The conditions written into the contracts of many of the emigrés have already been detailed; some of these could be described as "public service," in American parlance, rather than as scholarship. Some individuals were not properly prepared or suited for these conditions. Friedrich Dessauer, professor of radiology, is a case in point. Trained as a research scientist, Dessauer was confronted by as many as eighty cancer patients per day in need of the services of his clinic in Istanbul. The need was so overwhelming that he could not in good conscience refuse to treat these people. On the other hand, the demands of their treatment were so great that he was unable to carry on his research. Not surprisingly, Dessauer accepted an appointment at the University of Fribourg, Switzerland, three years after his arrival in Istanbul.[21]

Emigré Contributions

Negative cases of this kind were greatly outweighed by the positive aspects of the emigrés' experience. Some of the individual emigrés made outstanding—and highly appreciated—contributions to Turkish culture and society, and many went on to illustrious careers in Europe and America. Ernst Reuter seems to have literally created the field of urban planning in Turkey, laying the foundations for the Institute of Urbanism (which today bears his name) at the Political Science Faculty of Ankara University. In 1946, Reuter returned to Germany, ultimately to become the mayor of West Berlin.[22]

Paul Hindemith almost single-handedly paved the way for the establishment of the State Conservatory of Music in Ankara, despite the fact that he never really settled down in Turkey. He was recruited by Cevat Dursunoğlu, a prominent Turkish official then serving as education attaché in Berlin. Hindemith came to Ankara several times for periods of several months each, developed recommendations and project plans, and was responsible for the recruitment of a total of at least eleven colleagues and fellow artists. Carl Ebert, also recruited in Berlin, became the guiding spirit of the newly established State Opera in Ankara, and Ernst Praetorius established the Presidential Philharmonic Orchestra. Of equal importance, if less public prominence, was the establishment of vital academic departments at such institutions as the Faculty of Language, History and Geography in Ankara, where emigré faculty served as the first professors in such significant fields as Sumerology, Hittitology, Sinology, Hungarian studies, and Western classical languages and literatures.

Beyond the establishment of important academic institutions, the emigrés made immense contributions to Turkish society also in other ways. Several of the medical specialists conducted epidemiological and other studies in their fields, particularly Albert Eckstein in pediatrics and Marchionini in dermatology. Perhaps most significantly, these researchers trained one or more generations of Turkish students who were able to continue to work in their field after the emigré's departure. One of Eckstein's students, for example, was that prominent Turkish pediatrician İhsan Doğramacı. In other fields, too, emigrés had lasting influence. The Hittitologist Hans G. Güterbock (later of the Oriental Institute at the University of Chicago) designed and directed the reconstruction of a historic building in the old city of Ankara that became the core of a highly regarded Museum of Ethnography, which continues to thrive today.

Most of the emigrés remained in Turkey until the end of World War II. In the postwar period, many of them were invited to join the faculties of prominent European and American universities. In numerous cases these invitations served both to compensate for ill treatment under the Nazis and to rebuild the war-shattered German universities. For the emigrés, such invitations were extremely tempting, as they signified restitution for psychological and material damage caused by the disruption of their careers, and they provided an opportunity to return to the land of their birth.

Some of the emigrés, however, left Turkey involuntarily. The group associated with the History, Language, and Geography Faculty in Ankara stands out in this regard. Paradoxically, these individuals came under fire as part of the changing Turkish atmosphere associated with the shift from one-party rule to democracy following World War II. Officially their dismissals came about as the result of parliamentary action that eliminated their faculty positions from the university budget. But this parliamentary move was only a maneuver. It was clear that the five foreign professors were specifically targeted. Significantly, all but one of them were ultimately offered appointments at highly prestigious American universities: two at the Oriental Institute of the University of Chicago, and one each at Columbia University and the University of California at Berkeley.[23]

♦   ♦   ♦

The Turkish initiative of 1933 was both far-sighted and magnanimous. It was certainly most timely. In a classical political manner, it harnessed the interests of the Turkish state and society to the well-being of a number of highly skilled human beings—saving their careers, and probably their very lives. In some way, this was a symbolic reenactment, though numerically on a small scale, of the migration of Jews from Spain to the Ottoman Empire some five hundred years earlier. Even the bittersweet ending of the experience for some of the scholars does not diminish the significance of the human contribution represented by the Turkish initiative.

CHAPTER 15

Roads East

Turkey and the Jews of Europe during World War II

Stanford J. Shaw

The Ottoman Empire had for centuries provided a safe haven for Jewish refugees from Europe. The large-scale migrations of Jews from Spain, Portugal, and other European countries in the fifteenth and sixteenth centuries are well known and have been discussed in detail.[1] However, later Jewish population movements to the Ottoman Empire and republican Turkey are less well known. In the seventeenth and eighteenth centuries, the migration of Jews to the Ottoman Empire declined greatly in comparison with the earlier period. Still, over the years many European Jews, individually or in small groups, continued to settle in the Ottoman dominions for political, economic, or religious reasons.[2] In the nineteenth and early twentieth centuries, the influx of Jewish refugees into the shrinking boundaries of the Ottoman Empire rose again. This time the migration was caused mainly by persecution in the newly independent Balkan states as well as in eastern Europe.[3]

Still another chapter in the story of Turkish assistance to Jewish refugees began in the 1930s, when Turkey was in the process of modernizing its universities and scientific research institutions. Mustafa Kemal Atatürk and his minister of education, Reşit Galip, decided to invite to Turkey hundreds of refugee scholars and scientists, many of them Jews, who had fled Nazi Germany and Austria. These refugees, whose number included many of the most prominent scholars in their fields, made significant contributions to the development of Turkish universities and scientific institutions, as well as

246

to the fine arts and music. For most of the refugee scholars, the Turkish haven, in return, provided an escape from certain death and an opportunity to continue with their professional careers.[4]

When World War II broke out, Turkey found itself in an unusual situation. Before the war it had concluded a defensive treaty with both France and Britain, mainly against Italian and German expansionism. Turkey had entered these agreements on the assumption of Soviet friendliness, in view of Moscow's strong opposition to both Fascism and Nazism. But the German-Soviet pact of August 1939 and later the rapid Italian and German advances in the Balkans, East Europe, the Caucasus, and North Africa left Turkey increasingly isolated from its nominal allies and exposed to the full might of Axis power established along its borders. In addition, most Turks vividly remembered the tremendous losses and deprivations experienced as a result of the disasters of World War I, and they had no desire to go through that again, unless their country's interests were directly involved. For that reason, and in order to avoid provoking a German invasion, Turkey maintained an uneasy neutrality throughout most of the war. What it could not escape, however, were oppressive economic and financial hardships that resulted from the need to maintain a very large army against the possibility of a German attack at a time when most of its imports and exports were cut off because of the war.[5]

As a neutral power whose friendship was valued by Berlin and Vichy France, Turkey was placed in a unique position where it was able to provide assistance to Jews who were being persecuted throughout Nazi-occupied Europe. Turkey was one of the few neutral countries remaining in Europe able to maintain diplomatic representation in Germany as well as in most of the occupied countries, and its diplomats and consuls used their position to intervene on behalf of Turkish Jews resident in those countries. In France, for which we have most of the information, this work was carried out by the Turkish embassy, located at Vichy starting in 1941, as well as by the Turkish consulates-general in Paris and Marseilles. (The Marseilles consulate was transferred to Grenoble after Germany occupied much of southern France following Italy's withdrawal from the war in September 1943.) The Turkish diplomats who were most involved in this work—and who went to great lengths to protect Turkish Jews, often at the risk of their own lives—were at the two consulates. In Paris were Consul-General Cevdet Dülger, from 1939 until 1942; Consul-General Fikret Şefik Özdoğancı from 1942 until 1945; and Vice Consul Namık Kemal Yolga, who remained in Paris throughout the war. At Marseilles were Consul-General Bedi'i Arbel, from 1940 until 1943; Consul-General Mehmed Fuad Carım, from June 1943 until 1945; and Vice Consul Necdet Kent, who, like Yolga, remained in France until the end of the war.[6]

The Turkish consuls regularly applied to the German and French authorities to exempt Turkish Jews from the anti-Jewish laws introduced by the German occupation authorities and the Vichy government of unoccupied France, whose measures were sometimes harsher than those of the Germans. The Turkish claims for exemption were always based on the same principle, stated over and over again: that Turkey made no distinction among citizens of different religions. These diplomats intervened in all sorts of ways to assist Turkish Jews during the war. First and foremost, the diplomats kept the Jews' Turkish citizenship up to date by registering them and informing the authorities that they were Turkish citizens whenever it was necessary to assist them against Nazi and Vichy persecution. This was not as easy as it appears. There were about ten thousand Turkish Jews living in France at the start of the war, and about an equal number living elsewhere in Europe at the same time. Some of these Jews had left Turkey as early as 1921, in the company of the French army that evacuated the country following the Franklin-Bouillon Agreement. Other Turkish Jews went to France during the 1920s, in the early years of the Turkish Republic, when the country's future seemed uncertain; Atatürk was just beginning to put his secular reforms into place, and residence in France appeared to offer far greater economic opportunity. By 1940 many of these Turkish Jews living in France had married French Jews, had children and even grandchildren who were French citizens, and had in fact taken up French citizenship themselves. Some had retained their Turkish citizenship by registering with the Turkish consulates at least once every five years. Others had neglected this duty, and as a result they had lost their Turkish citizenship under terms of a law that required Turks abroad to register or forfeit their citizenship.

Up until the war, the loss of Turkish nationality had not seemed important to most Turkish Jews in France because they considered French citizenship preferable. However, when the Nazis came in and began persecuting French Jews, and when Turkish diplomats started intervening to exempt Turkish Jews from the racial laws, those Jews who had lost their Turkish citizenship suddenly discovered the benefits of their former nationality, and they began applying in large numbers to have their Turkish citizenship restored. This took time, however, since each application had to be referred to Ankara. In the meantime, these Turkish Jews were increasingly subjected to severe persecution unless they could produce Turkish papers. The Turkish diplomats responded to this situation in two ways. Sometimes they provided false papers, giving certificates of Turkish citizenship to Turkish Jews who were in imminent danger of being deported for forced labor or to concentration camps, and to those who were being threatened with seizure of their homes and businesses. Alternatively, the diplomats provided papers stating that the bearers were "irregular Turkish citizens" (*gayri muntazam vatandaş*), whose papers were being processed in Ankara, but who in the meantime had to be considered and treated as Turkish citizens, with all the protections and immunities provided to other Turkish citizens in France. The consular records indicate that the amount of paperwork involved was immense, but that the Turkish diplomats worked assiduously to handle all the cases and to protect those Jews who were in imminent danger.[7]

On 2 November 1940, the Turkish consulate general in Paris sent the following note to the German embassy in protest against a regulation forbidding Jews to own or operate businesses:

> To the Embassy of Germany:
>   The Consulate General of Turkey in Paris, basing itself on the fact that Turkish Constitutional Law makes no distinctions between its citizens on the basis of the religion to which they belong, has the honor of asking the German Embassy to give instructions to the competent department that the decision that has begun to affect certain merchants of Turkish nationality, because of the regulation of 18 October 1940, be reconsidered.[8]

The German replies generally accepted the Turkish argument; for example, that of 28 February 1941 stated: "Despite the general regulations . . . , the German Embassy is ready to support individual requests for exemptions of

Jews by the Turkish Consulate General when they have Turkish nationality."[9] The French government of unoccupied France, based at Vichy, was in
many ways more devious and difficult in these matters. On 16 June 1941,
Vichy made public a law requiring all Jews in unoccupied France, including
Turkish citizens, to register themselves and their property on pain of deportation to concentration camps. Following this decree, the Turkish ambassador to Paris (Vichy) sent a message to the French foreign ministry stating:

> The Embassy of Turkey has the honor of informing the Ministry of For-
> eign Affairs that its Government, having been informed of the text of law
> no. 2,333 of 2 June 1941, which, under pain of penal sanctions, orders the
> registration of Jews on a special record, along with a declaration which
> they must make regarding their properties, feels that the measures which it
> dictates are also applicable to Turkish citizens of Jewish origin established
> in France. Turkey itself does not discriminate among its citizens on the
> basis of race, religion or otherwise, and therefore feels with unease such
> discrimination imposed by the French government on those of its citizens
> who are established in France. Consequently the Turkish government en-
> tirely reserves its rights in what concerns those of the latter who are of the
> Jewish race.[10]

In response, Vichy insisted that a Jew was a Jew regardless of his nationality,
as in the note from the French foreign ministry to the Turkish embassy at
Vichy on 8 August 1941:

> The Ministry has the honor of informing the [Turkish] Embassy that by es-
> tablishing themselves in France, the individuals in question have implicitly
> agreed to submit themselves to the legislation of the country in which they
> are guests. This principle has sufficient force that the measures regarding
> persons of the Hebrew race apply to all Jews whether they are of French al-
> legiance or nationals of foreign countries.[11]

The United States embassy at Vichy advised American citizens in
France to accept the French official argument, on the grounds that it did not
discriminate among Jews.[12] Turkey, however, resolutely refused to accept
this principle on the following grounds: first, that it violated the treaties

signed between Turkey and France, which provided that nationals of Turkey were to enjoy the same civil rights in France that French citizens enjoyed in Turkey; and second, that it discriminated among Turkish citizens of different religions. The Turkish reply to this message, dated 9 September 1941, thus rejected this argument:

> While it is natural enough for foreigners to accept the laws of a country in which they live, in accordance with the strongly expressed view of the French Foreign Minister that a foreigner who has settled in a country can be assumed to have accepted the attachment of his state and future to that country's laws, our answer must be that we reserve our rights in regard to a law which discriminates among Turkish citizens of different religions.[13]

The Turkish consulates in Paris and Marseilles, therefore, regularly protested against the discriminatory laws issued both by the Nazi occupation authorities and the Vichy government. These laws required unemployed Jews to join forced labor gangs, prevented Jews from having telephones or radios in their homes, and required that Jewish businesses be Aryanized by turning them over to non-Jewish administrators or selling them to Aryans. These laws further resulted in the arrest of Jews on the flimsiest of pretexts, the seizure of their apartments and businesses, and their deportation to concentration camps in France or to death camps in eastern Europe. In such cases, the Turkish consuls sent official letters of protest and personally intervened with the German ambassador in Paris, Otto Abetz, and with French and German police officials, concentration camp commanders, S.S. and Gestapo officers, and the like. Although the German and French authorities were evasive in their response, ultimately the Turkish diplomats would receive the answer that if they could document that the Jews in question were in fact Turkish citizens, they would be released on the condition that they be repatriated to Turkey as rapidly as possible. At times, the Turkish consuls actually went to the concentration camps—most of the Jews in France were sent to the camp at Drancy, on the outskirts of Paris, from which they were sent on to Auschwitz for extermination.[14]

The situation of the Turkish Jews at Drancy and other concentration camps was difficult because they were scorned and persecuted not only by the Germans and the French police that guarded the camps but also by the French Jews, who somehow felt superior to the foreign Jews. The French Jews used their numerical superiority in the camp and their domination of the Jewish camp bureaucracy to favor their own in areas where they had influence, such as distributing food and assigning work. Also, when the Germans ordered that a thousand Jews a week be shipped east to the extermination camps, the French Jews arranged that most of those selected were foreign Jews. The following excerpts were recorded by different people who were inmates at Drancy during the war:

There were there Frenchmen, Poles, Turks and the like. I was chief of the room, and I never succeeded in being able to place myself between the Yiddishists and the Hispano-Turks, who constantly intrigued for a few more bits of bread. They lived by nationality, by groups, by compatriots. Each looked only after his own interests and not those of his neighbor.

The internees deplored that there was little solidarity among them. The most striking manifestation of this seemed to be the frequent arguments which pitted some against others, in particular French against foreign Jews. The French Jews blamed the foreigners for being the cause of their misfortunes, and the latter complained about France. Perhaps it is necessary to lay the responsibility at the door of the French Jews, many of whom came to the camp saying that they were superior Jews and that they would be released before the others. But one must recognize that their bitterness was justified, particularly when they were war veterans who had performed their duty for their country and who could not understand how they could be treated differently than their [French] fellow citizens.

The French and foreign Jews interned in the camp formed two hostile groups: the French Jews affirmed that their being there was the fault of the foreigners and they hoped for special treatment by the authorities which never came.

The French Jews believed that they would be freed soon, and they did not want to be seen in solidarity with the foreigners. . . . The French Jew

believed that it was because of the former that he was in the camp. He
spoke of the foreign Jew with disdain. . . . Their self-deception resulted in
more bitterness when they saw that the Germans made no distinction between Jews and Jews. . . . The foreign Jews, in turn, reproached the French
Jews for the attitude of France. This led to endless arguments that ended in
tumult and dispute.[15]

Whenever Turkish Jews were ordered to join French and other Jews in
forced-labor gangs, the Turkish diplomats advised them not to report, and
they sent protests to the French government, which usually led to the exemption of Turkish Jews. On 15 December 1942, Ambassador Behiç Erkin
(Vichy) reported to Ankara: "I have sent a telegram to the French Foreign
Ministry asking that Turkish Jewish citizens not be included in the decree
recently published in the newspapers by the Prefecture of Marseilles that all
foreign Jews who entered France since December 1933 and who are without work or in need, be gathered in foreign worker groups."[16] At the same
time Erkin sent the following instructions to the Turkish consul general in
Marseilles, Bedi'i Arbel: "Jewish citizens whose papers are in order cannot be
subjected to forced labor, and if such situations arise, it is natural that we
should provide them with protection. The prefects of police should be reminded of the relevant instructions and it is necessary to intervene with the
competent authorities when necessary."[17]

Turkish diplomats in France also spent a good deal of time organizing
train caravans to take Turkish Jews back to Turkey. This actually was encouraged by the Vichy government as well as the French authorities in German-
occupied France as the only way to make sure that Turkish Jews would not
be subjected to the racial laws applied to French Jews. On their part, the
Nazi occupation officials themselves were becoming increasingly unhappy
about the exemptions and were constantly demanding that they be brought
to an end. Thus the French foreign ministry wrote to the Turkish embassy at
Vichy on 13 January 1943, after the French had finally accepted the Turkish
argument that it was illegal for them to discriminate against Turkish citizens
of different religions: "To avoid the application of these measures to Turkish
citizens, the Ministry of Foreign Affairs would be disposed to look favorably

on the return of the interested parties to their countries of origin." [18] In mid-1943 the Nazi occupation authorities, inspired by Adolph Eichmann, finally issued an ultimatum to Turkey and to the other neutral countries: they would have to repatriate all their Jewish citizens by May 1944, after which all those who remained would be treated just like French Jews. Most of the neutral countries agreed to this right away and evacuated their Jews quickly because they were able to send them home directly, without having to arrange for them to cross through third countries. Turkey, however, was unable to do the same because with the Mediterranean closed to shipping, the only way to send Turkish Jews back was by train through southeastern Europe. The Nazis issued group visas for the evacuated Jews, but the various semi-independent countries located along the path of the train were not anxious to help Jews escape extermination. The worst of these were Croatia, Serbia, and Bulgaria, which caused all sorts of delays before the trains could start out from Paris. Finally, however, the Turkish diplomats were able to organize four train caravans during 1943 and eight more in 1944, which altogether transported some 2,000 Jews back to Turkey. Other Turkish Jews were helped to flee to the areas of southern France under Italian occupation, where they were treated much better until Mussolini fell and Italy was occupied by the Germans in September 1943. Still others were assisted in escaping across the Pyrenees into Franco's Spain, or across the Mediterranean to North Africa.

In late 1943 and early 1944 when the Vichy government, which at times was even more anti-Semitic than the Nazis, was considering the deportation of all 10,000 Turkish Jews living within its territory to East Europe for extermination, the Turkish foreign minister, Numan Menemencioğlu, intervened with Vichy, on the direct orders of President İsmet İnönü. Menemencioğlu maintained that such an act by Vichy would be considered by Turkey as unfriendly and would cause a major diplomatic incident. This argument convinced Vichy to abandon the plan, and it saved these Jews from almost certain death. The original correspondence in this matter has not yet been uncovered in either the Turkish or French archives. Turkey's key role, however, is well documented in other sources. The American ambassador in Ankara during the war, Laurence Steinhart, himself a Jew, wrote to the head of the Jewish Agency office in Istanbul, Chaïm (Charles) Barlas, on 9 February 1944:

> It has been a great satisfaction to me personally to have been in a position to have intervened with at least some degree of success on behalf of former Turkish citizens in France of Jewish origin. As I explained to you yesterday, while the Vichy Government has as yet given no commitment to the Turkish Government, there is every evidence that the intervention of the Turkish authorities has caused the Vichy authorities to at least postpone if not altogether abandon their apparent intention to exile these unfortunates to almost certain death by turning them over to the Nazi authorities.[19]

Steinhart's account is confirmed in the memoirs of his German counterpart, the well-known Franz von Papen, who, however, emphasized his own role in the affair:

> I learned through one of the German emigré professors that the Secretary of the Jewish Agency had asked me to intervene in the matter of the threatened deportation to camps in Poland of 10,000 Jews living in Southern France. Most of them were former Turkish citizens of Levantine origin. I promised my help and discussed the matter with M. Menemencioğlu. There was no legal basis to warrant any official action on his part, but he authorized me to inform Hitler that the deportation of these former Turkish citizens would cause a sensation in Turkey and endanger friendly relations between the two countries. This demarche succeeded in quashing the whole affair.[20]

Finally, one of Barlas's associates at the Jewish Agency office in Istanbul, Dr. Chaim Pazner, stated to the Second Yad Vashem International Historical Conference on Rescue Attempts during the Holocaust, held in Jerusalem in April 1974:

> In December 1943, Chaim Barlas notified me from Istanbul that he had received a cable from Isaac Weisman, representative of the World Jewish Congress in Lisbon, that approximately ten thousand Jews who were

Turkish citizens, but had been living in France for years and had neglected to register and renew their Turkish citizenship with the Turkish representation in France, were in danger of being deported to the death camps. Weisman requested that Barlas contact the competent Turkish authorities and attempt to save the above mentioned Jews. Upon receiving the telegram, Barlas immediately turned to the Turkish Foreign Ministry in Ankara, submitted a detailed memorandum on the subject, and requested urgent action by the Turkish legation in Paris. Upon being notified of the above, I promptly contacted Marc Jarblum, who was working in Geneva at the time, since the case involved Jews who lived in France. Jarblum immediately contacted his co-workers in France. We later received word from Istanbul and Paris that, with the exception of several score, these ten thousand Jews were saved from extermination.[21]

The Jewish Agency was also involved in what Turkey did to help East European Jews flee from persecution in countries such as Poland, Czechoslovakia, Romania, Hungary, Yugoslavia, and Bulgaria. Right from the start of the war, Turkey permitted the Jewish Agency to maintain a rescue office at the Pera Palace and other hotels in the Tepebaşı section of Istanbul under the direction of Chaïm (Charles) Barlas, one of the Agency's leading officials. In addition, other Jewish organizations in Palestine were allowed to establish representative offices in Istanbul. Kibbutzim sent emissaries with the purpose of rescuing their members from eastern and southeastern Europe. Their first task was to gather information on the conditions in those countries. For this purpose they sent agents from Istanbul. They also used the Turkish post office to correspond with Jews in these countries to gather information and to send packages of food and clothing. In these activities the Turkish ministry of finance provided them with the hard currency needed to meet their expenses, and the Turkish diplomats in the countries concerned provided their facilities when needed. With this help, the Jewish rescue groups were able to arrange for trains and steamboats to carry to safety, in Turkey and beyond, as many refugees as could leave.[22] In these activities Turkey was vigorously opposed by the British government, which feared, correctly, that most of the refugees would go on to Palestine. As a matter of fact, Turkey had made this a condition of its agreement to accept the refugees. Wartime shortages and the near-starvation conditions in the country severely limited the number of refugees that Turkey could admit in the course of the war. It did allow the Jewish Agency and other organizations to bring refugees through the country on their way to Palestine, permitting the Agency to send them illegally in small boats across the Mediterranean from southern Turkey. When the British were successful in preventing some of these refugees from going to Palestine, the Turkish government allowed them to remain in Turkey far beyond the limits of their transit visas—in many cases right until the end of the war. British obduracy and wartime conditions resulted in a number of tragic disasters, the worst of which was the sinking of the *Struma* in the Black Sea in February 1942, with the loss of 769 refugees from Romania. On the whole, however, the Turkish border guards allowed individual or small groups of Jews coming across the border on foot, or swimming across the Maritza, to enter Turkey even though most of them had no papers at all. Camps were set up for these refugees near Edirne, and ultimately they were allowed to continue to Istanbul and the Mediterranean coast of southern Turkey, from which most departed by small boats for Palestine.[23]

As is well known, the Vatican did very little to help persecuted European Jews, but this was not the case with its representative in Istanbul from 1935 until 1944: Monseigneur Angelo Roncalli, the papal nuncio, who later became Pope John XXIII. Roncalli was a very unusual person. When he first came to Turkey before the war, he taught his parishioners, including many Greeks and Armenians, that they should follow the precepts of Christian charity and love in dealing with Turks; that they should forget the hatred and bigotry of the past and work together with the Turks to build a new and modern republic. Roncalli himself learned Turkish, and at times recited the Christmas mass in Turkish in Istanbul. This greatly pleased the Turkish people. During the war Roncalli went much further than this. He had the Sisters of Sion order of nuns use their own network to help the Jewish Agency pass communications, clothing, and food to Jews, particularly in Hungary. Other Vatican couriers going from Istanbul to eastern Europe did the same thing as a result of Roncalli's instructions. He even arranged to send false certificates of baptism to Hungarian Jews to save them from the Nazis.[24]

Turkey also acted to help the Jews of Greece during the war. In those parts of Greece, including Athens, that fell under Italian control, the condition of the Jewish population was tolerable. However, in the German zone, including Salonica, anti-Jewish measures were implemented from the start. After Italy fell out of the war in September 1943 and the Germans took over entirely, the Jews were subjected to increasing persecution and to deportation to Auschwitz. From this point on, the condition of Jews in Greece became worse than almost anywhere else in Europe. While in other European countries (e.g., Holland, France, even Germany), many among the local population had helped Jews in different ways, at times concealing them for months and years, the Greeks, because of their long history of pervasive anti-Semitism, did almost nothing. Consequently, some 65,000 Greek Jews—about 85 percent of the total Jewish population—perished during World War II. The only Greeks who in any way helped Jews were the partisans fighting against the Nazis, who did assist Jews to escape from Greece across the Aegean and eastern Mediterranean to Turkey or Palestine, and by land across the Maritza river into Turkey.

The Turkish consuls in Greece—at Athens, Salonica, and Komotene (Gümülçine), as well as on the islands of Mytilene (Midilli) and Rhodes—provided the same sort of help that the Turkish consuls did in France. They also organized caravans to carry Jews to safety in Turkey and intervened with the German authorities to exempt Turkish Jews from persecution and extermination.[25] The most outstanding example of such help was that of Consul Selahattin Ülkümen in Rhodes, who in July 1944, at great personal risk, was able to save from deportation to extermination camps a group of forty-two Jews, including Turkish citizens as well as spouses and relatives who were not Turkish citizens. In January 1945 the Germans permitted the group to be evacuated to Turkey. In 1989, Ülkümen was honored by Yad Vashem in Jerusalem as a "Righteous Gentile," who had helped rescue Jews from Nazi persecution.[26]

Despite constant pressure from, on the one hand, the Nazis, who at times demanded that Turkey return Jewish refugees to them, and, on the other hand, the British, who wanted Turkey to stop admitting the refugees and in any case not to allow them to continue to Palestine, Turkey steadfastly refused these demands and throughout World War II it continued to assist

European Jews to escape from the Holocaust and, in most cases, to go on to Palestine. Of course, in the larger scheme of things, with six million Jews perishing in the Holocaust, the rescue efforts of Turkey and its diplomatic representatives were relatively insignificant. But to the thousands of individuals whose lives were saved, these actions were very significant indeed.

CHAPTER 16

Recipes of Magic–Religious Medicine as Expressed Linguistically

Marie-Christine Varol
Translated from the French by Franck Salameh

I n Istanbul of the 1980s, magic–religious recipes and medical witchcraft still constituted a knowledge that was deemed worthy of being handed down through the generations. This study will deal with several questions: Where did this knowledge originate, who passed it on and why, to whom was it passed on, and more importantly, how was it conveyed? This inquiry is not a survey of techniques or recipes used in the application of remedies. It is rather a study of the linguistic methods by which these recipes were handed down through a combination of Judeo-Spanish and spoken French and Turkish.[1] Between the end of the nineteenth century and the period during which my study was conducted, the Jewish community of Istanbul had gone through momentous changes, and the methods of handing down recipes had consequently adapted to these transformations.

Framework of the Inquiry

The first finding showed that it was mainly women who conveyed this knowledge. Accounts of miraculous healing were reported to me exclusively by women, with the exception of one man who directly quoted his wife's experience. The second finding showed that the women who transmitted these remedies were generally over the age of fifty at the time of the original survey (1982).[2] Out of twelve subjects, one was less than fifty years of age, and two were over seventy. All twelve women were Judeo-Spanish speakers, although they also spoke Turkish and French. They were generally well educated. Just one woman, from humble social origins, possessed only a primary education. Of the others, the older women had completed the high school of the Alliance Israélite Universelle, while the younger ones had had secondary schooling and two of them had gone on to college. In other words, these were not individuals alien to modernity. Normally, their first reaction to illness was to seek the advice of a physician, and almost all of them attempted to rationalize their decision to resort to magic-religious medicine only after attempting other methods, which we shall evaluate at a later stage.

Traditional Knowledge

The knowledge which these women transmitted stemmed primarily from personal recollections. The oldest women had not personally administered these remedies. This task had previously been the purview of so-called rabbis of lesser importance. Hence the expression *hahamiko,* or "little rabbi" (the diminutive), was often mentioned in the accounts. Some of the women spoke of the "lesser rabbi," using informal nicknames such as *haribi Moshon* (variant of the name Mosheh) or *haham Kochiko,* a diminutive meaning "the small limping one." [3] One of these "lesser rabbis," according to one account, had tremendous respect for the narrator's mother, who had been the daughter of a rabbi who used to be the *hahamiko's* teacher. So we are dealing here with a somewhat belittled or not much respected religious figure, one who seemingly belonged to a lower social class. Diminutives, as I had the opportunity to note elsewhere, are also used to refer to the realm of women (cooking, the home, children). [4]

These lesser rabbis consulted books in which they foresaw the future (*miravan goral*) so as to unveil the causes of problems, curses (literally, the evil eye, *el aynara*), or fright (*el sar* or *espanto*). The source of their skills was divine bestowal, a gift of prophecy, the *nevua del patron del mundo.* They set their patients out toward healing, or *salvasyon,* often referred to also as *refua.* The verb *amahar* (to alleviate or relieve) was also generally used to denote healing. These rabbis *aprekantavan,* muttered incantations (*prekantes* or *aprekantamyentos*), the most typical of which was: "In the name of God, Abraham, Isaac, and Jacob, I remove from you, (name), daughter of (name), the evil eye, evil talk, all evil, all fright; let them go to the bottom of the sea" [*Kon el nombre del Dyo, Avram, Izak i Yakov, X ija de X, te kito el ojo malo, el avla mala, todo el mal, todo el sar, ke se vayan a las profundinas de la mar].* They then prescribed medications, usually based on sugared water, which were to be administered in three doses or during a three-day period at predetermined hours of the day, while reciting benedictions. The rabbis would also prepare *kemeaikas* (small *kemeas,* or amulets). These practices, observed in Istanbul, were very similar to the rituals noted by Michaël Molho in Salonica of the end of the nineteenth century.[5] Customarily it was women who sent for the *hahamiko,* usually to attend to their children, but sometimes also for their sick mothers or husbands.

The Diminutive

The realm of women and home medicine were generally known as "little matters of the house," *kozikas de kaza.* Doctors would sometimes refer to them as "women's matters," *kozas de mujeres,* and they were characterized by the usage of diminutives, a feature that we shall encounter throughout the various accounts in this study.

For example, *una kemeaika,* a small amulet, is made out of a *handrajiko,* a small rag, rolled up *komo korasoniko,* like a small heart; one drinks *una auita,* a little water, or *una kutcharika de pishadika,* a small spoonful of a little urine; one uses *un livriko de Ley,* a small book of the Law, to cover *una kupika,* a small cup. One of the recipes is called *kaviko a la mezuza,* a little coffee within the mezuzah;[6] another one is called *kaviko al sereno,* a small cup of coffee left in the cool night's air; one serves *papelikos,* small pieces of paper, to drink; one places *una ridaika mojada,* a wet, small handkerchief, on the stomach.

The use of diminutives in Judeo-Spanish expresses the desire to minimize the importance of something. It also expresses the awareness of the speakers that they are handing down a socially devalued science.

Borrowings

As is well known, Judeo-Spanish is a language of countless borrowings from many languages. It is striking, therefore, that in the description of the procedures and recipes of magic-religious medicine, terms borrowed from French are almost completely absent. Out of all the accounts narrated throughout the survey, one could note only the euphemistic use of the term *urine* in French as a substitute for the Judeo-Spanish *pishado,* which was deemed inappropriate. One could also note a dearth of Turkish terms in contrast to an abundance of Hebrew words, which suggests that we are within the realm of religion. We should add, however, that the rarity in the usage of French and Turkish could also be attributed to other phenomena, such as the intercultural origins of certain techniques and their methods of conveyance.

A Specific Verb

The Judeo-Spanish verb *kreerse* (to believe, to give credit to), in its reflexive form, appears regularly in some contexts where religion is contrasted with popular belief, so as to point out one's reference to the *kozikas de kaza.* Hence, a Judeo-Spanish speaker would say: *"Mi marido es mui CROYANT, PRATIQUANT de la ley, ma este modo de kozas no se kree"* [My husband is very much a believer, and observant of the Law, however, he does not believe in those sorts of things]. Another speaker of the language, using a more cautious tone, would say: *"Ni me kreygo ni aprovo"* [I neither believe in it, nor do I use it], so as to accentuate her ambiguous attitude to these practices. So we are dealing here with a certain knowledge that is rooted in popular religious practices and beliefs and whose origins are somewhat disreputable. It used to be the realm of second-rate religious figures and was practiced only among women. However, the large-scale Jewish emigration of 1949, and the desertion of the traditional Jewish neighborhoods, coupled with the rise in literacy, have led to the disappearance of the *hahamikos,* which in turn left women as the sole holders and officiates of this knowledge.

Narration Techniques

Women would now transmit this kind of medicine, following a technique common among the Judeo-Spanish speakers of Istanbul. They would re-arrange their personal recollections and experiences into pedagogical accounts of a particular structure. Almost all of the accounts would exhibit the following characteristics:

1. A female family member, fearing the envy of others, or for some other unknown reason, suddenly takes ill.

2. The help of one or several doctors is sought, but no results are noticed. One of the doctors is even replaced on account of his youth. However, the diagnoses are evasive, and the doctors are unable to determine the cause of the illness. They prescribe medicines or suggest treatments, which still prove ineffective. They admit to their inability to help, and one doctor goes so far as to suggest seeking the help of some old wives' practices: *"aprova si keres koza de mujeres"* [try, if you wish, women's remedies].

3. A female neighbor, a female friend, an aunt, a family member, or an acquaintance, occasionally a stranger (say, a woman one meets on a bus), but in most cases a woman (except in the instance of the Jewish neighborhood grocer), advances a diagnosis and suggests a remedy. Generally, the remedy consists of a traditional recipe given specifically for the illness in question, although at times a specific recipe could be revealed in a dream. The certitude and precision with which the remedy and treatment are prescribed are contrasted with the doctors' uncertainty about both diagnosis and remedy.

4. The treatment proves effective, the patient is cured and the skeptics are convinced.

5. Through this process, the recipe is transmitted to another woman, *por zahud* (as a good deed), and the healer or narrator points out: "I am teaching you so that you would put it into practice."

6. Often in commenting upon the experience, the narrator rationalizes what would otherwise seem implausible.

The example that I have chosen to relate below is neither the most characteristic nor the most common, but rather the most edifying, in my opinion, although I should add that many of these accounts do indeed resemble each other. These modern and intelligent women do not convey their knowledge because of its scientific or folkloric value, but rather because they are convinced of the validity of their experiences, and this so long as family matriarchs feel obliged to compensate for modern medicine's insufficiencies. In fact, since the testimonies of the oldest subjects maintain that the *hahamikos* were able to cure all sorts of illnesses, whether alone or in concert with a physician, these women commonly believe that home remedies can heal all but inexplicable cases, or cases that are simply medicine-proof (e.g., bouts of fever, nervous breakdowns, insomnia, distress, irritability, as well as psychologically actuated warts). In the Istanbul of the 1980s, it was not common to seek the help of a psychiatrist unless one was incapacitated by mental illness or else seriously depressive. Psychotherapy was not commonplace; it was one's own social environment and circle of friends and relatives that would help to cope with problems.

Narrative Example

1. A healthy young woman, resident of one of the largest Jewish quarters of Istanbul in about 1920, has long been engaged to a young man with whom she is deeply in love. The marriage is delayed by the young man's family on the grounds that his elder siblings should be married first. Suddenly this young woman is gripped by nervous attacks followed by bouts of fainting resembling epileptic convulsions.

2. A young doctor is called in, but he is unable to determine the problem. The young woman herself is unable to describe her troubles and does not remember a thing, except for a recurring dream in which the dead are trying to drive bones into her abdomen. She is sent to a renowned Greek doctor, a specialist in nervous disorders, who, though unable to find anything abnormal with her, prescribes remedies and suggests therapy sessions at the Yalova spa. The young woman's condition does not improve, however, and the recurrent sudden and inexplicable attacks continue to grip her, prompting her fiancé's family to dissuade him from marrying her.

3. The mother of one of the young woman's female friends arrives on the scene. She has dreamed on three separate occasions about the cause and *refua* (cure) of the young woman's problems. She suggests that the young woman had sinned: having taken a stroll with her fiancé inside a Muslim

cemetery, she sat down with him on the tomb of a saint. In order to cure the young woman, her mother is required to make a *ziyara* (visit) to the Jewish cemetery at Hasköy on a day of torrential rain and there to collect in a cup the rainwater dripping from the Hebrew letters on a rabbi's tombstone. She must then give the water to her daughter to drink, together with a benediction.

4. The mother carries out her part; the young woman drinks the water and is cured. She is then promptly married off and never has a relapse.

5. The narrator then offers her opinion on the case, persuading her interlocutor that these sorts of things do in fact happen, that people have experienced them, and that they need to be taken into consideration.

6. Finally the narrator explains what has by now become obvious: that this disorder was psychological, and that it is conviction that cures. In any event, a little water never hurt anyone.

Commentary

We should note that the young woman's inner circle had carefully picked up on her dream and it was in a dream that the friend's mother had come upon the cure.[7] The task of the mediators, in this case the friend's mother and the mother of the young woman, is to reconcile the young woman (who had in a sense brought banishment upon herself) with the surrounding social group. The mediators could succeed in their work only by interpreting the dream and by taking into account the young woman's special circumstances. Through her interpretation of the dream, the friend's mother suggested, or rather imposed (given that the solution had presented itself through a dream on three different occasions, the tone here is somewhat categorical) upon the young woman's mother an interpretation that the latter would not have been able to advance on her own without otherwise dishonoring her daughter. By proposing to the young woman a symbolic procedure of reintegration into her social circle, the mediators were prompting her to make peace both with herself and with her group. Finally, and with much social savvy, the families proved to have learned the moral of this story by promptly marrying off the young couple. It should also be noticed that from the beginning, the young man's family, which was delaying the marriage, was being depicted as the prime culprit.

Contradictions and Language Changes

Although the women in my survey still felt the need to convey their knowledge to others, at the same time they were also aware of the contradiction between what was viewed to be within the realm of superstition and their status as women of the times, modern and skeptical. Hence they would point out this contradiction and attempt to resolve it by using various narrative and stylistic approaches.

In almost all of their accounts, the women took great pains to distance themselves from the experiences that they were relating. In order to assert their neutrality, they would abandon Judeo-Spanish, the language of tradition, and switch to French (in the case of the older women or those educated in French) or Turkish, both equally considered languages of modernity. Hence in the following passages one should note the ubiquity of borrowings and code alternations.

The women would, for instance, dissociate themselves from their subject matter by alternating between direct and indirect speech. In one case a speaker relates how years earlier her mother had urged their neighbor to conceal from the speaker what she was about to do, and comments: *"a mi ke no me lo diga porke [. . .] era mas MODERNa a mi FAÇON"* [so that she would not tell me because I was more modern, in my own way]. One also finds: *"Mi mama era MODERNa, ija de GRAND-RABBIN ama . . ."* [My mother was modern, a daughter of a Chief Rabbi, but . . .]; *"Yo no do muntcha IMPORTANsa"* [I do not pay too much attention to these things]. Hence we see in the preceding the usage of French borrowings as a rectifier.

The women take into account certain reservations and present them as legitimate, all in French: *"TU VOIS JE NE SAIS PAS SI TU SERAS CROYANTE"* [See, I am not sure whether you will be able to believe]; *"TU NE VAS PAS CROIRE CE QUE JE VAIS TE DIRE"* [You won't believe what I'm about to tell you]. Another woman uses French as follows: *"Mi marido no se kree, es PRATIQUANT de la ley, muy CROYANT, ma este modo de kozas no se kree"* [My husband does not give credit to these things; he is observant of the Law, he is very much a believer, but in these things he does not believe]. One can note in the preceding the use of the French CROYANT and PRATIQUANT in juxtaposition to the Judeo-Spanish *se kree* (infinitive *kreerse*, to believe) in connection with "magical belief." The same woman continues *"dize ke es [. . .] MAGIE"* [he says it is witchcraft].

They insist on the living truth of their accounts. One of them argues, in Turkish and repeatedly: *"BAK YAVRUM, BUNU BEN YAŞADIM"* [You see, dear, I have lived through this]. A little further in the account she adds, *"GÖRÜLDÜ, YANI BILMIYORUM* [This was already seen, I mean, I don't know . . .].

They give details in French or in Turkish about the doctor who was consulted or the treatment that was followed: *"UN DOCTEUR,* Doktor Z., SINIR MÜTEHASSISI" (Doctor Z., a neurologist); *"el DOCTEUR M. de Hasköy, un DERMATOLOGUE DOCTEUR"* (Doctor M. from Hasköy, a dermatologist); *"La yevi al doctor de ojos F."* (I took her to see an eye doctor, F.).

They point out the medical diagnoses using well-informed terminology. Hence we can find the following in French: OXYURES, DEPRESSION, HERNIE, MAUVAISE CIRCULATION DE SANG, CYSTITE; and in Turkish: SARI-LIK (jaundice), FITIK (hernia), KARACIĞER HASTALIĞI (liver disease), *manera de YANI . . . MALARYA* (a sort of, how should I say it, malaria), SARA NOBETI (a fit of epilepsy), BIR NEVI SARA HASTALIĞI (a type of epilepsy). They also expound on the causes of these ailments: *"una AMBITION ke no la decha bivir"* [an ambition that prevented her from living], or their symptoms: *"SALYALAR AKIYOR"* (saliva runs from his mouth), *"DEMANGEAISON, CRISE"* (itching, a fit). These terms are in sharp contrast with traditional family diagnoses and the names used to designate illnesses: *"me se arrebolto la sangre"* [my blood has turned sour], *barruguas* (warts), *la ijada* (cystitis), *friyos* (shivers), *kevradura* (hernia), *desrepozo* or *sıkıntı* (anguish or depression), the latter term having been integrated from Turkish. These terms are also in sharp contrast with the customary causes of illnesses as discussed above: *"M'espanti"* or *"Estuve asarada"* [I was scared]. On the other hand, the doctors consulted, not surprisingly, speak only either Turkish or French.

The women rationalize the effects of the treatments throughout their accounts: *"PSIKOLOJIK BIR ŞEY, BUNLAR HEP TELKINDIR"* [This is psychological, all of this is in the mind]; *"Esto es el kreer, ama era komo se yama ITIKAT"* [This is popular belief, but it is as if you said firm belief in God]. They insist on the fact that these remedies are used as a measure of last recourse for persons with many problems, *"ande el doktor no sta topando remedyo"* [for which the doctor is unable to find a remedy]. And finally they stress the point that their remedies are innocuous: *"Una auita, kualo ay?"* [a little water, nothing wrong with that], *"d'esto danyo no vyene"* [it could not hurt], *"todo era dulsuryas"* [this was nothing but sweets]. All this is usually followed by a commentary from one of the speakers, *"ÇOK FAYDALI ÇÜNKÜ"* [because it is very beneficial]; *haribi* Mosheh's book was *"komo un livro de MEDECINE"* [like a medical book]; *"porke la MEDECINE entera es de PLANTES ke azen las DROGas"* [because in all of medicine, it is with plants that drugs are made].

Religious and Medical Transgressions

Although so far we have not discussed the issue of crossing the bounds of normative religion, we must nevertheless point out that the conveyance and execution of this kind of popular knowledge are not limited to members of the Jewish community. One can seek the services of a HOCA, a Turkish man of religion, who might prescribe drinking a potion consisting of pieces of paper written in ESKİ TÜRKÇE (Ottoman Turkish). The upward social mobility of many Jews, which often led them to move from the old Jewish neighborhoods to distant suburbs, and the growing interaction among neighbors of different backgrounds have created many opportunities for encounters across community lines. Thus one of the speakers related that while riding on a bus, she was once given a recipe by a Turkish woman who had received it from a Christian priest while also traveling by bus. These encounters can be interpreted simultaneously along the lines of tradition and modernity. Tradition is expressed through the use of *mallah* (angel, from the Hebrew *mal'akh*): *"Es una mallah ke rekontri i eya rekontro al PRÉTRE"* [It comes from an angel that I met and she met a priest]. At the same time, the modern component in the interpretation of the encounter describes the meeting as a fortuitous coincidence, and expresses it in French, the language of rationalization: *"COINCIDENCE, un PRÉTRE al lado de mi"* [Coincidence, a priest next to me]. However, in this case, the fluctuation between the direct style of conversation and the strategic games of switching languages (where French seems to emphasize the speaker's reserve) are incompatible. The syncretism in this example is strengthened by the fact that the Turkish woman speaks Judeo-Spanish with French borrowings, and she concludes by recommending that each religious community use its own holy book: *"Los Turkos kon el CORAN, los CHRÉTIENes kon el EVANGILE i los djudyos kon la BIBLE."* In reality, however, we are unable to ascertain in this sentence whether it is the speaker rationalizing what could be construed as a religious transgression, whether it is the Christian priest speaking directly in French, or whether someone is simply relating verbatim the words of the Turkish woman. In most other accounts, however, the logic of the direct style is more closely maintained: a speaker gives a recipe to a young Turkish servant for her grandmother. The servant thanks the speaker with a benediction in Turkish; later, an incredulous Jewish husband utters a benediction in Turkish instead of Hebrew, which would normally have been considered blasphemous. In another account, a Turkish client *melda*—literally, "reads," which is a close translation of the Turkish OKUMAK (to study)—the warts of a Jewish shopkeeper.

Conclusion

The *kozikas de kaza* are part of a knowledge that is still considered worthy of being preserved and transmitted, and for that purpose it is still structured in Judeo-Spanish pedagogical narratives. These narratives expound two opposite conceptions of illness, which the speakers, well integrated into the modern world, attempt to reconcile. The first conception is a traditional one: in keeping with its sources, it is marked by an unusual preponderance of Hebrew-Aramaic borrowings, placing it thereby within the realm of religion. However, this is a peculiar domain of religion; lexically it is noted by the use of specific verbs such as *kreerse,* by the alternating use of Judeo-Spanish and French, and finally by the use of diminutives, which places this domain in what is considered a woman's world, inferior to men's realm of religion. The second conception of illness is a modern one, personified by doctors and marked by the ubiquity of borrowings from languages of culture and learning (French and Turkish in the case of the speakers).

The plurilingualism of the speakers allows the establishment of a link between the Judeo-Spanish of tradition and the languages of modernity as expressed in Turkish and French. The gamut of possibilities allows many variations. The most Hebraized forms of Judeo-Spanish are reserved for describing the causes traditionally attributed to illnesses and the recipes and methods for their treatment. In contrast, the change to Turkish or French is meant to emphasize the speaker's reserve, the rationalization of the experience, and the opinion of modern medicine. In between these extremes, very Frenchified or Turkified varieties of Judeo-Spanish allow for the naming of illnesses, their symptoms and their causes, in a modern fashion, and they simplify the review of treatments recommended by the doctors and the adoption of intercultural customs. The parallel usage of, on the one hand, Judeo-Spanish (a language of tradition and the past, a language of beliefs and superstitions, a language of women and popular culture) and, on the other hand, French and Turkish (languages of science and modernity, languages of men of affairs and of high culture) is particularly remarkable. Contrary to widespread belief and the expected conclusion, the purpose of this parallel usage is not to prove the superiority of one language over the other, but rather to demonstrate that Judeo-Spanish is not a language of useless, uninteresting, and superannuated knowledge. This parallel usage is possible only through the adoption by one language variety of the theoretical and linguistic points of view of the other. Judeo-Spanish, an intermediary language (*langue de truchement,* to use Jacques Hassoun's expression[8]), situated between many worlds, playing the stocks of the many languages within its reach, is able to express through the many lexical choices it enjoys a wide variety of subtle distinctions. The direct access to the languages of others, facilitated by the community's multilingualism, increases these lexical choices and possibilities. In concluding, it is only appropriate to pose a question: Will the conveyance of the specialized knowledge discussed in this article be able to withstand the disappearance of Judeo-Spanish, on the one hand, or that of the community's multilingualism, on the other?

CHAPTER 17

Mario Levi

A Young Jewish Author from Istanbul

Nedim Gürsel

Translated from the French by Franck Salameh

orn in Istanbul in 1957, Mario Levi is, as far as I know, the first modern Turkish-language writer who has openly flaunted his Jewish identity. Others have been more circumspect. For Sevim Burak (1931–84), for
instance, the search for identity was one of the major themes of her work.
Yet it seems somewhat disguised within biblical allusions, engendering a religious discourse, ostensibly universal, but in fact, disengaged from any specific social context.[1] For Mario Levi, however, the presence of a minority
Jewish community in Turkey and the self-awareness of belonging to that
community constitute the very foundation of his literary approach. Like any
other worthy writer, Levi is certainly considered to be on the fringe of society, indeed on the fringe in his country of residence, although he asserts that
his true homeland is the Turkish language. Paradoxically, he claims to have
become aware of that reality during his association with the newspaper
Şalom, the weekly organ of the Jewish community of Istanbul, which devotes one of its eight pages to articles written exclusively in Judeo-Spanish.
Here is how Levi speaks of his Jewishness:"Yes, I am Jewish. . . . Being Jewish is being, everywhere, a stranger."[2] However, he views this ethnic distinctiveness, with regard to his "adventure as a writer," to be a privilege of sorts,
even an advantage. This last point seems to me important if we are to understand Mario Levi, not so much as an individual, but rather as a writer whose

place in modern Turkish literature is defined in terms of a certain ethnocultural specificity. Levi says:

> This name which today I bear with a certain kind of pride, has it always been easy to bear in a country one of whose most unfortunate policies was once embodied in the slogan "Citizen, speak Turkish!"[3] Has it always been easy to put up with the ridicule to which my forebears were subjected, simply because they were—and for historical reasons—unable to adequately learn Turkish?

We can say that with few exceptions, the acculturation of Turkish Jews, who have lived in Turkey for centuries, is a relatively recent occurrence. Mario Levi, who seems to be an example of this acculturation, views it as the "logical outcome of a certain process." However, he objects to all forms of assimilation and stresses both the importance of democratization and the government's attitude toward its minorities. He defines himself at the closing of a centuries-long process as the voice of a traveler who has been left with few options concerning other geographies. In his own words, he is "a hoarse voice, somewhat quivery from the anxiety of a journey toward questions without answers."

If I chose to begin with Mario Levi's special position within contemporary Turkish literature, it is simply because Turkish literature has always had the tendency to either assimilate or reject any minority discourse. As I noted earlier, Levi is, as far as I know, the first writer of the Turkish language to have asserted his Jewish identity. This seems to me to be an important enough factor to turn Levi into a subject of discussion in spite of the fact that he is a young author whose work is still in its formative stages. I have to admit that being a writer myself, and only six years older than Levi, I find it difficult to discuss his work as that of an author who has already proved his mettle. I will therefore attempt to approach Mario Levi from the point of view of a fellow writer and friend rather than that of an academician.

Mario Levi has so far authored a book about Jacques Brel, *Bir Yalnız Adam* (A Solitary Man; published 1986); three collections of short stories: *Bir Şehre Gidememek* (To Be Unable to Go to a City; published 1990), *Madam*

Floridis Dönmeyebilir (Mrs. Floridis Cannot Come Back; published 1990), and *En Güzel Aşk Hikâyemiz* (Our Most Beautiful Love Story; published 1992);[4] and a novel, *İstanbul bir Masaldı* (Istanbul Was a Fable; published 1999).[5] The first collection of short stories won him the Haldun Taner Award, which introduced him to the general public. This recognition seems to have left a mark on the author with regard to his identity, for in the course of accepting the award, he expressed his pleasure:"This is the first time that a writer belonging to a minority has been recognized. Whether Armenian, Jewish, or Greek, from now on nobody can claim that an author has been left out of the competition simply because of his name." The judges' choice was rather well received, not only within the Jewish community but also among the literary circles, which recognized in the person of Levi a bursting new sensitivity within contemporary Turkish literature, the sensitivity of an author who looks at minorities from a new perspective and who regrets not having named his first book "The Minorities," a term that according to him designates all those who are shut out from the rest of society.

Of course, there were many authors before Levi, not least of whom was Sait Faik (1906–54), considered a pioneer of twentieth-century Turkish prose, who had depicted the cosmopolitan aspects of the city of Istanbul, stressing the world of the common people, those living on society's margins, and the minorities.[6] However, for Mario Levi, ethnic marginality—"the geography of minorities," as he calls it—constitutes the very essence of his work, which can be analyzed only through an understanding of two concepts dear to his heart: exile and writing. In fact, Levi depicts uprooted characters "in search of their author," to use Pirandello's expression. The narrator, who is often identified with the author, relates the shattered lives of those on the fringe and resists forgetfulness through the vehicle of writing. Most of Levi's characters are members of the Jewish and Greek communities of Istanbul who, for one reason or another, have been compelled to leave. The author follows them in their exile as well as throughout their past lives, and through their memories, he conjures up their lost loves. What Levi describes as "the geography of minorities" and "the irresistible attraction of writing," enables us to better grasp the imaginary world of a writer who discloses "the secret story" of the non-Muslim communities of Istanbul as well as their world of language. It is true that the latter had already been explored by other modern Turkish writers such as Sait Faik and Sevim Burak, who seem to have had a particularly strong influence on Mario Levi. But Levi went even further in his analysis of the minorities' sensitivities and in his evocation of their exile, an exile accepted as fate by some and as a type of existence by others. At the end of his first story, Levi concludes: "We must never forget that our own ghost follows us wherever we go, that in spite of all our efforts we are condemned to live in perpetual captivity and exile."[7] This reminds me of the famous verse by Ahmet Hasim, who also felt exiled in his own country:

> Uzak
> Ve mâi gölgeli bir beldeden cüdâ kalarak
> Bu nefy-ü hicret müebbed bu yerde mahkûmuz . . .

> (Far
> From a blue and shady country separated
> We are forever condemned to live this exile, right where we
> are . . .)[8]

But where does Levi's feeling of strangeness come from—this sense of the unspeakable misfortune of having to live one's life as if it were an inescapable fate, as if it were absolute helplessness? Perhaps it derives from the fact that most of the characters are in search of impossible love, and dream of departing, although they forever remain in their closed-off world.

Let us consider the case of Rachel and Eşref Bey. Eşref Bey is a high-school teacher of Turkish literature, a cultured and sensitive man. But he is also shy and a bit too withdrawn to succeed in life. He always puts off important matters, and in his loneliness he writes poetry that probably will never be published. He is, so to speak, like one of those characters we can easily find in a Chekhov short story or in Gorki's novels. His ordinary appearance masks the complexities of a tormented being, of base secrets and unsatisfied desires. Eşref Bey lives on a street where, beginning in the 1950s, Jewish families who had just grown wealthy started moving in. These families simply wanted to live in larger and more comfortable apartments now. And it is with Rachel, a young woman from one of these families, that Eşref

Bey will experience the love of his life. It is a young love, reciprocal, but forbidden. Eşref says to the narrator:

> I have to admit that my memories of Rachel are all that is left to me from my past and from all those distant days. . . . At the time we thought that happiness was possible by just living a simple life. We believed that we could overcome society's traditional values and principles. I, my name was Eşref and hers was Rachel, and we certainly had things in common, in spite of our given names.[9]

But they must separate. Rachel would set out for Israel to start a new life in a country that from now on she would consider as her own. Years later, however, she would admit to the narrator, who had visited her in Tel Aviv, that she should probably have stayed in Istanbul. In fact, the life she had in Israel was totally different from the one she probably would have had if she had remained in her native country. She never stopped cultivating her yearning for the city where she had lived before, with Eşref Bey, the love of her life. She had also perfected her knowledge of Turkish instead of slowly forgetting it, as was the case with most Jews who immigrated to Israel. The difficulties that all immigrants usually face are vividly revealed through the accounts given by Rachel, who is one of the most engaging characters in the book. She tells the narrator:

> No one received us with open arms in this country. My father, who had encountered some problems due to my relationship with Eşref, but also because of the decline of his small business, decided to bring us to this country on the heels of the events of the sixth and seventh of September.[10] At forty-six he still had the courage to work in a lime kiln. The foreman would ask him many times during the course of the day:"Hey Rafael! Are you still alive?" These were the first Hebrew words that we learned.[11]

The firsthand accounts of the lives of migrant laborers throughout Europe and the description of their problems of integration into alien societies constitute an important aspect of contemporary Turkish literature. But little is known about the experiences of the Jewish and Greek minorities of Istanbul who have left their homeland in search of a new life elsewhere. Hence-forth however, this "elsewhere" will have its place in our literature thanks to Mario Levi. He emphasizes the psychology of exile over its physical condi-tion, and especially stresses the split personality of the uprooted who live be-tween two countries, two cultures, and two languages. Their nostalgic discourse also reveals the harshness of exile for those cut off from their birth-place. While recalling her youth and the places she had visited with her Turkish lover, Rachel also evokes the possibility of a new day, personified in her child, born in Israel. She, however, would always remain obsessed with her past, "the green paradise of young lovers," as Baudelaire called it. In fact, almost all of Levi's characters are in search of times lost, for he considers Proust to be his great master and makes no secret of the influence that Proust has had on his writing. This explains Levi's efforts at constructing an elabo-rate syntax and articulating long Proustian sentences, skillfully equilibrated, in spite of the impediments of Turkish grammar. Mario Levi's style is beyond the scope of this study, although it could and should constitute the topic of another. For now, let us go back to his characters.

Mrs. Floridis, an Istanbul high-school librarian, is also part of the por-trait gallery meticulously painted by the author. Akin to her fellow charac-ters, she also dreams of leaving one day, although she knows that she will be back to "these lands to which the final return is inevitable." Levi describes Mrs. Floridis as an elderly woman who speaks poor Turkish, but a rather good French, and who dyes her hair blue. She is not highly educated but does appreciate popular writers such as Dumas and Cronin, whom she reads in their original versions. Divorced, she lives alone with her two cats in an apartment filled with objects that remind her of her past. The atmosphere created by the description of the character's universe exemplifies the author's penchant for nostalgia. Levi is not afraid to describe, one by one, every sin-gle old article that surrounds the daily life of Mrs. Floridis in her old cosmo-politan neighborhood of Istanbul: an old radio set with four tubes, barely functional; a turntable on which one could still play old vinyl singles; two couches whose old coverings are taken down only during holidays; letters from Salonica written in French; the smell of carnations; cooking recipes; Easter souvenirs of yesteryear, and so on. She has only one daughter, Sandra, born of an unhappy union to Telemako Eflambiu, a mysterious accordion player. All the members of this small family end up leaving: Telemako to Anatolia or elsewhere, Sandra to Paris, and Mrs. Floridis to Athens, following an amorous relationship with a Mr. Moiz, another lonely man whom we will ultimately find dead at his home.

One can read the texts in Mario Levi's works as if they constituted a single continuous narrative whose protagonists almost always keep coming back. The author has created a number of characters, and by moving them through the narrative, he makes them sometimes appear before us or emerge from the past, and at other times simply steal away in front of our very eyes. Nevertheless, they are always present, in spite of the pain they endure of separation and loneliness. In fact, loneliness is a second nature of sorts to most of his characters—a second nature, but also a pretext to evoke memories. In his stories Mario Levi inserts the narrator as a witness. This witness, who knows all these unfortunate characters, shares with us at some later time the story of their common miseries. The characters have all lived in the same neighborhood; they all loved and were loved, and then they have all separated. But it is up to the narrator to give form and meaning to these vanished lives. Only he, the true character, capable of crossing the narrative from one end to the other, seems to have escaped forgetfulness, *because he writes.* And thanks to his writing, the existence of the other characters is unveiled; the words of the narrator prevent these characters from forever sinking into oblivion. Hence, it is the narrator (as in the case of Proust) who becomes witness to an age that has gone by. At the same time, however, the narrator, in his capacity as a demiurge, omnipresent and identified with the author, is also the one who pulls the strings that move the characters. Hence the succession of prefaces that precede the narrative itself, and the digressions in time and space attributed not to the author but to a narrator conceived as a character. Although this method can be viewed as somewhat artificial, it does grant Levi's style an originality that could qualify as modern. I shall conclude my account by expressing the hope that Mario Levi, who maintains that he is "still in the midst of a long narration," will continue exploring the unknown world of minorities who still constitute—although not for much longer perhaps—the rare colors of our social fabric.

Appendixes

Notes

Bibliography

Index

APPENDIX A

Establishment of Jewish Girls' and Mixed Schools, 1840–1913

1840   Cairo (Adolphe Crémieux; closed 1860); Alexandria (Adolphe Crémieux; closed 1842)

1848   Jerusalem (Miss Cooper's Institution)

1854   Jerusalem (Rothschild)

1855   Jerusalem (Montefiore; closed 1857)

1862   Alexandria (Community)

1865   Alexandria (Aghion)

1870   Edirne (AIU)

1872   Aleppo (AIU; closed 1885; reopened 1889)

1874   Salonica (AIU)

1875   Cairo (Aghion); Kasaba (AIU-MX)

1877   Istanbul/Hasköy (AIU); Tripoli, Libya (Italian)

1878   Beirut (AIU); Izmir (AIU)

1879   Istanbul/Galata (AIU)

1880   Istanbul/Dağhamamı (AIU; transferred to Kuzguncuk 1895)

1882   Istanbul/Ortaköy (AIU); Istanbul/Balat (AIU)

1883   Damascus (AIU)

1884   Baghdad (AIU-V)

1886   Rishon le-Tziyon; Bursa (AIU)

1888   Dardanelles (AIU)

1889   Jaffa (Belkind-MX; closed 1891)

1891   Haifa (AIU); Safed (Private)

AIU = L'Alliance Israélite Universelle; HV = Hilfsverein der Deutschen Juden; KGTC = Kindergarten Teachers College; MX = Mixed; P = Popular (primary vocational); TC = Teachers College; V = Vocational

1892   Alexandria (Shadai Ya'azor)

1893   Baghdad (AIU); Jaffa (AIU/Hovevei Tziyon); Istanbul/Haydarpaşa (AIU-MX)

1894   Aleppo (AIU)

1895   Izmir/Karataş (AIU)

1896   Cairo (AIU); Manisa (AIU); Tripoli, Libya (AIU)

1897   Alexandria (AIU-MX); Cairo (Karaite; closed 1907); Safed (AIU); Salonica (AIU-P)

1900   Cairo (Zionist; closed 1903); Tiberias (AIU)

1902   Sidon (AIU-MX); Cairo/Abbasiyah (AIU-MX)

1904   Aydın (AIU); Rodosto (AIU-MX)

1905   Tanta (AIU-MX); Jerusalem (HV); Jaffa (Gymnasium-MX)

1906   Jerusalem (Betzalel-MX); Jerusalem (AIU)

1908   Bergama (AIU-MX); Gederah (HV-MX); Rehovot (HV-MX)

1909   Jerusalem (Gymnasium-MX); Jerusalem (HV-KGTC)

1910   Aleppo/Bahsita (AIU); Amarah (AIU); Haifa (HV-MX); Tire (AIU)

1911   Aleppo/Jemiliye (AIU); Çorlu (AIU-MX); Hillah (AIU); Khanaqin (AIU-MX); Kırkkilise (AIU)

1912   Mosul (AIU)

1913   Basra (AIU); Gelibolu (AIU-MX); Jaffa (HV); Jaffa (T/C)

Enrollment in Girls' Schools by City, 1840–1917

Aleppo (AIU)	192 (1906); 271 (1908)
Alexandria	
AIU	121 (1908); 203 (1913)
Community	70 (1862)
Crémieux	200 (1842)★
Shadai Ya'azor	365 (1916)
Baghdad	
AIU	28 (1894); 405 (1908); 780 (1912)
AIU-V	10–80 (1890–93)
Basra (AIU)	151 (1913)
Beirut (AIU)	242 (1908); 267 (1914)
Benghazi (Italian)	160 (1911)
Cairo	
AIU	67 (1897); 212 (1908); 77 (1912)
Crémieux	175 (1879); 500 (1908); 600? (1912)
Karaite	93 (1903)
Damascus (AIU)	236 (1908); 250 (1914)
Edirne (AIU)	551 (1908); 929 (1912)
Haifa	
AIU	172 (1912)
HV	64 (1912)
Hilla (AIU)	48 (1911)
Istanbul	
Balat (AIU)	160 (1882); 352 (1908); 497 (1911)
Galata (AIU)	92 (1879); 850 (1912)

★Data given for boys' and girls' schools together.
AIU = L'Alliance Israélite Universelle; HV = Hilfsverein der Deutschen Juden; KGTC = Kindergarten Teachers College; MX = Mixed; P = Popular; V = Vocational.

Hasköy (AIU)	20 (1877); 372 (1908)
Kuzguncuk (AIU)	213 (1898); 201 (1908); 270 (1912)
Ortaköy (AIU)	93 (1885); 215 (1908)
Izmir (AIU)	100 (1879); 351 (1908); 422 (1912)
Jaffa	
HV	120 (1914)
Hovevei Tziyon	410 (1910)
Jerusalem	
AIU	275 (1912)
Betzalel	45 (1906)
Cooper	160 (1854)
HV	83 (1906); 398 (1912)
HV-KGTC	23 (1912)
Montefiore	84–120 (1855–56)
Private (two schools)	123 (1875)
Rothschild	50 (1854); 275 (1912); 676 (1913)
Mosul (AIU)	115 (1914); 140 (1917)
Safed	
AIU	171 (1912)
Private	86 (1894)
Salonica	
AIU	625 (1912)
AIU-P	268 (1912)
Tanta (AIU-MX)	105 (1905)
Tiberias (AIU)	187 (1912)
Tripoli, Libya	
AIU	44 (1896); 150 (1908); 245 (1910)
Italian	348 (1911)

Enrollment in Mixed Schools by City, 1890–1914

Amara (AIU)	183 (1910)
Bursa (AIU)	287 (1911)
Cairo (Zionist)	100–40 (1900–1903)
Damascus (Zionist)	1200 (1914)
Jaffa	
Belkind	15 (1890)
Gymnasium	17 (1905)
Jerusalem (Gymnasium)	20 (1909); 110 (1912)
Khanaqin (AIU)	132 (1911)
Sidon (AIU)	143 (1902)

AIU = L'Alliance Israélite Universelle

Notes

Abbreviations

ABCFM	American Board of Commissioners, Foreign Missions, Cambridge, Mass.
AIU	L'Alliance Israélite Universelle, Paris
A&P	*Parliamentary Papers, Accounts and Papers,* Great Britain
AUB	American University of Beirut
BAIU	*Bulletin de l'Alliance Israélite Universelle*
BBA	Başbakanlık Arşivi, Istanbul
ED	Ecnebi Defterleri (registers of foreigners), BBA, Istanbul
EI	*Encyclopedia of Islam,* 2d ed.
FO	Foreign Office, Public Record Office Archive, London
HV	Hilfsverein der Deutschen Juden
IA	*İslam Ansiklopedisi*
İFM	*İktisat Fakültesi Mecmuası,* Istanbul University
IJMES	*International Journal of Middle Eastern Studies*
JEH	*Journal of Economic History*
JOS	*Journal of Ottoman Studies*
JTS	*Journal of Turkish Studies*
MES	*Middle Eastern Studies*
PRO	Public Record Office Archive, London
REJ	*Revue des Etudes Juives*
RRC	*Bulletin consulaire français. Recueil des rapports commerciaux adressés au Ministère des Affaires Etrangères par les agents diplomatiques et consulaires de France à l'étranger.* France
SiZ	*Studies in Zionism*
SP	State Papers, PRO, London.
TSAB	*Turkish Studies Association Bulletin*

Introduction

1. The introduction was published as *The Sephardim in the Ottoman Empire* (Princeton: Darwin Press, 1992). The full volume, including the introduction and twenty-eight articles, was published under the title *The Jews of the Ottoman Empire* (Princeton: Darwin Press, 1994).

2. Stanford J. Shaw, *The Jews of the Ottoman Empire and the Turkish Republic* (New York: New York Univ. Press, 1991).

3. Walter F. Weiker, *Ottomans, Turks and the Jewish Polity: A History of the Jews of Turkey* (Lanham, Md.: University Press of America, 1992).

4. Esther Benbassa and Aron Rodrigue, *The Jews of the Balkans: The Judeo-Spanish Community, Fifteenth to Twentieth Centuries* (Oxford: Blackwell, 1995). Reprinted as *Sephardi Jewry: A History of the Judeo-Spanish Community, 14th-20th Centuries* (Berkeley: Univ. of California Press, 2000). A French edition of this book was first published in 1993.

5. Cited in Paméla J. Dorn Sezgin, "*Hakhamim,* Dervishes, and Court Singers: The Relationship of Ottoman Jewish Music to Classical Turkish Music," in Levy, ed., *Jews of the Ottoman Empire,* 585.

1. Foundations of Ottoman-Jewish Cooperation

1. For Ottoman archival sources on minorities in general, see Halil İnalcık, "Ottoman Archival Materials on *Millets,*" in *Christians and Jews in the Ottoman Empire: The Functioning of a Plural Society,* ed. Benjamin Braude and Bernard Lewis (New York: Holmes and Meier, 1982), 1: 437–49. For Ottoman archival sources specifically on Jews, see sources cited in Halil İnalcık, "Jews in the Ottoman Economy and Finances, 1450–1500," in *Essays in Honor of Bernard Lewis: The Islamic World from Classical to Modern Times,* ed. C. E. Bosworth, Charles Issawi, et al. (Princeton: Darwin Press, 1988), 513–55; also see in *The Jews of the Ottoman Empire,* ed. Avigdor Levy (Princeton: Darwin Press, 1994), the contributions by Heath Lowry, Justin McCarthy, Kemal Karpat, Avigdor Levy, Amnon Cohen, and Fatma Müge Göçek.

2. See Halil İnalcık, "The Ottoman Empire and the Crusades," in *The Impact of the Crusades on Europe,* ed. Norman P. Zacour and Harry W. Hazard (Madison: Univ. of Wisconsin Press, 1989; vol. 6 of *A History of the Crusades,* gen. ed. Kenneth M. Setton; 6 vols. (Madison: Univ. of Wisconsin Press, 1989), 339–46.

3. Salo Wittmayer Baron, *A Social and Religious History of the Jews,* vol. 18, 2d ed. (New York: Columbia Univ. Press, 1983), 8–21.

4. See Halil İnalcık, "Mehmed II," *IA,* 7: 506–35.

5. Baron, *Social and Religious History,* 18: 20–21.

6. İnalcık, "Mehmed II," *IA,* 7: 506–11; idem, "Istanbul," *EI,* 4: 223–26.

7. David Jacoby, "Les Juifs vénetiens de Constantinople—Leur communauté du XIIIᵉ siècle jusqu'au milieu du XVᵉ siècle," *REJ* 131 (1972): 397–472.

8. Halil İnalcık, "Ottoman Galata, 1453–1553," in *Première rencontre internationale sur l'Empire Ottoman et la Turquie moderne,* ed. E. Eldem (Istanbul: Isis, 1991), 17–43.

9. Halil İnalcık, "Kutadgu Bilig'de Türk ve İran Siyaset Nazarıye ve Gelenekleri," *Reşid Rahmeti Arat İçin* (Ankara: Türk Kültürünü Araştirma Enstitüsü, 1966), 267–71.

10. See Werner Sombart, *The Jews and Modern Capitalism,* trans. M. Epstein (New York: B. Franklin, 1969), 328, n. 1; Baron, *Social and Religious History,* 18: 36–37, 457, n. 42; Avigdor Levy, introduction to *Jews of the Ottoman Empire,* ed. idem, 3–12.

11. İnalcık, "Istanbul," *EI,* 4: 234–38; Minna Rozen, "Individual and Community in the Jewish Society of the Ottoman Empire: Salonica in the Sixteenth Century," in Levy, ed., *Jews of the Ottoman Empire,* 215–73.

12. Amnon Cohen, "Ritual Murder Accusations against the Jews during the Days of Suleiman the Magnificent," *JTS* 10 (1986): 73–74.

13. See Levy, introduction to *Jews of the Ottoman Empire,* ed. idem, 21–31. *Responsa* (sing. *responsum*) are formal opinions written by rabbinic authorities in response to submitted questions or problems.

14. İnalcık, "Jews in the Ottoman Economy," 530 n. 27.

15. Ibid., 513–27.

16. Halil İnalcık, "Part I. The Ottoman State: Economy and Society, 1300–1600," in *An Economic and Social History of the Ottoman Empire, 1300–1914,* ed. Halil İnalcık with Donald Quataert (Cambridge: Cambridge Univ. Press, 1994), 209–16.

17. See Halil İnalcık, "Notes on N. Beldiceanu's Translation of the Kānūnnāme, fonds turc ancien 39, Bibliothèque Nationale, Paris," *Der Islam* 43 (1967): 154–57.

18. Baron, *Social and Religious History,* 18: 74–109; Halil İnalcık, "Capital Formation in the Ottoman Empire," *JEH* 29 (1969): 97–140.

19. İnalcık, "Jews in the Ottoman Economy," 529 n. 22.

20. Ibid., 525.

21. Feridun Bey, *Munşa'at al-Salatin* (Istanbul, 1265 H/1849), 450.

22. Benjamin Ravid, *Economics and Toleration in Seventeenth-Century Venice* (Jerusalem: American Academy for Jewish Research, 1978), 28–38. On this subject, see also Benjamin Arbel, *Trading Nations: Jews and Venetians in the Early Modern Eastern Mediterranean* (Leiden: Brill, 1995), 13–28 and passim.

23. Gilles Veinstein, "Une communauté ottomane: les Juifs d'Avlonya (Valona) dans la deuxième moitié du XVIᵉ siècle," in Gaetano Cozzi, *Gli Ebrei e Venezia, Secoli XIV-XVIII* (Milan: Edizioni comunità, 1987), 781–828.

24. J. Tadič, "Le commerce en Dalmatie et à Raguse et la décadence économique de Venise au XVIII siècle," in *Aspetti e Cause della Decadenza Economica Veneziana nel Secolo XVII* (Venice: Istituto per la Collaborazione Culturale, 1961), 238–74.

25. Mark Alan Epstein, *The Ottoman Jewish Communities and Their Role in the Fifteenth and Sixteenth Centuries* (Freiburg: Klaus Schwarz Verlag, 1980), 205.

26. Benjamin Ravid, "An Autobiographical Memorandum by Daniel Rodriga, *Inven-*

tore of the *Scala* of Spalato," in *The Mediterranean and the Jews: Banking, Finance and International Trade (Sixteenth to Eighteenth Centuries)*, ed. Ariel Simon Schwarzfuchs (Ramat Gan, Israel: Bar Ilan University Press, 1989), 189–213; idem, "Daniel Rodriga and the First Decade of the Jewish Merchants of Venice," in *Exile and Diaspora: Studies in the History of the Jewish People Presented to Prof. Chaim Beinart* (Latin alphabet volume), ed. A. Mirsky, A. Grossman and Y. Kaplan (Jerusalem: Mosad Ha-Rav Kook, 1991), 203–23; idem, "A Tale of Three Cities and Their Raison d'Etat: Ancona, Venice, Livorno and the Competition for Jewish Merchants in the Sixteenth Century," *Mediterranean Historical Review* 6 (1991–92): 138–62.

27. Baron, *Social and Religious History,* 18: 120–21.

2. Jews in Early Modern Ottoman Commerce

The author gratefully acknowledges funding from the Institute of Turkish Studies, Inc.; the National Endowment for the Humanities; the Office of Research at Ball State University; and the Social Science Research Council; as well as the assistance of the staffs of the Başbakanlık Archives, Istanbul; the British Library, London; the Bodleian Library, Oxford; and the Public Record Office, London.

1. Before the late sixteenth century, direct relations between western European and Ottoman Jewish merchants seem to have been relatively infrequent. See Aryeh Shmuelevitz, *The Jews of the Ottoman Empire in the Late Fifteenth and Sixteenth Centuries: Administrative, Economic, Legal and Social Relations as Reflected in the Responsa* (Leiden: Brill, 1984) 175–78.

2. The cities of Istanbul, Izmir, and Aleppo are compared in Edhem Eldem, Daniel Goffman, and Bruce Masters, *The Ottoman City Between East and West* (Cambridge: Cambridge Univ. Press, 1999).

3. Steven B. Bowman, *The Jews of Byzantium, 1204–1453* (Tuscaloosa: Univ. of Alabama Press, 1985), 171–77 and 189–95. Bowman has published translations of important documents from this period on pages 314–32.

4. Cecil Roth, *A History of the Marranos* (Philadelphia: Jewish Publication Society, 1947); Salo Baron, *The Ottoman Empire, Persia, Ethiopia, India and China,* vol. 18 of *A Social and Religious History of the Jews,* 2d ed. (New York: Columbia Univ. Press, 1983); Stanford J. Shaw, *The Jews of the Ottoman Empire and the Turkish Republic* (New York: New York Univ. Press, 1991), 25–40; and Avigdor Levy, introduction to *The Jews of the Ottoman Empire,* ed. idem (Princeton: Darwin Press, 1994), 1–37.

5. See the contribution by İnalcık in this volume. Mark Alan Epstein's *Ottoman Jewish Communities and Their Role in the Fifteenth and Sixteenth Centuries* (Freiburg: Klaus Schwartz Verlag, 1980), 53–100, is a study of this relationship at the level of leadership. See also his "Leadership of the Ottoman Jews in the Fifteenth and Sixteenth Centuries," in *The Central Lands,* vol. 1 of *Christians and Jews in the Ottoman Empire: The Functioning of a Plural Society,* ed. Benjamin Braude and Bernard Lewis (New York: Holmes and Meier, 1982), 101–16.

6. On the gnarled problem of the roots of Ottoman traditions, see Paul Wittek, *The Rise*

of the Ottoman Empire (London: Royal Asiatic Society, 1958); and Colin Heywood's critique, " 'Boundless Dreams of the Levant': Paul Wittek, the George-*Kries,* and the Writing of Ottoman History," *Journal of the Royal Asiatic Society* 1 (1989): 32–50. See also Speros Vryonis, Jr., *The Decline of Medieval Hellenism in Asia Minor and the Process of Islamization from the Eleventh through the Fifteenth Century* (Berkeley: Univ. of California Press, 1971); and Halil İnalcık, *The Ottoman Empire: The Classical Age, 1300–1600,* trans. Norman Itzkowitz and Colin Imber (London: Weidenfeld and Nicolson, 1973), 5–16 and passim.

7. The Ottomans of course complied with and adapted to their situation Islamic regulations concerning "People of the Book," Christians as well as Jews. On the perplexing question of *millet* as the Ottoman answer to Islamic strictures and the practicalities of governance, see Benjamin Braude, "Foundation Myths of the *Millet* System," in Braude and Lewis, eds., *Christians and Jews,* 1: 69–88.

8. Stanford Shaw's *Jews of the Ottoman Empire* honors this relationship, though it should not be revered uncritically. For a Turkish anti-Semitic polemic in the tradition of the *Protocols of the Elders of Zion,* see Hikmet Tanyu, *Tarih Boyunca Yahudiler ve Türkler,* 2d ed., 2 vols. (Istanbul: Bilge Yayınlar, 1979).

9. For an interesting treatment of Jewish entrepreneurship in the Ottoman Empire, see Ellis Rivkin, *The Shaping of Jewish History: A Radical New Interpretation* (New York: Scribner's, 1971), 140–58.

10. Halil İnalcık, "Jews in the Ottoman Economy and Finances, 1450–1500," in *The Islamic World from Classical to Modern Times: Essays in Honor of Bernard Lewis,* ed. C. E. Bosworth et al. (Princeton: Darwin Press, 1989), 513–50. See also Shaw, *Jews of the Ottoman Empire,* 93–96. The position Jews assumed in the commercial relations between the Ottoman Empire and Venice is discussed in Benjamin Arbel, *Trading Nations: Jews and Venetians in the Early Modern Eastern Mediterranean* (Leiden: Brill, 1995).

11. Benjamin Braude, "International Competition and Domestic Cloth in the Ottoman Empire, 1500–1650, A Study in Undevelopment," *Review: A Journal of the Fernand Braudel Center* 1 (1979): 437–54.

12. Halil İnalcık, "Istanbul," *EI,* 4: 224–48; and Edhem Eldem, "Istanbul: From Imperial to Peripheral Capital," in Eldem, Goffman, and Masters, *Ottoman City Between East and West.*

13. See Apostolos Euangelou Bakalopoulos, *A History of Thessaloniki,* trans. T. F. Carney (Thessaloniki: Institute of Balkan Studies, 1972), 76–78 and 88–90; Halil Sahillioğlu, "Yeniçeri çuhası ve II. Bayezid'in son yıllarında yeniçeri çuha muhasebesi," *Güney Doğu Avrupa Araştırmaları Dergisi* 2, no. 3 (1974): 415–23; Joseph Nehama, *Histoire des Israélites de Salonique,* 7 vols. (Salonica: Librairie Molho, 1935–78); and Isaac Samuel Emmanuel, *Histoire de l'industrie des tissues des Israélites de Salonique* (Paris: Librairie Lipschutz, 1935).

14. Cecil Roth, *The House of Nasi: The Duke of Naxos* (Philadelphia: Jewish Publication Society, 1948); and Halil İnalcık, "Capital Formation in the Ottoman Empire," *Journal of Economic History* 29 (1969): 97–140.

15. Philip D. Curtin, *Cross-Cultural Trade in World History* (Cambridge: Cambridge Univ.

Press, 1984), discusses this and other "trading diasporas," including the Armenian, Chinese, and Portuguese examples.

16. Gershom Scholem, *Major Trends in Jewish Mysticism,* 3d ed. (New York: Schocken, 1954); Moshe Idel, *Kabbalah: New Perspectives* (New Haven, Conn.: Yale Univ. Press, 1988); and Moshe Halbertal's review article "Varieties of Mysticism," *New Republic* (11 June 1990): 34–39.

17. Braude, "International Competition."

18. Şevket Pamuk, "Money in the Ottoman Empire, 1326 to 1914," in *An Economic and Social History of the Ottoman Empire, 1300–1914,* ed. Halil İnalcık with Donald Quataert (Cambridge: Cambridge Univ. Press, 1994), 947–80; Şevket Pamuk, *A Monetary History of the Ottoman Empire* (Cambridge: Cambridge Univ. Press, 2000). This is the most current and exhaustive analysis of the Ottoman monetary system.

19. Braude, "International Competition," and Sahıllıoğlu, "Yeniçeri çuhası."

20. BBA, Ecnebi Defterleri (registers of foreigners; hereafter ED) vol. 13/1, p. 35, no. 5.

21. On textiles in Safed, see Simon Schwarzfuchs, "La décadence de la Galilée juive de XVIᵉ siècle et la crise du textile au Proche Orient," *REJ* 121(1962): 169–79.

22. On Aleppo in the seventeenth and eighteenth centuries, see Ralph Davis, *Aleppo and Devonshire Square: English Traders in the Levant in the Eighteenth Century* (London: Macmillan, 1967); Bruce Masters, *The Origins of Western Economic Dominance in the Middle East: Mercantilism and the Islamic Economy in Aleppo, 1600–1750* (New York: New York Univ. Press, 1988); and Abraham Marcus, *The Middle East on the Eve of Modernity: Aleppo in the Eighteenth Century* (New York: Columbia Univ. Press, 1989).

23. On changes in seventeenth-century Ottoman tax collection, see Halil İnalcık, "Military and Fiscal Transformation in the Ottoman Empire, 1500–1700," *Archivum Ottomanicum* 6 (1980): 283–337; Suraiya Faroqhi, "Crisis and Change, 1590–1699," in İnalcık and Quataert, eds., *Ottoman Empire,* esp. 531–44. On Jewish customs collectors as tax farmers, see Epstein, *Ottoman Jewish Communities,* 113–38, and, most recently, Haim Gerber, "Jewish Tax Farmers in the Ottoman Empire in the Sixteenth and Seventeenth Centuries," *JTS* 10 (1986): 143–54.

24. Daniel Goffman, "The Ottoman Role in Patterns of Commerce in Aleppo, Chios, Dubrovnik, and Istanbul, 1600–1650," in *Decision Making and Change in the Ottoman Empire,* ed. Caesar E. Farah (Kirksville, Mo.: Thomas Jefferson Univ. Press, 1993), 139–48.

25. This incident and its repercussions are reported in letters from the English consul in Aleppo to the ambassador in Great Britain, Public Record Office (PRO), State Papers (SP) 110/54, fols. 121r–22v, fols. 122v-24v, fol. 137r, and fol. 147v.

26. PRO, SP 110/54, fol. 122v.

27. This money, which the Ottomans called *esed-i kuruş,* was the principal coinage of international exchange. See Lewes Roberts's superb guide to commerce, *The Merchants Mappe of Commerce* (London, 1638; reprint, London: Ralph Mabb, 1938), particularly chaps. 303–25

(on the lion dollar), 45 (on commerce in Izmir), 62 (on commerce in Aleppo), and 247 (on commerce in Istanbul); and Pamuk's "Money in the Ottoman Empire," 961–66.

28. Westerners referred to extraordinary levies that Ottoman officials imposed on merchants, consuls, or ambassadors as *avanias*. For further discussion of this term, see Merlijn Olnon, "Towards Classifying *Avanias:* A Study of Two Cases Involving the English and Dutch Nations in Seventeenth-Century Izmir," in *Friends and Rivals in the East: Studies in Anglo-Dutch Relations in the Levant from the Seventeenth to the Early Nineteenth Century,* eds. Alastair Hamilton, Alexander H. de Groot, and Maurits H. van den Boogert (Leiden: Brill, 2000), 159–86.

29. PRO, SP 110/54, fol. 147r.

30. See PRO, SP 110/54, fol. 147v (28 May 1641), fol. 148r (31 May 1641), fols. 149r–50r (17 June 1641), fols. 150v–51r (June-Aug. 1641), and fol. 155r (10 Dec. 1642). At one point, the Jewish collector himself went to Istanbul and appealed to Sackvile Crow, the English ambassador! See PRO, SP 110/54, fol. 157r-v. On Crow, see Daniel Goffman, *Britons in the Ottoman Empire, 1642–1660* (Seattle: Univ. of Washington Press, 1998), 68–124.

31. PRO, SP 110/54, fol. 160v. This *hatt-i şerif,* the English consul proclaimed, "particularly expressed what duties we ought justly to pay, upon all sorts of goods both inwards and outwards, at Aleppo and Scanderoon, the want of settling whereof by such authority had for the time past left us still open and exposed, to the mercy of the Customers, and our estates to be preyed upon by them, the 3 percent on monies, with which we have been unjustly burdened more than 20 years, contrary to the Capitulations, was by this means taken off, as likewise the exaction of $5 per bale on silk, paid by no Nation but ours, and their Jewish and still growing accommodations, which had no measure nor limits, but like a Canker went on still eating, with this Hattesheriff the Lord Ambassador dispatched one of his druggermen at whose arrival here without loss of time, it was by the Consul accompanied with all the Nation, presented to the Bassha and Caddee in public Divan." On the role of these decrees, see Cengiz Orhonlu, "Khatt-i sherif," *EI,* 4: 1131.

32. Halil İnalcık, "Tax Collection, Embezzlement, and Bribery in the Ottoman Empire," *TSAB* 15 (1991): 327–46.

33. BBA, Maliyeden Müdevver (various financial documents), no. 23308, p. 27, doc. 1. Proper names are transliterated from Ottoman sources as closely as possible, and copied directly from English sources.

34. PRO, SP 105/143, fol. 127r. On Bendysh, see Goffman, *Britons in the Ottoman Empire,* 98–211.

35. PRO, SP 105/174, pp. 521–23.

36. In the seventeenth-century context discussed here the term "nation" referred either to the nationals of a European country living throughout the Ottoman Empire, or to those dwelling in a single city in that empire. For a discussion, see Goffman, *Britons in the Ottoman Empire,* 13–44.

37. PRO, SP 105/174, p. 522. This belief that Jews wielded immense power in the Ottoman government was widespread among the English. On 12 March 1631, for example, Ambassador Wych wrote to his friend Lord Dorchester: "as all these Ministers are bought and soulde, wee speede the worse, the Jewes beinge our adversaries, doe make it a generall business amonge them, and have extraordinarie favour within the Seraglio" (PRO, SP 97/15, fol. 80v).

38. It is difficult to ascertain whether this perception of great wealth constituted a stereotypical assumption, in the tradition of Shylock, or was grounded in historical truth. We do know that in this period several Jewish concerns—including the one of Cargashan, Hekem, and Useph (see below)—faced bankruptcy and ultimate extinction.

39. PRO, SP 105/174, p. 347. This manifests a self-defense mechanism that is exhaustively documented among Jewish communities in Christian Europe (see, for instance, Jacob Katz, *Tradition and Crisis: Jewish Society at the End of the Middle Ages* [New York: Schocken, 1971], 18–28 and 35–42) as well as in the Ottoman Empire (see, for instance, Shmuelevitz, *Jews of the Ottoman Empire*, 68–73).

40. PRO, SP 105/174, pp. 495–96.

41. See, for instance, PRO, SP 105/174, pp. 353–54, where Bendysh imposes a commercial boycott on, or *battulates,* Isaac Soreson and his son Davide for not paying to William Gibbs 776 lion dollars in recompense for some cloths, and p. 365, where he battulates "Joseph Aluffe Jew and Company."

42. PRO, SP 110/55, pp. 27, 28, 32, 33, 34, 37, and 45.

43. This was the Armenian Bedik, on whom see Masters, *Origins of Western Economic Dominance,* 140–41.

44. PRO, SP 110/55, p. 28.

45. On this incident, see Mark Charles Fissel and Daniel Goffman, "Viewing the Scaffold from Istanbul: The Bendysh-Hyde Affair, 1647–51," *Albion* 22 (1990): 421–48.

46. PRO, SP 110/55, p. 37.

47. PRO, SP 110/55, p. 34.

48. BBA, ED 26, p. 102, no. 3. See also BBA, ED 26, p. 118, no. 2.

49. On the Ottoman side, see, for example, BBA, ED 13/1, p. 36; and ED 26/1, p. 5, no. 1, pp. 47–48, and p. 48, no. 2.

50. See *Calendar of State Papers and Manuscripts Relating to English Affairs Existing in the Archives and Collections of Venice, and in Other Libraries of Northern Italy* (London, 1864–1947), vol. 10, pp. 311 and 318; and BBA, ED 13/1, p. 63, no. 5.

51. See Daniel Goffman, *Izmir and the Levantine World, 1550–1650* (Seattle: Univ. of Washington Press, 1990), 50–76.

52. On migration, see, for example, R. Paul Shaw, *Migration Theory and Fact: A Review and Bibliography of Current Literature* (Philadelphia: Regional Science Research Institute, 1975), 17–19 and bibliography.

53. See in particular Niels Steensgaard, *The Asian Trade Revolution of the Seventeenth Century* (Chicago: Univ. of Chicago Press, 1974).

54. Goffman, *Izmir,* 68–75.

55. On Ottoman resettlements of populations in general, see Ömer Lutfi Barkan, "Les déportations comme methode de peuplement et de colonisation dans l'Empire Ottoman," *İFM* 11 (1949–50): 67–131.

56. See Daniel Goffman, "The Jews of Safed and the *Maktu'* System in the Sixteenth Century: A Study of Two Documents from the Ottoman Archives," *JOS* 3 (1982): 81–90.

57. Scholars such as Douglas A. Howard, in "Ottoman Historiography and the Literature of 'Decline' of the Sixteenth and Seventeenth Centuries," *Journal of Asian History* 22 (1988): 52–77; Cemal Kafadar, in "Les troubles monétaires de la fin du XVIᵉ siècle et la prise de conscience ottomane du déclin," *Annales, E.S.C.* [économies, sociétés, civilisations] (1991), 381–400, and "On the Purity and Corruption of the Janissaries," *TSAB* 15 (1991): 273–80; Rifa'at 'Ali Abou-El-Haj, *Formation of the Modern State: The Ottoman Empire, Sixteenth to Eighteenth Centuries* (Albany: State Univ. of New York Press, 1992); Karen Barkey, *Bandits and Bureaucrats: The Ottoman Route to State Centralization* (Ithaca: Cornell Univ. Press, 1994); Ariel Salzmann, "An *Ancien Regime* Revisited: Privatization and Political Economy in the Eighteenth-Century Ottoman Empire," *Politics and Society* 21 (1993): 393–423; and Madeline Zilfi, *The Politics of Piety: The Ottoman Ulema in the Postclassical Age (1600–1800)* (Minneapolis: Biblioteca Islamica, 1988) are questioning the decline model from a number of perspectives.

58. On the relationship between commerce and power, see Frederic C. Lane, "Economic Consequences of Organized Violence," *JEH* 18(1958): 401–17. On piracy in the Mediterranean, see Maurice Aymard, "XVI. Yüzyılın Sonunda Akdeniz'de Korsanlık ve Venedik," *İFM* 23 (1962–63): 219–38; and Alberto Tenenti, *Piracy and the Decline of Venice,* trans. Janet Pullen and Brian Pullan (Berkeley and Los Angeles: Univ. of California Press, 1967).

59. See Goffman, *Izmir,* 87–90.

60. BBA, ED 26/1, p. 17, no. 1.

61. BBA, ED 26/1, p. 22, no. 2.

62. BBA, ED 26/1, p. 20, no. 2.

63. Halil İnalcık, "Imtiyāzāt," *EI,* 3: 1179–89.

64. British Library, Egerton Manuscript 2541, fols. 300–302 and 316. See also Goffman, *Britons in the Ottoman Empire,* 51–60.

65. Fissel and Goffman, "Viewing the Scaffold," 428–30.

66. This dispute is reconstructed from PRO, SP 97/16, fols. 242r (Frances Reade to Sackvile Crow), 242v (Crow to Edward Stringer), 243r-v (English merchants of Izmir to Crow), 244r-v (Crow to Stringer), 245r (merchants of Izmir to Crow), 245v (Stringer to Crow), and 246r–47v (Crow to Stringer). We know that the religious "millets" were in no

sense politically or economically independent before the nineteenth century (on which see Daniel Goffman, "Ottoman Millets in the Early Seventeenth Century," *New Perspectives on Turkey* 11 (1994): 135–58). As much as various authorities—whether rabbinic or Ottoman—might have striven to secure communal autonomy, the walls they built were extremely porous. It might be argued that some of Ottoman Jewry's success derived from its ability to maneuver outside the Jewish world, and that the leadership's growing ability to seal the breaches from that world contributed to its loss of vigor and decline.

67. PRO, SP 97/16, fol. 243r.

68. Christian foreigners sometimes resisted utilizing Jews even in those employments for which they were renowned, such as brokerage or medicine. Thus Isaac Bagire, an exiled English Catholic who wandered the Middle East during the 1640s and 1650s, remarks that he had studied and practiced medicine because of "the iniquity of the Jews." See Bodleian Library, Clarendon Manuscript 46, fols. 73r–74r.

69. The best-known example of this phenomenon is Sabbatai Sevi's father, employed in the 1630s as an English broker. See Gershom Scholem, *Sabbatai Sevi: The Mystical Messiah, 1626–1676,* trans. R. J. Zwi Werblowsky (Princeton: Princeton Univ. Press, 1973), 106–108.

70. Also see Arbel, *Trading Nations,* 192–94. The stormy events of the early seventeenth century did not, however, utterly destroy Jewish commerce. Nevertheless, their descent from dominance forced them to share trade more equally with others. See, for example, Thomas Philipp, "French Merchants and Jews in the Ottoman Empire During the Eighteenth Century," in Levy, ed., *Jews of the Ottoman Empire,* 315–25.

3. The Development of Community Organizational Structures: The Case of Izmir

1. M. Tournfort, *A Voyage into the Levant* (London: D. Midwinter, 1712), 3: 333–36.

2. Necmi Ülker, "The Rise of Izmir" (Ph.D. diss., University of Michigan, 1975), 16–25; Daniel Goffman, *Izmir and the Levantine World 1550–1650* (Seattle: Univ. of Washington Press, 1990), 3–24. See also the contribution by Goffman in this volume.

3. Jacob Barnai, "The Origins of the Jewish Community in Izmir in the Ottoman Period" (in Hebrew), *Pe'amim* 12 (1982): 47–58.

4. Jacob Barnai, "Portuguese Marranos in Izmir in the Seventeenth Century" (in Hebrew), in *Nation and History,* ed. Menahem Stern (Jerusalem: Merkaz Zalman Shazar, 1983) 1: 289–98.

5. J. Can'ani, "Economic Life in Safed and Its Environs in the Sixteenth and the First Half of the Seventeenth Centuries" (in Hebrew), *Zion* (Yearbook) 6 (1934): 172–217; Shmuel Avitzur, "Safed: Center for the Manufacture of Woven Woolens in the Sixteenth Century" (in Hebrew), *Sefunot* 6 (1962): 41–70.

6. Shmuel Avitzur, "The Woolen Textile Industry in Salonica" (in Hebrew), *Sefunot* 12

(1971–78): 145–68; Joseph Hacker, "The Jewish Community in Salonica in the Fifteenth and Sixteenth Centuries" (in Hebrew; Ph.D. diss. Hebrew University, Jerusalem, 1978) 159 and passim; Benjamin Braude, "The Textile Industry in Salonica in the Context of the Eastern Mediterranean Economy" (in Hebrew), *Pe'amim* 15 (1983): 82–95.

7. Avraham Ya'ari, "Hebrew Printing Presses in Izmir" (in Hebrew), *Areshet* 1 (1959): 97–222; Joseph R. Hacker, "An Emissary of Louis XIV in the Levant and Ottoman Jewish Culture" (in Hebrew), *Zion* 52 (1987): 25–44.

8. Barnai, "Portuguese Marranos;" idem, "Jewish Congregations in Izmir in the Seventeenth Century" (in Hebrew), *Pe'amim* 48 (1991): 66–84; idem, "Organization and Leadership in the Jewish Community of Izmir in the Seventeenth Century," in *The Jews of the Ottoman Empire,* ed. Avigdor Levy (Princeton: Darwin Press, 1994), 275–84.

9. Hacker, "Jewish Community," 61 and ff.; idem, "Ottoman Policy toward the Jews and Jewish Attitudes toward the Ottomans during the Fifteenth Century," in *Christians and Jews in the Ottoman Empire* ed. Benjamin Braude and Bernard Lewis (New York and London: Holmes and Meier, 1982), 1: 117–26; Joseph Hacker, "The Ottoman System of Sürgün and Its Effect on Jewish Society in the Ottoman Empire" (in Hebrew), *Zion* 55 (1990): 27–82; Minna Rozen, "Individual and Community in the Jewish Society of the Ottoman Empire: Salonica in the Sixteenth Century," in Levy, ed., *Jews of the Ottoman Empire,* 215–24.

10. Leah Bornstein-Makovetzky, "Jewish Communal Leadership in the Near East from the Late Fifteenth to the Eighteenth Centuries" (in Hebrew; Ph.D. diss., Bar Ilan University, Ramat Gan, 1978); Haim Gerber, *The Jews of the Ottoman Empire in the Sixteenth and Seventeenth Centuries: Economy and Society* (in Hebrew; Jerusalem: Historical Society of Israel, 1982), 9–80; Avigdor Levy, introduction to *Jews of the Ottoman Empire,* ed. idem, 50–51.

11. Jacob Barnai, "Rabbi Joseph Escapa and the Rabbinate of Izmir" (in Hebrew), *Sefunot,* n.s. 3 (1985), 53–81.

12. David Tamar, *Studies in the History of the Jews in Palestine and the Oriental Countries* (in Hebrew; Jerusalem: Mosad Ha-Rav Kook, 1981), 119–35; Jacob Barnai, "R. Haim Benveniste and the Izmir Rabbinate" (in Hebrew), in *The Days of the Crescent: Chapters in the History of the Jews in the Ottoman Empire,* ed. Minna Rozen (Tel Aviv: Tel Aviv University, 1996), 151–91.

13. Fernand Braudel, *The Mediterranean and the Mediterranean World in the Age of Philip II,* trans. Siân Reynolds (New York: Harper and Row, 1973), 2: 1159; Meir Benayahu, "Moses Benveniste, Court Physician to the Sultan, and R. Judah Zarko's Poem on His Exile to Rhodes" (in Hebrew), *Sefunot* 12 (1971–78): 123–44.

14. Gershom Scholem, *Sabbatai Sevi: The Mystical Messiah, 1626–1676,* trans. R. J. Zwi Werblowsky (Princeton: Princeton Univ. Press, 1973), 103–11.

15. Jacob Barnai, "On the History of the Sabbatean Movement and Its Place in Jewish Life in the Ottoman Empire" (in Hebrew), *Pe'amim* 3 (1979): 59–71.

16. Scholem, *Sabbatai Sevi.*

17. Moshe Idel, " 'One from a Town, Two from a Clan'—The Diffusion of Lurianic

Kabbalah and Sabbateanism: A Re-Examination," *Jewish History* 7 (1993): 79–104; Jacob Barnai, "Christian Messianism and Portuguese Marranos: The Emergence of Sabbateanism in Smyrna," *Jewish History* 7 (1993): 119–26; idem, "The Outbreak of Sabbateanism—The Eastern European Factor," *Journal of Jewish Thought and Philosophy* 4 (1994): 171–83.

18. Richard H. Popkin, "R. Nathan Shapiro's Visit to Amsterdam in 1650," *Dutch Jewish History* 1 (1984): 185–205; Yosef Kaplan, Henry Mechoulan, and Richard H. Popkin, eds., *Menasseh Ben Israel and His World* (Leiden: Brill, 1989).

19. Menasseh Ben Israel, *Esperanca de Israel* (Izmir, 1659); Ya'ari, "Hebrew Printing Presses in Izmir," 102.

20. Scholem, *Sabbatai Sevi,* 427–30; Barnai, "Christian Messianism."

21. See n. 11 and 12 above.

22. Ralph S. Hattox, *Coffee and Coffeehouses* (Seattle: Univ. of Washington Press, 1985); Eliezer Bashan, "The Rise and Decline of the Sephardi Communities in the Levant: The Economic Aspects," in *The Sephardi Heritage,* ed. Richard D. Barnett and W. M. Schwab (London: Gibraltar Books, 1989), 2: 349–88.

23. R. Hayyim Benveniste, *Sheyarei Keneset Hagedola, Orah Hayyim* (Izmir, 1671), 64b; my translation.

24. R. Yitzhak Molkho, *Orhot Yosher* (Tel Aviv: Yeshivat Shuvi Nafshi, 1975), 35; Haim Gerber, "On the History of the Jews in Istanbul in the Seventeenth and Eighteenth Centuries" (in Hebrew), *Pe'amim* 12 (1982): 27–46.

25. Gershom Scholem, *The Messianic Idea in Judaism* (New York: Schocken, 1971), 142–66; Meir Benayahu, "The Great Conversion in Salonica" (in Hebrew), *Sefunot* 14 (1971–78): 77–108.

26. Ülker, "Rise of Izmir," 42–47; Eliezer Bashan, "Fires and Earthquakes in Izmir from the Seventeenth to the Nineteenth Centuries" (in Hebrew), *Miqqedem Umiyyam* 2 (1986): 13–28.

27. Ülker, "Rise of Izmir," 48–54.

28. A. Lutzky, "The 'Francos' and the Effect of the Capitulations on the Aleppo Jews" (in Hebrew), *Zion* 6 (1941): 46–79; Minna Rozen, "The Archives of the Marseilles Chamber of Commerce" (in Hebrew), *Pe'amim* 9 (1981): 112–24; Simon Schwarzfuchs, "The Salonica Balance Scales: The Conflict between the French and the Jewish Merchants" (in Hebrew), *Sefunot* 15 (1971–78): 77–102; Jacob Barnai, "The Jews in the Ottoman Empire" (in Hebrew), in *History of the Jews in Islamic Countries,* ed. Shmuel Ettinger (Jerusalem: Merkaz Zalman Shazar, 1986), 2: 254–58; Aron Rodrigue, *French Jews, Turkish Jews: The Alliance Israélite Universelle and the Politics of Jewish Schooling in Turkey, 1860–1939* (Bloomington: Indiana Univ. Press, 1990), 25; idem, "The Beginnings of Westernization and Community Reform Among Istanbul's Jewry, 1854–65," in Levy, ed., *Jews of the Ottoman Empire,* 439–56.

29. R. Joshua Abraham Judah, *Avodat Massa* (Salonica, 1846).

30. Ya'ari, "Hebrew Printing Presses in Izmir," 103–108, 125–44.

31. R. Hayyim Abulafia, *Hanan Elohim* (Izmir, 1736), last pages of the book (without page numbers).

32. Jacob Barnai, "The Development of Links between Izmir Jews and Palestine Jews in the Seventeenth and Eighteenth Centuries" (in Hebrew), *Shalem* 5 (1987): 95–114; idem, "The Eretz Israel Fund in Nineteenth-Century Izmir" (in Hebrew), in *Transaction and Change in Modern Jewish History: Essays Presented in Honor of Shmuel Ettinger,* ed. Shmuel Almog et al. (Jerusalem: Merkaz Zalman Shazar, 1987), 135–48.

33. Jacob Barnai, *The Jews in Palestine in the Eighteenth Century* (in Hebrew; Jerusalem: Ben-Zvi Institute, 1982), 34–40, 72–85; English edition, trans. Naomi Goldblum (Tuscaloosa: Univ. of Alabama Press, 1992), 35–36, 147–53.

34. Isaiah Tishby, *Paths of Belief and Heresy* (in Hebrew; Ramat Gan: Agudat Ha-Sofrim, 1964), 108–68; Avraham Ya'ari, *The Mystery of a Book* (in Hebrew; Jerusalem: Mosad Ha-Rav Kook, 1954), 83–96.

35. R. Isaac Hacohen Rapaport, *Batei Kehuna* (Izmir, 1736), 1: 76–86, 125–34.

36. R. Joseph Hazzan, *Hikrei Lev, Yoreh De'a* (Salonica, 1806), 81, 88.

37. Jacob Barnai, "On the Jewish Community of Izmir in the Late Eighteenth and Early Nineteenth Centuries" (in Hebrew), *Zion* 47 (1982): 56–76.

38. Jacob Barnai, "Jewish Guilds in Turkey from the Sixteenth to the Nineteenth Centuries" (in Hebrew), in *Jews in Economic Life,* ed. N. Gross (Jerusalem: Merkaz Zalman Shazar, 1985), 133–47.

39. Haim Gerber and Jacob Barnai, *The Jews in Izmir in the Nineteenth Century* (in Hebrew and Turkish; Jerusalem: Misgav Yerushalayim, 1984), 5–12, 21–22, 69–71; Avner Levi, "Changes in the Leadership of the Main Spanish Communities in the Nineteenth-Century Ottoman Empire" (in Hebrew) in Rozen, ed., *Days of the Crescent,* 237–54.

40. Jacob Barnai, "The Status of the Jerusalem General Rabbinate in the Ottoman Period" (in Hebrew), *Cathedra* 13 (1979): 47–69; Mazal Kennedy, "The Institution of the Hakham Bashi and the Hakham Haneh Constitution in Istanbul in the Light of Changes in the Nineteenth Century (1835–1914)" (in Hebrew; M.A. thesis, Haifa University, 1985). Recently doubt has been cast on the limits of Jewish judicial autonomy in the Ottoman Empire in the fifteenth to eighteenth centuries as well; see Joseph R. Hacker, "Jewish Autonomy in the Ottoman Empire: Its Scope and Limits," in Levy, ed., *Jews of the Ottoman Empire,* 153–202. For a different perspective of the chief rabbinate at this time, see Avigdor Levy, introduction to *Jews of the Ottoman Empire,* 105–108; and idem, *"Millet* Politics: The Appointment of a Chief Rabbi in 1835," in ibid., 425–38.

41. Barnai, "Jews in the Ottoman Empire," 238–67; Rodrigue, *French Jews, Turkish Jews,* 25–70.

42. I. Hassida, *R. Hayyim Palagi and His Books* (in Hebrew; Jerusalem: Hotsa'at Mokirei Maran Ha-Habif, 1968); S. Ekstein, "R. Hayyim Palagi's Life and Work and His Influence on the Izmir Jewish Community" (in Hebrew; Ph.D. diss., Yeshiva University, 1970).

43. Rodrigue, *French Jews, Turkish Jews,* 47–56.

44. Avner Levi, "Jewish Periodicals in Izmir" (in Hebrew), *Pe'amim* 12 (1982): 87–104; idem, "Judeo-Spanish (Ladino)" (in Hebrew), in *The Writings of Sephardi and Oriental Jewish Authors in Languages other than Hebrew,* ed. Itzhak Bezalel (Tel Aviv: Tel Aviv University, 1982), 227–54.

45. Jacob Landau, "Relations between Jews and Non-Jews in the Late Ottoman Empire: Some Characteristics," in Levy, ed., *Jews of the Ottoman Empire,* 539–46.

46. Jacob Barnai, "Blood Libels in the Ottoman Empire from the Fifteenth to the Nineteenth Century" (in Hebrew), in *Antisemitism through the Ages,* ed. Shmuel Almog (Jerusalem: Merkaz Zalman Shazar, 1980), 211–16; English edition (Oxford: Pergamon, 1988), 189–94.

4. Rabbinic Literature in the Late Byzantine and Early Ottoman Periods

1. Steven B. Bowman, *The Jews of Byzantium, 1204–1453* (Tuscaloosa: Univ. of Alabama Press, 1985).

2. A. S. Hartom and M. D. Cassuto, eds., *Takkanot Kandia: Statuta Judaeorum Candiae* (in Hebrew; Jerusalem: Mekizei Nirdamim, 1943), no. 47.

3. Meir Benayahu, *Rabbi Eliyahu Capsali of Crete* (in Hebrew; Jerusalem: Tel Aviv University, 1983), 20.

4. *Takkanot Kandia,* 45.

5. *Israelitische Annalen* 21 (1839): 162.

6. A. Geiger, *Kevutzat Ma'amarim* (in Hebrew; Warsaw: Tushiyah, 1910), 285–96; previously published in *He-Halutz* 2 (1853): 158–60; see also entry (without title) by J. L. Dukes in *Otzar Nehmad* 2 (1857): 90–94.

7. M. Steinschneider, "Candia, Cenni di Storia Letteraria Candia," *Mose* 2 (1879): 457, and 3 (1880): 282.

8. Joseph Shelomoh Delmedigo, *Eilim* (Amsterdam, 1628), 29.

9. *Behinat Hadat* was first published much later (Vienna, 1833).

10. *Takkanot Kandia,* 50.

11. Published by A. Jellinek in *Ginzei Hokhmat ha-Kabbalah* (Leipzig, 1853).

12. Naomi Goldfeld, "A Commentary on the Pentateuch by Yehudah ben Shemaryah, from a Genizah Manuscript" (in Hebrew), *Kovetz Al-Yad* 10 (1982): 123–60.

13. J. Sussman, "Two Halakhic Pamphlets by Rabbi Moses Botaril" (in Hebrew), *Kovetz Al-Yad* 6 (1966): 271–97.

14. The first printed edition of *Sefer ha-Agur* was Naples, 1490.

15. Samuel K. Mirsky, ed., *She'iltot de Rab Ahai Gaon,* vols. 1–5 (Jerusalem: Mosad Ha-Rav Kook, 1959–1977).

16. See Robert Brody, *The Textual History of the She'iltot* (in Hebrew; New York and Jerusalem: American Academy for Jewish Research, 1991), 194.

17. See C. Sirat, "A Letter on the Creation by R. Shemaryah b. Elijah Akriti" (in Hebrew), *Eshel Beer-Sheva* 2 (1980): 204.

18. See Shabetai Kolidetzky's introduction to his edition of *Safra Devei Rav with the Commentary of Rabbi Hillel b. Elyakim* (in Hebrew; Jerusalem, 1961).

19. Joseph Hacker, "The Jewish Community in Salonica in the Fifteenth and Sixteenth Centuries" (in Hebrew; Ph.D. diss., Hebrew Univ., Jerusalem, 1978), appendix 1.

5. Jewish Contributions to Ottoman Medicine, 1450–1800

1. Steven B. Bowman, *The Jews of Byzantium, 1204–1453* (Tuscaloosa: Univ. of Alabama Press, 1985), 25.

2. Abraham Galanté, *Médecins juifs au service de la Turquie* (Istanbul: Babock, 1938; reprint, Istanbul: Editions Isis, 1985—*Histoire des Juifs de Turquie,* vol. 9), 81.

3. See H. A. R. Gibb, trans., *The Travels of Ibn Batuta* (Cambridge: Hakluyt Society at the University Press, 1958–1971), 2: 442–43; also cited by Bowman, *Jews of Byzantium,* 214.

4. See Bernard Lewis, *The Muslim Discovery of Europe* (New York: Norton, 1982), 228; Stanford J. Shaw, *The Jews of the Ottoman Empire and the Turkish Republic* (New York: New York Univ. Press, 1991), 86.

5. The list of such "standard" accounts is infinitely expandable, but three titles may serve as examples: Morris S. Goodblatt, *Jewish Life in Turkey in the Sixteenth Century* (New York: Jewish Theological Seminary, 1952); Salo Wittmayer Baron, *A Social and Religious History of the Jews,* 2nd ed., vol. 18 (New York: Columbia Univ. Press, 1983); Aryeh Shmuelevitz, *The Jews of the Ottoman Empire in the Late Fifteenth and Sixteenth Centuries* (Leiden: Brill, 1984).

6. Heinrich Graetz, *History of the Jews* (Philadelphia: Jewish Publication Society, 1891–1895), 4: 630.

7. See, for example, A. Fabris, "Il Dottor Girolamo Fasaneo, alias Receb," *Archivio Veneto,* series 5, vol. 23(1989): 105–18, and F. Lucchetta and G. Lucchetta, "Un medico veneto in Siria nel cinquecento: Cornelio Bianchi," *Quaderni di Studi Arabi* 4 (1986): 1–56.

8. For an account of the contemporary publication history, see Harry Friedenwald, *Jewish Luminaries in Medical History* (Baltimore: Johns Hopkins Press, 1946), 35–37.

9. See in particular R. Taton, ed., *History of Science* (New York: Basic Books, 1963–1966), 2: 169 and 345; *Encyclopedia Judaica* (Jerusalem: Keter Publishing House, 1972), 2: 795–98.

10. For an account of the main figures of the Turkish branch of the ben Yahya family, see *The Jewish Encyclopedia* (New York, 1901–1905), 12: 584 (nos. 23–27).

11. See Lewis, *Muslim Discovery of Europe,* 228.

12. Perhaps the most celebrated example of the doctor/diplomat combination was not a member of the Hamon clan, but the case of Solomon Ashkenazi, a German Jew who migrated to the Ottoman Empire via Poland. In Istanbul he acquired a position as doctor to the Venetian mission and later became private physician to the grand vezir Sokollu Mehmed

Pasha; see M. Franco, *Essai sur l'histoire des Israélites de l'empire ottoman depuis les origines jusqu'à nos jours* (Paris, 1897; reprint, Paris: Centre d'Etudes Don Isaac Abravanel, 1981), 62. For the critical role played by Solomon in concluding the Venetian-Ottoman Peace Treaty of 1573, see J. von Hammer-Purgstall, *Geschichte des Osmanischen Reiches* (Pest, 1827–1835; reprint, Graz: Akademische Druck, 1963), 3: 601 and 789. See also *Jewish Encyclopedia*, 2: 201.

13. *Jewish Encyclopedia*, 6: 201–202, records the names of six members of the family, ending with Aaron ben Isaac Hamon, who practiced in Istanbul circa 1720. A list of forty physicians belonging to the palace corps of the *etibba-i Yahudiyan* in 1618 also includes the name of a certain "Yehuda fils de Hamon"; see Galanté, *Médecins juifs*, 89 (no. 21). Although their names are not known to us, it is highly probable that there were other Hamons practicing medicine who bridged the generational gap between the time of Joseph the Elder in the early sixteenth century and Aaron Hamon two centuries later.

14. Baron, *Social and Religious History*, 18: 74–77.

15. Ayn-i Ali, *Risale* (Istanbul, 1280 H/1863–1864), 94. See also the list of twenty-one doctors belonging to the *etibba-i hassa* in 1604 published by İ. H. Uzunçarşılı, *Osmanlı Devletinin Saray Teşkilatı* (Ankara: Türk Tarih Kurumu Basımevi, 1945; reprint, 1984), 364–65. The list clearly shows that while for administrative purposes the doctors were divided into two groups, the non-Jewish *etibba-i hassa* and the Jewish *etibba-i Yahudiyan*, the ranks of the former included a number of recent converts. Cf. the following names: Mevlana Frenk Mehmed, Muslim-i Nev, and Kara Yahudi-oğlu Mustafa.

16. Baron, *Social and Religious History*, 18: 262.

17. Uriel Heyd, "The Jewish Communities of Istanbul in the Seventeenth Century," *Oriens* 6 (1953): 299–314; see in particular p. 307.

18. See J. H. Elliot, *The Revolt of the Catalans: A Study in the Decline of Spain (1598–1640)* (Cambridge: Cambridge Univ. Press, 1963), 91. For a graphic description of conditions during the evacuation of Spain, see R. Watson and W. Thomson, *A History of the Reign of Philip the Third, King of Spain* (London, 1818), 132–55.

19. See in particular J. Yerushalmi, *The Re-education of Marranos in the Seventeenth Century* (Cincinnati: Judaic Studies Program, University of Cincinnati, 1980), 1.

20. A. Refik, *Hicri On Üçüncü Asırda İstanbul Hayatı (1200–1255)* (Istanbul: Matbaacılık ve Neşriyat T.A.Ş., 1932), 29–31.

21. See Graetz, *History of the Jews*, 4: 716–17. For an account of his brother Fernando's scholarly publications, see Friedenwald, *Jewish Luminaries*, 51–52.

22. See R. Landau, *Geschichte der Juedischen Aerzte* (Berlin, 1895), 89.

23. See Lewis, *Muslim Discovery of Europe*, 227–31.

24. Archivio di Stato di Venezia, Senato, Dispacci Constantinopoli, box 56, p. 9. See fig. 1 for a facsimile of this document. An English translation of the letter of Mehmed Ali Pasha is as follows:

Upon the arrival of this note *(tezkire)* to the pillar of the commanders of the Christian community [his excellency Francesco Contarini] *bailo* [of the Republic] of Venice [at Istanbul] (may his latter days end well) be ye advised that we desire that our physician Yakov Desakov, having long been in our service, should be treated with favor and protection. He has given service unstintingly at our side day and night and is unquestionably deserving of our protection. The aforementioned Doctor [Desakov] has dispatched commercial goods [to Venice] valued at 5,000 gold pieces. [We request that] when he arrives [in Venice] you bring about through your help and careful attention and your striving and persistence the granting of a customs exemption for his yearly trips [to Venice]. [In return for] our goodwill on behalf of your interests here [in the Ottoman Empire] the 5,000 gold-piece customs exemption for the aforementioned [Desakov] is no great matter. The aforementioned [Desakov] is working assiduously and continuously on your behalf in all matters concerning your interests here. [In recognition of his service on your behalf here and] for my sake you should expend all effort and care in the matter of securing the said Desakov's customs exemption; its granting is the firm object and desire of this party [i.e., the sultan's government]. Your full efforts and unquestioning cooperation are accordingly requested. [Be ye assured] that [like] efforts will be expended by this party on your behalf in all matters and particulars involving your interests arising here [in the Ottoman lands]. With that in mind be ye ever vigilant in efforts and attention to the matter of [the acquisition of] the customs exemption in the manner indicated. Be ye advised that we assign the highest priority to the achievement of this object and instruct you to act in accordance with the gist of this missive. In closing [we offer our] salutations to him who has followed [God's] guidance on the right path.

Francesco Contarini, to whom the note was addressed, was *bailo* at Istanbul from 1602 to 1604; see T. Bertele, *Il palazzo ambasciatori di Venezia a Constantinopoli* (Bologna: Apollo, 1932), 417. The form of address used in the salutation, "may his latter days end well," was standard for communications sent to non-Muslim dignitaries, implying the sender's pious wish that the addressee will eventually undergo a change of heart and accept the Islamic faith. This expression is complemented by the standard formula for the closing of letters addressed to non-Muslims. These paired phrases were conventionally used to invite the non-Muslim addressee to convert to Islam.

25. See Friedenwald, *Jewish Luminaries,* 159–60.

26. Galanté, *Médecins juifs,* 92.

27. See E. Carmoly, *Histoire des médecins juifs* (Brussels: Société Encyclographique des Sciences Médicales, 1844), 199 and 247.

28. See the section on the eighteenth century and n. 37, below.

29. *Encyclopedia Judaica,* 6: 1414 and *Jewish Encyclopedia,* 5: 429–30.

30. For the biography of Mustafa Feyzi (d. 1103 H/1691–1692), see Mehmed Süreyya, *Sicill-i Osmani* (Istanbul, 1308–1311 H/1890–1893; reprint, Westmead, England: Gregg, 1971; cited hereafter as *SO*), 4: 408. The life of his grandson, also called Mustafa, is recorded in *SO,* 4: 426–27. The biography of the younger Mustafa's brother, Mehmed Emin Efendi, is

found in *SO,* 1:406, while that of his associate *(kethüda)* is found in *SO,* 3:29. See also the accounts in Mehmed Tahir, *Osmanlı Müellifleri* (Istanbul: Matbaa-i Âmire, 1333–1342 H/1915–1924; reprint, Istanbul, 1975), 3:207, 224, and 230.

31. For a list of works by Mustafa Feyzi, see R. Şeşen et al., *Catalogue of the Islamic Medical Manuscripts in the Libraries of Turkey* (Istanbul: Markaz al-Abhath, 1984), 215–19.

32. For a list of Süleyman Efendi's works, see Şeşen, *Islamic Medical Manuscripts,* 212–14.

33. See Şeşen, *Islamic Medical Manuscripts,* 214.

34. See, in particular, his *Cevher al ferid fi al tibb al cedid,* completed in 1112 H/1700; Şeşen, *Islamic Medical Manuscipts,* 263–64, and Osman Şevki, *Beş Büçük Asırlık Türk Tebabet Tarihi* (Istanbul, 1314 H/1896–1897), 163–64 (no. 41).

35. See his *Destur-i vesim fi tibb al-cedid ve'l-kadim;* Şeşen, Islamic Medical Manuscripts, 387, and Şevki, *Tebabet Tarihi,* 169–70 (no. 58).

36. See C. Hannaway, "Medicine and Religion in Pre-Revolutionary France: Introduction," *Social History of Medicine* 2 (1989): 315–19.

37. For a summary of his ideas on the subject of medical reform, see Carmoly, *Médecins juifs,* 199ff.

38. On the various members of the Hayatizade dynasty, see n. 30, above. In 1754, when the *hekimbaşılık* passed out of the hands of the Hayatizade dynasty, the position was occupied for a three-year term, from 1754 to 1756, by another Jewish convert named Çelebi Mustafa Efendi. See *SO,* 4:434, and Şevki, *Tebabet Tarihi,* 176–77.

39. See Şevki, *Tebabet Tarihi,* 204–205, for the text of the document issued during the *hekimbaşılık* of Giridli Nuh Efendi Abdülmennan, a Greek convert to Islam. For the text of the document addressed to Mustafa Feyzi Efendi Hayatizade, a Jewish convert to Islam, see Şevki, *Tebabet Tarihi,* 214–15. Şevki, *op. cit.,* 218–19, also provides the text of another *ferman,* dated 1182 H/1768, whose contents confirm the tenor of the previous two edicts.

40. On these developments see Franco, *Israélites de l'empire ottoman,* 116 ff. See also Mesut Paşa, ed., *Muahedat Mecmuası* (Istanbul, 1292–1298 H/1876–1882), 3: 117 (art. 6), for the wording of the agreements permitting the establishment of Ottoman consulates in Austria.

41. Galanté, *Médecins juifs,* 94.

42. The principal scions of this family in the nineteenth century were Jacques de Castro (1802–1876), head of the military hospital that had been founded in Istanbul in 1827, and Abraham de Castro, chief doctor of the mental asylum in Istanbul in the late nineteenth century. For their biographies, see *Jewish Encyclopedia,* 3:611, and Galanté, *Médecins juifs,* 113. On the other branches of the de Castro family that also produced a number of distinguished physicians, see Harry Friedenwald, *The Jews and Medicine* (Baltimore: Johns Hopkins Press, 1944), 2:448–59.

6. Changing Patterns of Community Structures, with Special Reference to Ottoman Egypt

1. For a detailed study of the organization of the Jewish community in Egypt, see Leah Bornstein-Makovetzky, "The Community and Its Institutions" (in Hebrew), in *The Jews in Ottoman Egypt (1517–1914)*, ed. Jacob M. Landau (Jerusalem: Misgav Yerushalayim, 1988), 129–216. On Jewish community organization in the Ottoman Empire in general, until the early nineteenth century, see Avigdor Levy, introduction to *The Jews of the Ottoman Empire*, ed. idem (Princeton: Darwin Press, 1994), 42–70; and in the same volume the following articles: Joseph R. Hacker, "Jewish Autonomy in the Ottoman Empire: Its Scope and Limits. Jewish Courts from the Sixteenth to the Eighteenth Centuries," 153–202; Minna Rozen, "Individual and Community in the Jewish Society of the Ottoman Empire: Salonica in the Sixteenth Century," 215–73; Jacob Barnai, "Organization and Leadership in the Jewish Community of Izmir in the Seventeenth Century," 275–84; Daniel J. Schroeter, "Jewish Quarters in the Arab-Islamic Cities of the Ottoman Empire," 287–300. Also see the contribution by Jacob Barnai in this volume.

2. Cf. Norman A. Stillman, "Middle Eastern and North African Jewries Confront Modernity: Orientation, Disorientation, Reorientation," in *Sephardi and Middle Eastern Jewries: History and Culture in the Modern Era* (Bloomington: Indiana Univ. Press, 1996), 59–72; Paul Dumont, "Jewish Communities in Turkey during the Last Decades of the Nineteenth Century in the Light of the Archives of the Alliance Israélite Universelle," in *Christians and Jews in the Ottoman Empire: The Functioning of a Plural Society*, ed. Benjamin Braude and Bernard Lewis (New York: Holmes and Meier, 1982), 1:209–42; Charles Issawi, "The Transformation of the Economic Position of the *Millets* in the Nineteenth Century," in ibid., 261–85; Roderic H. Davison, "The *Millets* as Agents of Change in the Nineteenth-Century Ottoman Empire," in ibid., 319–37; Jacques Hassoun, "The Penetration of Modernization into Jewish Life in Egypt, 1870–1918" (in Hebrew), in Landau, ed., *Jews in Ottoman Egypt*, 559–76; Yehuda Nini, *From East and from West: Everyday Life of the Jews of Egypt* (in Hebrew; Tel Aviv: Tel Aviv University, 1980); Ali İhsan Bağış, *Osmanlı Ticaretinde Gayri Müslimler* (Ankara: Turhan Kitabevi, 1983). See also Maurice Mizrahi, *L'Egypte et ses Juifs: Le temps révolu* (Lausanne: M. Mizrahi, 1977), chap. 4.

3. For Istanbul, see Dumont, "Jewish Communities in Turkey," 210–14. For Egypt, see Sergio Della-Pergola, "The Jewish Population in the Nineteenth and Twentieth Centuries" (in Hebrew), in Landau, ed., *Jews in Ottoman Egypt,* 33–42. For some characteristic photographs of Cairo and Alexandria, see *Juifs d'Egypte: Images et Textes* (Paris: Editions du Scribe, 1984), 27, 46, and 78, ff. For other Arabic-speaking provinces, see Schroeter, "Jewish Quarters," 293–95; Rachel Simon, "Jewish Participation in the Reforms in Libya during the Second Ottoman Period, 1835–1911," in Levy, ed., *Jews of the Ottoman Empire,* 494–504; Norman A. Stillman, *The Jews of Arab Lands in Modern Times* (Philadelphia: Jewish Publication

Society, 1991), 37–41. Also see the contributions by Daniel J. Schroeter, Marie-Christine Varol, and Nedim Gürsel in this volume.

4. See Aron Rodrigue, "The Beginnings of Westernization and Community Reform Among Istanbul's Jewry, 1854–65," in Levy, ed., *Jews of the Ottoman Empire*, 439–56; Esther Benbassa, "Associational Strategies in Ottoman Jewish Society in the Nineteenth and Twentieth Centuries," in ibid., 457–84. For Zionism in Egypt, see Stillman, *Jews of Arab Lands in Modern Times*, 67–70; Gudrun Krämer, *The Jews in Modern Egypt, 1914–1952* (Seattle: Univ. of Washington Press, 1989), 182–204. For an exaggerated view, see Siham Nassar, *Al-Yahud al-Misriyyun bayn al-Misriyya wa-l-Sahyuniyya* (Beirut: Dar al-Wahda, 1980).

5. Jacob M. Landau, *Jews in Nineteenth-Century Egypt* (New York: New York Univ. Press, 1969), 51–70; Shimon Shamir, "The Evolution of the Egyptian Nationality Laws and Their Application to the Jews in the Monarchy Period," in idem, ed., *The Jews of Egypt: A Mediterranean Society in Modern Times* (Boulder, Colo.: Westview, 1987), 33–38.

6. Della-Pergola, "Jewish Population," 28–42.

7. Maurice Frageon, *Les Juifs en Egypte* (Cairo: Paul Barbey, 1938), 31; B. Taragan, *La Communauté Israélite d'Alexandrie* (Alexandria: Les Editions Juives d'Egypte, 1932), 92–93.

8. On the Karaites, see Yoseph El-Gamil, "Karaite Jews in Egypt, 1517–1918" (in Hebrew), in Landau, ed., *Jews in Ottoman Egypt*, 513–56.

9. Bornstein-Makovetzky, "Community and Its Institutions," 204–11; Hassoun, "Penetration of Modernization," 564–70.

10. Landau, *Jews in Nineteenth-Century Egypt*, 52–54.

11. So Albert Cohn claimed, in *Allgemeine Zeitung des Judenthums* 28, no. 36 (30 Aug. 1864): 559.

12. *Revue Israélite d'Egypte* 5, no. 21 (15–25 Nov. 1916): 193–96. The translator remains anonymous. The statutes have been reprinted in Landau, *Jews in Nineteenth-Century Egypt*, 161–65.

13. *Statuti della Communità Israelitica di Alessandria d'Egitto* (Alexandria, 1872); reprinted in Landau, *Jews in Nineteenth-Century Egypt*, 183–91.

14. For the Jewish hospital in Alexandria, see Fargeon, *Les Juifs en Egypte*, 254; Taragan, *La Communauté Israélite d'Alexandrie*, 145–46; Noury Farhi, *La Communauté juive d'Alexandrie* (Alexandria, 1946), 25. For the Cairo hospital, see B. L. Benas, *Report of His Travels in the East* (London: Anglo-Jewish Association, 1885), 6.

15. Landau, *Jews in Nineteenth-Century Egypt*, 58–70.

16. See *Jewish Chronicle*, 16 Apr. 1847, p. 115.

17. See letter from Alexandria published in the Hebrew weekly *Ha-Maggid* 15, no. 13 (29 Mar. 1871): 100; cf. Egypte, Ministère de l'Intérieur, *Statistique de l'Egypte—année 1873* (Cairo, 1873), 256. Also see Landau, *Jews in Nineteenth-Century Egypt*, 74–79 and passim.

18. Details in Jacob M. Landau, "The Beginnings of Modernization in Education: The Jewish Community in Egypt as a Case Study," in *The Beginnings of Modernization in the Middle*

East: The Nineteenth Century, ed. William R. Polk and Richard L. Chambers (Chicago: Univ. of Chicago Press, 1968), 299–312. See also the contribution by Rachel Simon in this volume.

19. Bornstein-Makovetzky, "Community and Its Institutions," 145–48; Landau, *Jews in Nineteenth-Century Egypt,* 23–24.

20. Bornstein-Makovetzky, "Community and Its Institutions," 173–74.

7. The Changing Relationship between the Jews of the Arab Middle East and the Ottoman State in the Nineteenth Century

1. For a detailed study that focuses on Christians and Jews specifically in the Arabic-speaking parts of the Ottoman Empire, published since the present paper was written, see Bruce Masters, *Christians and Jews in the Ottoman Arab World: Roots of Sectarianism* (Cambridge: Cambridge Univ. Press, 2001).

2. H. A. R. Gibb and Harold Bowen, *Islamic Society and the West* (London: Oxford Univ. Press, 1950–1957), pt. 2: 211–12.

3. Ibid., pt. 2: 217. The authors, in a footnote, acknowledge that the Jews were formally recognized as a *millet* only in 1839.

4. The early origins of the Jewish *millet,* with a chief rabbi as equal to the patriarch since early times, has until recently been an unchallenged assumption in the literature, including those authors who have focused on the Tanzimat. See, e.g., Roderic H. Davison, *Reform in the Ottoman Empire, 1856–1876* (Princeton: Princeton Univ. Press, 1963), 13.

5. Benjamin Braude, "Foundation Myths of the *Millet* System," in *Christians and Jews in the Ottoman Empire: The Functioning of a Plural Society,* ed. Benjamin Braude and Bernard Lewis (New York and London: Holmes and Meier, 1982), 1: 69 ff. It is surprising that there is no dialogue between this important revisionist article and the study in the same volume by Kemal H. Karpat, *"Millets* and Nationality: The Roots of the Incongruity of Nation and State in the Post-Ottoman Era," 141–69. Karpat essentially accepts the historicity of the "foundation myths" and here makes no revision from his previous monograph, *An Inquiry into the Social Foundations of Nationalism in the Ottoman State: From Social Estates to Classes, From Millets to Nations* (Princeton: Center of International Studies, Princeton University, 1973), 32–40.

6. Gülnihal Bozkurt, "An Overview on the Ottoman Empire-Jewish Relations," *Islam—Zeitschrift für Geschichte und Kultur des Islamischen Orient* 71 (1994): 255–60. How much this generalization would apply to the Ottoman provinces with Christian majorities still needs to be investigated.

7. See Maria Todorova, "The Ottoman Legacy in the Balkans," in *Imperial Legacy: The Ottoman Imprint on the Balkans and the Middle East,* ed. L. Carl Brown (New York: Columbia Univ. Press, 1996), 45–77.

8. Karpat, *"Millets* and Nationality," 149–50.

9. Ibid., 162–63.

10. Karpat, *Social Foundations of Nationalism,* 87–88.

11. Walter P. Zenner, "Jews in Late Ottoman Syria: External Relations," in *Jewish Societies in the Middle East: Community, Culture and Authority,* ed. Shlomo Deshen and Walter P. Zenner (Washington, D.C.: University Press of America, 1982), 168.

12. Stanford J. Shaw, *The Jews of the Ottoman Empire and the Turkish Republic* (New York: New York Univ. Press, 1991), 149. Also see Avram Galante [Abraham Galanté], *Histoire des Juifs de Turquie* (Istanbul: Editions Isis, n.d. [1985]), 5: 31–32.

13. Avigdor Levy, *"Millet* Politics: The Appointment of a Chief Rabbi in 1835," in idem, ed., *The Jews of the Ottoman Empire* (Princeton: Darwin Press, 1994), 425–38.

14. Avigdor, Levy, *The Sephardim in the Ottoman Empire* (Princeton: Darwin Press, 1992), 105–108; Shaw, *Jews of the Ottoman Empire,* 149–55.

15. The text of the statute is found in Galante, *Histoire des Juifs,* 5: 13–26.

16. Shaw, *Jews of the Ottoman Empire,* 166–70; Davison, *Reform,* 130.

17. Levy, *Sephardim in the Ottoman Empire,* 107; Aron Rodrigue, *French Jews, Turkish Jews: The Alliance Israélite Universelle and the Politics of Jewish Schooling in Turkey, 1860–1925* (Bloomington: Indiana Univ. Press, 1990), 43–44.

18. See Esther Benbassa and Aron Rodrigue, *Sephardi Jewry: A History of the Judeo-Spanish Community, 14th–20th Centuries* (Berkeley: Univ. of California Press, 2000), 68ff. On the failure to integrate non-Muslims into the new Ottoman civil institutions, see Fatma Müge Göçek, *Rise of the Bourgeoisie, Demise of Empire: Ottoman Westernization and Social Change* (Oxford: Oxford Univ. Press, 1996), 84–86.

19. Ibid., 150 ff.; Shaw, *Jews of the Ottoman Empire,* 172–73.

20. See the introduction to *Haim Nahum: A Sephardic Chief Rabbi in Politics, 1892–1923,* ed. Esther Benbassa (Tuscaloosa: Univ. of Alabama Press, 1995).

21. Zenner, "Jews in Late Ottoman Syria: External Relations," 167.

22. H. Z. Hirschberg, "The Oriental Jewish Communities," in *Religion in the Middle East: Three Religions in Concord and Conflict,* ed. A. J. Arberry (Cambridge: Cambridge Univ. Press, 1969), 1: 198–99; Levy, *Sephardim in the Ottoman Empire,* 107–108.

23. Davison, *Reform in the Ottoman Empire,* 137 ff.

24. Moshe Ma'oz, "Changes in the Position of the Jewish Communities of Palestine and Syria in Mid-Nineteenth Century," in idem, ed., *Studies on Palestine during the Ottoman Period* (Jerusalem: Magnes Press, 1975), 142–43.

25. Zenner, "Jews in Late Ottoman Syria: External Relations," 157–58.

26. Ibid., 163–64.

27. Isaiah Friedman, "The System of Capitulations and Its Effects on Turco-Jewish Relations in Palestine, 1856–1897," in *Palestine in the Late Ottoman Period: Political, Social and Economic Transformation,* ed. David Kushner (Jerusalem: Yad Izhak Ben-Zvi, 1986), 280–81.

28. Tudor Parfitt, *The Jews in Palestine, 1800–1882* (Woodbridge, Suffolk: Boydell Press, 1987), 127 ff.

29. Bozkurt, "Ottoman Empire-Jewish Relations," 266–69.

30. It has been demonstrated, contrary to a later popular notion, that *ha-rav ha-kolel* of Jerusalem did not have authority over communities in Palestine as a whole. The title *rishon le-tziyyon* was officially applied to *ha-rav ha-kolel* of Jerusalem only from the beginning of the nineteenth century. See Jacob Barnai, "The Status of the Jerusalem General Rabbinate in the Ottoman Period" (in Hebrew), *Cathedra* 13 (1979): 54–57.

31. Moshe Ma'oz, *Ottoman Reform in Syria and Palestine, 1840–1861: The Impact of the Tanzimat on Politics and Society* (Oxford: Clarendon Press, 1968), 90 ff.

32. Ma'oz, "Changes in the Position," 150–51. For an exhaustive study of the Damascus Affair, see Jonathan Frankel, *The Damascus Affair: "Ritual Murder," Politics, and the Jews in 1840* (Cambridge: Cambridge Univ. Press, 1997).

33. Ma'oz, *Ottoman Reform,* 195.

34. Ibid., 204.

35. Zenner, "Jews in Late Ottoman Syria: External Relations," 167.

36. Walter P. Zenner, "Jews in Late Ottoman Syria: Community, Family and Religion," in Deshen and Zenner, eds., *Jewish Societies,* 190.

37. Parfitt, *Jews in Palestine,* 161, referring to a letter from the British consulate dated 5 September 1849.

38. Archives of the Alliance Israélite Universelle, Liban I G 4, cited in Norman A. Stillman, *The Jews of Arab Lands in Modern Times* (Philadelphia: Jewish Publication Society, 1991), 231–34.

39. Barnai, "Status of the Jerusalem General Rabbinate," 60.

40. Ibid., 63.

41. Zenner, "Jews in Late Ottoman Syria: Community," 187 ff.

42. Jacob Saul Duwayk, *Derekh Emunah* (Aleppo, 1913/14), 120a–121a, cited in Stillman, *Jews of Arab Lands in Modern Times,* 223–24.

43. Israel Kolatt, "The Organization of the Jewish Population of Palestine and the Development of Its Political Consciousness before World War I," in *Studies on Palestine during the Ottoman Period,* ed. Moshe Ma'oz (Jerusalem: Magnes Press, 1975), 211 ff.; Barnai, "Status of the Jerusalem General Rabbinate," 63–65.

44. Daphne Tsimhoni, "On the Beginnings of Modernization among the Jews of Iraq in the Nineteenth Century until 1914" (in Hebrew), *Pe'amim* 36 (1988): 8.

45. Zvi Yehudah, "Social Relations between Jews and Muslims in Baghdad at the End of the Nineteenth Century According to Local Jewish Sources" (in Hebrew), in *A Nation and Its History,* ed. Shmuel Ettinger (Jerusalem: Merkaz Zalman Shazar, 1984), 56–58.

46. Bozkurt, "Ottoman Empire–Jewish Relations," 265.

47. Nissim Kazzaz, "The Political Activity of the Jews of Iraq at the End of the Ottoman Period" (in Hebrew), *Pe'amim* 36 (1988): 38; Hasan Kayalı, "Jewish Representation in the Ottoman Parliaments," in Levy, ed., *Jews of the Ottoman Empire,* 509–10.

48. Bozkurt, "Ottoman Empire–Jewish Relations," 266.

49. Shlomo Deshen, "La communauté juive de Bagdad à la fin de l'époque ottomane:

L'émergence de classes sociales et de la sécularisation," *Annales HSS* [*Annales, Histoire, Sciences Sociales*] 3 (1994): 681–703; see also Tsimhoni, "Beginnings of Modernization," 12–13.

50. David Solomon Sassoon, *A History of the Jews in Baghdad* (Letchworth, England: S. D. Sassoon, 1949), 138; Abraham Ben-Ya'akov, *The Jews of Iraq from the End of the Gaonic Period to Our Times (1038–1960),* 2d ed. (in Hebrew; Jerusalem: Kiryat Sefer, 1979), 156–58.

51. Tsimhoni, "Beginnings of Modernization," 14 n. 11.

52. Details on this strife are found in Ben-Ya'akov, *Jews of Iraq,* pp. 162–63; Sassoon, *Jews in Baghdad,* 157–64.

53. Ben-Ya'akov, *Jews of Iraq,* 165–66.

54. This point is stressed by both Deshen, "La communauté juive de Bagdad," 694–96, and Sassoon, *Jews in Baghdad,* 157.

55. Abdallah Ali Ibrahim, "Evolution of Government and Society in Tripolitania and Cyrenaica (Libya): 1835–1911" (Ph.D. diss., University of Utah, 1982), 8 ff.; Ali Abdullatif Ahmida, *The Making of Modern Libya: State Formation, Colonization and Resistance, 1830–1932* (Albany: State University of New York Press, 1994), 30–31.

56. Rachel Simon, "The Jews of Libya and the Non-Jewish Environment in the Late Ottoman Period," *Pe'amim* 3 (1979): 20.

57. Harvey E. Goldberg, ed., *The Book of Mordechai: A Study of the Jews of Libya* (Philadelphia: Institute for the Study of Human Issues, 1980), 141–43; Rachel Simon, "Jewish Participation in the Reforms in Libya during the Second Ottoman Period, 1835–1911," in Levy, ed., *Jews of the Ottoman Empire,* 490–93.

58. On these anecdotes, see Nahum Slouschz, *My Travels in Libya* (in Hebrew; Tel-Aviv, 1937–1943), 1: 233–35; idem, "La Tripolitaine sous la domination des Karamanlis," *Revue du Monde Musulman* 6 (1908): 448–51. Harvey E. Goldberg, "Ottoman Rule in Tripoli as Viewed by the History of Mordechai Hakohen," in *Les relations entre Juifs et Musulmans en Afrique du Nord, XIXe-XXe siècles* (Paris: Editions du Centre National de la Recherche Scientifique, 1980), 155.

59. Slouschz, *My Travels in Libya,* 2: 75.

60. Ibid., 1: 100, and 2: 60–61; H. Z. Hirschberg, *A History of the Jews in North Africa* (Leiden: Brill, 1974–1981), 2: 172–73; Simon, "Jewish Participation," 491.

61. Slouschz, *My Travels in Libya,* 1: 106.

62. Hirschberg, *Jews in North Africa,* 2: 173.

63. Ibrahim, "Evolution of Government," 187–89.

64. Goldberg, "Ottoman Rule in Tripoli," 150–51.

65. Simon, "Jews of Libya," 8–9; Ibrahim, "Evolution of Government," 187–89.

66. Ibrahim, "Evolution of Government," 187–89.

67. Goldberg, "Ottoman Rule in Tripoli," 151; Simon, "Jews of Libya," 8; on the establishment of the secular courts, see Ibrahim, "Evolution of Government," 198–201.

68. Hirschberg, *Jews in North Africa,* 2: 175–76; Simon, "Jews of Libya," 5–6; Harvey E. Goldberg, *Jewish Life in Muslim Libya* (Chicago: Univ. of Chicago Press, 1990), 21, 25.

69. Simon, "Jews of Libya," 5–6; idem, "Jewish Participation," 497.

70. Simon, "Jews of Libya," 5–6; Hirschberg, *Jews in North Africa*, 2: 176. The term *hahambaşı* may have been employed earlier. See Goldberg, "Ottoman Rule in Tripoli," 150.

71. Simon, "Jews of Libya," 31.

72. Maurice Roumani, "Zionism and Social Change in Libya at the Turn of the Century," *Studies in Zionism* 8, no. 1 (1987): 5.

73. Hirschberg, *Jews in North Africa*, 2: 182–84. Shabbetai was appointed *hahambaşı* in 1904. It is not clear when his appointment ended. Hacohen lists two acting *hahambaşıs* who served between Shabbetai's departure and Italy's invasion of Libya in 1911. Mordekhai Hacohen, *Higgid Mordekhai*, ed. Harvey Goldberg (in Hebrew; Jerusalem: Yad Yitzhaq Ben-Zvi, 1978), 147.

74. Cf. Goldberg, "Ottoman Rule in Tripoli," 154.

75. Renzo De Felice, *Jews in an Arab Land: Libya, 1835–1970* (Austin: Univ. of Texas Press, 1985), 18–24.

76. Benbassa, ed., *Haim Nahum,* 9–10; Feroz Ahmad, "Unionist Relations with the Greek, Armenian, and Jewish Communities of the Ottoman Empire, 1908–1914," in Braude and Lewis, eds., *Christians and Jews,* 1: 401–405, 425–28; Kayalı, "Jewish Representation," 511–12; M. Şükrü Hanioğlu, "Jews in the Young Turk Movement to the 1908 Revolution," in Levy, ed., *Jews of the Ottoman Empire,* 519–26.

77. Neville J. Mandel, *The Arabs and Zionism before World War I* (Berkeley: Univ. of California Press, 1976), 71 ff.; Ahmad, "Unionist Relations," 428.

78. Cf. Şerif Mardin, "Power, Civil Society and Culture in the Ottoman Empire," *Comparative Studies in Society and History* 11(1969): 258–81; and Ergun Özbudun, "The Continuing Ottoman Legacy and the State Tradition in the Middle East," in Brown, ed., *Imperial Legacy,* 136–37.

8. Changing Relations between Jews, Muslims, and Christians during the Nineteenth Century, with Special Reference to Ottoman Syria and Palestine

1. These figures are estimates: the numbers of Jews in Syria-Palestine have been worked out on the basis of various sources; for example, see Great Britain, Public Record Office (PRO), Foreign Office (FO) 78/495, Rose to Canning, no. 36, Beirut, 24 May 1842. Also see the contribution by Daniel Schroeter in this volume.

2. See Stanford J. Shaw, *The Jews of the Ottoman Empire and the Turkish Republic* (New York: New York Univ. Press, 1991), 86–92 and passim; Avigdor Levy, introduction to *The Jews of the Ottoman Empire,* ed. idem (Princeton: Darwin Press, 1994), 28–34, 76–78 and passim; and the contribution by Rhoads Murphey in this volume.

3. Abd al-Qadir al-Maghribi, "Yahud al-Sham mundhu Mi'at Am," *Majallat al-Majma al-Ilmi al-Arabi* 9 (1929): 642.

4. Bernard Lewis, *The Jews of Islam* (Princeton: Princeton Univ. Press, 1984), 137.

5. J. L. Burckhardt, *Travels in Syria and the Holy Land* (London: Darf Publishers, 1822), 180.

6. Ibrahim al-Awra, *Ta'rikh Wilayat Sulayman Basha al-Adil* (Sidon, 1936; reprint, Beirut: Dar Lahad Khatir, 1989), 477.

7. As'ad Mansur, *Ta'rikh al-Nasira* (Egypt: Matba'at al-Hilal, 1924), 59.

8. H. A. R. Gibb and Harold Bowen, *Islamic Society and the West* (London: Oxford University Press, 1950), pt. 1: 208.

9. See Moshe Ma'oz, *Ottoman Reform in Syria and Palestine, 1840–1861: The Impact of the Tanzimat on Politics and Society* (Oxford: Clarendon Press, 1968), 7.

10. Cf. Lewis, *Jews of Islam*, 139; Levy, Introduction to *Jews of the Ottoman Empire*, 21–23, 105–108; and the contribution by Halil İnalcık in this volume.

11. Roderic H. Davison, "Turkish Attitudes concerning Christian-Muslim Equality in the Nineteenth Century," *American Historical Review* 59 (1954): 846; Enver Ziya Karal, "Non-Muslim Representatives in the First Consitutional Assembly, 1876–1877," in *Christians and Jews in the Ottoman Empire: The Functioning of a Plural Society*, ed. Benjamin Braude and Bernard Lewis (New York: Holmes and Meier, 1982), 1: 388.

12. Feroz Ahmad, *The Young Turks: The Committee of Union and Progress in Turkish Politics, 1908–1914* (Oxford: Clarendon Press, 1969), 14–36, 57–64.

13. Moshe Ma'oz, "Communal Conflict in Ottoman Syria during the Reform Era: The Role of Political and Economic Factors," in Braude and Lewis, eds., *Christians and Jews*, 2: 92–95; Samir Khalaf, "Communal Conflict in Nineteenth-Century Lebanon," in ibid., 117–31.

14. Walter P. Zenner, "Jews in Late Ottoman Syria: External Relations," in *Jewish Societies in the Middle East: Community, Culture and Authority*, ed. Shlomo Deshen and Walter P. Zenner (Washington, D.C.: University Press of America, 1982), 157–68. See also the contribution of Daniel Schroeter in this volume.

15. Cf. PRO, FO 195/1945, Beirut, 21 Mar. 1842.

16. Mikha'il al-Dimashqi, *Ta'rikh Hawadith al-Sham wa-l-Lubnan* (Beirut: Al-Matba'ah al-Kathulikiyah, 1912); [Anon.] "Kitab al-Ahzan fi Ta'rikh al-Sham wa-Jabal Lubnan," American University of Beirut, MS no. 956.9 K62, KA, pp. 48–50.

17. Mikha'il Mishaqa, "Al-Jawab ala Iqtirah al-Ahbab," American University of Beirut, MS no. 956.9 M39, JA, pp. 170–71; Neophytus of Cyprus, *Annals of Palestine 1821–1841*, ed. S. N. Spyridon (Jerusalem: Ariel, 1938), 18–29.

18. See, respectively, PRO, FO 78/2494, Damascus, 20 Nov. 1876; PRO, FO 226/190, Aleppo, 19 Feb. 1877.

19. PRO, FO 78/1519, Haifa, 29 Aug. 1860.

20. PRO, FO 195/1410, Aleih, 2 July 1882.

21. Ahmed Cevdet, *Tezakir*, ed. C. Baysun (Ankara: Türk Tarih Kurumu Basımevi, 1953), 1: 67–68; English translation in Şerif Mardin, *The Genesis of Young Ottoman Thought: A Study of Modernization of Turkish Political Ideas* (Princeton: Princeton Univ. Press, 1962), 18.

22. PRO, FO 78/283, Campbell Report, p. 242, in Campbell to Palmerston, no. 29, Alexandria, 23 Aug. 1836.

23. Qustantin al-Basha, ed., *Mudhakkirat Ta'rikhiyya* (Lebanon: Matba'at al-Qiddis Bulus, n.d.), 77.

24. Charles Issawi, *The Economic History of the Middle East* (Chicago: Univ. of Chicago Press, 1960), 223. For a detailed discussion, see Ma'oz, "Communal Conflict," 96–98.

25. Laurence Oliphant, *The Land of Gilead* (New York: D. Appleton, 1880), 497.

26. PRO, FO 78/1520, no. 17, Damascus, 6 Sept. 1860.

27. PRO, FO 78/836, Beirut, 5 Nov. 1850.

28. M. Ubicini, *Letters on Turkey* (London, 1856; reprint, New York: Arno, 1973), 2:346.

29. Mishaqa, "Al-Jawab," 343.

30. Hayyim Cohen, *The Jews of the Middle East, 1860–1972* (in Hebrew; Jerusalem: Israel Universities Press, 1972), 25; Shaw, *Jews of the Ottoman Empire,* p. 160; Levy, introduction to *Jews of the Ottoman Empire,* ed. idem, 1–3, 124; İlber Ortaylı, "Ottomanism and Zionism during the Second Constitutional Period, 1908–1915," in Levy, ed., *Jews of the Ottoman Empire,* 532–33.

31. Ubicini, *Letters on Turkey,* 2:350.

32. PRO, FO 78/477, Damascus, 21 Aug. 1840, Werry to Bidwell.

33. Mishaqa, "Al-Jawab," 357; see also "Kitab al-Ahzan," p. 125.

34. Church Missionary Society, London, CM/028, from Bishop Gobat, 2 Aug. 1841; PRO, FO 78/714, no. 5, Damascus, 30 Apr. 1847; PRO, FO 78/1219, no. 33, Beirut, 14 July 1856; Mishaqa, *Al-Jawab,* 309; Harvey E. Goldberg, introduction to *Sephardi and Middle Eastern Jewries: History and Culture in the Modern Era,* ed. idem (Bloomington: Indiana Univ. Press, 1996), 14.

35. For an exhaustive study of the 1840 Damascus Affair, see Jonathan Frankel, *The Damascus Affair: "Ritual Murder," Politics, and the Jews in 1840* (Cambridge: Cambridge Univ. Press, 1997). Also see Moshe Ma'oz, "Changes in the Position of the Jewish Communities of Palestine and Syria in the Mid-Nineteenth Century," in *Studies on Palestine during the Ottoman Period,* ed. idem, (Jerusalem: Magnes Press, 1975), 149 ff. See also BBA, Iradeler Hariciye, no. 527, 3 Jumada I 1257/23 June 1841.

36. PRO, FO 195/170, No. 1, Damascus, 14 Jan. 1841; FO 78/447, Damascus, 21 Aug. 1841, Werry to Bidwell (private).

37. Ma'oz, "Changes in the Position," 152. For a recent detailed study of this period, see Yaron Harel, "Jewish-Christian Relations in Aleppo as Background for the Jewish Response to the Events of October 1850," *IJMES* 30 (1998): 77–96.

38. *Birjis Baris* (Paris), vol. 2, no. 32 (1860).

39. Avraham Ya'ari, *The Travels of an Emissary from Safed* (in Hebrew; Jerusalem, 1942), 19.

40. See, for example, Neville J. Mandel, *The Arabs and Zionism before World War I* (Berkeley: Univ. of California Press, 1976), 204–5, 211–12; *Al-Mashriq* (Beirut), second year, no. 23, 1 Dec. 1899, p. 1088.

41. Quoted in Ya'acov Ro'i, "The Zionist Attitude to the Arabs, 1908–1914," *MES* 1 (1968): 227.

9. A Tale of Two Women: Facets of Jewish Life in Nineteenth-Century Jerusalem as Seen through the Muslim Court Records

1. For a detailed discussion of this legal practice, see Gabriel Baer, "Ḥikr," *EI* (supplement, 1982).

2. Amnon Cohen, *Jewish Life under Islam: Jerusalem in the Sixteenth Century* (Cambridge, Mass.: Harvard Univ. Press, 1984): 110–27.

3. Amnon Cohen and Bernard Lewis, *Population and Revenue in the Towns of Palestine in the Sixteenth Century* (Princeton: Princeton Univ. Press, 1978), pp. 36, 68, 92–94; Amnon Cohen, *Jewish Life under Islam,* 199–205; idem, *Economic Life in Ottoman Jerusalem* (Cambridge: Cambridge Univ. Press, 1989), 1–10.

4. *Ha-Levanon* 2 (11), p. 162, dated June 1865.

5. See, for example, a report on repeated trips of fund-raising committees in the late fifties and early sixties in *Ha-Maggid* 4 (37), p. 148.

6. Yehoshua Ben-Arieh, *A City Reflected in Its Times—Jerusalem in the Nineteenth Century* (in Hebrew; Jerusalem: Yad Yitzhaq Ben-Zvi, 1977), 371–72.

7. Ibid., 372.

8. *Ha-Maggid* 7 (33), p. 260, dated April 1863.

9. Amnon Cohen, "Additional Documents on the Distribution of the Jewish Community's Debts in Jerusalem and Hebron in the Eighteenth Century" (in Hebrew), *Shalem* 1(1974): 317–30.

10. *Ha-Maggid* 8 (34), p. 268 and passim.

11. *Ha-Levanon* 3 (9), p. 133.

12. Two years later, in March 1867, *Ha-Levanon* 7 (7), p. 104, referred in the past tense to the renewed Ashkenazi slaughtering and the fact that Muslims were purchasing meat from Ashkenazi butchers.

13. *Ha-Levanon* 2 (15), p. 227, dated August 1865, cites a detailed report on this conflict, prepared at the same time as the case under discussion was being decided in court. See also *Ha-Maggid* 7 (42), p. 332, for another dispute dated late 1863.

14. *Ha-Maggid* 5 (14), p. 60 and 7 (17), p. 132.

10. Jewish Female Education in the Ottoman Empire, 1840–1914

1. For a general survey on education in the Ottoman Empire, see Yahya Akyüz, *Türk Eğitim Tarihi* (Ankara: Ankara Üniversitesi, Eğitim Bilimleri Fakültesi, 1982); Osman Ergin, *Türkiye Maarif Tarihi* (Istanbul: Esmer Matbaası, 1977).

2. Stanwood Cobb, *The Real Turk* (Boston: Pilgrim Press, 1914), 130–32; William E.

Strong, *The Story of the American Board* (New York: Arno, 1969), 221; Bertold Spuler, *Die Min-derheitenschulen der europäischen Türkei von der Reformzeit bis zum Weltkrieg* (Breslau: Verlag Priebatsch, 1936), 2.

3. Akyüz, *Türk Eğitim Tarihi*, 108–10.

4. Spuler, *Minderheitenschulen*, 71.

5. Akyüz, *Türk Eğitim Tarihi*, 100–101, 109, 118; Ergin, *Türkiye Maarif Tarihi*, 457–58.

6. Spuler, *Minderheitenschulen*, 72–73.

7. Akyüz, *Türk Eğitim Tarihi*, 108.

8. Ibid., 124, 183; Ergin, *Türkiye Maarif Tarihi*, 458–59, 668–79.

9. Akyüz, *Türk Eğitim Tarihi*, 175 (lists curriculum).

10. Ergin, *Türkiye Maarif Tarihi*, 686–90; Akyüz, *Türk Eğitim Tarihi*, 118.

11. Akyüz, *Türk Eğitim Tarihi*, 157.

12. Cobb, *Real Turk,* 74 and passim; Lucy M. J. Garnett, *The Women of Turkey and Their Folk-Lore* (London: David Nutt, n.d.), describes women of various ethnic groups.

13. John Bowring, *Report on the Commercial Statistics of Syria* (London: William Clowes and Sons, 1840), 105–106, 109.

14. Moshe Ma'oz, *Ottoman Reform in Syria and Palestine, 1840–1861* (Oxford: Claren-don Press, 1968), 241; Shmuel Avitsur, *Everyday Life in Eretz Yisrael in the Nineteenth Century* (in Hebrew; Jerusalem: Am Ha-Sefer, 1976), 145–46.

15. James Heyworth-Dunne, *An Introduction to the History of Education in Modern Egypt* (London: Luzac and Co., 1938), pp. 14–15.

16. Ibid., 132, 242, 323, 357, 392, 432, 441.

17. Ibid., 374–75. The Education Law of 7 November 1867 required parents to support the teachers' salaries and the cost of the equipment of the *kuttabs*. See ibid., 362–69.

18. It was unusual for Coptic girls in Cairo to attend school, but those in Upper Egypt did, together with boys until the age of eight or nine. In 1853, Patriarch Cyril IV opened girls' schools in Azbakiyah and in Harat al-Saqqa'in in Cairo, where reading, writing, arith-metic, and sewing were taught. In Upper Egypt, missionary schools offered Coptic girls ed-ucational opportunities. The Greek Orthodox community established schools for boys and girls in 1854 in Alexandria. In 1855, the girls' school had 120 pupils. Following the establish-ment of a Greek Orthodox community in Cairo, a school with separate sections for boys and girls was founded. The lower grades were apparently coeducational. In 1860 the school had 60 female students and in 1871 it had 95. In 1878 a girls' school was opened in Port Said. See Heyworth-Dunne, *Education in Modern Egypt,* 86–87, 310–11, 334–35, 413–14, 421, and the tables, 444 ff.

19. Ibid., 419.

20. American missionary activity in the region started in the early 1820s in Beirut. For details on American, and especially ABCFM, missionary activity in Lebanon, Syria, and Palestine, see A. L. Tibawi, *American Interests in Syria, 1800–1901* (Oxford: Oxford Univer-sity Press, 1966). On American activity in general, see Strong, *American Board.* On British ac-

tivity, see A. L. Tibawi, *British Interests in Palestine, 1800–1901* (Oxford: Oxford Univ. Press, 1961). On Catholic activity, see Tibawi's two books cited above. For activity in Egypt, see also Heyworth-Dunne, *Education in Modern Egypt*. For Russian activity, see Theofanis G. Stavrou, *Russian Interests in Palestine, 1882–1914* (Salonica: Institute for Balkan Studies, 1963), and Derek Hopwood, *The Russian Presence in Syria and Palestine, 1843–1914* (Oxford: Oxford Univ. Press, 1969).

The Church of England and Scottish Presbyterian missionaries to the Jews in the East operated several girls' schools. They provided an elementary education and taught English, French, needlework, and New Testament history. The missionaries realized that due to family influence, conversion was practically impossible, and that many Jews, including the rich, sent their daughters simply due to financial considerations; see Garnett, *Women of Turkey,* 2: 20. In some places missionary education was in Judeo-Spanish. On Jewish girls in missionary schools in Palestine, see Eliyahu Ze'ev Lewin-Epstein, *My Memoirs* (in Hebrew; Tel-Aviv: Levin-Epstein, 1932), 318. Bishop Samuel Gobat (the second Anglican Bishop of Jerusalem, 1846–1878) at first recruited Jewish girls to his school, but later he preferred to focus on Arab Christians; see Tibawi, *British Interests in Palestine,* 90–91; Yehoshua Ben-Arieh, *A City Reflected in Its Times—Jerusalem in the Nineteenth Century: The Old City* (in Hebrew; Jerusalem: Yad Yitzhak Ben Zvi, 1977), 294–96. The British girls' school in Jerusalem during 1857–1907 had a total of 774 pupils; see Tibawi, *British Interests in Palestine,* p. 209. The boys' school had at the same period 591 pupils, and 241 baptisms. In the sources, the original religion of the students in the girls' school and the boys' school is not indicated.

In 1879 the LJS girls' school in Jerusalem had 72 students, of whom only eight were not Jewish or of Jewish origin. A kosher kitchen provided the girls with food, and they "sang many hymns in English, in which Jewish phraseology was ingeniously applied to Christian dogma." Attached to the school was a workshop for Jewish women, where 21 women were instructed in sewing and earned some money; see Sydney S. Montagu, *Jewish Life in the East* (London: C. Kegan Paul & Co., 1881), 138–39. The workshop was apparently the one established by Miss Cooper. In Safed, a Scottish missionary opened a girls' school in 1887 and provided the students with food and clothing; see Rachel Elboim-Dror, *Hebrew Education in Eretz-Yisrael,* vol. 1, *1854–1914* (in Hebrew; Jerusalem: Yad Yitzhak Ben-Zvi, 1986), 102.

In Beirut, Jews paid 300 francs in tuition fees in order to have their daughters attend the German Deaconesses school in the 1870s, in spite of the availability of a Jewish alternative; see Narcisse Leven, *Cinquante ans d'histoire: L'Alliance Israélite Universelle (1860–1910)* (Paris: Librairie Félix Alcan, 1911–1920), 2: 205. In Egypt, Jews attended CMS institutions; see Heyworth-Dunne, *Education in Modern Egypt,* 283. In Istanbul some 550 Jewish children attended the LJS institutions in 1879; see Montagu, *Jewish Life in the East,* 176–77. In 1875, 472 girls studied in American missionary institutions in Palestine, Lebanon, and Syria, and the number grew to 1,262 in 1881; see Tibawi, *American Interests in Syria,* 228. During the same years these institutions had 1,707 and 3,725 boys, respectively; see ibid.

The Constantinople College for Women (established in 1871) severed its ties with the

ABCFM in 1908. In 1915–16 it also had Jews among its 227 students; see J. A. DeNovo, *American Interests and Policies in the Middle East, 1900–1939* (Minneapolis: Univ. of Minnesota Press, 1963), 16, 36, 95n.; Strong, *American Board,* passim. In 1899, there were 65 Russian schools in Palestine and Syria with 7,690 pupils, including 2,938 girls; see Stavrou, *Russian Interests in Palestine,* 164. On other Protestant, Catholic, and Greek Orthodox activities, see ibid., 61n.

21. Rachel Simon, "Between the Family and the Outside World: Jewish Girls in the Modern Middle East and North Africa," *Jewish Social Studies* 7 (2000): 81–108. For Iraq, see Hayyim J. Cohen, *The Jews of the Middle East, 1860–1972* (Jerusalem: Israel Universities Press, 1973), 113–14; Abraham Ben-Ya'akov, *The Jews of Iraq from the End of the Gaonic Period to Our Times (1038–1960)* (in Hebrew; Jerusalem: Ben-Zvi Institute, 1965), 233; Reeva S. Simon, "Education in the Jewish Community of Baghdad until 1914" (in Hebrew), *Pe'amim* 36 (1988): 54; Shaul Sehayik, "Changes in the Position of Urban Jewish Women in Iraq since the End of the Nineteenth Century" (in Hebrew), *Pe'amim* 36 (1988): 81; Zevi Scharfstein, *History of Jewish Education in Modern Times, vol. 5, Lands of the Mediterranean, the Balkans, and the East* (in Hebrew; Jerusalem: Re'uven Mas, 1966), 35. For Jerusalem, where the parents paid the teacher one shilling a week, see Montagu, *Jewish Life in the East,* 120; Eliezer Maneberg, "The Evolution of Jewish Educational Practices in the Sancak (Eyalet) of Jerusalem under Ottoman Rule" (Ph.D. diss., University of Connecticut, 1976), p. 100.

22. Leven, *Cinquante ans d'histoire,* 2: 127, 186; Moshe Rinott, *The Hilfsverein der Deutschen Juden in Palestine* (in Hebrew; Jerusalem: Bet Ha-Sefer Le-Hinukh Shel Ha-Universitah Ha-Ivrit, 1971), 81; Maneberg, "Jewish Educational Practices," 158; Shlomo Haramati, *The Beginning of Hebrew Education in Eretz Yisrael and Its Contribution to the Revival of Hebrew (1883–1914)* (in Hebrew; Jerusalem: Re'uven Mas, 1979), 340; Elboim-Dror, *Hebrew Education in Eretz-Yisrael,* 1: 159.

23. Ezra Laniado, in *The Jews of Mosul* (in Hebrew; Tirat Ha-Karmel: Ha-Makhon Le-Heker Yahadut Motsul, 1981), 61–68, includes part of Rabbanit Osnat's correspondence; Ben Ya'akov, *Jews of Iraq,* 86.

24. Ben-Ya'akov, *Jews of Iraq,* 338.

25. For some examples of female poetry in Libya, see Frigia Zuaretz, Amishadai Guetta et al, eds., *Libyan Jewry* (in Hebrew; Tel Aviv: Council of Libyan Jewish Communities in Israel 1982), 387–89. For Yemen, see Mishael Maswari Caspi, trans., *Daughters of Yemen* (Berkeley: Univ. of California Press, 1985).

26. In 1860 the school was taken over by the community. See Leven, *Cinquante ans d'histoire,* 2: 127; Jacob M. Landau, *Jews in Nineteenth-Century Egypt* (New York: New York Univ. Press, 1969), 73–74; H. Cohen, *Jews of the Middle East,* 109; Paul Silberman, "An Investigation of the Schools Operated by the Alliance Israélite Universelle from 1862 to 1940" (Ph.D. diss., New York University, 1973), 33; Heyworth-Dunne, *Education in Modern Egypt,* 272.

27. James Finn, *Stirring Times,* trans. Aharon Amir (in Hebrew; Jerusalem: Yad Yitzhak Ben-Zvi, 1980; originally published in English, London, 1878), 88, 233, 339, 357, 546;

Maneberg, "Jewish Educational Practices," 136, 302; Elboim-Dror, *Hebrew Education in Eretz-Yisrael,* 1: 76–77, 80, 86; Tibawi, *British Interests in Palestine,* 208 (for the 1880s).

28. Ben-Zion Gat, *The Jewish Population in Eretz-Yisrael during the Period 1840–1881* (in Hebrew; Jerusalem: Yad Yitzhak Ben Zvi, 1974), 242–44; Maneberg, "Jewish Educational Practices," 149–57; Daniel Carpi and Moshe Rinott, "A Journal of the Travels of a Jewish Female Teacher from Trieste to Jerusalem (1857–1865)" (in Hebrew), *Kevatzim le-Heker Toledot ha-Hinukh ha-Yehudi be-Yisrael uva-Tefutzot* 1(1982): 126, 128–30, 153; Kurt Grunwald, "Jewish Schools under Foreign Flags in Ottoman Palestine," in *Studies on Palestine during the Ottoman Period,* ed. Moshe Ma'oz (Jerusalem: Magnes Press, 1975), 168–71; Elboim-Dror, *Hebrew Education in Eretz-Yisrael,* 1:67, 88, 104, 111–14, 245, 292; Montagu, *Jewish Life in the East,* 144–45; Leven, *Cinquante ans d'histoire,* 2:213; Haramati, *Beginning of Hebrew Education,* 12–13; *The British Consulate in Jerusalem in Relation to the Jews of Palestine, 1838–1914,* ed. Albert M. Hyamson (London: E. Goldston, 1939–1941), 2: 428, 502–504, 514–22, 583–84.

29. Gat, *Jewish Population in Eretz-Yisrael,* 224; Hyamson, *British Consulate in Jerusalem,* 1: 234; Maneberg, "Jewish Educational Practices," 139–43, 306; Mary E. Rogers, *Domestic Life in Palestine,* trans. Shulamit Haran (in Hebrew; originally published in English, London, 1862; Tel-Aviv: Misrad ha-Bitahon, 1984), 274–77; Grunwald, "Jewish Schools," 170; Lucien Wolf, *Sir Moses Montefiore: A Centennial Biography with Extracts from Letters and Journals* (London: John Murray, 1884), 170; Elboim-Dror, *Hebrew Education in Eretz-Yisrael,* 1: 82, 86.

30. Landau, *Jews in Nineteenth-Century Egypt,* 74; Sergio Della-Pergola, "The Jewish Population in the Nineteenth and Twentieth Centuries" (in Hebrew), in *The Jews in Ottoman Egypt (1517–1914),* ed. Jacob M. Landau (Jerusalem: Misgav Yerushalayim, 1988), 53; Heyworth-Dunne, *Education in Modern Egypt,* 337, 422–23.

31. Yosef el-Gamil, "Karaite Jews in Egypt, 1517–1918" (in Hebrew), in Landau, ed., *Jews in Ottoman Egypt,* 538–40.

32. Landau, *Jews in Nineteenth-Century Egypt,* 79–80; Montagu, *Jewish Life in the East,* 8.

33. Leven, *Cinquante ans d'histoire,* 2: 131; Landau, *Jews in Nineteenth-Century Egypt,* 79; Scharfstein, *History of Jewish Education,* 52–53.

34. For Cairo, see Leven, *Cinquante ans d'histoire,* 2: 129–30; Landau, *Jews in Nineteenth-Century Egypt,* 86–88; Scharfstein, *History of Jewish Education,* 19, 58. For Alexandria: Leven, 2: 133; Landau, 88; Scharfstein, 19. There were 120 boys in 1908. For Tanta: Leven, 2: 134–35; Landau, 89–90; H. Cohen, *Jews of the Middle East,* 110; Scharfstein, 19.

35. For more details on AIU activities in the Ottoman Empire, see Leven, *Cinquante ans d'histoire;* André Chouraqui, *Cent ans d'histoire: l'Alliance Israélite Universelle et la renaissance juive contemporaine (1860–1960)* (Paris: Presses Universitaires de France, 1965); Gérard Israel, *L'Alliance Israélite Universelle 1860–1960* (Paris: AIU, 1960); Aron Rodrigue, *Images of Sephardi and Eastern Jewries in Transition: The Teachers of the Alliance Israélite Universelle, 1860–1939* (Seattle: Univ. of Washington Press, 1993); idem, *French Jews, Turkish Jews: The Alliance Israélite Universelle and the Politics of Jewish Schooling in Turkey, 1860–1925* (Bloomington:

Indiana Univ. Press, 1990); Esther Benbassa, "L'école de filles de l'Alliance Israélite Universelle à Galata," in *Première Rencontre Internationale sur l'Empire Ottoman et la Turquie Moderne* (Istanbul-Paris: Editions Isis, 1991), 203–36.

36. For details on the activities of the HV, see Rinott, *Hilfsverein der Deutschen Juden.*

37. Rachel Simon, *Change within Tradition among Jewish Women in Libya* (Seattle: Univ. of Washington Press, 1992), 108–53.

38. Landau, *Jews in Nineteenth-Century Egypt,* 81–82.

39. Scharfstein, *History of Jewish Education,* 18, 25, 27.

40. Elboim-Dror, *Hebrew Education in Eretz-Yisrael,* 1: 114. Still, schools often substituted instruction of *Pirkei Avot* for girls instead of the more demanding Talmud. Also, different crafts were taught to boys and girls.

41. Gat, *Jewish Population in Eretz-Yisrael,* 212.

42. Ibid., 244; Montagu, *Jewish Life in the East,* 145.

43. Chouraqui, *Cent ans d'histoire,* 190, 445–46 (a proclamation of AIU aims dating from 1865, including its position regarding female education); Leven, *Cinquante ans d'histoire,* 2: 38–39; Rodrigue, *Images of Sephardi and Eastern Jewries,* 80–93; Silberman, "Investigation of the Schools," 63.

44. Chouraqui, *Cent ans d'histoire,* 455; Leven, *Cinquante ans d'histoire,* 2: 56–57.

45. Leven, *Cinquante ans d'histoire,* 2: 178; Silberman, "Investigation of the Schools," 113.

46. Leven, *Cinquante ans d'histoire,* 2: 163.

47. Elboim-Dror, *Hebrew Education in Eretz-Yisrael,* 1: 137.

48. Leven, *Cinquante ans d'histoire,* 2: 36.

49. Gat, *Jewish Population in Eretz-Yisrael,* 224, 228; Israel, *L'Alliance Israélite Universelle,* 66.

50. Lewin-Epstein, *My Memoirs,* 318; Elboim-Dror, *Hebrew Education in Eretz-Yisrael,* 1: 102.

51. Landau, *Jews in Nineteenth-Century Egypt,* 84, citing a letter in *Ha-Magid,* 26 Apr. 1888, pp. 126–27.

52. Leven, *Cinquante ans d'histoire,* 2: 235; Chouraqui, *Cent ans d'histoire,* 171; Elboim-Dror, *Hebrew Education in Eretz-Yisrael,* 1: 99.

53. Laniado, *Jews of Mosul,* 188, relating to Mosul.

54. Ibid., 188.

55. For Iraq, see ibid., 164. A similar attitude was observed in Tripoli, Libya; see Mordekhai Hacohen, *Higgid Mordecai* (in Hebrew; Jerusalem: Yad Yitzhak Ben Zvi, 1978), 248–49, 337.

56. For Miss Cooper's Institution in Jerusalem (1848), see Elboim-Dror, *Hebrew Education in Eretz-Yisrael,* 1: 76–77, 86; for AIU, Baghdad (1884), see Yehezkel Yiftah, *Jewish Education in Iraq in Modern Times* (in Hebrew; Nahalal: Yad Eli'ezer Yafeh, 1984), 41; for AIU, Tripoli (1896), see Rachel Simon, *Change within Tradition,* 114–15.

57. Silberman, "Investigation of the Schools," 191; Gat, *Jewish Population in Eretz-Yisrael,* 241–44; Rogers, *Domestic Life in Palestine,* 274–77.

58. El-Gamil, "Karaite Jews in Egypt," 540.

59. Leven, *Cinquante ans d'histoire*, 2: 186; Rinott, *Hilfsverein der Deutschen Juden*, 81; Maneberg, "Jewish Educational Practices," 158; Haramati, *Beginning of Hebrew Education*, 340; Elboim-Dror, *Hebrew Education in Eretz-Yisrael*, 1: 159. See n. 22 above.

60. Elboim-Dror, *Hebrew Education in Eretz-Yisrael*, 159, 455 n.

61. Ibid., 159.

62. Haramati, *Beginning of Hebrew Education*, 216–19. For details, see also his chapter on kindergartens, 207–34.

63. Yehoshua Ben-Arieh, *A City Reflected in Its Times—New Jerusalem:The Beginnings* (in Hebrew; Jerusalem: Yad Yitzhak Ben Zvi, 1979), 582–83.

64. Yiftah, *Jewish Education in Iraq*, 41.

65. Leven, *Cinquante ans d'histoire*, 2: 166–67.

66. Rinott, *Hilfsverein der Deutschen Juden*, 80–88, 285, with data for 1907–1908.

67. Ibid., pp. 142–48; Ben-Arieh, *New Jerusalem*, 583.

68. Chouraqui, *Cent ans d'histoire*, 181.

69. Rinott, *Hilfsverein der Deutschen Juden*, 142–48.

70. Elboim-Dror, *Hebrew Education in Eretz-Yisrael*, 1: 312; Haramati, *Beginning of Hebrew Education*, 243.

71. Rinott, *Hilfsverein der Deutschen Juden*, 153.

72. Shelomoh Karmi, *Beginnings of Hebrew Education: The Hebrew Teachers Assembly in Palestine and Its Place in the History of Education, 1892–1896* (in Hebrew; Jerusalem: Re'uven Mas, 1986), 130–31, 195. In 1892 there were 23 Hebrew teachers in Palestine.

73. Rinott, *Hilfsverein der Deutschen Juden*, 175; Elboim-Dror, *Hebrew Education in Eretz-Yisrael*, 212, 224.

74. Among the twelve teachers at the gymnasium in Jerusalem there was one woman. See Ben-Arieh, *New Jerusalem*, 585–86.

75. Elboim-Dror, *Hebrew Education in Eretz-Yisrael*, 1: 224.

76. Ibid., p. 160. On the tortuous relations between the directress of the AIU school in Edirne and the community leadership, see the contribution by Avigdor Levy in this volume.

77. Karmi, *Hebrew Teachers Assembly*, 119.

78. Elboim-Dror, *Hebrew Education in Eretz-Yisrael*, 1: 305.

79. E.g., the AIU school in Galata also offered German; see Scharfstein, *History of Jewish Education*, 5: 122–23, and Benbassa, "L'école de filles," 212, 228. The Menasce school in Alexandria in addition to French also taught Hebrew, Arabic, and English; see Leven, *Cinquante ans d'histoire*, 2: 131. The Italian school in Tripoli also offered French; see Rachel Simon, *Change within Tradition*, 114–15. For a broader discussion of the politics of language, see Rachel Simon, "Language Change and Socio-Political Transformations: The Case of Nineteenth- and Twentieth-Century Libyan Jews," *Jewish History* 4 (1989): 101–21.

80. Yiftah, *Jewish Education in Iraq*, 52.

81. Silberman, "Investigation of the Schools," 111–12.

82. Elboim-Dror, *Hebrew Education in Eretz-Yisrael,* 1: 111.

83. Rogers, *Domestic Life in Palestine,* 274–77; Carpi and Rinott, "Travels of a Jewish Female Teacher," 126; Elboim-Dror, *Hebrew Education in Eretz-Yisrael,* 1: 115.

84. Silberman, "Investigation of the Schools," 113; Leven, *Cinquante ans d'histoire,* 2: 178.

85. Montagu, *Jewish Life in the East,* 181–82; Benbassa, "L'école de filles," 215.

86. For a discussion of the Language War, see Rinott, *Hilfsverein der Deutschen Juden,* 184–226. On the language issue in 1898, see Elboim-Dror, *Hebrew Education in Eretz-Yisrael,* 1: 203; on the language issue in the schools in Jerusalem in 1910, see Ben-Arieh, *New Jerusalem,* 581; for a list of sixty institutions in Palestine where Hebrew was dominant in 1914, see Haramati, *Beginning of Hebrew Education,* 244.

87. On choosing the Sephardi pronunciation, see Lewin-Epstein, *My Memoirs,* 212–15.

88. Haramati, *Beginning of Hebrew Education,* 29–30, quoting Ze'ev Smilanski. See also Lewin-Epstein, *My Memoirs,* 317–18, 328–29.

89. Carpi and Rinott, "Travels of a Jewish Female Teacher," 126; Rogers, *Domestic Life in Palestine,* 274–76; Elboim-Dror, *Hebrew Education in Eretz-Yisrael,* 1:115.

90. Benbassa, "L'école de filles," 207, 212.

91. Rinott, *Hilfsverein der Deutschen Juden,* 289.

92. Elboim-Dror, *Hebrew Education in Eretz-Yisrael,* 1: 50, citing a letter by Yehudah Leib Binshtock from Jaffa, 29 June 1892.

93. Lewin-Epstein, *My Memoirs,* 212–15.

94. Reeva Simon, "Baghdad," 54; Ben-Ya'akov, *Jews of Iraq,* 293, 343–44; Scharfstein, *History of Jewish Education,* 35. This was similar to the conditions prevailing among Muslims in some regions.

95. Sehayik, "Urban Jewish Women in Iraq," 83.

96. Elboim-Dror, *Hebrew Education in Eretz-Yisrael,* 1: 265 (in general); Leven, *Cinquante ans d'histoire,* 2: 135 (on Tanta, 1905), 195 (Kasaba, 1895), 196 (Bergama, 1908); Ben-Ya'akov, *Jews of Iraq,* 317 (Khanaqin, 1911); Haramati, *Beginning of Hebrew Education,* 59 (Gederah, 1899), 71 (Zikhron Ya'akov, 1902). On a Samaritan coeducational school in Arabe, see Rogers, *Domestic Life in Palestine,* 221–22.

97. Ben-Arieh, *New Jerusalem,* 362–63 (AIU school, Jerusalem).

98. Elboim-Dror, *Hebrew Education in Eretz-Yisrael,* 1: 132 (Belkind school in Jaffa, 1889), 243–44 (Hebrew Gymnasium in Jaffa, 1905), 247 (Hebrew Gymnasium in Jerusalem, 1909), 269 (Israel Belkind's Kiryat Sefer, 1903–1909); Karmi, *Hebrew Teachers Association,* 34 (Belkind in Jaffa).

99. Montagu, *Jewish Life in the East,* 176–77; Strong, *American Board,* 501; Haramati, *Beginning of Hebrew Education,* 268; Ben-Arieh, *Old City,* 294–96, DeNovo, *American Interests and Policies,* 13, 95 n, on the colleges for women which only the missionaries had. The ABCFM operated women's colleges in Istanbul, Marash, and Izmir, and some Jewish women

attended the first. See also Leven, *Cinquante ans d'histoire,* 2: 205 (on Beirut); Montagu, *Jewish Life in the East,* 134 (Jerusalem).

100. Montagu, *Jewish Life in the East,* 138–39, on the LJS school in Jerusalem.

101. Leven, *Cinquante ans d'histoire,* 2:114 (in the AIU school in Kuzguncuk Turks, Greeks, and Armenians were enrolled), 243 (Haifa); Haramati, *Beginning of Hebrew Education,* 88 (Jaffa, 1910); Benbassa, "L'école de filles," 207 (Galata).

102. Finn, *Stirring Times,* 88, 339, 357, 492–93, 546, on Miss Cooper's Institution; Rachel Simon, *Change within Tradition,* 114–15, on Tripoli.

103. Elboim-Dror, *Hebrew Education in Eretz-Yisrael,* 1: 104, 113–14 (on Evelina de Rothschild School); Leven, *Cinquante ans d'histoire,* 2: 213 (Evelina de Rothschild), 239–40 (Safed); Haramati, *Beginning of Hebrew Education,* 268 (on the terms demanded by parents of 200 girls in Jerusalem, in 1912, who were prepared to transfer their daughters from missionary to Jewish schools only if they would not lose their benefits).

104. Ben-Ya'akov, *Jews of Iraq,* 300–301; Sehayik, "Urban Jewish Women in Iraq," 81.

105. Elboim-Dror, *Hebrew Education in Eretz-Yisrael,* 1:245, following Yehudit Harari, a teacher at the gymnasium in Jaffa.

106. Elboim-Dror, *Hebrew Education in Eretz-Yisrael,* 1: 452, gives details on the parents' occupations.

107. Landau, *Jews in Nineteenth-Century Egypt,* 81–83, 88.

108. Rachel Simon, *Change within Tradition,* 122.

109. For Rehovot (1902) and Rosh Pinah (1903), see Haramati, *Beginning of Jewish Education,* 75–76, 154–55; for Damascus during World War I, see Scharfstein, *History of Jewish Education,* 27. On the establishment of societies of female graduates of the AIU schools, see Esther Benbassa, "Associational Strategies in Ottoman Jewish Society in the Nineteenth and Twentieth Centuries," in *The Jews of the Ottoman Empire,* ed. Avigdor Levy (Princeton: Darwin Press, 1994), 460 ff.

110. Haramati, *Beginning of Jewish Education,* 73–74 (on Zikhron Ya'akov, 1902), 75–76 (Rosh Pinah, 1903), 188–89 (Rishon le-Tziyon, 1902), 249 (Jerusalem, 1912), 231, 305 (in general); Elboim-Dror, *Hebrew Education in Eretz-Yisrael,* 1: 277 (Rehovot, 1913, for Yemenites).

111. Haramati, *Beginning of Jewish Education,* 78–80.

112. Ibid., 309–10.

113. Ben-Arieh, *New City,* 594.

114. For Iraq, see Sehayik, *Urban Jewish Women in Iraq,* 86; for Tripoli, see Rachel Simon, *Change within Tradition,* 110, 126. Most AIU schools staged public performances. The directress of the Rothschild school, Fortuna Behar, was known for the dance parties that took place at her home. See Elboim-Dror, *Hebrew Education in Eretz-Yisrael,* 1: 67.

11. The Siege of Edirne (1912–1913) as Seen by a Jewish Eyewitness: Social, Political, and Cultural Perspectives

1. On the Balkan Wars, see Carnegie Endowment for International Peace, *Report of the International Commission to Inquire into the Causes and Conduct of the Balkan Wars* (Washington, D.C.: The [Carnegie] Endowment, 1914); E. C. Helmreich, *The Diplomacy of the Balkan Wars, 1912–1913* (Cambridge, Mass.: Harvard Univ. Press, 1938); Richard C. Hall, *Bulgaria's Road to the First World War* (Boulder: East European Monographs, distributed by Columbia Univ. Press, New York, 1996); Richard C. Hall, *The Balkan Wars, 1912–1913: Prelude to the First World War* (London: Routledge, 2000); L. S. Stavrianos, *The Balkans since 1453* (New York: Holt, Rinehart and Winston, 1958), 533–39; Stanford J. Shaw and Ezel Kural Shaw, *Reform, Revolution and Republic, 1808–1975,* vol. 2 of *History of the Ottoman Empire and Modern Turkey* (Cambridge: Cambridge Univ. Press, 1977), 293–98; Charles Jelavich and Barbara Jelavich, *The Establishment of the Balkan National States, 1804–1920* (Seattle and London: Univ. of Washington Press, 1977), 216–21; Justin McCarthy, *Death and Exile: The Ethnic Cleansing of Ottoman Muslims, 1821–1922* (Princeton: Darwin Press, 1995), 135–77; Genel Kurmay Başkanlığı, *Balkan Harbi Tarihi,* 7 vols. (Istanbul and Ankara: Askeri Matbaa, 1938–1965); Yusuf Hikmet Bayur, *Türk İnkılâbı Tarihi,* vol. 2, pt. 2 (Ankara: Türk Tarih Kurumu Basımevi, 1943). On the siege of Edirne, in addition to the titles listed above, also see [Jean Frédéric Lucien] Piarron de Mondésir, *Siège et prise d'Andrinople (Novembre 1912-Mars 1913)* (Paris: Chapelot, 1914); Henry Mirande and Louis Olivier, *Sur la bataille: Journal d'un aviateur français à l'armée bulgare au siège d'Andrinople* (5th ed., Paris: L'Edition Moderne, n.d. [1913]); Remzi Yiğitgüden, *1912–13 Balkan Harbinde Edirne Kale Muharebeleri* (Istanbul: Askeri Matbaa, 1938); Bekir Sitki Baykal, "Edirne'nin Uğramış Olduğu İstilâlar," in *Edirne: Edirne'nin 600. Fetih Yıldönümü Armağan Kitabı,* ed. Türk Tarih Kurumu (Ankara: Türk Tarih Kurumu Basımevi, 1965), 179–95; Nazmi Çağan, "Balkan Harbinde Edirne," in ibid., 197–213. Also see sources listed in n. 2, 3, and 4 below.

2. Paul Christoff, *Journal du siège d'Andrinople: Notes quotidiennes d'un assiégé* (Paris: Charles-Lavauzelle, 1914). An early edition, or version, of this book was published in Edirne in 1913, shortly after the end of the siege, under the initials P.C. This edition, which quickly sold out, served as an important source for the Carnegie Report. See Carnegie Report, 110–11 and 111, n. 1.

3. Gustave Cirilli, *Journal du siège d'Andrinople (Impressions d'un assiégé)* 4th ed. (Paris: Chapelot, 1913).

4. Ratip Kazancıgil, ed., *Hafız Rakım Ertür'ün Anılarından: Balkan Savaşında Edirne Savunması Günleri* (Kırklareli: Sermet Matbaası, 1986). The editor of this volume has added to the original journal numerous notes and appendices. References to the original journal are hereafter cited as Ertür. References to the editor's notes and appendices are cited as Kazancıgil (Ertür). Kazancıgil added biographical notes on Ertür on pp. 110–11.

5. The journal is cataloged as follows: Turquie, IC3, Andrinople, Guéron, 1912. Writ-

ten in French, the journal comprises 80 pages typewritten on both recto and verso sides of 40 folios. The folios are numbered from 1 to 40. Throughout this article references to the journal are by folio number and are given parenthetically within the text. The journal's first entry is dated 30 October 1912 and the last 27 March 1913. All translations are my own.

Several of the journal's passages have been published in Aron Rodrigue, *Images of Sephardi and Eastern Jewries in Transition. The Teachers of the Alliance Israélite Universelle, 1860–1939* (Seattle and London: Univ. of Washington Press, 1993), 238–44, and the French and Hebrew editions of this book.

I would like to take this opportunity to thank the directors and staff of the library and archives of the Alliance Israélite Universelle in Paris for their assistance in the preparation of this article.

6. A.-H. Navon, *Les 70 ans de l'Ecole Normale Israélite Orientale (1865–1935)* (Paris: Librairie Durlacher, 1935), 166.

7. See n. 1.

8. M. Tayyib Gökbilgin, "Edirne," *IA,* 4: 108; McCarthy, *Death and Exile,* 135.

9. Baykal, "İstilâlar," 187, states that at the time Edirne had a population of 106,000. Other sources give somewhat higher estimates. See n. 10.

10. Cirilli, *Journal,* 31. According to this source, without European nationals, the total would be "close" to 111,000.

11. Christoff, *Journal,* 13, 31, 33, 78, 137, 204, and passim; Cirilli, *Journal,* 61, 72, 100, 123, 141, and passim.

12. On the history of the Jewish community of Edirne in the Ottoman period, see Haim Gerber, "Jews in Edirne (Adrianople) in the Sixteenth and Seventeenth Centuries" (in Hebrew), *Sefunot,* n.s., 3 (1985): 35–51; Shimon Marcus, "On the History of the Jews in Adrianople" (in Hebrew), *Sinai* 29 (1951): 7–23 and 318–44. These studies contain further references. Also see: Aron Rodrigue, *French Jews, Turkish Jews: The Alliance Israélite Universelle and the Politics of Jewish Schooling in Turkey, 1860–1925* (Bloomington and Indianapolis: Indiana Univ. Press, 1990), 50–52, 57–62, 91–92, 113–15, and passim; Stanford J. Shaw, *The Jews of the Ottoman Empire and the Turkish Republic* (New York: New York Univ. Press, 1991), 97–107, 156–68, 242–51, and passim; Ida Cowen, *Jews in Remote Corners of the World* (Englewood Cliffs, N.J.: Prentice-Hall, 1971), 276–84; Avner Levi, *History of the Jews in the Republic of Turkey* (in Hebrew; Jerusalem: Hotsa'at Lafir, 1992), 5–7, 12–14, and passim.

13. *Bulletin de l'Alliance Israélite Universelle* (hereafter *BAIU*), 2d ser., no. 25 (1900): 136; *BAIU,* no. 26 (1901): 116. According to Gökbilgin, "Edirne," 108, the number of Turks was approximately 47,000 (54 percent of the total), Greeks 20,000 (23 percent), Jews 15,000 (17 percent), Armenians 4,000 (4.6 percent), and Bulgarians 2,000 (2.3 percent).

14. Cf. McCarthy, *Death and Exile,* 86–88.

15. *BAIU,* no. 36 (1911): 89.

16. In modern times Rabbi Yakir Geron served as acting chief rabbi of Istanbul from

1863 to 1872. Rabbi Hayyim Moshe Bejerano (Becerano), after serving as chief rabbi of Edirne, became chief rabbi of Turkey from 1920 to 1931. See Marcus, "Jews in Adrianople," 328–34; Menahem Ezuz, "On the History of the Jews in the City of Adrianople" (in Hebrew), *Hemdat Yisrael* (Jerusalem, 1946), 157–68.

17. Marcus, "Jews in Adrianople," 334–39; Rodrigue, *French Jews, Turkish Jews,* 44–45, 50–52, 59–61, 81; Paul Silberman, "An Investigation of the Schools Operated by the Alliance Israélite Universelle from 1862 to 1940" (Ph.D. diss., New York University, 1974), 179–82.

18. *BAIU,* no. 36 (1911): 80–81; Marcus, "Jews in Adrianople," 335–38; Rodrigue, *French Jews, Turkish Jews,* 50–52, 59, 91–92.

19. See Gerber's "lament": Gerber, "Jews in Edirne," 35.

20. According to Alliance regulations, all the correspondence from the school directors to the Alliance headquarters in Paris had to be formally addressed to "Mr. President" *(Monsieur le President).* These instructions were printed on the Alliance stationery.

21. As was common then, Guéron consistently uses the names Constantinople and Andrinople (Adrianople), rendered here for the sake of uniformity as Istanbul and Edirne.

22. Bejerano was born in 1846 in Ottoman Eski Zagora, today in Bulgaria, in 1846. He received both a traditional and modern education and was believed to be close to Young Turk circles. He served as chief rabbi *(haham başı)* of Edirne from 1909 to 1920. In 1920 he was appointed chief rabbi of Istanbul and of Turkey. He served in that position until his death in 1931. Cf. Shaw, *Jews of the Ottoman Empire,* 243–46; Ezuz, "Jews in the City of Adrianople," 166; Avram Galante (Abraham Galanté), *Histoire des Juifs de Turquie* (9 vols, Istanbul: Editions Isis, n.d. [1985]), 1: 265–70.

23. Çağan, "Balkan Harbinde Edirne," 197–201; Baykal, "İstilâlar," 187; Cirilli, *Journal,* 11–14; Piarron, *Siège et prise d'Andrinople,* 50–62; Hall, *Balkan Wars,* 9–32.

24. Çağan, "Balkan Harbinde Edirne," 198–99; Baykal, "İstilâlar," 187.

25. Ertür, 7.

26. Cirilli, *Journal,* 13.

27. Ibid., 14.

28. Ibid., 20. Karaağaç was considered a wealthy suburb of Edirne. It was home to European nationals and members of minority communities. In addition, several foreign institutions, as well as the railroad station serving Edirne, were located at Karaağaç.

29. Christoff, *Journal,* 14.

30. Ibid., 25.

31. *BAIU,* 3d ser., no. 38 (1913): 79. On pp. 79–83 are published two lengthy excerpts from letters written by Moïse Mitrani following the war (hereafter cited as Mitrani, *BAIU*). They concisely discuss the condition of the Jewish community during the siege and immediately after it. In this context, Mitrani adds that the community felt the consequences of the absence of the well-to-do who could have contributed to the welfare and leadership of the Jewish population during the hard times of the siege. He points out, however, that the same

notables who had found shelter in Istanbul were also instrumental in aiding the community by soliciting funds and transfering them to Edirne by means of the wireless telegraph and the Ottoman Bank.

32. Baykal, "İstilâlar," 187; Christoff, *Journal,* 13.

33. Cirilli, *Journal,* 28.

34. Çağan, "Balkan Harbinde Edirne," 200; Cirilli, *Journal,* 65.

35. Piarron, *Siège et prise d'Andrinople,* 36–37.

36. Christoff, *Journal,* 106.

37. Çağan, "Balkan Harbinde Edirne," 200; Kazancıgil (Ertür), 11–12, following Yiğit-güden, *1912–13 Balkan Harbinde Edirne,* 46; Rifat Osman Tosyavizade, *Edirne Rehnüması* (Edirne: Vilayet Matbassı, 1920. A revised version of this book, in Roman characters, was published by Ratip Kazancıgil, Edirne: Türk Kütüphaneciler Derneği Edirne Şubesi, 1994. The references here are to the original edition.), 78.

38. Çağan, "Balkan Harbinde Edirne," 200; Kazancıgil (Ertür), 11–12. By the last phase of the siege, the Bulgarian and Serbian forces at Edirne had a total strength of 150,000 men, outnumbering the defenders by almost three to one. Hall, *Balkan Wars,* 90.

39. Kazancıgil (Ertür), 100; Cirilli, *Journal,* 15–16. The Istanbul correspondent of the British-Jewish weekly, *The Jewish Chronicle,* estimated in early October that 5,000 Jews had already been drafted to the Ottoman army and that in case of war, at least 10,000 would be called up for service. *The Jewish Chronicle,* no. 2271 (11 Oct. 1912), p. 1. A week later the same correspondent reported that "at Salonica and Adrianople, complete battalions have been organized by Jewish volunteers." *The Jewish Chronicle,* No. 2272 (18 October 1912), p. 12. Christoff occasionally gives information on the conduct of Jewish, Greek, and Bulgarian soldiers in the Ottoman army; see, for example, *Journal,* 25, 31, 86.

40. Cf. Christoff, *Journal,* 14, 31, 35, 37; Cirilli, *Journal,* 18, 52.

41. Although many of the minority communities serving in the Ottoman army remained loyal and even distinguished themselves in the Ottoman service, as the siege continued, desertion increased among the Christian soldiers. The Ottoman command disarmed many of the minority soldiers, using them as labor battalions (Cirilli, *Journal,* 71). According to Christoff (*Journal,* 158), by 1 January 1913, some 1,200 Ottoman soldiers had gone over to the enemy, the great majority of them Christians.

42. Cf. Ertür, 65; Christoff, *Journal,* 169. The latter source states that Bulgarian intelligence inside Edirne had been well organized years in advance and included not only Bulgarians, but also Greeks, Armenians, and even Turks; he does not mention Jews (see Christoff, *Journal,* 234). On this subject, see also Hall, *Balkan Wars,* 39, 88.

43. Christoff, *Journal,* 31.

44. Cirilli, *Journal,* 37. Piarron, also concurs with these assessments (*Siège et prise d'Andrinople,* 44. 181).

45. On Rosa Avigdor, see Navon, *L'Ecole Normale Israélite Oriental,* 167.

46. Barishac appears to have been one of the chief rabbi's most trusted aides. He was a

member of the school committees of the two Alliance schools. During 1910–1911 he edited a political-literary journal in Judeo-Spanish, *La Boz de la Verdad* (The Voice of Truth). See Shaw, *Jews of the Ottoman Empire,* 184; Moşe Grosman, *Dr. Markus (1870–1944). Osmanlıdan Cumhuriyete Geçişte Türk Yahudilerinden Görünümler* (Istanbul: As Matbaacılık, 1992), 399.

47. Cf. Christoff, *Journal,* 63–77; Cirilli, *Journal,* 96–117; Piarron, *Siège et prise d'Andrinople,* 59–74; Hall, *Balkan Wars,* 32–42.

48. The *okka* (also *oke*) was equal to 1,283 grams.

49. A comparison with Ertür's journal reveals that in the predominantly Muslim quarters conditions were even worse. Already on 5 December, Ertür records: "In front of the bakeries were crowds of Muslims only, . . . refugees and women without men. . . . Jewish or Christian women were not seen. Everyone noticed that. It can be easily understood. The institutions of the Jews and Christians are strong and well organized. They have funds for the poor. Commerce is in their hands. The grain that they gather . . . they distribute in an orderly fashion to their communities. Not one Christian woman has to make the effort to come to the bakeries to buy bread. . . . The miserable condition of the Muslims was everywhere exposed. The Muslims have no protector" (Ertür, 50).

50. Çağan, "Balkan Harbinde Edirne," 203; Baykal, "İstilâlar," 189. On this subject, see also Cirilli, *Journal,* 124–37; Tosyavizade, *Edirne,* 79–80; Hall, *Balkan Wars,* 70–78, 86.

51. Cf. Christoff, *Journal,* 116.

52. Ertür expresses similar sentiments at this time. See, for example, 56, 70–80.

53. From Mitrani's letter it would appear that the Alliance boys' school did not operate during most, or perhaps even all, of the period of the siege. He writes: "Following the first cannon shots of the [Bulgarian] army, . . . the school was taken over by more than 500 families which hoped to find there shelter from the murderous shells" (Mitrani, *BAIU:* 80).

54. Hilfsverein der Deutschen Juden was a German-Jewish aid organization founded in 1901 with the aim, similar to that of the Alliance, of helping the Jews of eastern Europe and the Middle East.

55. The Ottoman Public Debt Administration (in Turkish, *Duyun-u Umumiye Komisyonu*) was an international consortium founded in 1881 to represent European bondholders of Ottoman financial obligations. This body took control of some state revenues (including taxes imposed on salt and other products) and turned them over to European creditors.

56. The Fundukliyan flour mills company was the largest in Edirne. Cf. Ertür, 35.

57. Cf. Christoff, *Journal,* 137.

58. See also Çağan, "Balkan Harbinde Edirne," 203; Piarron, *Siège et prise d'Andrinople,* 110; Mirande and Olivier, *Sur la bataille,* 175–96.

59. Mitrani, *BAIU:* 80. Cirilli also visited the Alliance boys' school during this period. He estimated that it provided shelter for more than 600 families, or 3,000 to 4,000 individuals. He thought that the school could not comfortably accomodate more than 700 to 800 persons and that it was terribly crowded (Cirilli, *Journal,* 142).

60. Christoff gives his name as Hartfeld (Christoff, *Journal,* 137).

61. This school was apparently a much-desired shelter. Cirilli reports that he stayed there during the heavy bombardment in the latter part of November. At that time the school accommodated the Austrian nationals in town; the Austrian, British, and French consuls; the chief rabbi; the Protestant pastor; and "a multitude of families without religious or national distinction" (Cirilli, *Journal,* 98–100). In February 1913, Cirilli found shelter in a school administered by a Polish Catholic mission under French protection. He states that "all those who seek shelter are admitted without distinction. . . . Five to six hundred persons are already housed here and every day new refugees arrive" (Cirilli, *Journal,* 142).

62. Ertür reports that the searches were conducted by committees composed of police officers and civil servants. He was appointed as secretary to one committee, charged with conducting searches at the center of town. His committee discovered considerable quantities of hidden grain that were confiscated. He points out, however, that he carried out his duties against his better judgment, because he felt that only the rich and powerful, not the poor, would benefit from the confiscated goods (Ertür, 61–63). See also Christoff, *Journal,* 128–29, on this subject.

63. As of the end of February, Christoff gives numerous examples of the activities of war profiteers, Jews and non-Jews, who greatly increased the prices of basic commodities; see, for example, *Journal,* 181–82, 196, 205–207. When he reports about Jewish war profiteers, he usually adds commentary, sometimes with biblical allusions, such as: "Jacob always profits at the expense of Esau's hunger!" (Christoff, *Journal,* 207).

64. Ertür also writes disapprovingly about these phenomena, the corruption and ineffectiveness of the bureaucracy and the lack of discipline among military officers; see, for example, 50–51.

65. See also Mitrani, *BAIU,* 3d ser., no. 38 (1913): 79.

66. La Cercle de la Bienfaisance was a Jewish organization founded in Edirne in 1903, whose members were for the most part graduates of the Alliance schools. See Esther Benbassa, "Associational Strategies in Ottoman Jewish Society in the Nineteenth and Twentieth Centuries," in *The Jews of the Ottoman Empire,* ed. Avigdor Levy (Princeton: Darwin Press, 1994), 461.

67. Mitrani, *BAIU:* 79–81; see also Tosyavizade, *Edirne,* 80.

68. Çağan, "Balkan Harbinde Edirne," 205–207; Piarron, *Siège et prise d'Andrinople,* 112–70.

69. Çağan, "Balkan Harbinde Edirne," 211; Mitrani, *BAIU:* 79. It would appear that the Ottoman army reentered the city of Edirne only on 23 July, although the official date usually cited is 21 July. Cf. Hall, *Balkan Wars,* 118–19.

70. For an assessment of the Carnegie Report, see McCarthy, *Death and Exile,* 167–68, n. 22. In brief, McCarthy considers the report as pro-Bulgarian and hostile to Greece and the Ottoman Empire. McCarthy does not discuss the Jewish perspective.

71. Carnegie Report, 113.

72. Carnegie Report, 111–13, 326–28, 341–44. A report by the Russian journalist,

Machkov, first published on 20 August 1913 in the London *Daily Telegraph* and republished on 26 and 27 August in the Istanbul *Le Jeune Turc* is reprinted in the Carnegie Report as Appendix E (326–30). It states that in the first days following the Bulgarian occupation of Edirne, Turkish prisoners of war "died in hundreds every day" and that the total number of Turkish military and civilian losses *after the city's surrender* reached 10,000; Carnegie Report, 326. According to the deposition of a Turkish officer, the number of Turkish soldiers that died only in those first days was 3,000; Carnegie Report, 341 (Appendix G). According to Ottoman sources, Ottoman military losses in Edirne since the beginning of the siege totaled some 13,000 men, or approximately one quarter of the original military force; Kazancıgil (Ertür), 100. The total number of Bulgarian and Serbian casualties in the Edirne campaign was 18,282. Hall, *Balkan Wars,* 90.

73. Carnegie Report, 113, 327, 343.

74. Christoff, *Journal,* 232; Cirilli, *Journal,* 155–57. See also Tosyavizade, *Edirne,* 83–84.

75. Christoff, *Journal,* 227.

76. Ibid., 231–32.

77. Cirilli, *Journal,* 153.

78. Ibid., 154–55.

79. Carnegie Report, 113.

80. Ibid., 114–15.

81. See n. 2 above.

82. The Armenians of Edirne were generally regarded as sympathetic to the Bulgarians. However, they were a small and wealthy community, and it would appear that some of them also suffered from the consequences of the occupation. See Carnegie Report, 327; Christoff, *Journal,* 234.

83. Carnegie Report, 331 (Appendix F).

84. Carnegie Report, 326 (Appendix E).

85. Marcus, "Jews in Adrianople," 14, following *l'Univers Israélite,* no. 32 (18 Apr. 1913), p. 139, briefly states: "Following the Bulgarians' entry into Edirne . . . the Jews of Edirne suffered twofold: as civilians and as Jews, as a result of Greek attacks on them. The Jews of Bulgaria were concerned about the condition of their suffering brethren and they sent from Sophia a special delegation in order to investigate their condition."

86. A reference to the Committee of Union and Progress, the most important Young Turk group that was then in power.

87. Gökbilgin, "Edirne," 108.

88. In 1955, Edirne's population numbered 33,325; in 1965, 46,091; in 1975, 63,001; in 1985, 86,909. See Republic of Turkey, Prime Ministry State Institute of Statistics, *1985 Census of Population by Administrative Division* (Ankara, 1986).

89. See Mitrani's description of the impact of the war (Mitrani, *BAIU:* 81–82). As a result of territorial losses and emigration, the population of the Edirne province declined from almost 1,500,000 in 1912 to 631,000 in 1914. See Shaw, *Jews of the Ottoman Empire,* 274;

Kemal H. Karpat, *Ottoman Population 1830–1914: Demographic and Social Characteristics* (Madison: Univ. of Wisconsin Press, 1985), 190.

90. Mitrani, *BAIU:* 81; Shaw, *Jews of the Ottoman Empire,* 253–54; McCarthy, *Death and Exile,* 161; Cowen, *Jews in Remote Corners,* 276–84; Avner Levi, *Jews in the Republic of Turkey,* 11–19, 67–76.

91. Mitrani, *BAIU:* 82; Shaw, *Jews of the Ottoman Empire,* 176.

92. Marcus, "Jews in Adrianople," 8; Shaw, *Jews of the Ottoman Empire,* 176.

93. Hayyim J. Cohen, *The Jews of the Middle East, 1860–1972* (Jerusalem: Israel Universities Press, 1973), 77.

94. Gökbilgin, "Edirne," 108.

95. See Shaw, *Jews of the Ottoman Empire,* 285, and Shimon Marcus, "Adrianople," in *Encyclopaedia Judaica* (Jerusalem, 1971), 2: 310.

96. Cohen, *Jews of the Middle East,* 77.

97. Ibid. See also Cowen, *Jews in Remote Corners,* 278.

98. Şalom (Istanbul), no. 2404 (11 Oct. 1995): 10. See also Şalom, no. 2469 (15 Jan. 1997): 1, 8.

12. The Industrial Working Class of Salonica, 1850–1912

1. Samuel S. Cox, *Diversions of a Diplomat in Turkey* (New York: C. L. Webster, 1887), 187–88.

2. Centre de recherche sur le Judaïsme de Salonique, *Salonique. Ville-Mère en Israël* (in Hebrew with a very brief French summary; Jerusalem-Tel Aviv: Centre de recherches sur le Judaïsme de Salonque, 1967), 242–43. My thanks to Izhar Eliaz, State University of New York at Binghamton, for his translation from the Hebrew. Information in the French summary states that Isaac Broudo furnished the material on the porters, while A. Taggar provided the survey of the economy.

3. A different version of parts of the following section has been published in Donald Quataert, "Premières fumées d'usine," in *Salonique, 1850–1918: La "ville des Juifs" et le réveil des Balkans,* ed. Gilles Veinstein (Paris: Editions Autremont, 1992), 177–94.

4. Great Britain, Public Record Office (PRO), Foreign Office (FO) 195/293, Blunt at Salonica for 1849.

5. See, for example, *Selanik Vilayeti Salnamesi,* 1307 H/1889, p. 228; Great Britain, *Parliamentary Papers, Accounts and Papers* (hereafter *A&P*) 1873, vol. 67, no. 3655, Wilkinson, Salonica, 12 Aug. 1872; *A&P* 1897, vol. 94, no. 6016, Heathcote for 1895; Austria, Berichte der Königslichen und Kaiserlichen Österreich-Ungarischen Konsularämter über das Jahr, Vienna (hereafter Austria, *Berichte*), 1906, vol. 21, no. 3, Salonich.

6. Austria, *Berichte* 1906, vol. 21, no. 3, Salonich, and 1907, vol. 21, no. 5, Salonich; Germany, Ministry of Interior, *Berichte über Handel und Industrie* (Berlin, 1900–1915) (hereafter Germany, *Handel und Industrie*), vol. 19, no. 6, 13 Apr. 1913, pp. 444–46.

7. Ibid.

8. *A&P* 1893–94, vol. 97, no. 5581, Blunt, 30 Sept. 1893; *A&P* 1908, vol. 17, no. 7253, Salonica for 1907; *A&P* 1910, vol. 103, no. 7472; France, *Bulletin consulaire français. Recueil des rapports commerciaux adressés au Ministère des Affaires Étrangères par les agents diplomatiques et consulaires de France à l'étranger,* Paris (hereafter France, *RRC*) 1905, no. 515, Salonique, 1904; Austria, *Berichte* 1900, vol. 2, no. 7, Salonich; France, *RRC,* Library of Congress (hereafter LC) microfilm reel 33, Salonique for 1900, no. 76; reel 35, Salonique in 1903.

9. Austria, *Berichte* 1900, vol. 2, no. 7, Salonich and 1905, vol. 20, no. 6; *A&P* 1893–95, vol. 97, no. 5581, Salonica for 1891–92, Blunt, 30 Sept. 1893; France, *RRC* 1905, no. 515, Salonique for 1904, no. 927 for 1911, and no. 506, Smyrne for 1904.

10. See sources cited in n. 9 above and also Germany, *Handel und Industrie,* vol. 10, no. 9, 20 Aug. 1907; and *Board of Trade Journal,* 27 Mar. 1913.

11. PRO, FO 195/100, 31 Dec. 1838 and PRO, FO 195/176, 2 Feb. 1843, Blunt at Salonica; United States, Commercial Relations of the United States with Foreign Countries 1851, T 194, National Archives, reel 3; David Urquhart, *Turkey and Its Resources: Its Municipal Organization and Free Trade; the State and Prospects of English Commerce in the East* (London: Saunders and Otley, 1833), 180–81.

12. See the chapter on silk in Donald Quataert, *Ottoman Manufacturing in the Age of the Industrial Revolution* (Cambridge: Cambridge Univ. Press, 1993), 107–33.

13. Ibid.; PRO, FO 195/649, 12 June 1860, Calvert at Salonica; France, *RRC* 1878, 1 July 1878, pp. 838–40.

14. Heinrich Stich, *Die Weltwirtschaftlich Entwicklung der Anatolischen Produktion seit Anfangs des 19 Jahrhunderts* (Kiel: C. H. Jebens, 1929), 69–75; Germany, *Handel und Industrie* 1912, vol. 17, no. 7.

15. The Austro-Hungarian consular reports are perhaps the most useful in describing factory formation in Salonica; see, for example, Austria, *Berichte* 1906, vol. 21, no. 3 and 1907, vol. 21, no. 5, Salonich. Also see Germany, *Handel und Industrie* 1913, vol. 19, no. 6.

16. See sources cited in n. 15 above and also Stich, *Entwicklung der Anatolischen Produktion;* PRO, FO Annual Series 4579, for 1909.

17. Austria, *Berichte* 1900, vol. 2, no. 7; 1901, vol. 19, no. 2; 1902, vol. 18, no. 2; 1905, vol. 20, no. 6; 1906, vol. 21, no. 3; 1907, vol. 21, no. 5.

18. Germany, *Handel und Industrie* 1912, vol. 18, no. 7.

19. See, among others, the sources cited in n. 17 above; also, France, *RRC* 1888, Salonique, 25 July 1883.

20. Joseph Nehama, *Histoire des Israélites de Salonique,* vol. 7 (Salonica: Librairie Molho, 1978), 576. This important source for Jewish life in Salonica contains disappointingly little on matters relating to economic and labor history. Also see *Selanik Vilayeti Salnamesi* 1307/1889, p. 231.

21. PRO, FO 195/240, 27 Mar. 1846, Blunt at Salonica; France *RRC* 1888, Salonique, 25 July 1883; also see sources cited in n. 17 above.

22. PRO, FO 195/299, 27 Mar. 1846, Blunt at Salonica; *A&P* 1893–94, vol. 97, no. 5581, Salonica for 1891–92, Blunt at Salonica, 30 Sept. 1893; also see sources cited in n. 17 above.

23. France, *RRC,* LC microfilm reel 35, Salonique in 1902; Austria, *Berichte* 1900, vol. 20, no. 7 and 1901, vol. 19, no. 2.

24. *Salonique, Ville-Mère en Israël,* 237, also indicates that the Jewish workers at the port almost totally refused to work on Saturday, compelling foreign ships to change their schedules because the Greek workers were insufficient in number.

25. *A&P* 1893–94, vol. 97, no. 5581, Blunt at Salonica, 30 Sept. 1893.

26. Germany, *Handel und Industrie* 1912, vol. 18, no. 7, esp. pp. 331–37.

27. Germany, *Handel und Industrie* 1904, vol. 7, no. 4; Austria, *Berichte* 1906, vol. 21, no. 3 and 1907, vol. 21, no. 5.

28. PRO, FO Annual Series, 4597 for 1910; Germany, *Handel und Industrie* 1913, vol. 19, no. 6, p. 416 and ff. Paul Dumont has written extensively on post-1908 labor organizations in Salonica; see, for example, "Une organisation socialiste ottomane: La Fédération Ouvrière de Salonique (1908–1912)," *Etudes Balkaniques* 1 (1975): 76–88, and "Naissance d'un socialisme ottoman," in Veinstein, ed., *Salonique, 1850–1918,* 195–207.

29. See sources cited in n. 28 above.

30. See sources cited in n. 28 above; also Germany, *Handel und Industrie* 1912, vol. 18, no. 7, pp. 331–37.

13. The Special Relationship: The Committee of Union and Progress and the Ottoman Jewish Political Elite, 1908–1918

1. Feroz Ahmad, "Unionist Relations with the Greek, Armenian, and Jewish Communities of the Ottoman Empire, 1908–1914," in *Christians and Jews in the Ottoman Empire,* ed. Benjamin Braude and Bernard Lewis (New York: Holmes and Meier, 1982), 1: 402–403. The term *Unionist* refers to a member or follower of the Committee of Union and Progress (CUP), the main Young Turk organization.

2. Aron Rodrigue, *French Jews, Turkish Jews: The Alliance Israélite Universelle and the Politics of Jewish Schooling in Turkey, 1860–1925* (Bloomington: Indiana Univ. Press, 1990), 199 n. 33.

3. Ibid., 126.

4. Ibid., 136.

5. Walter F. Weiker, *The Unseen Israelis: The Jews from Turkey in Israel* (Lanham, Md.: University Press of America, 1988), 22.

6. Cf. Esther Benbassa, "Associational Strategies in Ottoman Jewish Society in the Nineteenth and Twentieth Centuries," in *The Jews of the Ottoman Empire* (Princeton: Darwin Press, 1994), ed. Avigdor Levy, esp. 465–77; also see Esther Benbassa and Aron Rodrigue, *The Jews of the Balkans: The Judeo-Spanish Community, Fifteenth to Twentieth Centuries* (Oxford: Blackwell, 1995), 116–34.

7. Rodrigue, *French Jews, Turkish Jews,* 132. On the next page Rodrigue notes that Abraham Galanté "accused the Central Committee [of the Alliance] of having nothing but contempt for 'the grievances of a Turkish Jew, a Savage!' " (133). The West showed a similar contempt for the Turks.

8. Cf. Avigdor Levy, introduction to *Jews of the Ottoman Empire,* ed. idem, 116–20; İlber Ortaylı, "Ottomanism and Zionism During the Second Constitutional Period, 1908–1915," in ibid., 527–37.

9. Hanna Weiner and Barnet Litvinoff, eds., *The Letters and Papers of Chaim Weizmann,* ser. A, vol. 5 (London and Jerusalem: Oxford University Press, 1974), 82 n. 1 and introduction, xxi-xxii.

10. Shabtai Teveth, *Ben-Gurion: The Burning Ground, 1886–1948* (Boston: Houghton Mifflin, 1987), 70. It seems that during his stay in Istanbul, Ben-Gurion did not have much contact with any of the prominent Jews in the Ottoman community; at least, such contacts are not mentioned by his biographer.

11. Rodrigue, *French Jews, Turkish Jews,* 125. On Haim Nahum's career, see Esther Benbassa, *Haim Nahum: A Sephardic Chief Rabbi in Politics, 1892–1923* (Tuscaloosa: Univ. of Alabama Press, 1995).

12. I owe this information to Madame Ter-Minassian, whose sources are Armenian writings from the contemporary press. See also Feroz Ahmad and Dankwart Rustow, "İkinci Meşrutiyet Döneminde Meclisler 1908–1918," *Güney-Doğu Avrupa Araştırmaları Dergisi* 4–5 (1976): 245–84.

13. Hasan Kayalı, "Jewish Representation in the Ottoman Parliaments," in Levy, ed., *Jews of the Ottoman Empire,* 511.

14. Abraham Galanté, *Turcs et Juifs* (Istanbul: Haim Rozio, 1932), 89; and Karasu's obituary in the *Times,* 8 June 1934, p. 19, entitled "Carasso Effendi: A Parasite of the Young Turks." See also Kayalı, "Jewish Representation," 511–12.

15. Isaiah Friedman, *Germany, Turkey, and Zionism, 1897–1918* (Oxford: Clarendon Press, 1977), 143; and Galanté, *Turcs,* 86–87.

16. Fevzi Demir, "İzmir Sancağında 1912 Meclis-i Mebusan Seçimleri," *Çağdaş Türkiye Tarihi Araştırmaları Dergisi* 1, no. 1 (1991): 158. Muslims had a population of 320,191 and Christians (Greek Orthodox and Gregorian Armenians) 277,657. The *sancak* of Izmir consisted of the *kaza*s of Izmir, Urla, Focateyn, Menemen, Çeşme, Kuşadası, Bergama, Seferhisar, Bayındır, Nif, Tire, and Ödemiş, as well as 24 boroughs (*kasaba*) and 710 villages.

17. Kayalı, "Jewish Representation," 512.

18. Galanté, *Turcs et Juifs,* 127–29; Kayalı, "Jewish Representation," 512–13.

19. Feroz Ahmad, *The Young Turks: The Committee of Union and Progress in Turkish Politics, 1908–1914* (Oxford: Clarendon Press, 1969), 50–52; Kayalı, "Jewish Representation," 512.

20. Friedman, *Germany, Turkey, and Zionism,* 148; Galanté, *Turcs et Juifs,* 116; T. Z. Tunaya, *Türkiye'de Siyasi Partiler, 1859–1952* (Istanbul, 1952), 412.

21. Galanté, *Turcs et Juifs,* 116–17; Ahmad, "Unionist Relations," 428.

22. Demir, "İzmir," 176.

23. Y. G. Çark, *Türk Devleti Hizmetinde Ermeniler, 1453–1953* (İstanbul: Yeni Matbaa, 1953).

24. Galanté, *Turcs et Juifs,* 123–24; Güngör Gönültaş, "Mahmut Şevket Paşa'nın Katillerini Vuran Polis Samuel Efendi Anıldı," *Milliyet,* 27 Dec. 1971; and Burhan Felek's column in *Milliyet,* 30 Dec. 1971. Felek, who had met Samuel Israel, describes him as an Ottoman patriot (*Osmanlı milliyetcisi*) and says: "He was self-sacrificing in duty because he was a Unionist." Felek himself was hostile to the CUP and was arrested as part of the 1913 conspiracy to overthrow the Unionist government.

25. See Elie Kedourie, "Young Turks, Freemasons and Jews," *MES* 7 (1971): 89–104; Bernard Lewis, *The Emergence of Modern Turkey,* 3rd ed. (New York: Oxford Univ. Press, 2002), 211–12.

26. Lowther's reports are quoted in Kedourie, "Young Turks": 99–100.

27. Friedman, *Germany, Turkey, and Zionism,* 146.

28. Ibid., 148.

29. Ibid. 141–42. The Zionists understood the relationship between the Unionists and the Jewish elite and did not take the elite for granted just because they were Jews. They appreciated their commitment to Ottomanism. When the question of Zionism threatening the integrity of the Ottoman Empire was raised, David Wolffsohn assured Russo and Mazliyah of Zionism's loyalty to Turkey. He added that "Zionism had nothing in common with the tendencies directed against the integrity of the Ottoman Empire. . . . Its realization is in full harmony with the interests of *your* homeland" (Ibid., 144, emphasis added).

30. Ibid., 148.

31. Ibid. 147.

32. Ibid., 148.

33. Parvus [Israel Helphand] *Türkiye'nin Can Daman: Devlet-i Osmaniye'nin Borçları ve İslahı* (İstanbul: Şems Matbaası, 1330/1914).

34. See Jacob Landau's excellent study, *Tekinalp: Turkish Patriot, 1883–1961* (Leiden: Publications de l'Institute historique et archéologique néerlandais de Stamboul, 1984). More studies of this kind are needed to illuminate the role of the Jewish community in Ottoman-Turkish life.

35. A. Cerrahoğlu, *Türkiye'de Sosyalizmin Tarihine Katkı* (İstanbul: May Yayınları, 1975), 73.

36. See the debate in the Assembly on 16/29 November 1909, in *Meclis-i Mebusan Zabıt Ceridesi,* vol. (*cilt*) 1, session (*devre*) I, year (*içtima senesi*) 2 (Ankara, 1985), 141–42.

37. H. Cemal, *Tekrar Başımıza Gelenler* (İstanbul: Kastas Yayınları, 1991), 122–23. On Jews and Christians in the Ottoman military during the Balkan Wars, see also the contribution by Avigdor Levy in this volume.

38. Quoted in Bilal Şimşir, ed., *Ege Sorunu, Belgeler,* vol. 1, *1912–1913* (Ankara: Türk Tarih Kurumu Basımevi, 1976), 591–94.

39. Richard G. Hovannisian, *Armenia on the Road to Independence, 1918* (Berkeley: Univ. of California Press, 1967), 31–32.

40. Neville Mandel, *The Arabs and Zionism before World War I* (Berkeley: Univ. of California Press, 1976), 95.

41. See Arnold J. Toynbee, *Acquaintances* (London and New York: Oxford Univ. Press, 1967), 149 ff.

42. Friedman, *Germany, Turkey, and Zionism*, 347 ff.

43. Ahmed Emin, "Filistin Meselesi," *Sabah*, 27 Aug. 1917.

44. "Osmanlı Devleti ve Museviler," *Tasvir-i Efkâr*, 27 Dec. 1917.

45. Quoted in Friedman, *Germany, Turkey, and Zionism*, 292–93.

46. Ibid., 261 and 405.

47. Isaiah Friedman, *The Question of Palestine*, 2d ed., rev. and enl. (New Brunswick, N.J.: Transaction Publishers, 1992), 298.

48. Galanté, *Turcs et Juifs*, 86–87.

49. Quoted in Friedman, *Germany, Turkey, and Zionism*, 397.

50. See n. 34 above.

14. German Jewish Emigrés in Turkey

1. Intellectual opposition to Atatürk included followers of the sociologist Ziya Gökalp. These well-educated and articulate individuals were not necessarily antimodern per se, but favored the retention of significant aspects of tradition (such as the Arabic script), whereas Atatürk wanted a completely clean slate (including replacement of the Arabic script with Latin letters). Cf. Joseph S. Szyliowicz, *Education and Modernization in the Middle East* (Ithaca: Cornell Univ. Press, 1973), 166–67, 216–19. In spite of its shortcomings, Bernard Lewis regards the opening of the Darülfünun in August 1900 as the initiation of "the first truly indigenous modern university in the Muslim world"; *The Emergence of Modern Turkey* (3d ed., New York: Oxford Univ. Press, 2002), 182.

2. The seventy-one senior professors who constituted about half of the dismissed faculty included roughly equal numbers in theology and philosophy, law, mathematics and natural sciences, medicine, and pharmacy and dentistry; Horst Widmann, *Exil und Bildungshilfe: Die deutschsprachige akademische Emigration in die Türkei nach 1933* (Bern: Herbert Lang, 1973), 50–51.

3. Volunteer and salaried personnel in Zurich worked fourteen-hour days to maintain the list of names. Later, the Rockefeller Foundation lent its support as well. The British Academic Assistance Council, formed specifically to aid academic refugees from Nazi Germany, also offered to help, suggesting that the operation be moved to London. This suggestion was finally accepted in 1936, when the activities of the two organizations were fused into the Academic Assistance Council; ibid., 53–54. Similar committees to aid displaced academics

and intellectuals were formed in France, Belgium, Holland, Denmark, and Sweden. The British Academic Assistance Council appears to have been the most successful, reportedly placing more than 500 scholars in 36 countries (including more than 150 in the United States), as well as another 300 in temporary positions; Laura Fermi, *Illustrious Immigrants* (Chicago: Univ. of Chicago Press, 1968), 63 ff.

4. Widmann, *Exil und Bildungshilfe,* 56, quoting the unpublished memoirs of Dr. Schwartz.

5. Ibid.

6. Among those who were freed from arrest due to Turkish intervention were Professors Gerhard Kessler (sociology), Friedrich Dessauer (radiology), and Alfred Kantorowicz (dentistry). Several others barely escaped arrest by leaving precipitously for Istanbul (e.g., Curt Kosswig, genetics), or fleeing to third countries and then proceeding to Turkey (e.g., Ernst Reuter, political science).

7. Widmann, *Exil und Bildungshilfe,* 57, 259, 271.

8. In 1930, Dr. Nissen reportedly performed the first operation in the world in which a patient's lung was removed. Author's interview with a Turkish surgeon trained at the Faculty of Medicine, University of Istanbul, Istanbul, April 1992.

9. Widmann, *Exil und Bildungshilfe,* 60, quoting the unpublished notes of Dr. Schwartz.

10. Ibid.

11. Ibid., 76 n.

12. Dr. Erich Uhlmann, conversation with the author, Michael Reese Hospital, Chicago, 1958.

13. Widmann, *Exil und Bildungshilfe,* 74.

14. Other sources indicate that 208 of the emigrés are known by name, along with 264 family members, constituting a total of 472 persons. In addition, Jan Cremer and Horst Przytulla maintain that others not known by name would bring the total to the range of 700 to 800. They also claim that 200 to 300 stayed in Turkey for only brief periods of time, some leaving after the German invasion of Greece. See Cremer and Przytulla, *Exil Türkei: Deutschsprachige Emigranten in der Türkei 1933–1945* (Munich: Verlag Karl M. Lipp, 1991). Stanford J. Shaw, *Turkey and the Holocaust: Turkey's Role in Rescuing Turkish and European Jewry from Nazi Persecution, 1933–1945* (New York: New York Univ. Press, 1993), 353–69 provides biographical details on fifty-four emigrés; see also ibid., 4–14.

15. The chancellor of this cabinet was to be Kurt von Schleicher, who together with Franz von Papen (who later served as Hitler's ambassador to Turkey) was largely responsible for bringing Hitler to power. Hitler characteristically reciprocated by ordering the murder of Schleicher in 1934. Rüstow returned to Germany after World War II and resumed an active scholarly and political career. See Dankwart A. Rustow, "A Biographical Sketch," in Alexander Rüstow, *Freedom and Domination: A Historical Critique of Civilization,* abbreviated translation by S. Attanasio, edited with an introduction by Dankwart A. Rustow (Princeton: Princeton Univ. Press, 1980), xvii ff.

16. It is in some cases difficult to determine whether a given individual was Jewish or not. Ordinarily such a determination would not matter except perhaps to adherents of such irrational and outrageously racist theories as Nazism. For that matter, many persons considered as Jews by the Nazis, following their official indicator of a single Jewish grandparent, were not considered as Jews by anyone else, least of all themselves. Some could have nevertheless been treated with consideration by the Nazis, e.g., by being credited with service on combat fronts during World War I, or being officially described as "non-Aryan but loyal," but all were vulnerable to the whims of the regime. The devastating political effectiveness of this system of classifying people has been widely noted in the literature on totalitarianism. Although this article deals specifically with Jewish refugees—making the question of identity relevant—non-Jews are not excluded from consideration in the discussion that follows. This approach is justified by the virtual absence of any distinction between Jews and non-Jews among the refugees, either in terms of their treatment by the Nazis who expelled them, or by the Turks who welcomed them, or in terms of their general problems and experiences.

17. Widmann, *Exil und Bildungshilfe*, 76, 178, 181 ff. The problems inherent in this situation surfaced as early as August 1933, even before the arrival of the first group of emigrés, when Dr. Schwartz was invited to an official reception at the summer residence of the German ambassador on the Bosphorus in Tarabya. Schwartz made it clear that he would not attend if any swastikas were displayed (ibid., 58).

18. Interviews by the author, October 1991 and April 1992.

19. See Klaus-Detlev Grothusen, ed., *Der Scurla Bericht: Die Tätigkeit deutscher Hochschullehrer in der Türkei 1933–1939* (Frankfurt am Main: Dagyeli Verlag, 1987). This small volume contains not only the verbatim record of the Scurla report, but a schedule of his two-week visit to Turkey, including the names of those with whom he met. The book also includes an introductory note by German President Richard von Weizsäcker, as well as comments by Fritz Neumark (one of the affected emigrés), an appreciation of Ernst Reuter by Professor Ruşen Keleş, and commentary by the editor. The Scurla report brims with reckless and haphazard political judgments typical of Nazi officialdom. Especially noteworthy is the scurrilous characterization of several of the non-Jewish scholars as Marxist. Clearly, if a politically undesirable individual could not be labeled as Jewish, the Marxist label would do almost as well.

20. Several of these individuals were offered positions in the United States. A few made their way to British-mandated Palestine. One of the latter, Otto Gerngross, had been working at the Higher Institute of Agriculture (later the Faculty of Agriculture of Ankara University). After World War II, he was invited to return to Ankara, this time to the Science Faculty. Widmann reports that Gerngross's departure was precipitated by the threat of internment, but local rumor had it that he was a token Jew at the institute and fell victim to pressure from the Nazi German embassy (*Exil und Bildungshilfe*, 159). This may be a rare example of Nazi success in influencing or controlling the recruitment of academics for service in Turkey. The Berlin regime objected to the appointment of Jews by the Turkish universities and tried to re-

strict the individual contract negotiations to official channels (a survivor of the Ankara emigré group, interview by author, April 1992). Widmann reports two Jews among the emigrés at the Institute of Agriculture (*Exil und Bildungshilfe,* 159–60).

21. Ibid., 82–83, 259.

22. For an appreciation of Ernst Reuter by one of the most prominent of his Turkish successors as Director of the Institute of Urbanism at the University of Ankara, see Ruşen Keleş, "Über Ernst Reuter," in Grothusen, *Der Scurla Bericht,* 61–66.

23. Widmann, *Exil und Bildungshilfe,* 171, 229. This attack on the university was linked to the resignation, in 1946, of Hasan-Ali Yücel, an exceptionally imaginative and innovative minister of education. His departure, in turn, was associated with the dismantling of the Village Institutes developed under his guidance. The leaders of Turkey's new opposition party thus exploited fears of communism for partisan political purposes at about the same time as some prominent American politicians were introducing the tactic in the United States. Other American institutions that recruited emigrés from Turkey included Yale (two), Southern California, Indiana, MIT, Harvard, and Long Island University.

15. Roads East: Turkey and the Jew of Europe during World War II

1. For some recent studies, see Stanford J. Shaw, *The Jews of the Ottoman Empire and the Turkish Republic* (New York: New York Univ. Press, 1991), 3–36; Avigdor Levy, introduction to *The Jews of the Ottoman Empire,* ed. idem (Princeton: Darwin Press, 1994), 3–34.

2. Shaw, *Jews of the Ottoman Empire,* 123–24, 130–31, 142–43, 145; Levy, introduction, 76–78, 83–84, 90.

3. The process by which the newly independent Balkan states persecuted their non-Christian populations is discussed in detail in Justin McCarthy, *Death and Exile: The Ethnic Cleansing of Ottoman Muslims, 1821–1922* (Princeton: Darwin Press, 1995). Cf. Shaw, *Jews of the Ottoman Empire,* 188–206. See also the contribution by Avigdor Levy in this volume.

4. Stanford J. Shaw, *Turkey and the Holocaust: Turkey's Role in Rescuing Turkish and European Jewry from Nazi Persecution, 1933–1945* (New York: New York Univ. Press, 1993), 4–14; Avner Levi, *History of the Jews in the Republic of Turkey* (in Hebrew; Jerusalem: Hotsa'at Lafir, 1992), 57–59. See also the contribution by Frank Tachau in this volume.

5. On Turkish neutrality during World War II, see Selim Deringil, *Turkish Foreign Policy during the Second World War: An Active Neutrality* (Cambridge: Cambridge Univ. Press, 1989).

6. Shaw, *Turkey and the Holocaust,* 46–99 and passim.

7. Ibid., 60–135.

8. Archives of the Turkish Embassy (henceforth ATE) (Paris), file 6127, Turkish Consulate General (Paris) to German Embassy (Paris) no. 605, 28 Dec. 1940.

9. ATE (Paris), file 6127, German Embassy (Paris) to Turkish Consulate General (Paris), no. 1334, 28 Feb. 1941.

10. ATE (Paris), file 6127, Turkish Embassy to Paris (Vichy) to French Ministry of Foreign Affairs (Vichy), no. 924, 31 July 1941.

11. ATE (Paris), file 6127, French Ministry of Foreign Affairs (Vichy) to Turkish Embassy (Vichy), no. 15722, 8 Aug. 1941.

12. ATE (Paris), file 6127, Maynard Barnes, First Secretary of the American Embassy to Turkish Consul General (Paris), 17 Oct. 1940.

13. ATE (Paris), file 6127, Turkish Embassy to Paris (Vichy) to French Ministry of Foreign Affairs, 9 Sept. 1941.

14. The Drancy prison camp was in fact a large housing development that was transformed into a prison by the French police. After the war it was returned to its original purpose, and it still remains under the name La Muette (Shaw, *Turkey and the Holocaust,* 123–35).

15. Maurice Rajsfus, *Drancy: Un camp de concentration très ordinaire, 1941–44* (Paris: Manya, 1991), 72–75, 226–27.

16. ATE (Paris), file 6127, Turkish Embassy to Paris (Vichy) to Turkish Foreign Ministry no. 1667, 15 Dec. 1942.

17. ATE (Paris), no. 27/1/4417/169, Turkish Ambassador to Paris (Vichy) to Turkish Consul General (Marseilles), no. 44–17, 27 Jan. 1944.

18. ATE (Paris) and Turkish Foreign Ministry (Ankara), French Ministry of Foreign Affairs (Vichy) to Turkish Embassy to Paris (Vichy) no. 101, 13 Jan. 1943.

19. Laurence Steinhart to Charles Barlas, Ankara Palace Hotel, 9 Feb. 1944. Quoted in Haim (Chaim, Chaïm, Charles) Barlas, *Rescue in the Days of the Holocaust* (in Hebrew; Tel Aviv: Bet Lohamei Ha-Geta'ot, 1975), supplement 8. Cf. also Laurence Steinhart Archives, Library of Congress, Washington, D.C.

20. Franz von Papen, *Memoirs* (London: A. Deutsch, 1952), 522.

21. Yad Vashem, *Rescue Attempts during the Holocaust. Proceedings of the Second Yad Vashem International Historical Conference, Jerusalem, April 8–11, 1974* (Jerusalem: Yad Vashem, 1977), 649.

22. Shaw, *Turkey and the Holocaust,* 255–304. For the saga of one such train, see A. N. Oppenheim, *The Chosen People: The Story of the "222 Transport" from Bergen-Belsen to Palestine* (Ilford, Essex: Vallentine Mitchell, 1996).

23. Bernard Wasserstein, *Britain and the Jews of Europe, 1939–1945* (Oxford: Oxford Univ. Press, 1979), 247; Dalia Ofer, *Escaping the Holocaust: Illegal Immigration to the Land of Israel, 1939–1944* (Oxford: Oxford Univ. Press, 1990), 162–64; Shaw, *Turkey and the Holocaust,* 278–81; Avner Levi, *Jews in the Republic of Turkey,* 87–88.

24. Roberto Morozzo della Rocca, "Roncalli Diplomatico in Turchia e Grecia, 1935–1944," *Cristianesimo nella Storia* 8 (1987): 33–72; Shaw, *Turkey and the Holocaust,* 277–78.

25. Shaw, *Jews of the Ottoman Empire,* 15–25, 196–206; idem, *Turkey and the Holocaust,* 250–54; Yitzhak Kerem, "Efforts to Rescue the Jews of Greece during the Second World War," (in Hebrew), *Pe'amim* 27 (1986): 77–109.

26. Consuls Namık Kemal Yolga (Paris) and Necdet Kent (Marseilles) have not been similarly honored despite the equally important contributions they made to rescuing Jews in France during World War II. See Shaw, *Turkey and the Holocaust,* 253–54; Marc D. Angel, *The Jews of Rhodes: The History of a Sephardic Community* (New York: Sepher-Hermon, 1980), 151–53; Joseph Nehama, *In Memoriam: Hommage aux victimes juives des Nazis en Grèce* (Salonica: Imp. N. Nicolaides, 1949), 2: 74–76; Naim Güleryüz, "Temmuz 1944—Rodos: Selahattin Ülkümen ve Matilde Turiel," *Şalom* (Istanbul), 25 Apr. 1990; idem, "Türk Konsolosu'nun Ölümünden Döndürdüğü 42 Yahudi," *Yaşam* (Istanbul), Aug. 1986, pp. 10–13.

16. Recipes of Magic-Religious Medicine as Expressed Linguistically

1. Judeo-Spanish terms and phrases are italicized throughout; in mixed-language passages French and Turkish words are in small capitals italic to distinguish them from Judeo-Spanish.

2. For further details on this survey, see Marie-Christine Bornes-Varol, "Le judéo-espagnol vernaculaire d'Istanbul (étude linguistique)" (Ph.D. diss., University of Paris III, 1992); idem, "The Balat Quarter and Its Image: A Study of a Jewish Neighborhood in Istanbul," in *The Jews of the Ottoman Empire,* ed. Avigdor Levy (Princeton: Darwin Press, 1994), 633–45.

3. Cf. Marie-Christine Varol, "Monsieur le rabbin—Termes d'adresse et désignation du rabbin en judéo-espagnol (Turquie)," in *Les interférences de l'hébreu dans les langues juives,* ed. J. Tedghi (Paris: Institute National des Langues et Civilisations Orientales, 1994), 87–109.

4. Bornes-Varol, "Le judéo-espagnol vernaculaire," 129–35.

5. Michaël Molho, *Usos y Costumbres de los Sefardíes de Salonica* (Madrid: Consejo Superior de Investigaciones Científicas (CSIC), 1950), 279 and passim.

6. A mezuzah consists of a small parchment scroll inscribed with verses from Deuteronomy and placed in a small case fixed to the doorpost of Jewish homes.

7. One should be reminded here that the subject of dreams, their nature and meaning, occupies an important place in Jewish literature, as well as in popular culture, from the Bible through the Talmud and medieval Jewish scholarship to modern times. The Talmud's tractate *Berakhot* 57b discusses how dreams are capable of revealing the truth, how they represent an admission of the dreamer's deeds and the owning up to mistakes, often of a sexual nature. Cf. A. Cohen, *Le Talmud* (Paris: Payot, 1986), 350 and passim; see also Samuel Kottek, "La maladie dans les sources de l'antiquité hébraïque," *Yod* 26 (1987): 17–31; Joseph Mergui, *Notions de psychopathologie et de médecine psychosomatique dans l'oeuvre de Maïmonide* (Ph.D. diss., University of Paris-Nord, 1984), 47, 56 and passim; Marc D. Angel, "Folk Wisdom and Intellectual Wisdom: A Study in Sephardic Culture," in *Hommage à Haïm Vidal Sephiha,* ed. Winfried Busse and Marie-Christine Varol-Bornes (Bern: Peter Lang, 1996), 391–97.

8. Cf. Jacques Hassoun, "A propos du possible lien existant entre la psychoanalyse et le

judaïsme," *Yod* 26 (1987): 63–69; idem, "Essai d'interprétation," *Combat pour la Diaspora* 22 (1988): 9–15.

17. Mario Levi: A Young Jewish Author from Istanbul

1. See Nedim Gürsel, "Some Jewish Characters in Modern Turkish Literature," in *The Jews of the Ottoman Empire,* ed. Avigdor Levy (Princeton: Darwin Press, 1994), 647–65. On Sevim Burak, who was half Jewish on her mother's side, and her work, see 661–62.

2. This and other quotations throughout the article, unless otherwise indicated, are based on conversations of the author with Mario Levi.

3. The "speak Turkish" campaign in the early years of republican Turkey was intended to integrate the minorities into Turkish society, but it resulted in state intervention in the minorities' educational systems, business practices, and other areas of life. These measures and the social pressures that they engendered were greatly resented by many among the minority communities.

4. All were published by AFA Yayınevi, Istanbul.

5. Published by Remzi, Istanbul.

6. On Sait Faik and some of his Jewish characters, see Gürsel, "Some Jewish Characters," 655–56.

7. Mario Levi, *Bir Şehre Gidememek* (Istanbul: AFA, 1990), 32.

8. Ahmet Hasim (1884–1933), a symbolist poet, is best known for his collection *Göl Saatleri* (The Hours of the Lake). Written in Ottoman Turkish, his work remains little known in contemporary Turkey. The quotation is from his poem "O Belde" (That Country).

9. Mario Levi, *Bir Şehre Gidememek,* 41.

10. A crisis on Cyprus touched off, on 6 and 7 September 1955, demonstrations in Istanbul in the course of which Greek places of business—as well as those belonging to other minorities, including Jews—were ransacked. This led to the emigration of several thousand Jews from Turkey, mostly to Israel.

11. Mario Levi, *Bir Şehre Gidememek,* 67.

Bibliography

Abou-El-Haj, Rifa'at 'Ali. *Formation of the Modern State: The Ottoman Empire, Sixteenth to Eighteenth Centuries.* Albany: State University of New York Press, 1992.

Abulafia, R. Hayyim. *Hanan Elohim.* Izmir: 1736.

Adler, Cyrus, Gotthard Deutsch et al. *The Jewish Encyclopedia.* 12 vols. New York: Funk and Wagnalls, 1901–1905.

Adler, Elkan Nathan. *Jews in Many Lands.* Philadelphia: Jewish Publication Society, 1905.

———. *Jewish Travellers.* London: Routledge and Sons, 1930.

Ahmad, Feroz. *The Young Turks: The Committee of Union and Progress in Turkish Politics, 1908–1914.* Oxford: Clarendon Press, 1969.

———. "Unionist Relations with the Greek, Armenian, and Jewish Communities of the Ottoman Empire, 1908–1914." In *Christians and Jews in the Ottoman Empire: The Functioning of a Plural Society,* edited by Benjamin Braude and Bernard Lewis, 1: 401–34. New York: Holmes and Meier, 1982.

Ahmad, Feroz, and Dankwart Rustow. "İkinci Meşrutiyet Döneminde Meclisler 1908–1918." *Güney-Doğu Avrupa Araştırmaları Dergisi* 4–5 (1976): 245–84.

Ahmida, Ali Abdulaatif. *The Making of Modern Libya: State Formation, Colonization and Resistance, 1820–1932.* Albany: State University of New York Press, 1994.

Akyüz, Yahya. *Türk Eğitim Tarihi.* Ankara: Ankara Üniversitesi Eğitim Bilimleri Fakültesi, 1982.

Alderson, A. D. *The Structure of the Ottoman Dynasty.* Oxford: Clarendon Press, 1956.

Anderson, M. S. *The Eastern Question, 1774–1923.* London: Macmillan, 1966.

Angel, Marc D. *The Jews of Rhodes: The History of a Sephardic Community.* New York, 1978. 2d ed. New York: Sepher-Hermon, 1980.

———. "Folk Wisdom and Intellectual Wisdom: A Study in Sephardic Culture." In

Hommage à Haïm Vidal Sephiha, edited by Winifried Busse and Marie-Christine Varol-Bornes, 391–97. Bern: Peter Lang, 1996.

Arbel, Benjamin. *Trading Nations: Jews and Venetians in the Early Modern Eastern Mediterranean.* Leiden: Brill, 1995.

Armistead, Samuel G., and Joseph H. Silverman. *The Judeo-Spanish Ballad Chapbooks of Yacob Abraham Yona.* Folk Literature of the Sephardic Jews no. 1. Berkeley: Univ. of California Press, 1971.

————. *Judeo-Spanish Ballads from Bosnia.* University of Pennsylvania Publications in Folklore and Folklife No. 4. Philadelphia: Univ. of Pennsylvania Press, 1971.

Ashtor, Eliyahu. *The Jews and the Mediterranean Economy, Tenth-Fifteenth Centuries.* London: Variorum, 1983.

————. *The Jews of Moslem Spain,* translated by A. Klein and J. M. Klein. 3 vols. Philadelphia: Jewish Publication Society, 1973–84.

————. *The Levant Trade in the Later Middle Ages.* Princeton: Princeton Univ. Press, 1983.

Avitsur, Shmuel. *Everyday Life in Eretz Yisrael in the Nineteenth Century* (in Hebrew). Jerusalem: Am Ha-Sefer, 1976.

————. "Safed—Center of the Manufacture of Woven Woolens in the Fifteenth Century" (in Hebrew). *Sefunot* 6 (1962): 41–69.

————. "The Woolen Textile Industry in Salonica" (in Hebrew). *Sefunot* 12 (1971–78): 145–68.

Awra, Ibrahim al-. *Ta'rikh Wilayat Sulayman Basha al-Adil.* Sidon, 1936; reprint, Beirut: Dar Lahad Khatir, 1989.

Aymard, Maurice. "XVI. Yüzyılın Sonunda Akdeniz'de Korsanlık ve Venedik." *İFM* 23 (1962–63): 219–38.

Ayn-i Ali. *Risale.* Istanbul, 1280 H/1863–1864.

Baer, Gabriel. "The Administrative, Economic and Social Functions of Turkish Guilds." *IJMES* 1 (1970): 28–50.

Baer, Yitzhak. *A History of the Jews in Christian Spain.* 2 vols. Philadelphia: Jewish Publication Society, 1961–66.

Bağış, Ali İhsan. *Osmanlı Ticaretinde Gayri Müslimler.* Ankara: Turhan Kitabevi, 1983.

Bakalopoulos, Apostolos Euangelou. *A History of Thessaloniki.* Translated by T. F. Carney. Thessaloniki: Institute of Balkan Studies, 1972.

Barkan, Ömer Lütfi. "Les déportations comme méthode de peuplement et de colonisation dans l'Empire Ottoman." *İFM* 11 (1949–50): 67–131.

————. "The Price Revolution of the Sixteenth Century: A Turning Point in the Economic History of the Near East." *IJMES* 6 (1975): 3–28.

Barkey, Karen. *Bandits and Bureaucrats: The Ottoman Route to State Centralization.* Ithaca, N.Y.: Cornell Univ. Press, 1994.

Barlas, Haim (Chaim, Chaïm, Charles). *Rescue in the Days of the Holocaust* (in Hebrew). Tel Aviv: Beit Lohamei Ha-Geta'ot, 1975.

Barnai, Jacob. "Blood Libels in the Ottoman Empire from the Fifteenth to the Nineteenth Century" (in Hebrew). In *Antisemitism through the Ages,* edited by Shmuel Almog, 211–16. Jerusalem: Merkaz Zalman Shazar, 1980. English edition (Oxford: Pergamon, 1988), 189–94.

———. "Christian Messianism and Portuguese Marranos: The Emergence of Sabbateanism in Smyrna." *Jewish History* 7 (1993): 119–26.

———. "The Development of Links between Izmir Jews and Palestine Jews in the Seventeenth and Eighteenth Centuries" (in Hebrew). *Shalem* 5 (1991): 95–114.

———. "The Eretz Israel Fund in Nineteenth-Century Izmir" (in Hebrew). In *Transaction and Change in Modern Jewish History: Essays Presented in Honor of Shmuel Ettinger,* edited by Shmuel Almog et al., 135–48. Jerusalem: Merkaz Zalman Shazar, 1987.

———. "The Financial Administration of the Jewish Community of Jerusalem in the Second Half of the Eighteenth Century" (in Hebrew). *Shalem* 7 (2002): 195–217.

———. "Jewish Congregations in Izmir in the Seventeenth Century" (in Hebrew). *Pe'amim* 48 (1991): 66–84.

———. "Jewish Guilds in Turkey from the Sixteenth to the Nineteenth Centuries" (in Hebrew). In *Jews in Economic Life,* edited by N. Gross, 133–47. Jerusalem: Merkaz Zalman Shazar, 1985.

———. "The Jews in the Ottoman Empire" (in Hebrew). In *History of the Jews in Islamic Countries,* edited by Shmuel Ettinger, vol. 2, pp. 183–297. Jerusalem: Merkaz Zalman Shazar, 1986.

———. *The Jews in Palestine in the Eighteenth Century under the Patronage of the Istanbul Committee of Officials for Palestine.* Translated by Naomi Goldblum. Tuscaloosa: Univ. of Alabama Press, 1992. Original edition in Hebrew (Jerusalem: Ben-Zvi Institute, 1982).

———. "Notes on the Jewish Community of Istanbul in the Eighteenth Century" (in Hebrew). *Miqqedem Umiyyyam* 1 (1981): 53–56.

———. "On the History of the Relations between the Jews of Izmir and the Jews of Palestine in the Seventeenth and Eighteenth Centuries" (in Hebrew). *Shalem* 5 (1987): 95–114.

———. "On the History of the Sabbatean Movement and Its Place in Jewish Life in the Ottoman Empire" (in Hebrew). *Pe'amim* 3 (1979): 59–71.

———. "On the Jewish Community of Izmir in the Late Eighteenth and Early Nineteenth Centuries" (in Hebrew). *Zion* 47 (1982): 56–76.

———. "Organization and Leadership in the Jewish Community of Izmir in the Seventeenth Century." In *The Jews of the Ottoman Empire,* edited by Avigdor Levy, 275–84. Princeton: Darwin Press, 1994.

———. "The Origins of the Jewish Community in Izmir in the Ottoman Period" (in Hebrew). *Pe'amim* 12 (1982): 47–58.

———. "The Outbreak of Sabbateanism—The Eastern European Factor." *Journal of Jewish Thought and Philosophy* 4(1994): 171–83.

———. "Portuguese Marranos in Izmir in the Seventeenth Century" (in Hebrew). In *Nation and History,* edited by Menahem Stern, vol. 1, pp. 289–98. Jerusalem: Merkaz Zalman Shazar, 1983.

———. "R. Haim Benveniste and the Izmir Rabbinate" (in Hebrew). In *The Days of the Crescent: Chapters in the History of the Jews in the Ottoman Empire,* edited by Minna Rozen, 151–91. Tel Aviv: Tel Aviv University, 1996.

———. "Rabbi Joseph Escapa and the Rabbinate of Izmir" (in Hebrew). *Sefunot,* n.s., 3 (1985): 53–81.

———. "Relation and Disengagement between the Scholars of Turkey and the Scholars of Poland and Central Europe in the Seventeenth Century" (in Hebrew). *Gal'ed* 9 (1986): 13–26.

———. "The Status of the Jerusalem General Rabbinate in the Ottoman Period." (in Hebrew). *Cathedra* 13 (1979): 47–69.

Baron, Salo Wittmayer. *A Social and Religious History of the Jews.* 2d ed. Vol. 18, *The Ottoman Empire, Persia, Ethiopia, India and China.* New York: Columbia Univ. Press, 1983.

Basha, Qustantin al-, ed. *Mudhakkirat Ta'rikhiyya.* Lebanon: Matba'at al-Qiddis Bulus, n.d.

Bashan, Eliezer. "Economic Life from the Sixteenth to the Eighteenth Century" (in Hebrew). In *The Jews in Ottoman Egypt,* edited by Jacob M. Landau, 63–112. Jerusalem: Misgav Yerushalayim, 1988.

———. "Fires and Earthquakes in Izmir from the Seventeenth to the Nineteenth Centuries" (in Hebrew). *Miqqedem Umiyyam* 2 (1986): 13–27.

———. "The Rise and Decline of the Sephardi Communities in the Levant: The Economic Aspects." In *The Sephardi Heritage,* edited by Richard D. Barnett and W. M. Schwab, 2: 349–88. London: Gibraltar Books, 1989.

Baykal, Bekir Sitki. "Edirne'nin Uğramış Olduğu İstilâlar." In *Edirne: Edirne'nin 600. Fetih Yıldönümü Armağan Kitabı,* edited by Türk Tarih Kurumu, 179–95. Ankara, 1965.

Bayur, Yusuf Hikmet. *Türk İnkilâbı Tarihi,* vol 2, pt. 2. Ankara: Türk Tarih Kurumu Basımevi, 1943.

Beinart, Haim. *Conversos on Trial: The Inquisition in Cuidad Real.* Jerusalem: Magnes Press, 1981.

Benardete, Mair Jose. *Hispanic Culture and Character of the Sephardic Jews.* Corrected and augmented by Marc D. Angel. 2d ed. New York: Sepher-Hermon Press, 1982.

Ben-Arieh, Yehoshua. *A City Reflected in Its Times—Jerusalem in the Nineteenth Century: The Old City* (in Hebrew). Jerusalem: Yad Yitzhak Ben Zvi, 1977.

———. *A City Reflected in Its Times—New Jerusalem: The Beginnings* (in Hebrew). Jerusalem: Yad Yitzhak Ben Zvi, 1979.

———. *Jerusalem in the Nineteenth Century.* 2 vols. New York: St. Martin's, 1984–1986.

Benas, B. L. *Report of His Travels in the East.* London: Anglo-Jewish Association, 1885.

Benayahu, Meir. "The Great Conversion in Salonica" (in Hebrew). *Sefunot* 14 (1971–1978): 77–108.

———. "Moses Benveniste, Court Physician to the Sultan, and R. Judah Zarko's Poem on His Exile to Rhodes." (in Hebrew). *Sefunot* 12 (1971–78): 123–44.

———. *Rabbi Eliyahu Capsali of Crete* (in Hebrew). Jerusalem: Tel Aviv University, 1983.

Benbassa, Esther. *Un grand rabbin sepharade en politique, 1892–1923.* Paris: Presses du CNRS, 1990. English edition, *Haim Nahum: A Sephardic Chief Rabbi in Politics, 1892–1923.* (Tuscaloosa: Univ. of Alabama Press, 1995).

———. "Zionism in the Ottoman Empire at the End of the Nineteenth and the Beginning of the Twentieth Century." *SiZ* 11 (1990): 127–40.

———. "L'école de filles de l'Alliance Israélite Universelle à Galata." In *Première Rencontre Internationale sur L'Empire Ottoman et la Turquie Moderne,* edited by E. Eldem, 203–36. Istanbul and Paris: Editions Isis, 1991.

———. "Associational Strategies in Ottoman Jewish Society in the Nineteenth and Twentieth Centuries," translated by Eric Fassin and Avigdor Levy. In *The Jews of the Ottoman Empire,* edited by Avigdor Levy, 457–84. Princeton: Darwin Press, 1994.

Benbassa, Esther, and Aron Rodrigue. *The Jews of the Balkans: The Judeo-Spanish*

Community, Fifteenth to Twentieth Centuries. Oxford: Blackwell, 1995. Reprinted as *Sephardi Jewry: A History of the Judeo-Spanish Community, 14th–20th Centuries.* Berkeley: Univ. of California Press, 2000. Originally published as *Juifs des Balkans: espaces judéo-ibériques XVᵉ-XXᵉ siècle* (Paris: Editions La Découverte, 1993).

Ben Israel, Menasseh. *Esperanca de Israel.* Izmir 1659.

Benvenisti, David. *The Jews of Salonica in the Last Generations* (in Hebrew). Jerusalem: Kiryat Sefer, 1973.

Benveniste, R. Hayyim. *Sheyarei Keneset Hagedola, Orah Hayyim.* Izmir 1671.

Ben-Ya'akov, Abraham. *The Jews of Iraq from the End of the Gaonic Period to Our Times (1038–1960)* (in Hebrew). Jerusalem: Ben-Zvi Institute, 1965. 2d rev. ed. Jerusalem: Kiryat Sefer, 1979.

Ben-Zvi, Itzhak (Izhak). *Eretz-Israel under Ottoman Rule* (in Hebrew). Jerusalem: Yad Yitshak Ben-Zvi, 1962.

———. *The Exiled and the Redeemed.* Rev. ed. Philadelphia: Jewish Publication Society, 1961.

Berkes, Niyazi. *The Development of Secularism in Turkey.* Montreal: McGill Univ. Press, 1964.

Bertele, T. *Il palazzo ambasciatori di Venezia a Constantinopoli.* Bologna: Apollo, 1932.

Blumenfeld, I., ed. *Otzar Nehmad* (in Hebrew) 2 vols. Vienna, 1856–63.

Bornstein-Makovetzky, Leah. "The Community and Its Institutions" (in Hebrew). In *The Jews in Ottoman Egypt,* edited by Jacob M. Landau, 129–216. Jerusalem: Misgav Yerushalayim, 1988.

———. "Eighteenth- and Nineteenth-Century Court Records from Istanbul as a Mirror of the Social and Economic Life of the City's Jews" (in Hebrew). *Shevet Va'am,* 2d ser., 5 (1984): 101–109.

———. "Jewish Brokers in Constantinople during the Seventeenth Century According to Hebrew Documents." In *The Mediterranean and the Jews: Banking, Finance and International Trade (Sixteenth-Eighteenth Centuries),* edited by Ariel Toaff and Simon Schwarzfuchs, 75–104. Ramat Gan: Bar Ilan University Press, 1989.

———. "Jewish Communal Leadership in the Near East from the Late Fifteenth to the Eighteenth Centuries" (in Hebrew). Ph.D. diss., Bar Ilan University, Ramat Gan, 1978.

———. "Remnants of the Register of the Court of Balat in Istanbul, 1839" (in Hebrew). *Sefunot,* n.s., 4 (1989): 53–122.

Bowman, Steven B. *The Jews of Byzantium, 1204–1453*. Tuscaloosa: Univ. of Alabama Press, 1985.

Bowring, John. *Report on the Commercial Statistics of Syria*. London: William Clowes and Sons, 1840.

Bozkurt, Gülnihal. "An Overview on the Ottoman Empire-Jewish Relations." *Islam—Zeitschrift für Geschichte und Kultur des Islamischen Orient* 71 (1994): 255–60.

Braude, Benjamin. "Foundation Myths of the *Millet* System." In *Christians and Jews in the Ottoman Empire: The Functioning of a Plural Society*, edited by Benjamin Braude and Bernard Lewis, 1: 69–88. New York: Holmes and Meier, 1982.

———. "International Competition and Domestic Cloth in the Ottoman Empire, 1500–1650: A Study in Undevelopment." *Review: A Journal of the Fernand Braudel Center* 1 (1979): 437–54.

———. "The Textile Industry in Salonica in the Context of the Eastern Mediterranean Economy" (in Hebrew). *Pe'amim* 15 (1983): 82–95.

Braude, Benjamin, and Bernard Lewis, eds. *Christians and Jews in the Ottoman Empire: The Functioning of a Plural Society*. 2 vols. New York: Holmes and Meier, 1982.

Braudel, Fernand. *Civilization and Capitalism: Fifteenth-Eighteenth Century*. Translated by Siân Reynolds. 2 vols. New York: Harper and Row, 1982.

———. *The Mediterranean and the Mediterranean World in the Age of Philip II*. Translated by Siân Reynolds. 2 vols. New York: Harper and Row, 1966, 1973.

Brody, Robert. *The Textual History of the She'iltot* (in Hebrew). New York and Jerusalem: American Academy for Jewish Research, 1991.

Brown, Carl L., ed. *Imperial Legacy: The Ottoman Imprint on the Balkans and the Middle East*. New York: Columbia Univ. Press, 1996.

Burckhardt, J. L. *Travels in Syria and the Holy Land*. London: Darf Publishers, 1822.

Cahen, Claude. *Pre-Ottoman Turkey: A General Survey of the Material and Spiritual Culture, c. 1071–1330*. Translated by J. Jones-Williams. London: Sidgwick and Jackson, 1968.

Çark, Y. G. *Türk Devleti Hizmetinde Ermeniler, 1453–1953*. Istanbul: Yeni Matbaa, 1953.

Carmoly, E. *Histoire des médecins juifs*. Brussels: Société Encyclographique des Sciences Medicales, 1844.

Carnegie Endowment for International Peace. *Report of the International Commission to Inquire into the Causes and Conduct of the Balkan Wars*. Washington, D.C.: The [Carnegie] Endowment, 1914.

Carpi, Daniel, and Moshe Rinott. "A Journal of the Travels of a Jewish Female Teacher from Trieste to Jerusalem (1857–1865)" (in Hebrew). In *Kevatzim le-Heker Toledot ha-Hinukh ha-Yehudi be-Yisrael uva-Tefutzot,* 1 (1982): 115–59.

Caspi, Mishael Maswari, trans. *Daughters of Yemen.* Berkeley: Univ. of California Press, 1985.

Çelik, Zeynep. *The Remaking of Istanbul: Portrait of an Ottoman City in the Nineteenth Century.* Seattle: Univ. of Washington Press, 1986.

Cemal, H. *Tekrar Başımıza Gelenler.* Istanbul: Kastas Yayınları, 1991.

Centre de recherche sur la Judaïsme de Salonique. *Salonique. Ville-Mère en Israël* (in Hebrew with a very brief French summary). Jerusalem-Tel Aviv: Centre de recherche sur le Judaïsme de Salonique, 1967.

Cerrahoğlu, A. *Türkiye'de Sosyalizmin Tarihine Katkı.* Istanbul: May Yayınları, 1975.

Cevdet, Ahmed. *Tezakir.* Edited by C. Baysun. Ankara: Türk Tarih Kurumu Basımevi, 1953.

Chouraqui, André. *Cent ans d'histoire: L'Alliance Israélite Universelle et la renaissance juive contemporaine (1860–1960).* Paris: Presses Universitaires de France, 1965.

Christoff, Paul. *Journal du siège d'Andrinople: Notes quotidiennes d'un assiégé.* Paris: Charles-Lavauzelle, 1914.

Cirilli, Gustave. *Journal du siège d'Andrinople (Impressions d'un assiégé).* 4th ed. Paris: Chapelot, 1913.

Cna'ani, J. "Economic Life in Safed and Its Environs in the Sixteenth and the First Half of the Seventeenth Centuries" (in Hebrew). *Zion* (Yearbook) 6 (1934): 172–217.

Cobb, Stanwood. *The Real Turk.* Boston: Pilgrim Press, 1914.

Cohen, A. *Le Talmud.* Paris: Payot, 1986.

Cohen, Amnon. "Additional Documents on the Distribution of the Jewish Community's Debts in Jerusalem and Hebron in the Eighteenth Century" (in Hebrew). *Shalem* 1 (1987): 317–30.

———. *Economic Life in Ottoman Jerusalem.* Cambridge: Cambridge Univ. Press, 1989.

———. *Jewish Life under Islam: Jerusalem in the Sixteenth Century.* Cambridge, Mass.: Harvard Univ. Press, 1984.

———. *Palestine in the Eighteenth Century: Patterns of Government and Administration.* Jerusalem: Magnes Press, 1973.

———. "Ritual Murder Accusations against the Jews during the Days of Suleiman the Magnificent." *JTS* 10 (1986): 73–78.

————. "Ottoman Sources for the History of Ottoman Jews: How Important?" In *The Jews of the Ottoman Empire*, edited by Avigdor Levy, 687–704. Princeton: Darwin Press, 1994.

Cohen, Amnon, and Bernard Lewis. *Population and Revenue in the Towns of Palestine in the Sixteenth Century.* Princeton: Princeton Univ. Press, 1978.

Cohen, Hayyim J. *The Jews of the Middle East, 1860–1972.* Jerusalem: Israel Universities Press, 1973. Hebrew Edition: Israel Universities Press, 1972.

Cohen, Mark R. *Jewish Self-Government in Medieval Egypt.* Princeton: Princeton Univ. Press, 1980.

Cohen, Richard I., ed. *Vision and Conflict in the Holy Land.* Jerusalem: Yad Yitzhak Ben-Zvi, 1985.

Cook, M. A., ed. *Studies in the Economic History of the Middle East.* London: Oxford Univ. Press, 1970.

————. *A History of the Ottoman Empire to 1730.* Cambridge: Cambridge Univ. Press, 1976.

Cowen, Ida. *Jews in Remote Corners of the World.* Englewood Cliffs, N.J.: Prentice-Hall, 1971.

Cox, Samuel S. *Diversions of a Diplomat in Turkey.* New York: C. L. Webster, 1887.

Cremer, Jan, and Horst Przytulla. *Exil Türkei: Deutschsprachige Emigranten in der Türkei 1933–1945.* Munich: Verlag Karl M. Lipp, 1991.

Curtin, Philip D. *Cross-Cultural Trade in World History.* Cambridge: Cambridge Univ. Press, 1984.

Dankoff, Robert (translation and commentary), and Rhoads Murphey (historical introduction). *The Intimate Life of an Ottoman Statesman, Melek Ahmed Pasha (1588–1662), as Portrayed in Evliya Çelebi's Book of Travels (Seyahat-Name).* Albany: State University of New York Press, 1991.

Davis, Ralph. *Aleppo and Devonshire Square: English Traders in the Levant in the Eighteenth Century.* London: Macmillan, 1967.

Davison, Roderic H. "The *Millet*s as Agents of Change in the Nineteenth-Century Ottoman Empire." In *Christians and Jews in the Ottoman Empire: The Functioning of a Plural Society,* edited by Benjamin Braude and Bernard Lewis, 1: 319–37. New York: Holmes and Meier, 1982.

————. *Reform in the Ottoman Empire, 1856–1876.* Princeton: Princeton Univ. Press, 1963.

————. "Turkish Attitudes concerning Christian-Muslim Equality in the Nineteenth Century." *American Historical Review* 59 (1954): 844–64.

De Felice, Renzo. *Jews in an Arab Land: Libya, 1835–1970.* Austin: Univ. of Texas Press, 1985.

Della-Pergola, Sergio. "The Jewish Population in the Nineteenth and Twentieth Centuries" (in Hebrew). In *The Jews in Ottoman Egypt (1517–1914),* edited by Jacob M. Landau, 27–62. Jerusalem: Misgav Yerushalayim, 1988.

Della Roca, Roberto Morozzo. "Roncalli Diplomatico in Turchia e Grecia, 1935–44." *Cristianesimo nella Storia* 8 (1987): 33–72.

Demir, Fevzi. "İzmir Sancağında 1912 Meclis-i Mebusan Seçimleri." *Çağdaş Türkiye Tarihi Araştırmaları Dergisi* 1, no. 1 (1991): 158–76.

DeNovo, J. A. *American Interests and Policies in the Middle East, 1900–1939.* Minneapolis: Univ. of Minnesota Press, 1963.

Deringil, Selim. *Turkish Foreign Policy during the Second World War: An Active Neutrality.* Cambridge: Cambridge Univ. Press, 1989.

Deshen, Shlomo. "La communauté juive de Bagdad à la fin de l'époque ottomane: L'émergence de classes sociales et de la sécularisation." *Annales HSS* [Histoire, Sciences Sociales] 3 (1994): 681–703.

Devereux, Robert. *The First Ottoman Constitutional Period: A Study of the Midhat Constitution and Parliament.* Baltimore: Johns Hopkins Press, 1963.

Dimashqi, Mikha'il al-. *Ta'rikh Hawadith al-Sham wa-l-Lubnan.* Beirut: Al-Matba'ah Al-Kathulikiya, 1912.

Dumont, Paul. "Jewish Communities in Turkey during the Last Decades of the Nineteenth Century in the Light of the Archives of the Alliance Israélite Universelle." In *Christians and Jews in the Ottoman Empire: The Functioning of a Plural Society,* edited by Benjamin Braude and Bernard Lewis, 1: 209–42. New York: Holmes and Meier, 1982.

———. "Naissance d'un socialisme ottoman." In *Salonique, 1850–1918. La "ville des Juifs" et le réveil des Balkans,* edited by Gilles Veinstein, 195–207. Paris: Editions Autrement, 1992.

———. "Une organisation socialiste ottomane: La Féderation Ouvrière de Salonique (1908–1912)." *Etudes Balkaniques* 1 (1975): 76–88.

Duwayk, Jacob Saul. *Derekh Emunah.* Aleppo: n.p., 1913–14.

Ekstein, S. "R. Hayyim Palagi's Life and Work and His Influence on the Izmir Jewish Community" (in Hebrew). Ph.D. diss., Yeshiva University, 1970.

Elazar, Daniel J., et al. *The Balkan Jewish Communities.* Lanham, Md.: University Press of America, 1984.

Elboim-Dror, Rachel. *Hebrew Education in Eretz-Yisrael.* Vol. 1, *1854–1914* (in Hebrew). Jerusalem: Yad Yitzhak Ben-Zvi, 1986.

Eldem, Edhem, Daniel Goffman, and Bruce Masters. *The Ottoman City between East and West.* Cambridge: Cambridge Univ. Press, 1999.

El-Gamil, Yosef. "Karaite Jews in Egypt, 1517–1918" (in Hebrew). In *The Jews in Ottoman Egypt (1517–1914),* edited by Jacob M. Landau, 513–56. Jerusalem: Misgav Yerushalayim, 1988.

Elliot, J. H. *The Revolt of the Catalans: A Study in the Decline of Spain (1598–1640).* Cambridge: Cambridge Univ. Press, 1963.

Emin, Ahmed. "Filistin Meselesi." *Sabah,* 27 Aug. 1917.

Emmanuel, Isaac Samuel. *Histoire de l'industrie des tissus des Israélites de Salonique.* Paris: Librairie Lipschutz, 1935.

———. *Histoire des Israélites de Salonique.* Paris: Librairie Lipschutz, 1936.

Encyclopedia Judaica Research Foundation. *Encyclopedia Judaica.* 16 vols. Jerusalem: Keter, 1972.

Engelhardt, Ed. *La Turquie et le Tanzimat.* 2 vols. Paris: A. Cotillon et Cie, 1882–1884.

Epstein, Mark Alan. "The Leadership of the Ottoman Jews in the Fifteenth and Sixteenth Centuries." In *Christians and Jews in the Ottoman Empire: The Functioning of a Plural Society,* edited by Benjamin Braude and Bernard Lewis, 1: 101–15. New York: Holmes and Meier, 1982.

———. *The Ottoman Jewish Communities and Their Role in the Fifteenth and Sixteenth Centuries.* Freiburg: Klaus Schwarz Verlag, 1980.

Ergin, Osman. *Türkiye Maarif Tarihi.* Istanbul: Esmer Matbaası, 1977.

Eton, William. *A Survey of the Turkish Empire.* 2d ed. London, 1799. Reprint, West-mead, England: Gregg, 1972.

Ezuz, Menahem. "On the History of the Jews in the City of Adrianople" (in Hebrew). *Hemdat Yisrael,* 157–68. Jerusalem, 1946.

Fabris, A. "Il Dottor Girolamo Fasaneo, alias Receb." *Archivio Veneto,* ser. 5, vol. 23 (1989): 105–18.

Farhi, David. "The Jews of Salonica in the Young Turk Revolution" (in Hebrew). *Sefunot* 15 (1971–1981): 135–52.

Farhi, Noury. *La Communauté juive d'Alexandrie.* Alexandria: n.p., 1946.

Faroqhi, Suraiya. "Crisis and Change, 1590–1699." In *An Economic and Social History of the Ottoman Empire, 1300–1914,* edited by Halil İnalcık and Donald Quataert, 411–636. Cambridge: Cambridge Univ. Press, 1994.

Fattal, Antoine. *Le statut légal des non-Musulmans en pays d'Islam.* Beirut: Imprimerie Catholique, 1958.

Feridun Bey. *Munşa'at al-Salatin.* Istanbul, 1265H/1849.

Fermi, Laura. *Illustrious Immigrants.* Chicago: Univ. of Chicago Press, 1968.

Findley, Carter V. *Bureaucratic Reform in the Ottoman Empire: The Sublime Porte, 1789–1922.* Princeton: Princeton Univ. Press, 1980.

Finn, James. *Stirring Times.* London, 1878. Hebrew translation by Aharon Amir. Jerusalem: Yad Yitzhaq Ben-Zvi, 1980.

Fischer-Galati, Stephen A. *Ottoman Imperialism and German Protestantism.* Cambridge, Mass.: Harvard Univ. Press, 1959.

Fissel, Mark Charles, and Daniel Goffman. "Viewing the Scaffold from Istanbul: The Bendysh-Hyde Affair, 1647–51." *Albion* 22 (1990): 421–48.

Fleischer, Cornell H. *Bureaucrat and Intellectual in the Ottoman Empire: The Historian Mustafa Ali (1541–1600).* Princeton: Princeton Univ. Press, 1986.

Frageon, Maurice. *Les Juifs en Egypte.* Cairo: Paul Barbey, 1938.

Franco, M. *Essai sur l'histoire des Israélites de l'empire ottoman depuis les origines jusqu'à nos jours.* Paris, 1897. Reprint, Paris: Centre d'Etudes Don Isaac Abravanel, 1981.

Frankel, Jonathan. *The Damascus Affair: "Ritual Murder," Politics, and Jews in 1840.* Cambridge: Cambridge Univ. Press, 1997.

Frankl, Ludwig August. *The Jews in the East.* 2 vols. Westport, Conn.: Greenwood, 1975. Originally published as *Nach Jerusalem* (London: Hurst and Blackett, 1859).

Friedenwald, Harry. *Jewish Luminaries in Medical History.* Baltimore: Johns Hopkins Press, 1946.

———. *The Jews and Medicine: Essays.* 2 vols. Baltimore: Johns Hopkins Press, 1944.

Friedman, Isaiah. *Germany, Turkey and Zionism, 1897–1918.* Oxford: Clarendon Press, 1977.

———. *The Question of Palestine.* 2d ed., rev. and enl. New Brunswick, N.J.: Transaction Publishers, 1992.

———. "The System of Capitulations and Its Effects on Turco-Jewish Relations in Palestine, 1856–1897." In *Palestine in the Late Ottoman Period: Political, Social, and Economic Transformation,* edited by David Kushner, 280–93. Jerusalem: Yad Izhak Ben-Zvi, 1986.

Galante, Avram [Galanté, Abraham]. *Histoire des Juifs de Turquie.* 9 vols. Reprint, Istanbul: Editions Isis [1985]. A reprint of Galante's main works.

———. *Médecins juifs au service de la Turquie.* Istanbul: Babock, 1938. Reprint, Istanbul: Editions Isis [1985]: *Histoire des Juifs de Turquie,* vol. 9.

———. *Turcs et Juifs.* Istanbul: Haim Rozio, 1932.

Garnett, Lucy M. J. *The Women of Turkey and Their Folk-Lore*. 2 vols. London: David Nutt, 1890–91.

Gat, Ben-Zion. *The Jewish Population in Eretz-Yisrael during the Period 1840–1881* (in Hebrew). Jerusalem: Yad Yitzhak Ben Zvi, 1974.

Geiger, A. *Kevutzat Ma'amarim* (in Hebrew). Warsaw: Tushiyah, 1910.

Geller, Yaakov. "Inter-Community Relations in the Ottoman Empire" (in Hebrew). *Miqqedem Umiyyam* 2 (1986): 29–54.

Genel Kurmay Başkanlığı. *Balkan Harbı Tarihi*. 7 vols. Istanbul: Askeri Matbaa, 1938–1965.

Gerber, Haim. "Entrepreneurship and International Commerce in the Economic Activity of the Jews of the Ottoman Empire in the Sixteenth-Seventeenth Centuries" (in Hebrew). *Zion* 43 (1978): 38–67.

———. "Guilds in Seventeenth-Century Anatolian Bursa." *Asian and African Studies* 11 (1976): 59–86.

———. "Jewish Tax Farmers in the Ottoman Empire in the Sixteenth and Seventeenth Centuries." *JTS* 10 (1986): 143–54.

———. "Jews and Money-Lending in the Ottoman Empire." *Jewish Quarterly Review* 72 (1981): 100–118.

———. "Jews in the Economic Life of the Anatolian City Bursa in the Seventeenth Century: Notes and Documents" (in Hebrew). *Sefunot*, n.s., 1 (1980): 235–72.

———. "Jews in Edirne (Adrianople) in the Sixteenth and Seventeenth Centuries" (in Hebrew). *Sefunot*, n.s., 3 (1985): 35–51.

———. *The Jews of the Ottoman Empire in the Sixteenth and Seventeenth Centuries: Economy and Society* (in Hebrew). Jerusalem: Historical Society of Israel, 1982.

———. "On the History of the Jews in Istanbul in the Seventeenth and Eighteenth Centuries" (in Hebrew). *Pe'amim* 12 (1982): 27–46.

———. *The Social Origins of the Modern Middle East*. Boulder, Colo.: Lynne Rienner, 1987.

Gerber, Haim, and Jacob Barnai. *The Jews in Izmir in the Nineteenth Century* (in Hebrew and Turkish). Jerusalem: Misgav Yerushalayim, 1984.

Gibb, H. A. R. *The Travels of Ibn Batuta*. 3 vols. Cambridge: Hakluyt Society at the University Press, 1958–1971.

Gibb, H. A. R., and Harold Bowen. *Islamic Society and the West*. One volume in two parts. London: Oxford Univ. Press, 1950–1957.

Göçek, Fatma Müge. *East Encounters West: France and the Ottoman Empire in the Eighteenth Century*. Oxford: Oxford Univ. Press, 1987.

————. "Ottoman Archival Information on Jews: The Inheritance Register of the Chief Rabbi of Galata (1770)." In *The Jews of the Ottoman Empire,* edited by Avigdor Levy, 705–16. Princeton: Darwin Press, 1994.

————. *Rise of the Bourgeoisie, Demise of Empire: Ottoman Westernization and Social Change.* Oxford: Oxford Univ. Press, 1996.

Goffman, Daniel. *Britons in the Ottoman Empire, 1642–1660.* Seattle: Univ. of Washington Press, 1998.

————. *Izmir and the Levantine World, 1550–1650.* Seattle: Univ. of Washington Press, 1990.

————. "The Jews of Safed and the *Maktu'* System in the Sixteenth Century: A Study of Two Documents from the Ottoman Archives." *JOS* 3 (1982): 81–90.

————. "Ottoman Millets in the Early Seventeenth Century." *New Perspectives on Turkey* 11 (1994): 135–58.

————. "The Ottoman Role in Patterns of Commerce in Aleppo, Chios, Dubrovnik, and Istanbul, 1600–1650." In *Decision Making and Change in the Ottoman Empire,* edited by Caesar E. Farah, 139–48. Kirksville, Mo.: Thomas Jefferson Univ. Press, 1993.

Goldberg, Harvey E. *Jewish Life in Muslim Libya.* Chicago: Univ. of Chicago Press, 1990.

————. "Ottoman Rule in Tripoli as Viewed by the History of Mordechai Hakohen." In *Les relations entre Juifs et Musulmans en Afrique du Nord, XIXᵉ-XXᵉ siècles,* 143–59. Paris: Editions du Centre National de la Recherche Scientifique, 1980.

Goldberg, Harvey E., ed. *The Book of Mordechai: A Study of the Jews of Libya.* Philadelphia: Institute for the Study of Human Issues, 1980.

————. *Sephardi and Middle Eastern Jewries: History and Culture in the Modern Era.* Bloomington: Indiana University Press, 1996.

Goldfeld, N. "A Commentary on the Pentateuch by Yehudah ben Shemaryah, from a Genizah Manuscript" (in Hebrew). *Kovetz Al-Yad* 10 (1982): 123–60.

Goldman, Israel M. *The Life and Times of Rabbi David Ibn Abi Zimra.* New York: Jewish Theological Seminary, 1970.

Gönültaş, Güngör. "Mahmut Şevket Paşa'nın Katillerini Vuran Polis Samuel Efendi Anıldı." *Milliyet,* 27 Dec. 1971.

Goodblatt, Morris S. *Jewish Life in Turkey in the Sixteenth Century.* New York: Jewish Theological Seminary, 1952.

Graetz, Heinrich. *History of the Jews.* 6 vols. Philadelphia: Jewish Publication Society, 1891–1895.

Grosman, Moşe. *Dr. Markus (1870–1944). Osmanlıdan Cumhuriyete Geçişte Türk Yahudilerinden Görünümler.* Istanbul: As Matbaacılık, 1992.

Grothusen, Klaus-Detlev, ed. *Der Scurla Bericht: Die Tätigkeit deutscher Hochschullehrer in der Türkei 1933–1939.* Frankfurt am Main: Dagyeli Verlag, 1987.

Grunebaum-Ballin, Paul. *Joseph Naci, duc de Naxos.* Paris: Mouton, 1968.

Grunwald, Kurt. "Jewish Schools under Foreign Flags in Ottoman Palestine." In *Studies on Palestine during the Ottoman Period,* edited by Moshe Ma'oz, 164–74. Jerusalem: Magnes Press, 1975.

Güleryüz, Naim. "Temmuz 1944—Rodos: Selahattin Ülkümen ve Matilde Turiel." *Şalom,* 25 Apr. 1990.

———. "Türk Konsolosu'nun Ölümünden Döndürdüğü 42 Yahudi." *Yaşam* (Aug. 1986): 10–13.

Gürsel, Nedim. "Some Jewish Characters in Modern Turkish Literature." In *The Jews of the Ottoman Empire,* edited by Avigdor Levy, 647–65. Princeton: Darwin Press, 1994.

Gutman, Yisrael, and Efraim Zuroff, eds. *Rescue Attempts During the Holocaust. Proceedings of the Second Yad Vashem International Historical Conference, Jerusalem, April 8–11, 1974.* Jerusalem: Yad Vashem, 1977.

Hacker, Joseph. "The 'Chief Rabbinate' in the Ottoman Empire in the Fifteenth and Sixteenth Centuries" (in Hebrew). *Zion* 49 (1984): 225–63.

———. "An Emissary of Louis XIV in the Levant and Ottoman Jewish Culture" (in Hebrew) *Zion* 52 (1987): 25–44.

———. "Jewish Autonomy in the Ottoman Empire: Its Scope and Limits." In *The Jews of the Ottoman Empire,* edited by Avigdor Levy, 153–202. Princeton: Darwin Press, 1994.

———. "The Jewish Community in Salonica in the Fifteenth and Sixteenth Centuries" (in Hebrew). Ph.D. diss., Hebrew University, Jerusalem, 1978.

———. "The Intellectual Activity of the Jews of the Ottoman Empire during the Sixteenth and Seventeenth Centuries." In *Jewish Thought in the Seventeenth Century,* edited by Isadore Twersky and Bernard Septimus, 99–135. Cambridge, Mass.: Harvard Univ. Press, 1987.

———. "Links between Spanish Jewry and Palestine, 1391–1492." In *Vision and Conflict in the Holy Land,* edited by Richard I. Cohen, 111–39. Jerusalem: Yad Yitzhak Ben-Zvi, 1985.

———. "Ottoman Policy toward the Jews and Jewish Attitudes toward the Ottomans during the Fifteenth Century." In *Christians and Jews in the Ottoman Em-*

pire: The Functioning of a Plural Society, edited by Benjamin Braude and Bernard Lewis, 1: 117–26. New York: Holmes and Meier, 1982.

———. "The Ottoman System of Sürgün and Its Effect on Jewish Society in the Ottoman Empire" (in Hebrew). *Zion* 55 (1990): 27–82.

Hacohen, Mordekhai. *Higgid Mordekhai* (in Hebrew). Edited by Harvey Goldberg. Jerusalem: Yad Yitzhak Ben-Zvi, 1978.

Halbertal, Moshe. "Varieties of Mysticism." *New Republic* (11 June 1990): 34–39.

Hall, Richard C. *The Balkan Wars, 1912–1913: Prelude to the First World War.* London: Routledge, 2000.

———. *Bulgaria's Road to the First World War.* Boulder, Colo.: East European Monographs, distributed by Columbia Univ. Press, New York, 1996.

Hammer-Purgstall, J. von. *Geschichte des Osmanischen Reiches.* 10 vols. Pest, 1827–1835; reprint, Graz: Akademische Druck, 1963.

Hanioğlu, M. Şükrü. "Jews in the Young Turk Movement to the 1908 Revolution." In *The Jews of the Ottoman Empire,* edited by Avigdor Levy, 519–26. Princeton: Darwin Press, 1994.

———. *The Young Turks in Opposition.* Oxford: Oxford Univ. Press, 1995.

Hannaway, C. "Medicine and Religion in Pre-Revolutionary France: Introduction." *Social History of Medicine* 2 (1989): 315–19.

Haramati, Shlomo. *The Beginning of Hebrew Education in Eretz Yisrael and Its Contribution to the Revival of Hebrew (1883–1914)* (in Hebrew). Jerusalem: Re'uven Mas, 1979.

Harel, Yaron. "Le Consul de France et l'Affaire de Damas à la lumière de nouveaux documents." *Revue d'histoire diplomatique* 2 (1999): 143–70.

———. "Jewish-Christian Relations in Aleppo as Background for the Jewish Response to the Events of October 1850." *IJMES* 30 (1998): 77–96.

Hartom, A. S., and M. D. Cassuto, eds. *Takkanot Kandia: Statuta Judaeorum Candiae* (in Hebrew). Jerusalem: Mekizei Nirdamim, 1943.

Hassida, I. *R. Hayyim Palagi and His Books* (in Hebrew). Jerusalem: Hotsa'at Mokirei Maran Ha-Habif, 1968.

Hassoun, Jacques. "A propos du possible lien existant entre la psychoanalyse et le judaïsme." *Yod* 26 (1987): 63–69.

———. "Essai d'interprétation." *Combat pour la Diaspora* 22 (1988): 9–15.

———. "The Penetration of Modernization into Jewish Life in Egypt, 1870–1918" (in Hebrew). In *The Jews in Ottoman Egypt (1517–1914),* edited by Jacob M. Landau, 559–76. Jerusalem: Misgav Yerushalayim, 1988.

Hattox, Ralph S. *Coffee and Coffeehouses.* Seattle and London: Univ. of Washington Press, 1985.

Havlin, Shlomo Zalman. "Intellectual Creativity" (in Hebrew). In *The Jews in Ottoman Egypt,* edited by Jacob M. Landau, 245–310. Jerusalem: Misgav Yerushalayim, 1988.

Hazzan, R. Joseph. *Hikrei Lev, Yoreh De'a.* Salonica, 1806.

Helmreich, E. C. *The Diplomacy of the Balkan Wars, 1912–1913.* Cambridge, Mass.: Harvard Univ. Press, 1938.

Hess, Andrew C. *The Forgotten Frontier: A History of the Sixteenth Century Ibero-African Frontier.* Chicago: Univ. of Chicago Press, 1978.

Heyd, Uriel. "The Jewish Communities of Istanbul in the Seventeenth Century." *Oriens* 6 (1953): 299–314.

———. "Moses Hamon, Chief Jewish Physician to Sultan Süleyman the Magnificent." *Oriens* 16 (1963): 152–70.

———. *Ottoman Documents on Palestine, 1552–1615.* London: Oxford Univ. Press, 1960.

———. "Ritual Murder Accusations in Fifteenth- and Sixteenth-Century Turkey" (in Hebrew). *Sefunot* 5 (1961): 135–50.

Heywood, Colin. " 'Boundless Dreams of the Levant': Paul Wittek, the George-Kries, and the Writing of Ottoman History." *Journal of the Royal Asiatic Society* 1 (1989): 32–50.

Heyworth-Dunne, James. *An Introduction to the History of Education in Modern Egypt.* London: Luzac and Co., 1938.

Hirschberg, H. Z. *A History of the Jews in North Africa.* 2 vols. Leiden: Brill, 1974–1981.

———. "The Oriental Jewish Communities." In *Religion in the Middle East: Three Religions in Concord and Conflict,* edited by A. J. Arberry, 1: 119–225. Cambridge: Cambridge Univ. Press, 1969.

Hopwood, Derek. *The Russian Presence in Syria and Palestine, 1843–1914.* Oxford: Oxford Univ. Press, 1969.

Hovannisian, Richard G. *Armenia on the Road to Independence, 1918.* Berkeley: Univ. of California Press, 1967.

Howard, Douglas A. "Ottoman Historiography and the Literature of 'Decline' of the Sixteenth and Seventeenth Centuries." *Journal of Asian History* 22 (1988): 52–77.

Hyamson, Albert M., ed. *The British Consulate in Jerusalem in Relation to the Jews of Palestine, 1838–1914.* 2 vols. London: E. Goldston, Ltd., 1939–1941.

Ibrahim, Abdallah Ali. "Evolution of Government and Society in Tripolitania and Cyrenaica (Libya): 1835–1911." Ph.D. diss., University of Utah, 1982.

Idel, Moshe. *Kabbalah: New Perspectives.* New Haven, Conn.: Yale Univ. Press, 1988.

———. " 'One from a Town and Two from a Family'—A New Look at the Problem of the Dissemination of Lurianic Kabbalah and the Sabbatean Movement" (in Hebrew). *Pe'amim* 44 (1990): 5–30. An English version of this article was published as " 'One from a Town, Two from a Clan'—The Diffusion of Lurianic Kabbalah and Sabbateanism: A Re-Examination," *Jewish History* 7 (1993): 79–104.

İnalcık, Halil. "Capital Formation in the Ottoman Empire." *Journal of Economic History* 29 (1969): 97–140.

———. *Essays in Ottoman History.* Istanbul: Eren, 1998.

———. "Jews in the Ottoman Economy and Finances, 1450–1500." In *Essays in Honor of Bernard Lewis: The Islamic World from Classical to Modern Times,* edited by C. E. Bosworth, Charles Issawi, et al., 513–50. Princeton: Darwin Press, 1989.

———. "Kutadgu Bilig'de Türk ve İran Siyaset Nazariye ve Gelenekleri." *Reşid Rahmeti Arat İçin,* 267–71. Ankara: Türk Kültürünü Araştırma Enstitüsü, 1966.

———. "Military and Fiscal Transformation in the Ottoman Empire, 1500–1700." *Archivum Ottomanicum* 6 (1980): 283–337.

———. "Notes on N. Beldiceanu's Translation of the Kānūnāme, fonds turc ancien 39, Bibliothèque Nationale, Paris." *Der Islam* 43 (1967): 139–57.

———. "Ottoman Archival Materials on *Millets.*" In *Christians and Jews in the Ottoman Empire: The Functioning of a Plural Society,* edited by Benjamin Braude and Bernard Lewis, 1: 437–49. New York: Holmes and Meier, 1982.

———. "The Ottoman Economic Mind and Aspects of the Ottoman Economy." In *Studies in the Economic History of the Middle East,* edited by M. A. Cook, 207–18. London: Oxford Univ. Press, 1970.

———. *The Ottoman Empire: The Classical Age, 1300–1600.* Translated by Norman Itzkowitz and Colin Imber. London: Weidenfeld and Nicolson, 1973.

———. "The Ottoman Empire and the Crusades." In *The Impact of the Crusades on Europe,* edited by Norman P. Zacour and Harry W. Hazard, 339–46. Madison: Univ. of Wisconsin Press, 1989 (vol. 6 of *A History of the Crusades,* gen. ed. Kenneth M. Setton, 6 vols. Madison: Univ. of Wisconsin Press, 1969–1989).

———. "Ottoman Galata, 1453–1553." In *Première rencontre internationale sur l'Empire Ottoman et la Turquie moderne,* edited by E. Eldem, 8–21. Istanbul: Isis, 1991.

———. "The Socio-Political Effects of the Diffusion of Fire-Arms in the Middle East." In *War, Technology and Society in the Middle East,* edited by V. J. Parry and M. E. Yapp, 195–217. London: Oxford Univ. Press, 1975.

———. "Tax Collection, Embezzlement, and Bribery in the Ottoman Empire." *TSAB* 15 (1991): 327–46.

———. "The Turkish Impact on the Development of Modern Europe." In *The Ottoman State and Its Place in World History,* edited by Kemal H. Karpat, 51–58. Leiden: Brill, 1974.

İnalcık, Halil, ed., with Donald Quataert. *An Economic and Social History of the Ottoman Empire, 1300–1914.* Cambridge: Cambridge Univ. Press, 1994.

İslamoğlu-İnan, Huri, ed. *The Ottoman Empire and the World-Economy.* Cambridge: Cambridge Univ. Press, 1987.

Israel, Gérard. *L'Alliance Israélite Universelle 1860–1960.* Paris: AIU, 1960.

Israel, Salvator. "Solomon Avraam Rozanes—Originator of the Historiography of the Bulgarian Jews (1862–1938)." In Social, Cultural and Educational Association of the Jews in the People's Republic of Bulgaria, Central Board, *Annual* 19 (Sofia, 1984): 343–71.

Issawi, Charles. *The Economic History of the Middle East.* Chicago: Univ. of Chicago Press, 1960.

———. *The Economic History of Turkey, 1800–1914.* Chicago: Univ. of Chicago Press, 1980.

———. "The Transformation of the Economic Position of the *Millets* in the Nineteenth Century." In *Christians and Jews in the Ottoman Empire: The Functioning of a Plural Society,* edited by Benjamin Braude and Bernard Lewis, 1: 261–85. New York: Holmes and Meier, 1982.

Jacoby, David. "Les Juifs vénetiens de Constantinople—Leur communauté du XIIIe siècle jusqu'au milieu du XVe siècle." *REJ* 131 (1972): 397–472.

Jelavich, Charles, and Barbara Jelavich. *The Establishment of the Balkan National States, 1804–1920.* Seattle: Univ. of Washington Press, 1977.

Jellinek, A. *Ginzei Hokhmat ha-Kabbalah.* Leipzig, 1853.

Judah, R. Joshua Abraham. *Avodat Massa.* Salonica, 1846.

Juhasz, Esther, ed. *Sephardi Jews in the Ottoman Empire: Aspects of Material Culture.* Jerusalem: Israel Museum, 1990.

Juifs d'Egypte: Images et Textes. Paris: Editions du Scribe, 1984.

Kafadar, Cemal. "On the Purity and Corruption of the Janissaries." *TSAB* 15 (1991): 273–80.

———. "Les troubles monétaires de la fin du XVIe siècle et la prise de conscience ottomane du déclin." *Annales, E.S.C.* [économies, sociétés, civilisations] (1991): 381–400.

Kalderon, Albert E. *Abraham Galante: A Biography.* New York: Sepher-Hermon Press, 1983.

Kamen, Henry. "The Mediterranean and the Expulsion of Spanish Jews in 1492." *Past and Present* 119 (1988): 30–55.

Kaplan, Yosef, Henry Mechoulan, and Richard H. Popkin, eds. *Menasseh ben Israel and His World.* Leiden: Brill, 1989.

Karal, Enver Ziya. "Non-Muslim Representatives in the First Constitutional Assembly, 1876–1877." In *Christians and Jews in the Ottoman Empire: The Functioning of a Plural Society,* edited by Benjamin Braude and Bernard Lewis, 1: 387–400. New York: Holmes and Meier, 1982.

Karmi, Shelomoh. *Beginnings of Hebrew Education: The Hebrew Teachers Assembly in Palestine and Its Place in the History of Education, 1892–1896* (in Hebrew). Jerusalem: Re'uven Mas, 1986.

Karpat, Kemal H., ed. *An Inquiry into the Social Foundations of Nationalism in the Ottoman State: From Social Estates to Classes, From Millets to Nations.* Princeton: Center of International Studies, Princeton University, 1973.

———. "*Millet*s and Nationality: The Roots of the Incongruity of Nation and State in the Post-Ottoman Era." In *Christians and Jews in the Ottoman Empire: The Functioning of a Plural Society,* edited by Benjamin Braude and Bernard Lewis, 1: 141–69. New York: Holmes and Meier, 1982.

———. *Ottoman Population, 1830–1914: Demographic and Social Characteristics.* Madison: Univ. of Wisconsin Press, 1985.

———. *The Ottoman State and Its Place in World History.* Leiden: Brill, 1974.

———. "Jewish Population Movements in the Ottoman Empire, 1862–1914." In *The Jews of the Ottoman Empire,* edited by Avigdor Levy, 399–415. Princeton: Darwin Press, 1994.

Kasaba, Reşat. *The Ottoman Empire in the World Economy: The Nineteenth Century.* Albany: State University of New York Press, 1988.

Katz, Jacob. *Tradition and Crisis: Jewish Society at the End of the Middle Ages.* New York: Schocken, 1971.

Kayalı, Hasan. "Jewish Representation in the Ottoman Parliaments." In *The Jews of the Ottoman Empire,* edited by Avigdor Levy, 507–517. Princeton: Darwin Press, 1994.

Kazamias, Andreas M. *Education and the Quest for Modernity in Turkey.* Chicago: Univ. of Chicago Press, 1966.

Kazancıgil, Ratip, ed. *Hafız Rakım Ertür'ün Anılarından: Balkan Savaşında Edirne Savunması Günleri.* Kırklareli: Sermet Matbaası, 1986.

Kazzaz, Nissim. "The Political Activity of the Jews of Iraq at the End of the Ottoman Period" (in Hebrew). *Pe'amim* 36 (1988): 35–51.

Kedourie, Elie. *England and the Middle East: The Destruction of the Ottoman Empire, 1914–1921.* London: Bowes and Bowes, 1956; reprint, London Mansell Publishing, 1987.

———. "Young Turks, Freemasons, and Jews." *MES* 7 (1971): 89–104.

Keleş, Ruşen. "Über Ernst Reuter." In *Der Scurla Bericht: Die Tätigkeit deutscher Hochschullehrer in der Türkei 1933–1939,* edited by Klaus-Detlev Grothusen, 61–66. Frankfurt am Main: Dagyeli Verlag, 1987.

Kerem, Yitzhak. "Efforts to Rescue the Jews of Greece during the Second World War" (in Hebrew). *Pe'amim* 27 (1986): 77–109.

Kennedy, Mazal. "The Institution of the Hakham Bashi and the Hakham Haneh Constitution in Istanbul in the Light of Changes in the Nineteenth Century (1835–1914)" (in Hebrew). M.A. thesis, Haifa University, 1985.

Khalaf, Samir. "Communal Conflict in Nineteenth-Century Lebanon." In *Christians and Jews in the Ottoman Empire: The Functioning of a Plural Society,* edited by Benjamin Braude and Bernard Lewis, 2: 107–134. New York: Holmes and Meier, 1982.

Kolidetzky, Shabetai, ed. *"Safra Devei Rav" with the Commentary of Rabbi Hillel b. Elyakim* (in Hebrew). Jerusalem 1961.

Kolatt, Israel. "The Organization of the Jewish Population of Palestine and the Development of Its Political Consciousness before World War I." In *Studies on Palestine during the Ottoman Period,* edited by Moshe Ma'oz, 211–45. Jerusalem: Magnes Press, 1975.

Kottek, Samuel. "La maladie dans les sources de l'antiquité hébraïque." *Yod* 26 (1987): 17–31.

Krämer, Gudrun. *The Jews in Modern Egypt, 1914–1952.* Seattle: Univ. of Washington Press, 1989.

Küçük, Abdurrahman. *Dönmeler ve Dönmelik Tarihi.* Istanbul: Otüken Neşriyat, [1980?].

Kunt, I. Metin. *The Sultan's Servants: The Transformation of Ottoman Provincial Government, 1550–1650.* New York: Columbia Univ. Press, 1983.

———. "Transformation of *Zimmi* into *Askeri.*" In *Christians and Jews in the Ottoman Empire: The Functioning of a Plural Society,* edited by Benjamin Braude and Bernard Lewis, 1: 55–67. New York: Holmes and Meier, 1982.

Kushner, David, ed. *Palestine in the Late Ottoman Period: Political, Social and Economic Transformations.* Jerusalem: Yad Izhak Ben-Zvi, 1986.

Landau, Jacob M. "The Beginnings of Modernization in Education: The Jewish Community in Egypt as a Case Study." In *The Beginnings of Modernization in the Middle East:The Nineteenth Century,* edited by William R. Polk and Richard L. Chambers, 299–312. Chicago: Univ. of Chicago Press, 1968.

————. *Jews in Nineteenth-Century Egypt.* New York: New York Univ. Press, 1969.

————. "Relations between Jews and Non-Jews in the Late Ottoman Empire: Some Characteristics." In *The Jews of the Ottoman Empire,* edited by Avigdor Levy, 539–46. Princeton: Darwin Press, 1994.

————. *Tekinalp:Turkish Patriot, 1883–1961.* Leiden: Publications de l'Institute historique et archéologique néerlandais de Stamboul, 1984.

Landau, Jacob M., ed. *The Jews in Ottoman Egypt (1517–1914)* (in Hebrew). Jerusalem: Misgav Yerushalayim, 1988.

Landau, R. *Geschichte der Juedischen Aerzte.* Berlin: S. Karger, 1895.

Landshut, S. *Jewish Communities in the Muslim Countries of the Middle East.* London: Jewish Chronicle, 1950.

Lane, Frederic C. "Economic Consequences of Organized Violence." *JEH* 18 (1958): 401–17.

Laniado, Ezra. *The Jews of Mosul* (in Hebrew). Tirat ha-Karmel: Ha-Makhon Le-Heker Yahadut Motsul, 1981.

Laskier, Michael M. *The Alliance Israélite Universelle and the Jewish Communities of Morocco, 1862–1962.* Albany: State University of New York Press, 1983.

Leven, Narcisse. *Cinquante ans d'histoire: L'Alliance Israélite Universelle (1860–1910).* 2 vols. Paris: Librairie Félix Alcan, 1911–1920.

Levi, Avner. "Changes in the Leadership of the Main Spanish Communities in the Nineteenth-Century Ottoman Empire" (in Hebrew). In *The Days of the Crescent: Chapters in the History of the Jews in the Ottoman Empire,* edited by Minna Rozen, 237–54. Tel Aviv: Tel Aviv University, 1996.

————. *History of the Jews in the Republic of Turkey* (in Hebrew). Jerusalem: Hotsa'at Lafir, 1992.

————. "Jewish Periodicals in Izmir" (in Hebrew). *Pe'amim* 12 (1982): 87–104.

————. "Judeo-Spanish (Ladino)" (in Hebrew). In *The Writings of Sephardi and Oriental Jewish Authors in Languages other than Hebrew,* edited by Itzhak Bezalel, 227–54. Tel Aviv: Tel Aviv University, 1982.

Levi, Mario. *BirYalnız Adam.* Istanbul: AFA Yayınevi, 1986.

————. *Bir Şehre Gidememek.* Istanbul: AFA Yayınevi, 1990.

————. *En Güzel Aşk Hikâyemiz*. Istanbul: AFA Yayınevi, 1992.

————. *İstanbul bir Masaldı*. Istanbul: Remzi, 1999.

————. *Madam Floridis Dönmeyebilir*. Istanbul: AFA Yayınevi, 1990.

Levy, Avigdor. "Military Reform and the Problem of Centralization in the Ottoman Empire in the Eighteenth Century." *MES* 18 (1982): 227–49.

————. "*Millet* Politics: The Appointment of a Chief Rabbi in 1835." In *The Jews of the Ottoman Empire,* edited by idem, 425–38. Princeton: Darwin Press, 1994.

————. "Ottoman Attitudes to the Rise of Balkan Nationalism." In *War and Society in East Central Europe,* edited by Béla K. Király and Gunther E. Rothenberg, 1: 325–45. New York: Brooklyn College Press, 1979.

————. *The Sephardim in the Ottoman Empire*. Princeton: Darwin Press, 1992.

Levy, Avigdor, ed. *The Jews of the Ottoman Empire*. Princeton: Darwin Press, 1994.

Lewin-Epstein, Eliyahu Ze'ev. *My Memoirs* (in Hebrew). Tel-Aviv: Levin-Epstein, 1932.

Lewis, Bernard. *The Emergence of Modern Turkey*. London: Oxford Univ. Press, 1961; 2d ed., London: Oxford Univ. Press, 1968; 3d ed., New York: Oxford Univ. Press, 2002.

————. *Istanbul and the Civilization of the Ottoman Empire*. Norman: Univ. of Oklahoma Press, 1963.

————. *The Jews of Islam*. Princeton: Princeton Univ. Press, 1984.

————. *The Muslim Discovery of Europe*. New York: Norton, 1982.

————. *Notes and Documents from the Turkish Archives*. Jerusalem: Israel Oriental Society, 1952.

————. "The Privilege Granted by Mehmed II to His Physician." *Bulletin of the School of Oriental and African Studies* 14 (1952): 550–63.

Loeb, Isidore. *La situation des Israélites en Turquie, en Serbie et en Roumanie*. Paris: Joseph Baer et Cie., 1877.

Lowry, Heath. " 'From Lesser Wars to the Mightiest War': The Ottoman Conquest and Transformation of Byzantine Urban Centers in the Fifteenth Century." In *Continuity and Change in Late Byzantine and Early Ottoman Society,* edited by Anthony Bryer and Heath Lowry, 323–38. Birmingham, Eng., and Washington, D.C.: Dumbarton Oaks, 1986.

————. "When Did the Sephardim Arrive in Salonica? The Testimony of the Ottoman Tax-Registers, 1478–1613." In *The Jews of the Ottoman Empire,* edited by Avigdor Levy, 203–213. Princeton: Darwin Press, 1994.

Löwy, A. *The Jews of Constantinople: A Study of Their Communal and Educational Status*. London: Anglo-Jewish Association, 1890.

Lucchetta, F., and G. Lucchetta. "Un medico veneto in Siria nel cinquecento: Cornelio Bianchi." *Quaderni di Studi Arabi* 4 (1986): 1–56.

Lutzky, A. "The 'Francos' and the Effect of the Capitulations on the Aleppo Jews" (in Hebrew). *Zion* 6 (1940): 46–79.

Maghribi, Abd al-Qadir al-. "Yahud al-Sham mundhu Mi'at Am." *Majallat al-Majma al-Ilmi al-Arabi* 9(1929): 640–55.

Mandel, Neville J. *The Arabs and Zionism before World War I.* Berkeley: Univ. of California Press, 1976.

Maneberg, Eliezer. "The Evolution of Jewish Educational Practices in the Sancak (Eyalet) of Jerusalem under Ottoman Rule." Ph.D. diss., Univ. of Connecticut, 1976.

Mansur, As'ad. *Ta'rikh al-Nasira.* Egypt: Matba'at al-Hilal, 1924.

Ma'oz, Moshe. "Changes in the Position of the Jewish Communities of Palestine and Syria in the Mid-Nineteenth Century." In *Studies on Palestine during the Ottoman Period,* edited by idem, 142–63. Jerusalem: Magnes Press, 1975.

———. "Communal Conflict in Ottoman Syria during the Reform Era: The Role of Political and Economic Factors." In *Christians and Jews in the Ottoman Empire: The Functioning of a Plural Society,* edited by Benjamin Braude and Bernard Lewis, 2: 91–105. New York: Holmes and Meier, 1982.

———. *Ottoman Reform in Syria and Palestine, 1840–1861: The Impact of the Tanzimat on Politics and Society.* Oxford: Clarendon Press, 1968.

Ma'oz, Moshe, ed. *Studies on Palestine during the Ottoman Period.* Jerusalem: Magnes Press, 1975.

Marcus, Abraham. *The Middle East on the Eve of Modernity: Aleppo in the Eighteenth Century.* New York: Columbia Univ. Press, 1989.

Marcus, Shimon. "On the History of the Jews in Adrianople" (in Hebrew). *Sinai* 29 (1951): 7–23 and 318–44.

Mardin, Şerif. *The Genesis of Young Ottoman Thought: A Study of the Modernization of Turkish Political Ideas.* Princeton: Princeton Univ. Press, 1962.

———. "Power, Civil Society and Culture in the Ottoman Empire." *Comparative Studies in Society and History* 11 (1969): 258–81.

Masters, Bruce. *Christians and Jews in the Ottoman Arab World: Roots of Sectarianism.* Cambridge: Cambridge Univ. Press, 2001.

———. *The Origins of Western Economic Dominance in the Middle East: Mercantilism and the Islamic Economy in Aleppo, 1600–1750.* New York: New York Univ. Press, 1988.

Matkovski, Alexandar. *A History of the Jews in Macedonia*. Translated by David Arney. Skopje: Macedonian Review Editions, 1982.

McCarthy, Justin. *Death and Exile: The Ethnic Cleansing of Ottoman Muslims, 1821–1922*. Princeton: Darwin Press, 1995.

———. "Jewish Population in the Late Ottoman Period." In *The Jews of the Ottoman Empire*, edited by Avigdor Levy, 375–94. Princeton: Darwin Press, 1994.

———. *Muslims and Minorities: The Population of Ottoman Anatolia and the End of the Empire*. New York: New York Univ. Press, 1983.

McGowan, Bruce. *Economic Life in Ottoman Europe: Taxation, Trade and the Struggle for Land, 1600–1800*. Cambridge: Cambridge Univ. Press, 1981.

Mears, Eliot Grinnell, ed. *Modern Turkey: A Politico-Economic Interpretation, 1908–1923*. New York: Macmillan, 1924.

Mehmed Pasha, Sarı. *Ottoman Statecraft: The Book of Counsel for Vezirs and Governors*. Translated with an introduction and notes by Walter Livingston Wright, Jr. Princeton: Princeton Univ. Press, 1935; reprint, Westport, Conn.: Greenwood, 1971.

Mergui, Joseph. "Notions de psychopathologie et de médecine psychosomatique dans l'oeuvre de Maïmonide." Ph.D. diss., Univ. of Paris-Nord, 1984.

Mesut Paşa, ed. *Muahedat Mecmuası*. 5 vols. Istanbul, 1292–1298 H/1876–1882.

Mirande, Henry, and Louis Olivier. *Sur la bataille: Journal d'un aviateur français à l'armée bulgare au siège d'Andrinople*. 5th ed. Paris: L'Edition Moderne, n.d. [1913].

Mirsky, Samuel K., ed. *She'iltot de Rab Ahai Gaon*. Vols. 1–5. Jerusalem: Mosad Ha-Rav Kook, 1959–1977.

Mizrahi, Maurice. *L'Egypte et ses Juifs: Le temps révolu*. Lausanne: M. Mizrahi, 1977.

Molho, Michaël. *Usos y Costumbres de los Sefardíes de Salonica*. Madrid: Consejo Superior de Investigaciones Científicas (CSIC), 1950.

Molkho, R. Yitzhak. *Orhot Yosher*. Tel Aviv: Yeshivat Shuvi Nafshi, 1975.

Montagu, Sydney S. *Jewish Life in the East*. London: C. Kegan Paul & Co., 1881.

Mordtmann, J. H. "Die jüdischen kira im Serai der Sultane." in *Mitteilungen des Seminars für orientalischen Sprachen* (Berlin) 32, no. 2 (1929): 1–38.

Nahoum, Haim. "Jews." In *Modern Turkey: A Politico-Economic Interpretation, 1908–1923*, edited by Eliot Grinnell Mears, 86–97. New York: Macmillan, 1924.

Nassar, Siham. *Al-Yahud al-Misriyyun bayn al-Misriyya wa-l-Sahyuniyya*. Beirut: Dar Al-Wahda, 1980.

Navon, A-H. *Les 70 ans de l'Ecole Normale Israélite Orientale (1865–1935)*. Paris: Librairie Durlacher, 1935.

Nehama, Joseph. *Histoire des Israélites de Salonique*. 7 vols. Salonica: Librairie Molho, 1935–1978.

————. *In Memoriam: Hommage aux victimes juives des Nazis en Grèce*. 2 vols. Salonica: Imp. N. Nicolaides, 1949.

Neophytus of Cyprus [monk]. *Annals of Palestine, 1821–1841*. Edited by S. N. Spyridon. Jerusalem: Ariel, 1938.

Nicolay, Nicholas de. *The Navigations, Peregrinations, and Voyages, made into Turkie by Nicholas Nicholay etc.* Translated by T. Washington. London, 1585; reprint, Amsterdam: Da Capo Press, 1968.

Nini, Yehuda. *From East and from West: Everyday Life of the Jews of Egypt* (in Hebrew). Tel Aviv: Tel Aviv University, 1980.

Ofer, Dalia. *Escaping the Holocaust: Illegal Immigration to the Land of Israel, 1939–1944*. Oxford: Oxford Univ. Press, 1990.

Öke, Mim Kemal. "The Ottoman Empire, Zionism and the Question of Palestine (1880–1908)." *IJMES* 14 (1982): 329–41.

————. *Siyonizm ve Filistin Sorunu (1880–1914)*. Istanbul: Üçdal Neşriyat, 1982.

————. "Young Turks, Freemasons, Jews and the Question of Zionism in the Ottoman Empire (1908–1913)." *SiZ* 7 (1986): 199–218.

Okyar, Osman, and Halil İnalcık, eds. *Social and Economic History of Turkey (1071–1920). Papers Presented to the First International Congress on the Social and Economic History of Turkey, Hacettepe University, Ankara, July 11–13, 1977*. Ankara: Meteksan, 1980.

Oliphant, Laurence. *The Land of Gilead*. New York: D. Appleton, 1881.

Olnon, Merlijn. "Toward Classifying *Avanias*: A Study of Two Cases Involving the English and the Dutch Nations in Seventeenth-Century Izmir." In *Friends and Rivals in the East: Studies in Anglo-Dutch Relations in the Levant from the Seventeenth to the Early Nineteenth Century*, edited by Alastair Hamilton, Alexander H. de Groot, and Maurits van den Boogert, 159–86. Leiden: Brill, 2000.

Olson, Robert W. "Jews in the Ottoman Empire in Light of New Documents." *Jewish Social Studies* 41 (1979): 75–88.

————. "The Young Turks and the Jews: A Historiographical Revision." *Turcica* 18 (1986): 219–35.

Oppenheim, A. N. *The Chosen People: The Story of the "222 Transport" from Bergen-Belsen to Palestine*. Ilford, Essex: Vallentine Mitchell, 1996.

Ortaylı, İlber. "Ottomanism and Zionism during the Second Constitutional Period,

1908–1915," translated by Ayşegül Acar. In *The Jews of the Ottoman Empire,* edited by Avigdor Levy, 527–37. Princeton: Darwin Press, 1994.

Oscanyan, C. *The Sultan and His People.* New York: Derby and Jackson, 1857.

Özbudun, Ergun. "The Continuing Ottoman Legacy and the State Tradition in the Middle East." In *Imperial Legacy: The Ottoman Imprint on the Balkans and the Middle East,* edited by L. Carl Brown, 133–57. New York: Columbia Univ. Press, 1996.

Pamuk, Şevket. *A Monetary History of the Ottoman Empire.* Cambridge: Cambridge Univ. Press, 2000.

———. "Money in the Ottoman Empire, 1326–1914." In *The Economic and Social History of the Ottoman Empire, 1300–1914,* edited by Halil İnalcık and Donald Quataert, 947–80. Cambridge: Cambridge Univ. Press, 1994.

Papen, Franz von. *Memoirs.* London: A. Deutsch, 1952.

Parfitt, Tudor. *The Jews in Palestine, 1800–1882.* Woodbridge, Suffolk: Boydell Press, 1987.

Parry, V. J. and M. E. Yapp, eds. *War, Technology, and Society in the Middle East.* London: Oxford Univ. Press, 1975.

Parvus [Israel Helphand]. *Türkiye'nin Can Damları: Devlet-i Osmaniye'nin Borçları ve İslahı.* Istanbul: Şems Matbaası, 1330H/1914.

Philipp, Thomas. "The Farhi Family and the Changing Position of the Jews in Syria and Palestine, 1750–1860" (in Hebrew). *Cathedra* 34 (1985): 97–114.

———. "French Merchants and Jews in the Ottoman Empire during the Eighteenth Century." In *The Jews of the Ottoman Empire,* edited by Avigdor Levy, 315–25. Princeton: Darwin Press, 1994.

Piarron de Mondésir, Jean Frédéric Lucien. *Siège et prise d'Andrinople (Novembre 1912-Mars 1913).* Paris: Chapelot, 1914.

Pitcher, Donald Edgar. *An Historical Geography of the Ottoman Empire from Earliest Times to the End of the Sixteenth Century.* Leiden: Brill, 1972.

Polk, William R., and Richard L. Chambers, eds. *Beginnings of Modernization in the Middle East: The Nineteenth Century.* Chicago: Univ. of Chicago Press, 1968.

Popkin, Richard H. "R. Nathan Shapiro's Visit to Amsterdam in 1657." *Dutch Jewish History* 1 (1984): 185–205.

Puryear, Vernon John. *International Economics and Diplomacy in the Near East: A Study of British Commercial Policy in the Levant, 1834–1853.* Berkeley: Univ. of California Press, 1935; reprint, Archon Books, 1969.

Quataert, Donald. *Ottoman Manufacturing in the Age of the Industrial Revolution.* Cambridge: Cambridge Univ. Press, 1993.

———. "Premières fumées d'usine." In *Salonique, 1850–1918. La "ville des Juifs" et le réveil des Balkans,* edited by Gilles Veinstein, 177–94. Paris: Editions Autrement, 1992.

———. *Social Disintegration and Popular Resistance in the Ottoman Empire, 1881–1908: Reactions to European Economic Penetration.* New York: New York Univ. Press, 1983.

Quataert, Donald, ed. *Consumption Studies and the History of the Ottoman Empire, 1550–1922. An Introduction.* Albany: State Univ. of New York Press, 2000.

Rajsfus, Maurice. *Drancy: Un camp de concentration très ordinaire, 1941–44.* Paris: Manya, 1991.

Ramsaur, E. E. *The Young Turks: Prelude to the Revolution of 1908.* Princeton: Princeton Univ. Press, 1957.

Rapaport, R. Isaac Hacohen. *Batei Kehuna.* Vol. 1. Izmir, 1736.

Ravid, Benjamin. "An Autobiographical Memorandum by Daniel Rodriga, *Inventore* of the *Scala* of Spalato." In *The Mediterranean and the Jews: Banking, Finance and International Trade (Sixteenth to Eighteenth Centuries),* edited by A. Toaff and S. Schwarzfuchs, 189–213. Ramat Gan, Israel: Bar Ilan University Press, 1989.

———. "Daniel Rodriga and the First Decade of the Jewish Merchants of Venice." In *Exile and Diaspora: Studies in the History of the Jewish People Presented to Prof. Chaim Beinart* (Latin alphabet volume), edited by A. Mirsky, A. Grossman and Y. Kaplan, 203–223. Jerusalem: Ben Zvi Institute and Hebrew University Press, 1991.

———. *Economics and Toleration in Seventeenth-Century Venice.* Jerusalem: American Academy for Jewish Research, 1978.

———. "Money, Love, and Power Politics in Sixteenth-Century Venice: The Perpetual Banishment and Subsequent Pardon of Joseph Nasi." In *Italia Judaica: Atti del I Convegno Internazionale, Bari, 1981,* edited by Vittore Colorni et al., 159–81. Rome: Ministero per i Beni Culturali e Ambientali, 1983.

———. "A Tale of Three Cities and Their Raison d'Etat: Ancona, Venice, Livorno and the Competition for Jewish Merchants in the Sixteenth Century." *Mediterranean Historical Review* 6 (1991–92): 138–62.

Refik, A. *Hicri On Üçüncü Asırda İstanbul Hayatı (1200–1255).* Istanbul: Matbaacılık ve Neşriyat T.A.Ş., 1932.

Renard, Raymond. *Sepharad: Le monde et la langue judéo-espagnole des Séphardim.* Mons, Belgium: Annales Universitaires de Mons, [1966?].

Rinott, Moshe. *The Hilfsverein der Deutschen Juden in Palestine* (in Hebrew). Jerusalem: Bet Ha-Sefer Le-Hinukh Shel Ha-Universitah Ha-Ivrit, 1971.

Rivkin, Ellis. *The Shaping of Jewish History: A Radical New Interpretation.* New York: Scribner's, 1971.

Roberts, Lewes. *The Marchants Mappe of Commerce.* London, 1638; reprint, London: Ralph Mabb, 1938.

Rodrigue, Aron. "The Beginnings of Westernization and Community Reform Among Istanbul's Jewry, 1854–65." In *The Jews of the Ottoman Empire,* edited by Avigdor Levy, 439–56. Princeton: Darwin Press, 1994.

———. *De l'instruction à l'émancipation: Les enseignants de l'Alliance Israélite Universelle et les Juifs d'Orient, 1860–1939.* Paris: Calmann-Lévy, 1989. Expanded English edition, *Images of Sephardi and Eastern Jewries in Transition: The Teachers of the Alliance Israélite Universelle, 1860–1939.* Seattle: Univ. of Washington Press, 1993.

———. *French Jews, Turkish Jews: The Alliance Israélite Universelle and the Politics of Jewish Schooling in Turkey, 1860–1925.* Bloomington: Indiana Univ. Press, 1990.

Rodrigue, Aron, ed. *Ottoman and Turkish Jewry: Community and Leadership.* Bloomington: Indiana University Turkish Studies 12, 1992.

Rogers, Mary E. *Domestic Life in Palestine.* London 1862. Hebrew translation by Shulamit Haran. Tel-Aviv: Misrad Ha-Bitahon, 1984.

Ro'i, Ya'acov. "The Zionist Attitude to the Arabs, 1908–1914." *MES* 4 (1968): 198–242.

Rosanes, Solomon A. [Rozanes, Shelomoh]. *History of the Jews in the Ottoman Empire* (in Hebrew). 6 vols. Vol. 1–3 were first published in Husijatin, 1907–1911. A second revised edition of vol. 1 was published in Tel Aviv: Devir, 1930. A second edition of volumes 2 and 3 was published in Sofia, 1937–1938. The second edition of vol. 3 and vols. 4–6 were published under the title *History of the Jews in Turkey and the Lands of the East* (in Hebrew). Volumes 4 and 5 were published in Sofia, 1934–1937; vol. 6 was published in Jerusalem: Rabbi Kook Institute, 1945.

Roth, Cecil. *A History of the Marranos.* Philadelphia: The Jewish Publication Society, 1947. Reprinted with a new introduction by Herman P. Salomon. New York: Sepher-Hermon Press, 1974.

———. *The House of Nasi: Doña Gracia.* Philadelphia: Jewish Publication Society, 1947.

———. *The House of Nasi: The Duke of Naxos.* Philadelphia: Jewish Publication Society, 1948; reprint, New York: Greenwood, n.d.

Roumani, Maurice. "Zionism and Social Change in Libya at the Turn of the Century." *SiZ* 8 (1987): 1–24.

Rozen, Minna. "The Archives of the Marseilles Chamber of Commerce" (in Hebrew). *Pe'amim* 9 (1981): 112–24.

———. "France and the Jews of Egypt: An Anatomy of Relations, 1683–1801" (in Hebrew). In *The Jews in Ottoman Egypt,* edited by Jacob M. Landau, 421–70. Jerusalem: Misgav Yerushalayim, 1988.

———. "Individual and Community in the Jewish Society of the Ottoman Empire: Salonica in the Sixteenth Century." In *The Jews of the Ottoman Empire,* edited by Avigdor Levy, 215–73. Princeton: Darwin Press, 1994.

———. *The Jewish Community of Jerusalem in the Seventeenth Century* (in Hebrew). Tel Aviv: Tel Aviv University, 1984.

Rozen, Minna, ed. *The Days of the Crescent: Chapters in the History of the Jews in the Ottoman Empire* (in Hebrew). Tel Aviv: Tel Aviv University, 1996.

Runciman, Steven. *The Fall of Constantinople, 1453.* London: Cambridge Univ. Press, 1965.

Ruppin, Arthur. *The Jews of To-Day.* Translated by Margery Bentwich. London: G. Bell and Sons, 1913.

Rüstow, Alexander. *Freedom and Domination: A Historical Critique of Civilization.* Abbreviated translation by S. Attanasio, edited with an introduction by Dankwart A. Rustow. Princeton: Princeton Univ. Press, 1980.

Rustow, Dankwart A. "A Biographical Sketch." In *Freedom and Domination: A Historical Critique of Civilization,* by Alexander Rüstow, xiii–xxii. Princeton: Princeton Univ. Press, 1980.

Sahıllıoğlu, Halil. "Yeniçeri çuhası ve II. Bayezid'in son yıllarında yeniçeri çuha muhasebesi." *Güney-Doğu Avrupa Araştırmaları Dergisi* 2–3 (1974): 415–23.

Salzmann, Ariel. "An *Ancien Regime* Revisted: Privatization and Political Economy in the Eighteenth-Century Ottoman Empire." *Politics and Society* 21 (1993): 393–423.

Sassoon, David Solomon. *A History of the Jews in Baghdad.* Letchworth, England: S. D. Sassoon, 1949.

Scharfstein, Zevi. *History of Jewish Education in Modern Times.* Vol. 5, *Lands of the Mediterranean, the Balkans, and the East* (in Hebrew). Jerusalem: Re'uven Mas, 1966.

Scholem, Gershom. *Major Trends in Jewish Mysticism.* 3d ed. New York: Schocken, 1954.

———. *The Messianic Idea in Judaism.* New York: Schocken, 1971.

———. *Sabbatai Şevi, The Mystical Messiah, 1626–1676.* Translated by R. J. Zwi Werblowsky. Princeton: Princeton Univ. Press, 1973.

Schroeter, Daniel J. "Jewish Quarters in the Arab-Islamic Cities of the Ottoman Empire." In *The Jews of the Ottoman Empire,* edited by Avigdor Levy, 287–300. Princeton: Darwin Press, 1994.

Schwarzfuchs, Simon. "La décadence de la Galilée juive de XVIᵉ siècle et la crise du textile au Proche Orient." *REJ* 121 (1962): 169–79.

———. "The Salonica Balance Scales: The Conflict between the French and the Jewish Merchants" (in Hebrew). *Sefunot* 15 (1971–1981): 77–102.

Sciaky, Leon. *Farewell to Salonica: Portrait of an Era.* New York: Current Books, 1946.

Sehayik, Shaul. "Changes in the Position of Urban Jewish Women in Iraq since the End of the Nineteenth Century" (in Hebrew). *Pe'amim* 36 (1988): 64–88.

Şeşen, R., et al. *Catalogue of the Islamic Medical Manuscripts in the Libraries of Turkey.* Istanbul: Markaz al-Abhath, 1984.

Şevki, Osman. *Beş Büçük Asırlık Türk Tebabet Tarihi.* Istanbul: Matbaa-yi Âmire, 1314 H/1896–1897.

Shamir, Shimon. "The Evolution of the Egyptian Nationality Laws and Their Application to the Jews in the Monarchy Period." In *The Jews of Egypt: A Mediterranean Society in Modern Times,* edited by idem, 33–67. Boulder, Colo.: Westview, 1987.

Shaw, R. Paul. *Migration Theory and Fact: A Review and Bibliography of Current Literature.* Philadelphia: Regional Science Research Institute, 1975.

Shaw, Stanford J. *Between Old and New: The Ottoman Empire under Sultan Selim III, 1789–1807.* Cambridge, Mass.: Harvard Univ. Press, 1971.

———. *History of the Ottoman Empire and Modern Turkey. Vol. 1, Empire of the Gazis, 1280–1808.* Cambridge: Cambridge Univ. Press, 1976.

———. *The Jews of the Ottoman Empire and the Turkish Republic.* New York: New York Univ. Press, 1991.

———. "The Nineteenth Century Ottoman Tax Reforms and Revenue System." *IJMES* 6 (1975): 421–59.

———. "The Ottoman Census System and Population, 1831–1914." *IJMES* 9 (1978): 325–38.

———. "The Population of Istanbul in the Nineteenth Century." *Türk Tarih Dergisi* 32 (1979): 403–14.

———. *Turkey and the Holocaust: Turkey's Role in Rescuing Turkish and European Jewry from Nazi Persecution, 1933–1945.* New York: New York Univ. Press, 1993.

Shaw, Stanford J., and Ezel Kural Shaw. *History of the Ottoman Empire and Modern Turkey.* Vol. 2, *Reform, Revolution and Republic, 1808–1975.* Cambridge: Cambridge Univ. Press, 1977.

Shmuelevitz, Aryeh. *The Jews of the Ottoman Empire in the Late Fifteenth and Sixteenth Centuries*. Leiden: Brill, 1984.

Silberman, Paul. "An Investigation of the Schools Operated by the Alliance Israélite Universelle from 1862 to 1940." Ph.D. diss., New York University, 1974.

Simon, Rachel. "Between the Family and the Outside World: Jewish Girls in the Modern Middle East and North Africa." *Jewish Social Studies* 7 (2000): 81–108.

———. *Change within Tradition among Jewish Women in Libya*. Seattle: Univ. of Washington Press, 1992.

———. "Jewish Participation in the Reforms in Libya during the Second Ottoman Period, 1835–1911." In *The Jews of the Ottoman Empire*, edited by Avigdor Levy, 485–506. Princeton: Darwin Press, 1994.

———. "The Jews of Libya and the Non-Jewish Environment in the Late Ottoman Period." *Pe'amim* 3 (1979): 5–36.

———. "Language Change and Socio-Political Transformations: The Case of Nineteenth- and Twentieth-Century Libyan Jews." *Jewish History* 4 (1989): 101–21.

Simon, Reeva S. "Education in the Jewish Community of Baghdad until 1914" (in Hebrew). *Pe'amim* 36 (1988): 52–63.

Şimşir, Bilal, ed. *Ege Sorunu, Belgeler*. Vol. 1, *1912–1913*. Ankara: Türk Tarih Kurumu Basımevi, 1976.

Sirat, C. "A Letter on the Creation by R. Shemaryah b. Elijah Akriti" (in Hebrew). *Eshel Beer-Sheva* 2 (1980): 199–227.

Skilliter, S. A. "Three Letters from the Ottoman 'Sultana' Safiye to Queen Elizabeth I." In *Oriental Studies III. Documents from Islamic Chanceries. First Series,* edited by S. M. Stern, 119–57. Cambridge, Mass.: Harvard Univ. Press, 1965.

Slouschz, Nahum. *My Travels in Libya* (in Hebrew). 2 vols. Tel-Aviv, 1937–1943.

———. "La Tripolitaine sous la domination des Karamanlis." *Revue du Monde Musulman* 6 (1908): 448–51.

Sombart, Werner. *The Jews and Modern Capitalism*. Translated by M. Epstein. New York: B. Franklin, 1969.

Spuler, Bertold. *Die Minderheitenschulen der europäischen Türkei von der Reformzeit bis zum Weltkrieg*. Breslau: Verlag Priebatsch, 1936.

Stavrianos, L. S. *The Balkans since 1453*. New York: Holt, Rinehart and Winston, 1958.

Stavrou, Theofanis G. *Russian Interests in Palestine, 1882–1914*. Salonica: Institute for Balkan Studies, 1963.

Steensgaard, Niels. *The Asian Trade Revolution of the Seventeenth Century.* Chicago: Univ. of Chicago Press, 1974.

Steinschneider, M. "Candia, Cenni di Storia Letteraria Candia." *Mose* 2 (1879): 457, and 3 (1880): 282.

Stich, Heinrich. *Die Weltwirtschaftlich Entwicklung der Anatolischen Produktion seit Anfangs des 19 Jahrhunderts.* Kiel: C. H. Jebens, 1929.

Stillman, Norman A. *The Jews of Arab Lands: A History and Sourcebook.* Philadelphia: Jewish Publication Society, 1979.

———. *The Jews of Arab Lands in Modern Times.* Philadelphia: Jewish Publication Society, 1991.

———. "Middle Eastern and North African Jewries Confront Modernity: Orientation, Disorientation, Reorientation." In *Sephardi and Middle Eastern Jewries: History and Culture in the Modern Era,* edited by Harvey E. Goldberg, 59–72. Bloomington: Indiana Univ. Press, 1996.

Strong, William E. *The Story of the American Board.* New York: Arno, 1969.

Sugar, Peter. *Southeastern Europe under Ottoman Rule, 1354–1804.* Seattle: Univ. of Washington Press, 1977.

Süreyya, Mehmed. *Sicill-i Osmani.* 4 vols. Istanbul, 1308–1311 H/1890–1893; reprint, Westmead, England: Gregg, 1971.

Sussman, J. "Two Halakhic Pamphlets by Rabbi Moses Botaril" (in Hebrew). *Kovetz Al-Yad* 6 (1966): 271–97.

Szyliowicz, Joseph S. *Education and Modernization in the Middle East.* Ithaca: Cornell Univ. Press, 1973.

Tadič, J. "Le commerce en Dalmatie et à Raguse et la décadence économique de Venise au XVIII siècle." In *Aspetti e Cause della Decadenza Economica Veneziana nel Secolo XVII,* 238–74. Venice: Istituto per la Collaborazione Culturale, 1961.

Tahir, Mehmed. *Osmanlı Müellifleri.* 3 vols. Istanbul: Matbaa-i Âmire, 1333–1342 H/1915–1924; reprint, Istanbul: Meral, 1975.

Tamar, David. *Studies in the History of the Jews in Palestine and the Oriental Countries* (in Hebrew). Jerusalem: Mosad Ha-Rav Kook, 1981.

Tamir, Vicki. *Bulgaria and Her Jews: The History of a Dubious Symbiosis.* New York: Sepher-Hermon Press, 1979.

Tanyu, Hikmet. *Tarih Boyunca Yahudiler ve Türkler.* 2d ed. 2 vols. Istanbul: Bilge Yayınlar, 1979.

Taragan, B. *La Communauté Israélite d'Alexandrie.* Alexandria: Les Editions Juives d'-Egypte, 1932.

Taton, R., ed. *History of Science*. 4 vols. New York: Basic Books, 1963–1966.

Temperley, Harold. *England and the Near East: The Crimea*. London: Longmans, Green and Co., 1936.

Tenenti, Alberto. *Piracy and the Decline of Venice*. Translated by Janet Pullan and Brian Pullan. Berkeley: Univ. of California Press, 1967.

Teveth, Shabtai. *Ben-Gurion: The Burning Ground, 1886–1948*. Boston: Houghton Mifflin, 1987.

Tibawi, A. L. *American Interests in Syria, 1800–1901*. Oxford: Oxford Univ. Press, 1966.

————. *British Interests in Palestine, 1800–1901*. Oxford: Oxford Univ. Press, 1961.

Tishby, Isaiah. *Paths of Belief and Heresy* (in Hebrew). Ramat Gan: Agudat Ha-Sofrim, 1964.

Toaff, Ariel, and Simon Schwarzfuchs, eds. *The Mediterranean and the Jews: Banking, Finance and International Trade (Sixteenth-Eighteenth Centuries)*. Ramat Gan: Bar Ilan Univ. Press, 1989.

Todorov, Nikolai. *The Balkan City, 1400–1900*. Seattle: Univ. of Washington Press, 1983.

Todorova, Maria. "The Ottoman Legacy in the Balkans." In *Imperial Legacy: The Ottoman Imprint on the Balkans and the Middle East,* edited by L. Carl Brown, 45–77. New York: Columbia Univ. Press, 1996.

Tosyavizade, Rifat Osman. *Edirne Rehnüması*. Edirne: Vilayet Matbaası, 1920. A revised version in Roman characters was published by Ratip Kazancıgil. Edirne: Türk Kütüphaneciler Derneği Edirne Şubesi, 1994.

Tournfort, M. *A Voyage into the Levant*. Vol. 3. London: Printed for D. Midwinter, 1712.

Toynbee, Arnold J. *Acquaintances*. London: Oxford Univ. Press, 1967.

Tritton, A. S. *The Caliphs and their Non-Muslim Subjects: A Critical Study of the Covenant of 'Umar*. London: Oxford Univ. Press, 1930.

Tsimhoni, Daphne. "On the Beginnings of Modernization among the Jews of Iraq in the Nineteenth Century until 1914" (in Hebrew). *Pe'amim* 36 (1988): 7–34.

Tunaya, T. Z. *Türkiye'de Siyasi Partiler, 1859–1952*. Istanbul 1952.

Turkey, Republic of. *Balkan Harbı Tarihi*. 7 vols. Istanbul and Ankara: Askeri Matbaa, 1938–1965.

Twersky, Isadore, and Bernard Septimus, eds. *Jewish Thought in the Seventeenth Century*. Cambridge, Mass.: Harvard University Press, 1987.

Ubicini, A. *Lettres sur la Turquie*. 2 vols. Paris, 1854. Translated as *Letters on Turkey*. (London, 1856; reprint, Arno, 1973).

Udovitch, Abraham L., and Lucette Valensi. *The Last Arab Jews: The Communities of Jerba, Tunisia.* Chur, Switzerland: Harwood Academic Publishers, 1984.

Ülker, Necmi. "The Rise of Izmir." Ph.D. diss., University of Michigan, 1975.

Urquhart, David. *Turkey and Its Resources: Its Municipal Organization and Free Trade; the State and Prospects of English Commerce in the East.* London: Saunders and Otley, 1833.

Usque, Samuel. *Consolation for the Tribulations of Israel.* Translated by Martin A. Cohen. Philadelphia: Jewish Publication Society, 1965.

Uzunçarşılı, İ. H. *Osmanlı Devletinin Saray Teşkilatı.* Ankara: Türk Tarih Kurumu Basımevi, 1945; reprint, 1984.

Varol, Marie-Christine. "The Balat Quarter and Its Image: A Study of a Jewish Neighborhood in Istanbul." In *The Jews of the Ottoman Empire,* edited by Avigdor Levy, 633–45. Princeton: Darwin Press, 1994.

———. "Le judéo-espagnol vernaculaire d'Istanbul (étude linguistique)." Ph.D. diss., Univ. of Paris III, 1992.

———. "Monsieur le rabbin—Termes d'adresse et désignation du rabbin en judéo-espagnol (Turquie)." In *Les interférences de l'hébreu dans les langues juives,* edited by J. Tedghi, 87–109. Paris: Institut national des Langes et Civilisations Orientales, 1994.

Veinstein, Gilles, ed. *Salonique, 1850–1918: La "ville des Juifs" et le réveil des Balkans.* Paris: Editions Autrement, 1992.

Veinstein, Gilles. "Une communanté ottomane: Les Juifs d'Avlonya (Valona) dans la deuxième moitié du XVIᵉ siècle." In *Gli Ebrei e Venezia, Secoli XIV-XVIII,* edited by Gaetano Cozzi, 781–828. Milano: Edizioni Comunità, 1987.

Vryonis, Speros, Jr. *The Decline of Medieval Hellenism in Asia Minor and the Process of Islamization from the Eleventh through the Fifteenth Century.* Berkeley: Univ. of California Press, 1971.

Ward, Robert E., and Dankwart A. Rustow, eds. *Political Modernization in Japan and Turkey.* Princeton: Princeton Univ. Press, 1964.

Wasserstein, Bernard. *Britain and the Jews of Europe, 1939–1945.* Oxford: Oxford Univ. Press, 1979.

Watson, R., and W. Thomson, *A History of the Reign of Philip the Third, King of Spain.* London, 1818.

Weiker, Walter F. *Ottomans, Turks and the Jewish Polity: A History of the Jews of Turkey.* Lanham, Md.: Univ. Press of America, 1992.

———. *The Unseen Israelis: The Jews from Turkey in Israel.* Lanham, Md.: Univ. Press of America, 1988.

Weiner, Hanna, and Barnet Litvinoff, eds. *The Letters and Papers of Chaim Weizmann.* Series A, vol. 5. London and Jerusalem: Oxford Univ. Press, 1974.

Werblowsky, R. J. Z. *Joseph Karo, Lawyer and Mystic.* London: Oxford Univ. Press, 1962.

Widmann, Horst. *Exil und Bildungshilfe: Die deutschsprachige akademische Emigration in die Türkei nach 1933.* Bern: Herbert Lang, 1973.

Winter, Michael. "The Relations of Egyptian Jews with the Authorities and with the Non-Jewish Society" (in Hebrew). In *The Jews in Ottoman Egypt,* edited by Jacob M. Landau, 371–420. Jerusalem: Misgav Yerushalayim, 1988.

Wittek, Paul. *The Rise of the Ottoman Empire.* London: Royal Asiatic Society, 1958.

Wolf, Lucien. *Sir Moses Montefiore: A Centennial Biography with Extracts from Letters and Journals.* London: John Murray, 1884.

Ya'ari, Avraham. *Hebrew Printing in Istanbul* (in Hebrew). Jerusalem: Magnes Press, 1967.

———. "Hebrew Printing Presses in Izmir" (in Hebrew). *Areshet* 1 (1959): 97–222.

———. *The Mystery of a Book* (in Hebrew). Jerusalem: Mosad Ha-Rav Kook, 1954.

———. *The Travels of an Emissary from Safed* (in Hebrew). Jerusalem, 1942.

Yad Vashem. *Rescue Attempts during the Holocaust. Proceedings of the Second Yad Vashem International Historical Conference, Jerusalem, April 8–11, 1974.* Jerusalem: Yad Vashem, 1977.

Yehudah, Zvi. "Social Relations between Jews and Muslims in Baghdad at the End of the Nineteenth Century According to Local Jewish Sources" (in Hebrew). In *A Nation and Its History,* edited by Shmuel Ettinger, 2: 55–64. Jerusalem: Merkaz Zalman Shazar, 1984.

Yerushalmi, J. *The Re-education of Marranos in the Seventeenth Century.* Cincinnati: Judaic Studies Program, University of Cincinnati, 1980.

Yiftah, Yehezkel. *Jewish Education in Iraq in Modern Times* (in Hebrew). Nahalal: Yad Eli'ezer Yafeh, 1984.

Yiğitgüden, Remzi. *1912–13 Balkan Harbinde Edirne Kale Muharebeleri.* Istanbul: Askeri Matbaa, 1938.

Zenner, Walter P. "Jews in Late Ottoman Syria: Community, Family and Religion." In *Jewish Societies in the Middle East: Community, Culture, and Authority,* edited by Shlomo Deshen and Walter P. Zenner, 187–209. Washington, D.C.: Univ. Press of America, 1982.

———. "Jews in Late Ottoman Syria: External Relations." In *Jewish Societies in the Middle East: Community, Culture, and Authority,* edited by Shlomo Deshen and

Walter P. Zenner, 155–86. Washington, D.C.: University Press of America, 1982.

Zilfi, Madeline. *The Politics of Piety: The Ottoman Ulema in the Postclassical Age (1600–1800)*. Minneapolis: Biblioteca Islamica, 1988.

Zinberg, Israel. *A History of Jewish Literature.* Translated and edited by Bernard Martin. Volume 5, *The Jewish Center of Culture in the Ottoman Empire.* Cincinnati: Hebrew Union College Press, 1974.

Zuaretz, Frigia, Amishadai Guetta et al., eds. *Libyan Jewry* (in Hebrew). Tel Aviv: Council of Libyan Jewish Communities in Israel, 1982.

Index

Other titles in the Modern Jewish History series
Henry L. Feingold, ed.